History

For UGC-NET/SLET/JRF

Paper I, II and III

Objective Type Questions

Previous Years Solved Papers

History

For UGC-NET/SLET/JRF

Paper I, II and III

Objective Type Questions

Previous Years Solved Papers

Atlantic Research Division

Published by

ATLANTIC

PUBLISHERS & DISTRIBUTORS (P) LTD

7/22, Ansari Road, Darya Ganj,
New Delhi-110002
Phones : +91-11-40775252, 23273880, 23275880, 23280451
Fax : +91-11-23285873
Web : www.atlanticbooks.com
E-mail : orders@atlanticbooks.com

Branch Office
5, Nallathambi Street, Wallajah Road,
Chennai-600002
Phones : +91-44-64611085, 32413319
E-mail : chennai@atlanticbooks.com

Disclaimer:

The author and the publisher have taken every effort to the maximum of their skill, expertise and knowledge to provide correct answers to questions in the book. Even then if some mistakes persist in the content of the book the publisher does not take responsibility for the same. The publisher shall have no liability to any person or entity with respect to any loss or damage caused, or alleged to have been caused directly or indirectly, by the information contained in this book. Hence, the book should be taken as a general guide only.

The publisher has fully tried to follow the copyright law. However, if any work is found to be similar, it is unintentional and the same should not be used as defamatory or to file legal suit against the author/publisher.

If the readers find any mistakes we shall be grateful to them for pointing those to us so that they can be corrected in the next edition.

All disputes are subject to the jurisdiction of Delhi court only.

Printed in India at Nice Printing Press, A-33/3A, Site-IV,
Industrial Area, Sahibabad, Ghaziabad, U.P.

Preface

The University Grants Commission (UGC) conducts National Eligibility Test (NET) on various subjects twice every year, once each in June and December, to determine eligibility for college and university level lectureship and for award of Junior Research Fellowship (JRF), for Indian nationals in order to ensure minimum standards for the entrants in the teaching profession and research.

The book contains previous years solved papers (objective type questions) on the subject of History, from June 2005 to June 2013. It covers all three papers (Paper I, II and III). In Paper I (General Paper on Teaching and Research Aptitude), and Paper II (Elective), solved papers have been included from June 2005. In Paper III (Core and Elective), solved papers of objective type questions have been included from June 2012, conforming to the existing UGC-NET pattern. In addition, five sets of Mock Tests for Paper I, II and III have been included in the book under Practice Papers. Answers have been given at the end of each set for self-check.

It will be useful for those preparing for UGC-NET/SLET/JRF in the subject of History. It will give them a feel of the type of questions asked in NET in this subject, i.e. Multiple-choice, Matching type, True/False, Assertion-Reasoning type, etc. The papers included in this book will enable the students to judge their own level of competence besides adding to their knowledge. It will also help them revise the important questions in the entire syllabus and enhance their self-confidence. Suggestions for further improvement of the book are, however, welcome.

Atlantic Research Division

Contents

JUNE–2013

Note: This paper contains sixty (60) multiple choice questions, each question carrying two (2) marks. Candidate is expected to answer any fifty (50) questions. In case more than fifty (50) questions are attempted, only the first fifty (50) questions will be evaluated.

PAPER–I

1. Which one of the following references is written as per Modern Language Association (MLA) format?
   (a) Hall, Donald. Fundamentals of Electronics,
   New Delhi: Prentice Hall of India, 2005
   (b) Hall, Donald, Fundamentals of Electronics,
   New Delhi: Prentice Hall of India, 2005
   (c) Hall, Donald, Fundamentals of Electronics,
   New Delhi: Prentice Hall of India, 2005
   (d) Hall, Donald. Fundamentals of Electronics.
   New Delhi: Prentice Hall of India, 2005

2. A workshop is
   (a) a conference for discussion on a topic.
   (b) a meeting for discussion on a topic.
   (c) a class at a college or a university in which a teacher and the students discuss a topic.
   (d) a brief intensive course for a small group emphasizing the development of a skill or technique for solving a specific problem.

3. A working hypothesis is
   (a) a proven hypothesis for an argument.
   (b) not required to be tested.
   (c) a provisionally accepted hypothesis for further research.
   (d) a scientific theory.

Read the following passage carefully and answer the questions (4 to 9):

The Taj Mahal has become one of the world's best known monuments. This domed white marble structure is situated on a high plinth at the southern end of a four-quartered garden, evoking the gardens of paradise, enclosed within walls measuring 305 by 549 metres. Outside the walls, in an area known as Mumtazabad, were living quarters for attendants, markets, serais and other structures built by local merchants and nobles. The tomb complex and the other imperial structures of Mumtazabad were maintained by the income of thirty villages given specifically for the tomb's support. The name Taj Mahal is unknown in Mughal chronicles, but it is used by contemporary Europeans in India, suggesting that this was the tomb's popular name. In contemporary texts, it is generally called simply the Illuminated Tomb (Rauza-i-Munavvara).

Mumtaz Mahal died shortly after delivering her fourteenth child in 1631. The Mughal court was then residing in Burhanpur. Her remains were temporarily buried by the griefstricken emperor in a spacious garden known as Zainabad on the bank of the river Tapti. Six months later her body was transported to Agra, where it was interred in land chosen for the mausoleum. This land, situated south of the Mughal city on the bank of the Jamuna, had belonged to the Kachhwaha rajas since the time of Raja Man Singh and was purchased from the then current raja, Jai Singh. Although contemporary chronicles indicate Jai Singh's willing cooperation in this exchange, extant *farmans* (imperial commands) indicate that the final price was not settled until almost two years after the mausoleum's commencement. Jai Singh's further cooperation was insured by imperial orders issued between 1632 and 1637 demanding that he provide stone masons and carts to transport marble from the mines at Makrana, within his "ancestral domain", to Agra where both the Taj Mahal and Shah Jahan's additions to the Agra fort were constructed concurrently.

Work on the mausoleum was commenced early in 1632. Inscriptional evidence indicates much of the tomb was completed by 1636. By 1643, when Shah Jahan most lavishly celebrated the 'Urs ceremony for Mumtaz Mahal', the entire complex was virtually complete.

4. Marble stone used for the construction of the Taj Mahal was brought from the ancestral domain of Raja Jai Singh. The name of the place where mines of marble is
   (a) Burhanpur (b) Makrana
   (c) Amber (d) Jaipur
5. The popular name Taj Mahal was given by
   (a) Shah Jahan
   (b) Tourists
   (c) Public
   (d) European travellers
6. Point out the true statement from the following:
   (a) Marble was not used for the construction of the Taj Mahal.
   (b) Red sand stone is non-visible in the Taj Mahal complex.
   (c) The Taj Mahal is surrounded by a four-quartered garden known as Chahr Bagh.
   (d) The Taj Mahal was constructed to celebrate the 'Urs ceremony for Mumtaz Mahal'.
7. In the contemporary texts the Taj Mahal is known
   (a) Mumtazabad
   (b) Mumtaz Mahal
   (c) Zainabad
   (d) Rauza-i-Munavvara
8. The construction of the Taj Mahal was completed between the period
   (a) 1632 – 1636 A.D.
   (b) 1630 – 1643 A.D.
   (c) 1632 – 1643 A.D.
   (d) 1636 – 1643 A.D.
9. The documents indicating the ownership of land, where the Taj Mahal was built, known as
   (a) Farman
   (b) Sale Deed
   (c) Sale-Purchase Deed
   (d) None of the above
10. In the process of communication, which one of the following is in the chronological order?
    (a) Communicator, Medium, Receiver, Effect, Message
    (b) Medium, Communicator, Message, Receiver, Effect
    (c) Communicator, Message, Medium, Receiver, Effect
    (d) Message, Communicator, Medium, Receiver, Effect
11. Bengal Gazette, the first Newspaper in India was started in 1780 by
    (a) Dr. Annie Besant
    (b) James Augustus Hicky
    (c) Lord Cripson
    (d) A.O. Hume

12. Press censorship in India was imposed during the tenure of the Prime Minister
(a) Rajeev Gandhi
(b) Narasimha Rao
(c) Indira Gandhi
(d) Deve Gowda

13. Communication via New media such as computers, teleshopping, internet and mobile telephony is termed as
(a) Entertainment
(b) Interactive communication
(c) Developmental communication
(d) Communitarian

14. Classroom communication of a teacher rests on the principle of
(a) Infotainment
(b) Edutainment
(c) Entertainment
(d) Enlightenment

15. ________ is important when a teacher communicates with his/her student.
(a) Sympathy (b) Empathy
(c) Apathy (d) Antipathy

16. In a certain code GALIB is represented by HBMJC. TIGER will be represented by
(a) UJHFS (b) UHJSF
(c) JHUSF (d) HUJSF

17. In a certain cricket tournament 45 matches were played. Each team played once against each of the other teams. The number of teams participated in the tournament is
(a) 8 (b) 10
(c) 12 (d) 14

18. The missing number in the series 40, 120, 60, 180, 90,?, 135 is
(a) 110 (b) 270
(c) 105 (d) 210

19. The odd numbers from 1 to 45 which are exactly divisible by 3 are arranged in an ascending order. The number at 6th position is
(a) 18 (b) 24
(c) 33 (d) 36

20. The mean of four numbers a, b, c, d is 100. If c = 70, then the mean of the remaining numbers is
(a) 30 (b) $\frac{85}{2}$
(c) $\frac{170}{3}$ (d) 110

21. If the radius of a circle is increased by 50%, the perimeter of the circle will increase by
(a) 20% (b) 30%
(c) 40% (d) 50%

22. If the statement 'some men are honest' is false, which among the following statements will be true. Choose the correct code given below:
(i) All men are honest.
(ii) No men are honest.
(iii) Some men are not honest.
(iv) All men are dishonest.

Codes:
(a) (i), (ii) and (iii)
(b) (ii), (iii) and (iv)
(c) (i), (iii) and (iv)
(d) (ii), (i) and (iv)

23. Choose the proper alternative given in the codes to replace the question mark.
Bee – Honey, Cow – Milk, Teacher –?
(a) Intelligence (b) Marks
(c) Lessons (d) Wisdom

24. P is the father of R and S is the son of Q and T is the brother of P. If R is the sister of S, how is Q related to T?
(a) Wife
(b) Sister-in-law
(c) Brother-in-law
(d) Daughter-in-law

25. Which of the codes given below contains only the correct statements?

Statements:

(i) Venn diagram is a clear method of notation.

(ii) Venn diagram is the most direct method of testing the validity of categorical syllogisms.

(iii) In Venn diagram method the premises and the conclusion of a categorical syllogism is diagrammed.

(iv) In Venn diagram method the three overlapping circles are drawn for testing a categorical syllogism.

Codes:

(a) (i), (ii) & (iii)
(b) (i), (ii) & (iv)
(c) (ii), (iii) & (iv)
(d) (i), (iii) & (iv)

26. Inductive reasoning presupposes
(a) unity in human nature
(b) integrity in human nature
(c) uniformity in human nature
(d) harmony in human nature

Read the table below and based on this table answer questions from 28 to 33:

Area under Major Horticulture Crops
(in lakh hectares)

Year	Fruits	Vegetables	Flowers	Total Horti-culture Area
2005-06	53	72	1	187
2006-07	56	75	1	194
2007-08	58	78	2	202
2008-09	61	79	2	207
2009-10	63	79	2	209

27. Which of the following two years have recorded the highest rate of increase in area under the total horticulture?
(a) 2005–06 & 2006–07
(b) 2006-07 & 2008-09
(c) 2007-08 & 2008-09
(d) 2006-07 & 2007-08

28. A definition put forward to resolve a dispute by influencing attitudes or stirring emotions is called
(a) Lexical (b) Persuasive
(c) Stipulative (d) Precisions

29. Shares of the area under flowers, vegetables and fruits in the area under total horticulture are respectively:
(a) 1, 38 and 30 percent
(b) 30, 38 and 1 percent
(c) 38, 30 and 1 percent
(d) 35, 36 and 2 percent

30. Which of the following has recorded the highest rate of increase in area during 2005-06 to 2009-10?
(a) Fruits
(b) Vegetables
(c) Flowers
(d) Total horticulture

31. Find out the horticultural crop that has recorded an increase of area by around 10 percent from 2005-06 to 2009-10
(a) Fruits
(b) Vegetables
(c) Flowers
(d) Total horticulture

32. What has been the share of area under fruits, vegetables and flowers in the area under total horticulture in 2007-08?
(a) 53 percent (b) 68 percent
(c) 79 percent (d) 100 percent

33. In which year, area under fruits has recorded the highest rate of increase?
(a) 2006-07 (b) 2007-08
(c) 2008-09 (d) 2009-10

34. 'www' stands for
(a) work with web
(b) word wide web
(c) world wide web
(d) worth while web

35. A hard disk is divided into tracks which is further subdivided into
(a) Clusters (b) Sectors
(c) Vectors (d) Heads

36. A computer program that translates a program statement by statement into machine language is called a/an
(a) Compiler (b) Simulator
(c) Translator (d) Interpreter

37. A Gigabyte is equal to
(a) 1024 Megabytes
(b) 1024 Kilobytes
(c) 1024 Terabytes
(d) 1024 Bytes

38. A Compiler is a software which converts
(a) characters to bits
(b) high level language to machine language
(c) machine language to high level language
(d) words to bits

39. Virtual memory is
(a) an extremely large main memory.
(b) an extremely large secondary memory.
(c) an illusion of extremely large main memory.
(d) a type of memory used in super computers.

40. The phrase 'tragedy of commons' is in the context of
(a) tragic event related to damage caused by release of poisonous gases.
(b) tragic conditions of poor people.
(c) degradation of renewable free access resources.
(d) climate change.

41. Kyoto Protocol is related to
(a) Ozone depletion
(b) Hazardous waste
(c) Climate change
(d) Nuclear energy

42. Which of the following is a source of emissions leading to the eventual formation of surface ozone as a pollutant?
(a) Transport sector
(b) Refrigeration and Airconditioning
(c) Wetlands
(d) Fertilizers

43. The smog in cities in India mainly consists of
(a) Oxides of sulphur
(b) Oxides of nitrogen and unburnt hydrocarbons
(c) Carbon monoxide and SPM
(d) Oxides of sulphur and ozone

44. Which of the following types of natural hazards have the highest potential to cause damage to humans?
(a) Earthquakes
(b) Forest fires
(c) Volcanic eruptions
(d) Droughts and Floods

45. The percentage share of renewable energy sources in the power production in India is around
(a) 2-3% (b) 22-25%
(c) 10-12% (d) < 1%

46. In which of the following categories the enrolment of students in higher education in 2010-11 was beyond the percentage of seats reserved?
(a) OBC students
(b) SC students
(c) ST students
(d) Woman students

47. Which one of the following statements is not correct about the University Grants Commission (UGC)?
(a) It was established in 1956 by an Act of Parliament.

(b) It is tasked with promoting and coordinating higher education.
(c) It receives Plan and Non-Plan funds from the Central Government.
(d) It receives funds from State Governments in respect of State Universities.

48. Consider the statement which is followed by two arguments (I) and (II):
Statement: Should India switch over to a two party system?
Arguments: (I) Yes, it will lead to stability of Government.
(II) No, it will limit the choice of voters.
(a) Only argument (I) is strong.
(b) Only argument (II) is strong.
(c) Both the arguments are strong.
(d) Neither of the arguments is strong.

49. Consider the statement which is followed by two arguments (I) and (II):
Statement: Should persons with criminal background be banned from contesting elections?
Arguments: (I) Yes, it will decriminalise politics.
(II) No, it will encourage the ruling party to file frivolous cases against their political opponents.
(a) Only argument (I) is strong.
(b) Only argument (II) is strong.
(c) Both the arguments are strong.
(d) Neither of the arguments is strong.

50. Which of the following statement(s) is/are correct about a Judge of the Supreme Court of India?
1. A Judge of the Supreme Court is appointed by the President of India.
2. He holds office during the pleasure of the President.
3. He can be suspended, pending an inquiry.
4. He can be removed for proven misbehaviour or incapacity.
Select the correct answer from the codes given below:
Codes:
(a) 1, 2 and 3 (b) 1, 3 and 4
(c) 1 and 3 (d) 1 and 4

51. In the warrant of precedence, the Speaker of the Lok Sabha comes next only to
(a) The President
(b) The Vice-President
(c) The Prime Minister
(d) The Cabinet Ministers

52. The black-board can be utilised best by a teacher for
(a) putting the matter of teaching in black and white
(b) making the students attentive
(c) writing the important and notable points
(d) highlighting the teacher himself

53. Nowadays the most effective mode of learning is
(a) self study
(b) face-to-face learning
(c) e-learning
(d) blended learning

54. At the primary school stage, most of the teachers should be women because they
(a) can teach children better than men.
(b) know basic content better than men.
(c) are available on lower salaries.
(d) can deal with children with love and affection.

55. Which one is the highest order of learning?
(a) Chain learning
(b) Problem-solving learning

(c) Stimulus-response learning
(d) Conditioned-reflex learning

56. A person can enjoy teaching as a profession when he
(a) has control over students.
(b) commands respect from students.
(c) is more qualified than his colleagues.
(d) is very close to higher authorities.

57. "A diagram speaks more than 1000 words." The statement means that the teacher should
(a) use diagrams in teaching.
(b) speak more and more in the class
(c) use teaching aids in the class.
(d) not speak too much in the class.

58. A research paper
(a) is a compilation of information on a topic.
(b) contains original research as deemed by the author.
(c) contains peer-reviewed original research or evaluation of research conducted by others.
(d) can be published in more than one journal.

59. Which one of the following belongs to the category of good 'research ethics'?
(a) Publishing the same paper in two research journals without telling the editors.
(b) Conducting a review of the literature that acknowledges the contributions of other people in the relevant field or relevant prior work.
(c) Trimming outliers from a data set without discussing your reasons in a research paper.
(d) Including a colleague as an author on a research paper in return for a favour even though the colleague did not make a serious contribution to the paper.

60. Which of the following sampling methods is not based on probability?
(a) Simple Random Sampling
(b) Stratified Sampling
(c) Quota Sampling
(d) Cluster Sampling

ANSWERS

1. (d)	2. (d)	3. (c)	4. (b)	5. (d)
6. (c)	7. (d)	8. (c)	9. (a)	10. (c)
11. (b)	12. (c)	13. (b)	14. (b)	15. (b)
16. (a)	17. (b)	18. (b)	19. (c)	20. (d)
21. (d)	22. (b)	23. (d)	24. (b)	25. (b)
26. (c)	27. (d)	28. (b)	29. (a)	30. (c)
31. (b)	32. (b)	33. (a)	34. (c)	35. (b)
36. (d)	37. (a)	38. (b)	39. (c)	40. (c)
41. (c)	42. (a)	43. (b)	44. (d)	45. (c)
46. (a)	47. (d)	48. (c)	49. (a)	50. (d)
51. (c)	52. (c)	53. (d)	54. (d)	55. (d)
56. (b)	57. (c)	58. (c)	59. (b)	60. (c)

PAPER–II

Note: This paper contains fifty (50) objective type questions, each question carrying two (2) marks. All questions are compulsory.

1. Match List I (Name of the book) with List II (Author of the book) and select the correct answer from the codes given below:
List I
(A) Sketch of Political History of India (1811)
(B) The History of British India (1881)
(C) The History of India (1841)
(D) The Early History of India (1904)

List II

(i) V.A. Smith
(ii) John Malcolm
(iii) James Mill
(iv) Elphistone

Codes:	A	B	C	D
(a)	(ii)	(iii)	(iv)	(i)
(b)	(iii)	(ii)	(i)	(iv)
(c)	(iv)	(i)	(iii)	(iv)
(d)	(i)	(iv)	(ii)	(iii)

2. Given below are two statements, one is labelled as Assertion (A) and the other is labelled as Reason (R).
   Assertion (A): Neolithic age was followed by the age of metals.
   Reason (R): For some time the use of stone implements continued side by side.
   Read the above statements and select the correct answer from the codes given below:
   Codes:
   (a) Both (A) and (R) are true and (R) is the correct explanation of (A).
   (b) Both (A) and (R) are true, but (R) is not correct explanation of (A).
   (c) (A) is true, but (R) is false.
   (d) (A) is false, but (R) is true.

3. Match List I with List II and select the correct answer from the code given below:

List I	List II
(A) Terracotta horse figure	(i) Banawali
(B) Terracotta spoked wheel	(ii) Mohenjodaro
(C) Fire altar	(iii) Harappa
(D) Cemetery-H	(iv) Kalibangan

Codes:	A	B	C	D
(a)	(ii)	(i)	(iv)	(iii)
(b)	(i)	(iii)	(iv)	(ii)
(c)	(ii)	(iv)	(iii)	(i)
(d)	(ii)	(iii)	(iv)	(i)

4. The concept of 'Oriental Despotism' in Indian history was introduced by whom?
   (a) James Mill
   (b) Lamberg-Karlovsky
   (c) H.G. Rawlinson
   (d) C.H. Philips

5. Match List I with List II and select the correct answer with the help of the codes given below:
   List I
   (A) William Jones
   (B) James Prinsep
   (C) Cunningham of Indus Script
   (D) Sir John Marshall
   List II
   (i) Indus Civilistion
   (ii) Indian Coins
   (iii) Decipherment
   (iv) Asiatic Society of Bengal

Codes:	A	B	C	D
(a)	(iv)	(iii)	(ii)	(i)
(b)	(iii)	(ii)	(i)	(iv)
(c)	(ii)	(i)	(iv)	(iii)
(d)	(i)	(iv)	(iii)	(ii)

6. Match List I (King) with List II (Kingdom) and select the correct answer with the help of the code given below:

List I (King)	List II (Kingdom)
(A) Brahmadatta	(i) Kekaya
(B) Jarasandha	(ii) Kuru
(C) Janamejaya	(iii) Kāśi
(D) Asvapati	(iv) Magadha

Codes:	A	B	C	D
(a)	(i)	(iii)	(iv)	(ii)
(b)	(iii)	(iv)	(ii)	(i)
(c)	(ii)	(i)	(iii)	(iv)
(d)	(iv)	(ii)	(i)	(iii)

7. The earliest available Indian coins were made of

(a) Gold
(b) Silver
(c) Copper
(d) Copper and Silver

8. In Mauryan period 'Sita tax' was imposed on
(a) Forest land only.
(b) Agricultural land under private control.
(c) Agricultural land under State control.
(d) Both (b) and (c).

9. Arrange the following rulers in the chronological order:
(I) Agnimitra (II) Pushyamitra
(III) Sumitra (IV) Sujeshta
Codes:
(a) (I) (II) (III) (IV)
(b) (II) (I) (IV) (III)
(c) (III) (IV) (I) (II)
(d) (IV) (III) (II) (I)

10. The *Romaka* Sidhānta in Indian astronomy shows signs of
(a) Roman influence
(b) Greek influence
(c) Iranian influence
(d) Arabian influence

11. Match the List I with List II and select the correct answer from the codes given below:

List I	**List II**
(A) Vikramashila	(i) Gujarat
(B) Valabhi	(ii) Madhya Pradesh
(C) Besnagar	(iii) Andhra Pradesh
(D) Nagarjunakonda	(iv) Bihar

Codes:	**A**	**B**	**C**	**D**
(a)	(iv)	(i)	(ii)	(iii)
(b)	(i)	(ii)	(iii)	(iv)
(c)	(ii)	(iii)	(iv)	(i)
(d)	(iii)	(iv)	(i)	(ii)

12. Which one of the following inscriptions provides the earliest epigraphical evidence of *Sati*?
(a) Mathura Inscription of Huvishka.
(b) Junagarh Inscription of Rudradaman.
(c) Eran Pillar Inscription of Bhanugupta.
(d) Banskhera Inscription of Harsh.

13. Match List I (Rulers) with List II (Inscriptions) and select the correct answer with the help of the codes given below:

List I	**List II**
(A) Kumaragupta I	(i) Uttaramerur Inscription
(B) Kumargupta II	(ii) Bilsad Inscription
(C) Budhagupta	(iii) Sarnath Inscription
(D) Parantaka II	(iv) Eran Inscription

Codes:	**A**	**B**	**C**	**D**
(a)	(ii)	(iii)	(iv)	(i)
(b)	(iii)	(iv)	(ii)	(i)
(c)	(iv)	(iii)	(ii)	(i)
(d)	(i)	(ii)	(iii)	(iv)

14. Arrange the following into sequential order and select the correct answer from the codes given below:
(i) Simha Vishnu
(ii) Parameswaravarman II
(iii) Narasimhavarman I
(iv) Mahendravarman I
Codes:
(a) (i), (iv), (iii), (ii)
(b) (ii), (iii), (iv), (i)
(c) (iii), (iv), (ii), (i)
(d) (iv), (ii), (i), (iii)

15. The rulers of South India constantly fought with each other, because of
(a) Imperialistic ambition.
(b) Old dynastic rivalry.
(c) Desire to control the rivers like Godavari, Krishna and their valleys.
(d) Monopolistic ambition to control sea routes.

16. Consider the following statements about Amir Khusrau:
   (i) He was a disciple of the Sufi Saint Shaikh Nizamuddin Auliya.
   (ii) He is said to have written several treatises on music.
   (iii) His work *Khazain-ul Futuh* deals with the reign of Sultan Kaiqubad.
   (iv) The musical instrument *Sitar* is regarded as his invention.

   Which of the statements given above are correct? Select your answer from the codes given below:
   Codes:
   (a) (i), (iv)
   (b) (i), (ii), (iii)
   (c) (i), (ii), (iv)
   (d) (i), (iii), (iv)
17. Which Sultan of Delhi got Qutubminar repaired, cleaned the derelict Hauz Khas and erected on its bank a specious madrasah?
   (a) Iltutmish (b) Alauddin Khalji
   (c) Firuz Tughlaq (d) Sikandar Lodi
18. Match List I with List II and select the correct answer from the codes given below:

List I (Saint-Poets)	List II (Compositions)
(A) Kabir	(i) *Vinaya Patrika*
(B) Surdas	(ii) *Bijak*
(C) Eknath	(iii) *Bhramar-Geet*
(D) Tulsidas	(iv) *Bhavartha Ramayana*

Codes:	A	B	C	D
(a)	(i)	(iii)	(ii)	(iv)
(b)	(ii)	(iii)	(iv)	(i)
(c)	(ii)	(iv)	(i)	(iii)
(d)	(i)	(ii)	(iii)	(iv)

19. Who among the following writers claim that Muhammad bin Tughlaq had designated Firuz Shah as his heir?
   (a) Ziauddin Barani
   (b) Shams-i-Siraj Afif
   (c) Ibn Battuta
   (d) Yahia bin Ahmad Sirhindi
20. Match List I with List II and select the correct answer from the codes given below:

   List I (Regional Kingdoms of Sultanate period)
   (A) Gujarat Sultanate
   (B) Bahmani Sultanate
   (C) Kashmir Sultanate
   (D) Malwa Sultanate

   List II (Ruler)
   (i) Mahmud Khalji I
   (ii) Mahmud Beghra
   (iii) Sultan Sikandar
   (iv) Ahmad Shah I

Codes:	A	B	C	D
(a)	(ii)	(iii)	(iv)	(i)
(b)	(ii)	(i)	(iii)	(iv)
(c)	(iv)	(ii)	(iii)	(i)
(d)	(ii)	(iv)	(iii)	(i)

21. Who among the following rulers divided his troops into units of fifty, two hundred, two hundred fifty and five hundred?
   (a) Sikandar Lodi (b) Sher Shah
   (c) Islam Shah (d) Akbar
22. Arrange the followings in correct chronological order:
   (i) Conquest of Gujarat by Akbar.
   (ii) Battle of Haldighati.
   (iii) Introduction of the *dagh* system.
   (iv) Introduction of the *Ilahi* era.

   Select the correct answer from the codes given below:
   Codes:
   (a) (ii), (i), (iv), (iii)
   (b) (i), (ii), (iii), (iv)
   (c) (i), (iii), (ii), (iv)
   (d) (ii), (iii), (i), (iv)

23. Identify the dynasty which Rai Singh Panj Hajari belonged to '
(a) Rathore of Bikaner
(b) Rathore of Jodhpur
(c) Rathore of Kishangarh
(d) Rathore of Ratlam

24. Which one of the following pairs is correctly matched?
(a) Second Battle of Panipat : Akbar Vs. Ibrahim Lodi
(b) Battle of Haldighati : Akbar Vs. Rana Udai Singh
(c) Battle of Dharmat : Aurangzeb Vs. Dara
(d) Battle of Samugarh : Aurangzeb Vs. Shuja

25. Match List I with List II and select the correct answer from the codes given below:
List I
(A) Khasa-i-sharifa (B) Sihbandi
(C) Talab (D) Zakat
List II
(i) Trooper hired for the occasion
(ii) Emperor's own establishment
(iii) Transit duty
(iv) Mansabdar's pay claim

Codes:	A	B	C	D
(a)	(ii)	(i)	(iv)	(iii)
(b)	(i)	(ii)	(iii)	(iv)
(c)	(iii)	(i)	(ii)	(iv)
(d)	(ii)	(iii)	(i)	(iv)

26. 'The cities look attractive from a distance, but inside them all the splendour is lost in the narrowness of the streets and the bustling of the crowds.'
The above comment on the Mughal Indian cities was made by
(a) Father Monserrate
(b) Sir Thomas Roe
(c) Peter Mundi
(d) Tavernier

27. Who stated that "Twenty thousand men worked incessantly to construct Taj Mahal"?
(a) Mannuci
(b) Abdul Hamid Lahori
(c) Tavernier
(d) Shah Nawaz Khan

28. Given below are two statements, one labelled Assertion (A) and other labelled Reason (R).
Assertion (A): Many Mughal nobles carried on trade in their own name, or in partnership with merchants.
Reason (R): As Governor of Bengal, Mir Jumla tried to monopolise trade in all important commodities.
In the context of the above two statements, which one of the following is correct? Select your answer from the codes given below:
Codes:
(a) Both (A) and (R) are true and (R) is the correct explanation of (A).
(b) Both (A) and (R) are true, but (R) is not the correct explanation of (A).
(c) (A) is true, but (R) is false.
(d) (A) is false, but (R) is true.

29. Which historian called the Indian merchants engaged in over-seas trade as pedlars?
(a) N. Steensgaard
(b) Om Prakash
(c) Van Leur
(d) Ashin Das Gupta

30. Which of the following pairs is not correctly matched?

	Authors		Books
(a)	Sunil Kumar	:	*The Emergence of the Delhi Sultanate*
(b)	Catherine B. Asher and Cynthia B. Talbot	:	*India Before Europe*

(c) Harbans Mukhia	:	*The Mughals of India*
(d) Farhat Hasan	:	*Writing the Mughal World*

31. Consider the names of the following Mughal emperors of the Eighteenth century:
 (i) Alamgir II
 (ii) Ahmad Shah
 (iii) Jahandar Shah
 (iv) Muhammad Shah

 Which among the following sequences represents the correct chronological order of these Mughal emperors? Select your answer from the codes given below:

 Codes:
 (a) (ii), (i), (iii), (iv)
 (b) (i), (ii), (iii), (iv)
 (c) (iii), (iv), (ii), (i)
 (d) (iii), (iv), (i), (ii)

32. Which of the following was not true of James Augustus Hickey?
 (a) He was the pioneer of Indian Journalism.
 (b) He was the founder of the *Bengal Chronicle.*
 (c) He always worked for the press freedom.
 (d) He was sent to prison by Company Government for being fearless journalist.

33. Who of the following Governor Generals started the Indian Civil Services?
 (a) William Bentinck
 (b) Wellesley
 (c) Cornwallis
 (d) Warren Hastings

34. At which place 'Women's Indian Association' was founded?
 (a) Bombay (b) Calcutta
 (c) Madras (d) Jaipur

35. Who authored the book "Stree-Purush Tulana" (A Comparison between Women and Men)?
 (a) Tarabai Shinde
 (b) Ramabai Ranade
 (c) Savitribai Phule
 (d) Aanandibai Joshi

36. Match List I with List II and select the correct answer with the help of the codes given below:

List I (Movement)	**List II (Area)**
(A) Pabna Movement	(i) Maharashtra
(B) Moplah Rebellion	(ii) East Bengal
(C) Deccan Riots	(iii) Gujarat
(D) Bardoli Movement	(iv) Malabar

Codes:	**A**	**B**	**C**	**D**
(a)	(i)	(ii)	(iv)	(iii)
(b)	(ii)	(iv)	(i)	(iii)
(c)	(iii)	(iv)	(ii)	(i)
(d)	(iv)	(i)	(iii)	(ii)

37. In which year the book *Hind Swaraj* was written?
 (a) 1907 (b) 1908
 (c) 1909 (d) 1910

38. Who of the following was known as 'Socrates of Maharashtra'?
 (a) N.M. Joshi
 (b) M.G. Ranade
 (c) G.H. Deshmukh
 (d) G.K. Gokhale

39. As a result of the Poona Pact the number of seats reserved for the depressed classes out of general electorate seats were
 (a) Decreased (b) Increased
 (c) Retained (d) Abolished

40. The Gujarat Sabha led by Gandhi played a leading role in the
(a) Ahmedabad Mill Workers' Strike
(b) Peasant Agitation of Kheda
(c) Bardoli Agitation
(d) Salt Satyagraha

41. Who of the following set up Mahila Arya Samaj to improve Women's Education?
(a) Pandita Ramabai
(b) Sister Nivedita
(c) D.K. Karve
(d) G.S. Agarkar

42. In which year Sharda Act was passed?
(a) 1927 (b) 1928
(c) 1929 (d) 1930

43. Rani Gardinulu who fought against the British was from
(a) Tripura (b) Assam
(c) Nagaland (d) Manipur

44. Which one of the following was not associated with Indian National Army?
(a) Rashbihari Bose
(b) Lakshmi Sehgal
(c) Rashbihari Ghosh
(d) General Mohan Singh

45. In February 1947 Prime Minister Attlee declared that the British would quit India by
(a) May 1948 (b) June 1948
(c) July 1948 (d) August 1948

46. The generals of the I.N.A. Shah Nawaz, Gurdial Singh Dhillon and Prem Sehgal, were formerly officers of the
(a) British Indian Army
(b) British Army
(c) Kashmiri Army
(d) Punjab Army

47. The Constitution of India introduced on 26th January, 1950 laid down certain basic principles and values. Which of the following was not part of it?
(a) India will be a secular and democratic republic.
(b) It will be a Parliamentary system based on adult franchise.
(c) It guarantees all citizens equality before law.
(d) It provides free education for girls.

48. The Moplahs were the poor peasants and agricultural labourers of South Malabar. They were mainly converts to Islam from the lower castes like
(a) Tiyya, Cheruma
(b) Ramdasiya, Mehtar
(c) Mahar, Mang
(d) Mala, Madiga

49. In the context of Cold War, which one of the following statements is not correct?
(a) USA planned to use the Island of Cuba, as a base for launching her nuclear weapons.
(b) Both USA and Soviet Union sent weapons and troops to other countries to fight.
(c) The Russians built the huge Berlin Wall to prevent the people of East Berlin from moving into West Berlin.
(d) NATO and Warsaw Pact came into being in due response to the Cold War situation.

50. Consider the following observations concerning 'new history' and select the correct answer.
(a) It focussed attention on manners, customs and beliefs of whole people.
(b) It tried to displace political history from the centre of historical attention.
(c) It employed the methods and insights of sociology and other sciences.
(d) All of the above.

ANSWERS

1. (a)	2. (a)	3. (a)	4. (c)	5. (a)
6. (b)	7. (d)	8. (b)	9. (b)	10. (b)
11. (a)	12. (c)	13. (a)	14. (a)	15. (c)
16. (c)	17. (c)	18. (b)	19. (a)	20. (d)
21. (c)	22. (b)	23. (a)	24. (c)	25. (a)
26. (a)	27. (c)	28. (b)	29. (c)	30. (d)
31. (c)	32. (b)	33. (c)	34. (c)	35. (a)
36. (b)	37. (c)	38. (b)	39. (b)	40. (b)
41. (a)	42. (c)	43. (c)	44. (c)	45. (b)
46. (a)	47. (d)	48. (a)	49. (a)	50. (d)

PAPER–III

Note: This paper contains seventy five (75) objective type questions of two (2) marks each. All questions are compulsory.

1. Match List I (authors) with List II (definitions of history) and select the correct answer with the help of the codes given below:

   List I (Authors)
   (A) Oakshott (B) Travelyan
   (C) Colling (D) Bury

   List II (Definitions of History)
   (i) All history is history of thought.
   (ii) History is herself simply a science, no less and no more.
   (iii) The fact is wood that the past in history varies with the present.
   (iv) The value of history is not scientific. Its true value is educational.

Codes:	A	B	C	D
(a)	(iii)	(iv)	(i)	(ii)
(b)	(ii)	(iii)	(iv)	(i)
(c)	(iv)	(ii)	(iii)	(i)
(d)	(iv)	(iii)	(i)	(ii)

2. Match List I with List II and select the correct answer from the code given below:

List I	List II
(A) Palaeolithic	(i) Ground stone tools
(B) Mesolithic	(ii) Rock painting
(C) Neolithic	(iii) Flaked stone tools
(D) Upper Palaeolithic	(iv) Microlithic tools

Codes:	A	B	C	D
(a)	(i)	(iv)	(ii)	(iii)
(b)	(iii)	(i)	(iv)	(ii)
(c)	(iii)	(iv)	(i)	(ii)
(d)	(ii)	(iii)	(iv)	(i)

3. The largest number of Harappan sites have been found on the bank of the river
   (a) Indus (b) Satluj
   (c) Saraswati (d) Ravi

4. What was the unique feature of the Harappan civilization which was unknown to other contemporary civilizations?
   (a) Cotton Cloth
   (b) Palatial Houses
   (c) Steatite Seals
   (d) Carnelian Beads

5. Match List I (Place name) with List II (Geographical location) and select the correct answer from the code given below:

List I	List II
(A) Meluha	(i) Bahrin
(B) Dilmun	(ii) Indus Region
(C) Makan	(iii) Central Asia
(D) Kurgaon	(iv) Makaran Coast

Codes:	A	B	C	D
(a)	(i)	(iii)	(iv)	(ii)
(b)	(iv)	(i)	(ii)	(iii)
(c)	(ii)	(i)	(iv)	(iii)
(d)	(iii)	(i)	(iv)	(ii)

6. Who was the first to propound the theory of Aryan invasion on India?
   (a) R.E.M. Wheeler
   (b) Gorden V. Childe

(c) J. Marshall
(d) R.P. Chanda

7. The famous philosopher king of the kingdom of Panchala during the later Vedic period was
(a) Ajatasatru
(b) Parikshita
(c) Pravahana Jaivali
(d) Svetaketu

8. Who among the following Dharmasutra writers does not approve the system of Niyoga?
(a) Gautama (b) Apastamba
(c) Baudhayana (d) Vasishtha

9. Several names of Kautilya have been mentioned in which one of the following?
(a) Devi-Chandra-Guptam
(b) Dasa-Kumara-Charita
(c) Mudrarakshasa
(d) Abhidhana-Chintamani

10. Which among the following places is not associated with the Megalithic culture?
(a) Chandragiri (b) Brahmagiri
(c) Adichchanallur (d) Utnur

11. What is the correct chronological order of the following Greco-Roman authors?
(a) Ktesias (b) Pliny
(c) Strabo (d) Ptolemy
(a) (b), (c), (d), (a)
(b) (a), (c), (b), (d)
(c) (c), (d), (a), (b)
(d) (d), (b), (c), (a)

12. The seat of the third great Sangam of Tamil authors was at
(a) Gangaikond Cholapuram
(b) Kanchi
(c) Madura
(d) Tanjavur

13. Which among the following was not a port city during the ancient period?
(a) Tuticorin (b) Poompuhar
(c) Tamralipti (d) Nagapatnam

14. Match List I with List II and select the correct answer from the code given below:

List I	List II
(A) Romaka Sidhanta	(i) Arabian's influence
(B) Rouletted Ware	(ii) Greek's influence
(C) Surkhi	(iii) Roman's influence
(D) Algebra	(iv) Kushan's influence

Codes:	A	B	C	D
(a)	(ii)	(iii)	(iv)	(i)
(b)	(iii)	(ii)	(iv)	(i)
(c)	(iv)	(ii)	(iii)	(i)
(d)	(i)	(iii)	(ii)	(iv)

15. Which one of the following inscriptions mentions the names of both Chandragupta and Ashoka?
(a) Allahabad Pillar inscription of Samudragupta.
(b) Junagarh inscription of Rudradaman.
(c) Shahbajgarhi inscription of Ashoka.
(d) Hathigumpha inscription of Kharvela.

16. Match List I with List II and select the correct answer from the code given below:

List I	List II
(A) Nyāya	(i) Jamini
(B) Vaiseshika	(ii) Kapila
(C) Sānkhya	(iii) Kanāda
(D) Mimansa	(iv) Gautam

Codes:	A	B	C	D
(a)	(iii)	(iv)	(ii)	(i)
(b)	(ii)	(iii)	(i)	(iv)
(c)	(iv)	(iii)	(ii)	(i)
(d)	(iv)	(i)	(iii)	(ii)

17. In connection with Satvahana coins which one of the following statement is *not correct*?
(a) They did not issue gold coins.
(b) They issued gold coins.

(c) They issued lead coins.
(d) They issued potin coins.

18. Match List I with List II and select the correct answer from codes given below:

List I	List II
(A) Kodumanal	(i) Pallava Temple
(B) Gangaikondan	(ii) Port City
(C) Mahabalipuram	(iii) Trade Centre
(D) Poompuhar	(iv) Chola Seat of Power

Codes:	A	B	C	D
(a)	(ii)	(iv)	(i)	(iii)
(b)	(i)	(ii)	(iii)	(iv)
(c)	(ii)	(iii)	(iv)	(i)
(d)	(iii)	(iv)	(i)	(ii)

19. With which of the following eras was the Malava-reckoning identical?
(a) Vikrama (b) Śaka
(c) Gupta (d) Kali

20. In which among the following a reference to the trading activities of the Tamils is found?
(a) Mullaippattu (b) Nedunalvadai
(c) Silappadigaram (d) Manimekhalai

21. The writer of Kural, the famous Deccan epic was
(a) Kamban (b) Ottakuttan
(c) Puglenid (d) Tiru-Valluvar

22. Match List I with List II and select the correct answer from the code given below:

List I	List II
(A) Tolkāppiyama	(i) Jain Philosophy
(B) Tirūkkural	(ii) Love Story
(C) Silappadikāram	(iii) Tamil Grammar
(D) Paripādal	(iv) Philosophy

Codes:	A	B	C	D
(a)	(iii)	(ii)	(i)	(iv)
(b)	(iii)	(i)	(ii)	(iv)
(c)	(i)	(iii)	(ii)	(iv)
(d)	(ii)	(i)	(iii)	(iv)

23. Which Indian epigraph yields the first evidence of zero?
(a) Apsad inscription of Adityasena.
(b) Gwalior inscription of Bhojdeva.
(c) Nasik inscription of Gotamiputra Satkarni.
(d) Hathigumpha inscription of Kharvela.

24. Given below are two statements, one labelled as Assertion (A) and the other labelled as Reason (R):
Assertion (A): Pallava King Mahendra-Varman I built some of the finest rock-cut Hindu temples, including, those at Mahabalipuram.
Reason (R): Mahendra-Varman I began life as a Jaina but was converted to Shaivism.
In the context of the above two statements, which one of the following is correct?
(a) Both (A) and (R) are true, and (R) is the correct explanation of (A).
(b) Both (A) and (R) are true, but (R) is not the correct explanation of (A).
(c) (A) is true, but (R) is false.
(d) (A) is false, but (R) is true.

25. Arrange the following into sequential order and select the correct answer from the codes given below:
(i) Rajaraja Chola I
(ii) Aditya Chola
(iii) Rajendra Chola
(iv) Parantaka Chola I
Codes:
(a) (i), (ii), (iii), (iv)
(b) (ii), (iv), (i), (iii)
(c) (iii), (iv), (ii), (i)
(d) (iv), (iii), (i), (ii)

26. Which of the following statements are not correct?
1. Iltutmish's tomb is an indication of the mixing of the Hindu and Muslim traditions of architecture.

2. First true arch was used in the tomb of Sultan Nasiruddin Mahmud.
3. The horse shoe arch was used for the first time in the construction of Alai Darwaza.
4. Architectural device known as double dome was not used in any building constructed during the Sultanate period.

Select your answer from the codes given below:

Codes:

(a) 1, 3, 4 (b) 2, 4
(c) 1, 3 (d) 2, 3, 4

27. The period from 1236 to 1296 witnessed the reign of
(a) Five Sultans (b) Seven Sultans
(c) Ten Sultans (d) Twelve Sultans

28. Which of the following statements is not correct?
(a) In Delhi Sultanate use of slave labour in craft production was significant.
(b) Slaves were also used for unskilled, domestic work.
(c) Sultan Firuz Tughlaq had 12,000 artisans among his slaves.
(d) Immigrant Muslim masons were employed for the construction of Sultanate buildings, including both mosques and tombs.

29. Which crops were not cultivated in India during the Sultanate period?
1. Potato 2. Barley
3. Sesame 4. Maize

Select your answer from the codes given below:

Codes:

(a) 1, 2, 3 (b) 1, 2
(c) 1, 4 (d) 3, 4

30. Match List I with List II and select the correct answer from the codes given below:

List I (Rulers of Delhi Sultanate)
(A) Jalaluddin Khalji
(B) Alauddin Khalji
(C) Ghiyasuddin Tughlaq
(D) Firuz Shah Tughlaq

List II (Measure or event)
(i) Conquest of Bengal
(ii) Establishment of the Department of Public Works
(iii) Execution of Sidi Maula
(iv) Conquest of Malwa and Gujarat

Codes:	**A**	**B**	**C**	**D**
(a)	(i)	(iv)	(iii)	(ii)
(b)	(iii)	(iv)	(i)	(ii)
(c)	(iv)	(iii)	(i)	(ii)
(d)	(i)	(iii)	(iv)	(ii)

31. The names of the three successors of Khizr Khan, the founder of the Saiyyid dynasty, are given below:
(i) Mabarak Shah
(ii) Alauddin Alam Shah
(iii) Muhammad Shah

Which of the following sequences represents the correct chronological order?
(a) (i), (ii), (iii) (b) (i), (iii), (ii)
(c) (iii), (ii), (i) (d) (ii), (iii), (i)

32. Match List I with List II and select the correct answer from the codes given below:

List I (Sufi terminology)
(A) Futuh (B) Sama
(C) Barkat (D) Malfuz

List II (Meaning)
(i) Sufi musical gathering
(ii) Conversations of Sufi saints
(iii) Unasked for charity
(iv) Spiritual grace acquired by a Sufi

Codes:	**A**	**B**	**C**	**D**
(a)	(i)	(iii)	(ii)	(iv)
(b)	(iii)	(i)	(iv)	(ii)

(c) (iii) (ii) (i) (iv)
(d) (iv) (iii) (ii) (i)

33. Who calls the political economy of the Vijayanagara regime of the sixteenth century as feudal?
(a) N. Karashima
(b) Burton Stein
(c) K.V. Ramesh
(d) N. Venkataramanyya

34. Constider the following statements:
(i) Guru Nanak was interested in all the major forms of contemporary religious beliefs and practices whether "Hindu" or "Muslim".
(ii) Guru Nanak was soft on the Jain monks.
(iii) He considered ritual reading of scriptures as waste of time.
(iv) During the last fifteen years of his life Guru Nanak settled at Kiratpur.

Which of the above statements are not correct? Select your answer from the codes given below:

Codes:

(a) (i) and (ii) (b) (i) and (iv)
(c) (ii) and (iii) (d) (ii) and (iv)

35. Given below are two statements, one labelled as Assertion (A) and the other labelled as Reason (R):
Assertion (A): Like his father and Surs, Humayan was not willing to recognize any power politically superior to him.
Reason (R): He himself assumed the title of Khalifa. In the context of the above two statements, which one of the followings is correct?
Codes:
(a) Both (A) and (R) are true and (R) is the correct explanation of (A).
(b) Both (A) and (R) are true, but (R) is not the correct explanation of (A).
(c) (A) is true, but (R) is false.
(d) (A) is false, but (R) is true.

36. Who stated that the 'best place for a woman is the *purdah* or the grave?
(a) Amir Khusrau
(b) Isami
(c) Badauni
(d) Shaikh Ahmad Sirhindi

37. Who justified Mughal attack on Malwa by saying that Baz Bahadur occupied himself with "unlawful and vicious practices"?
(a) Nizamuddin Ahmad
(b) Abdul Qadir Badauni
(c) Arif Qandhari
(d) Abul Fazl

38. Given below are two statements, one labelled as Assertion (A) and the other labelled as Reason (R):
Assertion (A): The art of painting reached its highest watermark during Jahanagir's reign.
Reason (R): He was not interested in other forms of art.
In the context of the above two statements, which one of the following is correct?
Codes:
(a) Both (A) and (R) are true and (R) is the correct explanation of (A).
(b) Both (A) and (R) are true, but (R) is not the correct explanation of (A).
(c) (A) is true, but (R) is false.
(d) (A) is false, but (R) is true.

39. Given below are two statements, one labelled as Assertion (A) and other labelled as Reason (R).
Assertion (A): The advent of the European trading companies in India adversely affected India's export trade during the seventeenth century.
Reason (R): Large quantities of silver found its way into India due to the trading activities of the English East India Company in the seventeenth century.

In the context of the above two statements, which one of the following is correct?

Select the correct answer from the codes given below:

Codes:

(a) Both (A) and (R) are true and (R) is the correct explanation of (A).

(b) Both (A) and (R) are true, but (R) is not the correct explanation of (A).

(c) (A) is true, but (R) is false.

(d) (A) is false, but (R) is true.

40. Which of the following officers was *not* associated with the administration of cities in the Mughal empire?

(a) Nazim (b) Qazi

(c) Mir-i-adl (d) Kotwal

41. Consider the following statements:

(i) Shah Jahan discontinued Jharokha darshan and tula dana.

(ii) Shah Jahan refused to grant land to Shanti Das, the leading Jain Jeweller and banker of Ahmedabad to build a resting place for Jain saints.

(iii) Shah Jahan banned mixed marriages between Hindus and Muslims in Kashmir.

(iv) Shah Jahan exempted the theologians from offering Sijda.

Which of the above statements are not correct. Select the correct answer from the codes given below:

Codes:

(a) (i) and (ii) (b) (ii) and (iii)

(c) (ii) and (iv) (d) (i) and (iv)

42. Which Mughal Court Chronicle gives an account of the Ahom Kingdom of Assam?

(a) *Padshahnama*

(b) *Alamgirnama*

(c) *Futuhat-i-Alamgiri*

(d) *Maasir-i-Alamgiri*

43. Which historian has spoken of tripartite relationship between zamindars, jagirdars and peasants as the reason for the crisis of the Mughal Empire and its decline?

(a) Stephan P. Blake

(b) M. Athar Ali

(c) Satish Chandra

(d) C.A. Bayly

44. Consider the following statements:

(i) Shivaji could check the Deccan power from intruding into his swaraj territory.

(ii) He could plunder Surat in 1664.

(iii) He could withstand the attacks of Shaista Khan and Mirza Raja Jai Singh.

(iv) Bijapur and Golkunda were annexed by the Mughals to undermine the position of Shivaji.

Which of the above statements are not correct. Select the correct answer from the codes given below:

Codes:

(a) (i) and (iii) (b) (i) and (iv)

(c) (ii) and (iii) (d) (iii) and (iv)

45. Which of the following pairs is not correctly matched?

(a) Ahdi	Gentleman trooper
(b) Ashraf	A person of noble birth
(c) Jama-i-Kamil	Assessment of revenue at normal rate
(d) Siwanah Nigar	News reporter

46. Which of the following statements is not correct?

(a) Horses constituted a very large item of India's overland import.

(b) Virji Vohra was one of the prominent merchants of Surat during the 17th century.

(c) The Portuguese dominated India's maritime trade during the 17th century.
(d) Many Mughal nobles participated in trade and commerce during the 17th century.

47. Which of the following statements is not correct?
(a) Monetary system of the Mughals was largely based on silver rupaiya.
(b) The Mughal rulers from Babur to Shahjahan continued to harbour territorial ambitions in Central Asia.
(c) There was no middle class in Mughal India.
(d) The period 1605-1658 witnessed significant changes in the *Mansab* and *Jagir* systems.

48. Given below are two statements, one labelled as Assertion (A) and the other labelled as Reason (R):
Assertion (A): With the acquisition of Diwani of Bengal the Company directly organised the 'drain of wealth'.
Reason (R): The Company began to send to England the revenue of Bengal through what were called "Investment".
In the context of the above two statements, which one of the following is correct?
(a) Both (A) and (R) are true and (R) is the correct explanation of (A).
(b) Both (A) and (R) are true, but (R) is not the correct explanation of (A).
(c) (A) is true, but (R) is false.
(d) (A) is false, but (R) is true.

49. The biggest British capital investment in India was made in
(a) The Jute Mills
(b) The Railways, Banking, Insurance and Shipping.
(c) The Tea and Coffee Plantations.
(d) The Indigo Plantations.

50. Who said: "The misery hardly finds a parallel in the history of commerce. The bones of the cotton weavers are bleaching the plains of India."?
(a) William Bentinck
(b) G.M. Travelyan
(c) C. Metcalfe
(d) Lord. Auckland

51. Who said, "Imparting education to natives is our moral duty"?
(a) Warren Hastings
(b) Wellesly
(c) William Bentinck
(d) Lord Moira

52. After 1833 the single biggest source of drain of Indian wealth to Britain was
(a) Export of opium
(b) Export of indigo
(c) British capital investment in India
(d) Export of cotton

53. Which of the following is not one of the causes responsible for the rise of moneylenders in British India?
(a) New Revenue Policy
(b) New Legal System
(c) New Educational System
(d) Commercialization of Agriculture

54. What was the common feature between the Wahabi and Kuka movements?
(a) Both began as religious movement, but drifted to became political movement.
(b) Both were political and economical movement.
(c) Both followed the path of Ahinsa.
(d) Both not suffered from certain weaknesses, such as communal passions, fanaticism and division with ranks.

55. Who of the following was the biographer of Raja Rammohan Roy?
(a) Armstrong
(b) Mary Carpenter

(c) David Havel
(d) Lawrence

56. The LexLoci Act gave
(a) no right over the ancestral properties for the Christian converts.
(b) the Christian converts, the right to inherit their ancestral properties.
(c) no right over the ancestral properties for the converts from Budhist religion.
(d) the right to inherit the ancestral properties for the converts from Jain religion.

57. Due to whose efforts Widow Remarriage Act was passed?
(a) Raja Rammohan Roy
(b) Ishwarchandra Vidyasagar
(c) D.K. Karve
(d) M.G. Ranade

58. In which year the Indian association for the cultivation of science was established?
(a) 1874 (b) 1875
(c) 1876 (d) 1877

59. The Act Prohibiting Child Marriages was passed in 1891 due to the efforts of
(a) Ishwar Chandra Vidyasagar and Jyotiba Phule.
(b) Mahadev Govind Ranade and Jyotiba Phule.
(c) Keshab Chandra Sen and Behramji Malabari.
(d) Keshab Chandra Sen and Mahadev Govind Ranade.

60. Shri Narayan Dharma Paripalana Yogam of Kerala worked for
(a) Upliftment of dalits and peasants.
(b) Women's education.
(c) Eradication of child labour.
(d) The Hindu widow remarriage.

61. The name 'Indian National Congress' was given by
(a) Dadabhai Naoroji
(b) M.G. Ranade
(c) S.N. Bannerjee
(d) A.O. Hume

62. Match List I with List II and select the correct answer with the help of the codes given below:

List I (Name)	List II (Newspaper)
(A) Abul Kalam Azad	i Bombay Chronicle
(B) Pheroze Shah Mehta	ii Al Hilal
(C) Mrs. Annie Besant	iii Young India
(D) Mahatma Gandhi	iv New India

Codes:	A	B	C	D
(a)	ii	i	iv	iii
(b)	i	ii	iv	iii
(c)	ii	i	iii	iv
(d)	iv	i	ii	iii

63. Given below are two statements, one labelled as Assertion (A) and the other labelled as Reason (R).
Assertion (A): *Avesta* is the sacred book of Parsis.
Reason (R): Madam Cama made significant contribution in reforming the Parsi society and uplifting the Parsi women.
In the context of the above two statements, which one of the following is correct?
(a) Both (A) and (R) are true and (R) is the correct explanation of (A).
(b) Both (A) and (R) are true, but (R) is not a correct explanation of (A).
(c) (A) is true, but (R) is false.
(d) (A) is false, but (R) is true.

64. The first woman who got nominated to the Madras Legislative Council in 1927 was
(a) Muthulakshmi Reddy
(b) Sister Subbalakshmi

(c) Mehribai Tata
(d) Margaret Counsins

65. The Indian National Congress became a real mass based political party after the
(a) Nagpur Session of the Congress in 1891.
(b) Nagpur Session of the Congress in 1920.
(c) Kanpur Session of the Congress in 1928.
(d) Faizpur Session of the Congress in 1936.

66. Given below are two statements, one labelled as Assertion (A) and the other labelled as Reason (R).
Assertion (A): Soon after the resignation of the Congress Ministries in the provinces in 1939, the Muslim League observed a deliverance day.
Reason (R): Ambedkar supported it. In the context of the above two statements, which one of the following is correct?
(a) Both (A) and (R) are true and (R) is the correct explanation of (A).
(b) Both (A) and (R) are true and (R) is not the correct explanation of (A).
(c) (A) is true, but (R) is false.
(d) (A) is false, but (R) is true.

67. Given below are two statements, one labelled as Assertion (A) and the other labelled as Reason (R).
Assertion (A): After the Civil War in U.S.A. blacks faced difficulty regarding voting right.
Reason (R): Some Southern States of U.S.A. made it mandatory to have either the name of grandfather or father in the electoral list of 1860.
(a) Both (A) and (R) are true and (R) is the correct explanation of (A).
(b) Both (A) and (R) are true, but (R) is not the correct explanation of (A).
(c) (A) is true and (R) is false.
(d) (A) is false and (R) is true.

68. Who among the following said: "To define the postmodernism is not just to define a term. It is to characterize the present age and to assess how we should respond to it."?
(a) J.F. Lyotard
(b) Arran Gare
(c) J.G. Merquior
(d) None of the above

69. Consider the following statements and point out the one which is incorrect in the context of research methodology:
(a) Subjective approach in Historical writing makes it possible to present a true picture of the past.
(b) External and internal criticism helps the historian to establish the authenticity of the records.
(c) To critically analyse the past happenings the historian needs to know the order of their occurance.
(d) Historical records of the past may not be wholly authentic or genuine to ascertain facts.

70. Consider the following statement: 'Before the scientific revolution of 17th century, history writing in the west suffered from certain weaknesses.'
Which one of the following justifies the above?
(a) Most of the writers were ignorant about the idea of change through time.
(b) The subject matter of history was treated more or less as a branch of literature or philosophy.
(c) Both (a) and (b)
(d) None of the above

The recruitment of the company's army in the eighteenth century was not just building on the existing traditions of the North Indian military labour market; those traditions were being adopted to British imperial preferences. The recruitment system for example, endorsed the traditional British preference for peasants as best potential recruits and followed the colonial stereotypes that wheat-eating Indians rather than the rice-eating groups were physically more suitable for the job, although such ethnic stereotyping became a much more important factor in army recruitment in the late nineteenth century rather than in the eighteenth. During the initial formative phase, Hastings did not want to disturb the existing caste rules in the affairs of the army. So the Company's army consisted mainly of upper caste Brahman and Rajput landed peasants from Awadh and the Rajput and Bhumihar Brahman peasants from north and south Bihar-both wheat-eating regions. These people joined the Company's army because the pay, allowances, pension and resettlement provisions offered by the Company were much better than those offered by the regional States, and what was most important, salaries were paid regularly. The deliberate policy of respecting caste, dietary, travel and others religious practices of the Sepoys fostered a high caste identity of the Company's army. By joining it many of the upcoming socially ambitious castes like the Bhumihar-Brahmans could fulfill their aspirations for social mobility. Cornwallis, despite his preference for Anglicisation, did not disturb this specific organization of the army, and as a result, the Company came to possess a high caste army, which was prone to revolt when their social privileges and pecuniary benefits were cut from the 1820s. As the Company's territories expanded to the west beyond the Bengal frontiers into the mountainous Jungle Terai, in the 1770s and then into the Ceded and Conquered Districts in 1802 there was another attempt to recruit from among the hill tribes. While in the plains the Company ran permanent recruitment centres, in the hills recruitment was made through local notables and payment was offered through the Mughal system of ghatwali service tenures. The defeat of the Indian States, particularly of Mysore in the late eighteenth and of the Marathas in the early nineteenth centuries created another vast reservoir of surplus armed manpower to recruit from; but the Company's army could not absorb all the disbanded soldiers of the Indian princes. Then from 1815 there was another experiment to recruit Gurkha soldiers from among the Nepalis, Garwahlis, and Sirmouri hill men. A skilful blending of the Nepali martial tradition and European training and discipline made the Gurkhas the most trusted soldiers in the British army.

71. The recruitment of the Company's army was based on
   (a) The existing traditions of military labour market.
   (b) Preferred peasants as best potential recruits.
   (c) Colonial stereotypes.
   (d) Physically suitable.

72. The Company's army consisted of
   (a) Upper Caste Brahman and Rajput.
   (b) Landed Peasants from Bihar and Bengal.
   (c) People from rice eating regions.
   (d) People only from South.

73. What kind of payment system British followed in army recruitment?
   (a) Malgujari (b) Ghatwali
   (c) Mahalwari (d) Yadgari

74. Company could not absorb disbanded soldiers after early nineteenth century because
   (a) It had surplus army.
   (b) Company was weak economically.

(c) Company did not want more Indian force.
(d) Of religious considerations.

75. Gurkhas became most trusted soldiers because
(a) They were experts in martial art.
(b) They were hill men.
(c) They were disciplined.
(d) They were experts in Guerilla war.

ANSWERS

1. (a)	2. (c)	3. (c)	4. (a)	5. (c)
6. (d)	7. (c)	8. (b)	9. (d)	10. (d)
11. (b)	12. (c)	13. (a)	14. (a)	15. (b)
16. (c)	17. (b)	18. (d)	19. (a)	20. (c)
21. (d)	22. (b)	23. (b)	24. (a)	25. (b)
26. (b)	27. (c)	28. (d)	29. (c)	30. (b)
31. (b)	32. (b)	33. (a)	34. (d)	35. (c)
36. (c)	37. (a)	38. (c)	39. (d)	40. (a)
41. (a)	42. (b)	43. (c)	44. (d)	45. (c)
46. (c)	47. (c)	48. (a)	49. (b)	50. (a)
51. (d)	52. (c)	53. (c)	54. (a)	55. (b)
56. (b)	57. (b)	58. (c)	59. (c)	60. (a)
61. (a)	62. (a)	63. (b)	64. (a)	65. (b)
66. (b)	67. (a)	68. (b)	69. (a)	70. (c)
71. (a)	72. (a)	73. (b)	74. (a)	75. (a)

DECEMBER–2012

Note: This paper contains sixty (60) multiple choice questions, each question carrying two (2) marks. Candidate is expected to answer any fifty (50) questions. In case more than fifty (50) questions are attempted, only the first fifty (50) questions will be evaluated.

PAPER–I

1. The English word 'Communication' is derived from the words
   (a) Communis and Communicare
   (b) Communist and Commune
   (c) Communism and Communalism
   (d) Communion and Common sense

2. Chinese Cultural Revolution leader Mao Zedong used a type of communication to talk to the masses is known as
   (a) Mass line communication
   (b) Group communication
   (c) Participatory communication
   (d) Dialogue communication

3. Conversing with the spirits and ancestors is termed as
   (a) Transpersonal communication
   (b) Intrapersonal communication
   (c) Interpersonal communication
   (d) Face-to-face communication

4. The largest circulated daily newspaper among the following is
   (a) The Times of India
   (b) The Indian Express
   (c) The Hindu
   (d) The Deccan Herald

5. The pioneer of the silent feature film in India was
   (a) K.A. Abbas
   (b) Satyajit Ray
   (c) B.R. Chopra
   (d) Dada Sahib Phalke

6. Classroom communication of a teacher rests on the principle of
   (a) Infotainment (b) Edutainment
   (c) Entertainment (d) Power equation

7. The missing number in the series:
   0, 6, 24, 60, 120, ?, 336, is
   (a) 240 (b) 220
   (c) 280 (d) 210

8. A group of 7 members having a majority of boys is to be formed out of 6 boys and 4 girls. The number of ways the group can be formed is
   (a) 80 (b) 100
   (c) 90 (d) 110

9. The number of observations in a group is 40. The average of the first 10 members is 4.5 and the average of the remaining 30 members is 3.5. The average of the whole group is
   (a) 4 (b) 15/2
   (c) 15/4 (d) 6

10. If MOHAN is represented by the code KMFYL, then COUNT will be represented by
   (a) AMSLR (b) MSLAR
   (c) MASRL (d) SAMLR

11. The sum of the ages of two persons A and B is 50. 5 years ago, the ratio of their ages was 5/3. The present age of A and B are
(a) 30, 20 (b) 35, 15
(c) 38, 12 (d) 40, 10

12. Let a means minus (–), b means multiplied by (×), C means divided by (÷) and D means plus (+). The value of 90 D 9 a 29 C 10 b 2 is
(a) 8 (b) 10
(c) 12 (d) 14

13. Consider the Assertion I and Assertion II and select the right code given below:
Assertion I : Even Bank-lockers are not safe. Thieves can break them and take away your wealth. But thieves cannot go to heaven. So you should keep your wealth in heaven.
Assertion II: The difference of skin-colour of beings is because of the distance from the sun and not because of some permanent traits. Skin-colour is the result of body's reaction to the sun and its rays.
Codes:
(a) Both the assertions I and II are forms of argument.
(b) The assertion I is an argument but the assertion II is not.
(c) The assertion II is an argument but the assertion I is not.
(d) Both the assertions are explanations of facts.

14. By which of the following proposition, the proposition 'some men are not honest' is contradicted?
(a) All men are honest.
(b) Some men are honest.
(c) No men are honest.
(d) All of the above.

15. A stipulative definition is
(a) always true
(b) always false
(c) sometimes true sometimes false
(d) neither true nor false

16. Choose the appropriate alternative given in the codes to replace the question mark.
Examiner – Examinee, Pleader – Client, Preceptor – ?
(a) Customer (b) Path-finder
(c) Perceiver (d) Disciple

17. If the statement 'most of the students are obedient' is taken to be true, which one of the following pair of statements can be claimed to be true?
I. All obedient persons are students.
II. All students are obedient.
III. Some students are obedient.
IV. Some students are not disobedient.
Codes:
(a) I & II (b) II & III
(c) III & IV (d) II & IV

18. Choose the right code:
A deductive argument claims that:
I. The conclusion does not claim something more than that which is contained in the premises.
II. The conclusion is supported by the premise/premises conclusively.
III. If the conclusion is false, then premise/premises may be either true or false.
IV. If premise/combination of premises is true, then conclusion must be true.
Codes:
(a) I and II (b) I and III
(c) II and III (d) All the above

On the basis of the data given in the following table, give answers to questions from 19 to 24:

Government Expenditures on Social Services
(As per cent of total expenditure)

Sl.No.	Items	2007-08	2008-09	2009-10	2010-11
	Social Services	11.06	12.94	13.06	14.02
(a)	Education, sports & youth affairs	4.02	4.04	3.96	4.46
(b)	Health & family welfare	2.05	1.91	1.90	2.03
(c)	Water supply, housing, etc.	2.02	2.31	2.20	2.27
(d)	Information & broadcasting	0.22	0.22	0.20	0.22
(e)	Welfare to SC/ST & OBC	0.36	0.35	0.41	0.63
(f)	Labour and employment	0.27	0.27	0.22	0.25
(g)	Social welfare & nutrition	0.82	0.72	0.79	1.06
(h)	North-eastern areas	0.00	1.56	1.50	1.75
(i)	Other social services	1.29	1.55	1.87	1.34
	Total Government expenditure	100.00	100.00	100.00	100.00

19. How many activities in the social services are there where the expenditure has been less than 5 percent of the total expenditures incurred on the social services in 2008-09 ?
(a) One (b) Three
(c) Five (d) All the above

20. In which year, the expenditures on the social services have increased at the highest rate?
(a) 2007-08 (b) 2008-09
(c) 2009-10 (d) 2010-11

21. Which of the following activities remains almost stagnant in terms of share of expenditures?
(a) North-eastern areas
(b) Welfare to SC/ST & OBC
(c) Information & broadcasting
(d) Social welfare and nutrition

22. Which of the following item's expenditure share is almost equal to the remaining three items in the given years?
(a) Information & broadcasting
(b) Welfare to SC/ST and OBC
(c) Labour and employment
(d) Social welfare & nutrition

23. Which of the following items of social services has registered the highest rate of increase in expenditures during 2007-08 to 2010-11?
(a) Education, sports & youth affairs
(b) Welfare to SC/ST & OBC
(c) Social welfare & nutrition
(d) Overall social services

24. Which of the following items has registered the highest rate of decline in terms of expenditure during 2007-08 to 2009-10?
(a) Labour and employment
(b) Health & family welfare
(c) Social welfare & nutrition
(d) Education, sports & youth affairs

25. ALU stands for
(a) American Logic Unit
(b) Alternate Local Unit
(c) Alternating Logic Unit
(d) Arithmetic Logic Unit

26. A Personal Computer uses a number of chips mounted on a circuit board called
(a) Microprocessor (b) System Board
(c) Daughter Board (d) Mother Board

27. Computer Virus is a
(a) Hardware (b) Bacteria
(c) Software (d) None of these

28. Which one of the following is correct?
(a) $(17)_{10} = (17)_{16}$
(b) $(17)_{10} = (17)_{8}$
(c) $(17)_{10} = (10111)_{2}$
(d) $(17)_{10} = (10001)_{2}$

29. The file extension of MS-Word document in Office 2007 is .
(a) .pdf (b) .doc
(c) .docx (d) .txt

30. _______ is a protocol used by e-mail clients to download e-mails to your computer.
(a) TCP (b) FTP
(c) SMTP (d) POP

31. Which of the following is a source of methane?
(a) Wetlands
(b) Foam Industry
(c) Thermal Power Plants
(d) Cement Industry

32. 'Minamata disaster' in Japan was caused by pollution due to
(a) Lead (b) Mercury
(c) Cadmium (d) Zinc

33. Biomagnification means increase in the
(a) concentration of pollutants in living organisms
(b) number of species
(c) size of living organisms
(d) biomass

34. Nagoya Protocol is related to
(a) Climate change
(b) Ozone depletion
(c) Hazardous waste
(d) Biodiversity

35. The second most important source after fossil fuels contributing to India's energy needs is
(a) Solar energy (b) Nuclear energy
(c) Hydropower (d) Wind energy

36. In case of earthquakes, an increase of magnitude 1 on Richter Scale implies
(a) a ten-fold increase in the amplitude of seismic waves.
(b) a ten-fold increase in the energy of the seismic waves.
(c) two-fold increase in the amplitude of seismic waves.
(d) two-fold increase in the energy of seismic waves.

37. Which of the following is not a measure of Human Development Index?
(a) Literacy Rate
(b) Gross Enrolment
(c) Sex Ratio
(d) Life Expectancy

38. India has the highest number of students in colleges after
(a) the U.K. (b) the U.S.A.
(c) Australia (d) Canada

39. Which of the following statement(s) is/are not correct about the Attorney General of India?
1. The President appoints a person, who is qualified to be a Judge of a High Court, to be the Attorney General of India.
2. He has the right of audience in all the Courts of the country.
3. He has the right to take part in the proceedings of the Lok Sabha and the Rajya Sabha.
4. He has a fixed tenure.
Select the correct answer from the codes given below:

Codes:
(a) 1 and 4 (b) 2, 3 and 4
(c) 3 and 4 (d) 3 only

40. Which of the following prefix President Pranab Mukherjee desires to be

discontinued while interacting with Indian dignitaries as well as in official notings?

1. His Excellency 2. Mahamahim
3. Hon'ble 4. Shri/Smt.

Select the correct answer from the codes given below:

Codes:

(a) 1 and 3 (b) 2 and 3
(c) 1 and 2 (d) 1, 2 and 3

41. Which of the following can be done under conditions of financial emergency?

1. State Legislative Assemblies can be abolished.
2. Central Government can acquire control over the budget and expenditure of States.
3. Salaries of the Judges of the High Courts and the Supreme Court can be reduced.
4. Right to Constitutional Remedies can be suspended.

Select the correct answer from the codes given below:

Codes:

(a) 1, 2 and 3 (b) 2, 3 and 4
(c) 1 and 2 (d) 2 and 3

42. Match List I with List II and select the correct answer from the codes given below:

List I

(A) Poverty Reduction Programme
(B) Human Development Scheme
(C) Social Assistance Scheme
(D) Minimum Need Scheme

List II

(i) Mid-day Meals
(ii) Indira Awas Yojana (IAY)
(iii) National Old Age Pension (NOAP)
(iv) MNREGA

Codes:	**A**	**B**	**C**	**D**
(a)	(iv)	(i)	(iii)	(ii)
(b)	(ii)	(iii)	(iv)	(i)
(c)	(iii)	(iv)	(i)	(ii)
(d)	(iv)	(iii)	(ii)	(i)

43. For an efficient and durable learning, learner should have

(a) ability to learn only
(b) requisite level of motivation only
(c) opportunities to learn only
(d) desired level of ability and motivation

44. Classroom communication must be

(a) Teacher centric
(b) Student centric
(c) General centric
(d) Textbook centric

45. The best method of teaching is to

(a) impart information
(b) ask students to read books
(c) suggest good reference material
(d) initiate a discussion and participate in it

46. Interaction inside the classroom should generate

(a) Argument (b) Information
(c) Ideas (d) Controversy

47. "Spare the rod and spoil the child", gives the message that

(a) punishment in the class should be banned.
(b) corporal punishment is not acceptable.
(c) undesirable behaviour must be punished.
(d) children should be beaten with rods.

48. The type of communication that the teacher has in the classroom, is termed as

(a) Interpersonal
(b) Mass communication
(c) Group communication
(d) Face-to-face communication

49. Which one of the following is an indication of the quality of a research journal?

(a) Impact factor (b) h-index
(c) g-index (d) i10-index

50. Good 'research ethics' means
   (a) Not disclosing the holdings of shares/stocks in a company that sponsors your research.
   (b) Assigning a particular research problem to one Ph.D./research student only.
   (c) Discussing with your colleagues confidential data from a research paper that you are reviewing for an academic journal.
   (d) Submitting the same research manuscript for publishing in more than one journal.

51. Which of the following sampling methods is based on probability?
   (a) Convenience sampling
   (b) Quota sampling
   (c) Judgement sampling
   (d) Stratified sampling

52. Which one of the following references is written according to American Psychological Association (APA) format?
   (a) Sharma, V. (2010). Fundamentals of Computer Science.
   New Delhi: Tata McGraw Hill
   (b) Sharma, V. 2010. Fundamentals of Computer Science.
   New Delhi: Tata McGraw Hill
   (c) Sharma.V. 2010. Fundamentals of Computer Science,
   New Delhi: Tata McGraw Hill
   (d) Sharma, V. (2010), Fundamentals of Computer Science,
   New Delhi: Tata McGraw Hill

53. Arrange the following steps of research in correct sequence:
   1. Identification of research problem
   2. Listing of research objectives
   3. Collection of data
   4. Methodology
   5. Data analysis
   6. Results and discussion

   (a) 1, 2, 3, 4, 5, 6 (b) 1, 2, 4, 3, 5, 6
   (c) 2, 1, 3, 4, 5, 6 (d) 2, 1, 4, 3, 5, 6

54. Identify the incorrect statement:
   (a) A hypothesis is made on the basis of limited evidence as a starting point for further investigations.
   (b) A hypothesis is a basis for reasoning without any assumption of its truth.
   (c) Hypothesis is a proposed explanation for a phenomenon.
   (d) Scientific hypothesis is a scientific theory.

Read the following passage carefully and answer the questions (55 to 60):

The popular view of towns and cities in developing countries and of urbanization process is that despite the benefits and comforts it brings, the emergence of such cities connotes environmental degradation, generation of slums and squatters, urban poverty, unemployment, crimes, lawlessness, traffic chaos etc. But what is the reality? Given the unprecedental increase in urban population over the last 50 years from 300 million in 1950 to 2 billion in 2000 in developing countries, the wonder really is how well the world has coped, and not how badly.

In general, the urban quality of life has improved in terms of availability of water and sanitation, power, health and education, communication and transport. By way of illustration, a large number of urban residents have been provided with improved water in urban areas in Asia's largest countries such as China, India, Indonesia and Philippines. Despite that, the access to improved water in terms of percentage of total urban population seems to have declined during the last decade of 20th century, though in absolute numbers, millions of additional urbanites, have been provided improved services. These countries have made significant progress in the provision of sanitation services too, together, providing for an additional population of more than 293 million citizens within a decade (1990-2000). These improvements must be viewed against the backdrop of rapidly increasing urban population, fiscal crunch and strained human resources and efficient and quality-oriented public management.

55. The popular view about the process of urbanization in developing countries is
    (a) Positive (b) Negative
    (c) Neutral (d) Unspecified

56. The average annual increase in the number of urbanites in developing countries, from 1950 to 2000 A.D. was close to
    (a) 30 million (b) 40 million
    (c) 50 million (d) 60 million

57. The reality of urbanization is reflected in
    (a) How well the situation has been managed.
    (b) How badly the situation has gone out of control.
    (c) How fast has been the tempo of urbanization.
    (d) How fast the environment has degraded.

58. Which one of the following is not considered as an indicator of urban quality of life?
    (a) Tempo of urbanization
    (b) Provision of basic services
    (c) Access to social amenities
    (d) All of the above

59. The author in this passage has tried to focus on
    (a) Extension of Knowledge
    (b) Generation of Environmental Consciousness
    (c) Analytical Reasoning
    (d) Descriptive Statement

60. In the above passage, the author intends to state
    (a) The hazards of the urban life
    (b) The sufferings of the urban life
    (c) The awareness of human progress
    (d) The limits to growth

ANSWERS

1. (a)	2. (d)	3. (a)	4. (a)	5. (d)
6. (b)	7. (d)	8. (b)	9. (c)	10. (a)
11. (a)	12. (d)	13. (a)	14. (a)	15. (d)
16. (c)	17. (c)	18. (c)	19. (d)	20. (d)
21. (c)	22. (d)	23. (d)	24. (b)	25. (d)
26. (d)	27. (c)	28. (d)	29. (b)	30. (d)
31. (a)	32. (b)	33. (a)	34. (d)	35. (c)
36. (a)	37. (c)	38. (b)	39. (d)	40. (c)
41. (c)	42. (a)	43. (d)	44. (b)	45. (d)
46. (c)	47. (c)	48. (c)	49. (a)	50. (a)
51. (d)	52. (a)	53. (b)	54. (d)	55. (b)
56. (a)	57. (a)	58. (a)	59. (d)	60. (d)

PAPER–II

Note: This paper contains fifty (50) objective type questions, each question carrying two (2) marks. All questions are compulsory.

1. Match List I with List II and select the correct answer from the codes given below:

List I	List II
A. Mesolithic site	i. Langhnaj
B. Microlith	ii. Bagor (Rajasthan)
C. Beginning of settled Agriculture	iii. Birbhanpur
D. Chalcedony	iv. Chopni Mando

Codes:	**A**	**B**	**C**	**D**
(a)	ii	i	iii	iv
(b)	i	ii	iii	iv

(c)	iii	ii	i	iv
(d)	ii	iii	iv	i

2. In which one of the following places the centre of stone tool manufacture is found?
(a) Mehbubanagar (b) Malaprabha
(c) Isampur (d) Palaghat

3. Match the List I with List II and select the correct answer from the codes given below:

List I	List II
A. Rigveda	i. Kanva
B. Yajurveda	ii. Ranayaniya
C. Samaveda	iii. Pippalada
D. Atharvaveda	iv. Shakala

Codes:	A	B	C	D
(a)	iv	iii	ii	i
(b)	ii	i	iii	iv
(c)	iv	i	ii	iii
(d)	i	ii	iii	iv

4. Excavations at the sites of the places mentioned in the Mahabharata are related to which one of the following cultures?
(a) Northern Black polished ware
(b) Red and Black polished ware
(c) Painted grey ware
(d) None of the above

5. Which, one of the following places, is not associated with mature Harappan settlement?
(a) Dhalewan (b) Lakhmirwala
(c) Surkotda (d) Sarai Khola

6. Recently in which place broken relief sculpture of King Ashoka has been discovered?
(a) Kanaganahalli in Karnataka
(b) Mahasthan in Uttar Pradesh
(c) Kumrahar in Bihar
(d) Nittur in Karnataka

7. In which Buddhist scripture religious practices in the contemporary period of Buddha has been mentioned?
(a) Ambattha Sutta
(b) Mahavamsa
(c) Bhaddasala Jataka
(d) Brahmajala Sutta

8. Which, one of the following, is not the anthology of Sangam literature?
(a) Ettutokai (b) Tirrukkurala
(c) Pattupattu (d) Ahinanuru

9. Match the List I with List II and select the correct answer from the codes given below:

List I	List II
A. Al-Biruni	i. Mc Crindle
B. Megasthenes	ii. Beal
C. Faxian	iii. Legge
D. Xuanzang	iv. Sachau

Codes:	A	B	C	D
(a)	iv	i	iii	ii
(b)	i	ii	iii	iv
(c)	ii	iii	i	iv
(d)	iv	ii	iii	i

10. Given below are two statements, one is labelled as Assertion (A) and the other is labelled as Reason (R).
Assertion (A): North India between 750 A.D. and 1200 A.D. witnessed the emergence and full growth of a new politicosocio-economic structure.
Reason (R): There is total unanimity among historians to describe this new structure as 'feudalism'.
Codes:
(a) (A) is correct but (R) is false.
(b) (A) is incorrect but (R) is correct.
(c) Both are correct and (R) is the correct explanation of (A).
(d) Both are correct but (R) is not the correct explanation of (A).

11. Match the List I with List II and select the correct answer from the codes given below:

List I	List II
A. Ashvaghosha	i. Kumarpala Charita
B. Bhasa	ii. Mudrarakshasa
C. Vishakhadatta	iii. Balacharita
D. Hemachandra	iv. Buddhacharita

Codes:	A	B	C	D
(a)	i	ii	iii	iv
(b)	iv	iii	ii	i
(c)	ii	iii	iv	i
(d)	iii	ii	iv	i

12. In which year the first English translation of Arthashastra was published?
(a) 1905 (b) 1909
(c) 1915 (d) 1960

13. Arrange the following Nanda Kings in chronological sequential order and select the correct answer from the codes given below:
(a) Govishanka (b) Panduka
(c) Ugrasena (d) Dhana

Codes:
(a) (b) (c) (a) (d)
(b) (c) (b) (a) (d)
(c) (a) (b) (c) (d)
(d) (b) (c) (d) (a)

14. Select the incorrect answer from the following statements:
(a) The reign of Kumaragupta faced the Huna invasion.
(b) The first Huna Chief Toramana managed to conquer Western India and area around Eran in Central India.
(c) Toramana adopted the Jaina faith.
(d) Mihirakula managed to conquer Sri Lanka.

15. Arrange the following names in chronological order and select the correct answer from the codes given below:
(a) Yoshomati (b) Pushyabhuti
(c) Naravardhan (d) Rajyashri

Codes:
(a) (c) (b) (d) (a)
(b) (b) (c) (a) (d)
(c) (b) (a) (c) (d)
(d) (a) (d) (c) (b)

16. Match the List I with List II and select the correct answer from the codes given below:

List I	List II
A. Pallava Dynasty	i. Lingaraja Temple
B. Somavamsa	ii. Vedanarayan Temple
C. Chalukya Dynasty	iii. Mukteshwar Temple
D. Chola Dynasty	iv. Lad Khan Temple

Codes:	A	B	C	D
(a)	iii	i	iv	ii
(b)	i	ii	iii	iv
(c)	ii	iii	i	iv
(d)	iv	iii	ii	i

17. Match the List I with List II and select the right answer from the codes given below:

List I (Founder)
A. Bhandarkar
B. Chandabardai
C. Colonel Tod
D. Gaurishankar Ojha

List II (Theories)
i. Origin of Rajputs from Kshatriyas
ii. Foreign origin of Rajputs
iii. Origin of Rajputs from Agni-Kunda
iv. Huna origin of Rajputs

Codes:	A	B	C	D
(a)	iv	iii	ii	i
(b)	i	ii	iii	iv
(c)	i	iii	iv	ii
(d)	i	ii	iv	iii

18. The Sultan Ghari was built as the mausoleum of
   (a) Qutubuddin Aibak
   (b) Ruknuddin Firoz
   (c) Balban
   (d) Nasiruddin Mahmud

19. Match List I with List II and select the correct answer from the codes given below:

List I (Sufi Terminology)	List II (Meanings)
A. Futuh	i. Sufi hospice
B. Khanqah	ii. Conversation of a Sufi Saint
C. Barkat	iii. Unasked for Charity
D. Malfuz	iv. Spiritual grace acquired by a Sufi

Codes:	A	B	C	D
(a)	i	iii	ii	iv
(b)	iii	i	iv	ii
(c)	iii	ii	i	iv
(d)	iv	iii	ii	i

20. Who separated the office of the *Wali* and *Amir*?
   (a) Balban
   (b) Alauddin Khalji
   (c) Ghiyasuddin Tughlaq
   (d) Muhammad Tughlaq

21. 'The pivot of the Kingdom of Delhi rests on wheat and barley, while the foundation of the Sultanate of Gujarat rests on corals and pearls, because there are eighty four ports under this Sultan.' The above remark is attributed by the author of *Mirat-i-Sikandari* to
   (a) Sultan Khizr Khan
   (b) Sikandar Lodi
   (c) Babur
   (d) Humayun

22. Match List I with List II and select the correct answer from the codes given below:

List I (Name of coin)	List II (Kingdom in which the coin circulated)
A. Mahmudi	i. Sur Kingdom
B. Rupaiah	ii. Delhi Sultanate
C. Pagoda	iii. Vijayanagar
D. Tanka	iv. Gujarat Sultanate

Codes:	A	B	C	D
(a)	i	ii	iii	iv
(b)	ii	i	iv	iii
(c)	iv	i	iii	ii
(d)	iv	ii	iii	i

23. Which of the following statements is not true?
   (a) Sultan Zainul-Abidin never allowed the Saiyids to grab dictatorial power in his court.
   (b) He called himself Amir ul-Muminin.
   (c) He took immense interest in agricultural production and expansion.
   (d) He abolished the post of Shaikh ul-Islam.

24. Which of the following statements about the activities of the Portuguese traders in India during the early sixteenth century is not correct?
   (a) The Portuguese were the first Europeans to reach India via Red Sea route.
   (b) The Portuguese made huge profits by selling Indian spices in European markets.
   (c) The Portuguese captured many places on the coasts of the Indian Ocean and built their fortresses there.
   (d) The Portuguese declared that other traders could not bring their ships into the Indian Ocean without their permission.

25. Vijayanagara exhibited 'Protopatrimonialism'. Who expressed this view?

(a) N. Karashima
(b) Burton Stein
(c) K.A. Nilkanta Sastri
(d) B.A. Saletore

26. Match List I with List II and select the correct answer from the codes given below:

List I (Foreign Travellers)	List II (Rulers)
A. Abdur Razaq	i. Akbar
B. Ibn Battuta	ii. Muhammad bin Tughlaq
C. Sidi Ali Reis	iii. Jahangir
D. William Finch	iv. Deva Raya II

Codes:	A	B	C	D
(a)	iv	ii	iii	i
(b)	iii	ii	iv	i
(c)	iii	ii	i	iv
(d)	iv	ii	i	iii

27. Consider the following statements about the Jaziya tax in the Mughal period:
(i) Akbar abolished the Jaziya in 1564.
(ii) Akbar re-imposed the Jaziya in 1575.
(iii) Akbar abolished the Jaziya again in 1579-80.
(iv) Aurangzeb re-imposed the Jaziya in 1679.
Which are the correct statement from the above.
(a) (i), (ii)
(b) (i), (ii), (iii)
(c) (i), (ii), (iii), (iv)
(d) (i), (iv)

28. Arrange the following in chronological order and select the correct answer from the codes given below:
(i) Conquest of Orissa by Akbar.
(ii) Introduction of *Dagh* system.
(iii) Creation of the twelve *Subahs* (provinces)
(iv) Introduction of the dual rank (the *Zat* and the *Sawar*)
Codes:
(a) (iii) (i) (ii) (iv) (b) (i) (iii) (iv) (ii)
(c) (ii) (iii) (i) (iv) (d) (iii) (iv) (i) (ii)

29. Who among the following painters were considered by Jahangir as masters without rival in their particular spheres?
(i) Abul Hasan (ii) Bishan Das
(iii) Ustad Mansur (iv) Manohar
Select the correct answer from the codes given below:
Codes:
(a) (i), (ii), (iv) (b) (i), (iii)
(c) (ii), (iv) (d) (i), (iii), (iv)

30. Which of the following States of North-East India was/were invaded by the Mughals?
(i) The Dimasa (ii) The Meitei
(iii) The Ahom (iv) The Koch
Select the correct answer from the codes given below:
(a) (i) and (iii) (b) (ii) only
(c) (iii) and (iv) (d) (i), (ii), (iii)

31. Match List I with List II and select the correct answer from the codes given below:

List I (Book)	List II (Author)
A. Gulshan-i-Ibrahimi	i. Gulam Murtaza
B. Basatin-us-Salatin	ii. Fuzuni Astrabadi
C. Futuhat-i-Adilshahi	iii. Bhimsen
D. Nuskha-i-Dilkusha	iv. Muhammad Qasim Firishta

Codes:	A	B	C	D
(a)	i	iii	ii	iv
(b)	ii	iii	iv	i
(c)	iv	iii	ii	i
(d)	iv	i	ii	iii

32. Match List I with List II and select the correct answer from the codes given below:

List I (Book)
A. Early Mughal Painting
B. A History of Sultanate Architecture
C. Mughal Painters and their works
D. Mughal Architecture An Outline of its History and Development (1526-1858)

List II (Author)
i. Somprakash Verma
ii. Ebba Koch
iii. Milo Cleveland Beach
iv. R. Nath

Codes:	A	B	C	D
(a)	iii	iv	i	ii
(b)	iv	ii	iii	i
(c)	i	ii	iv	iii
(d)	ii	i	iii	iv

33. Given below are two statements, one is labelled as Assertion (A) and other is labelled as Reason (R):
Assertion (A): Many Sanskrit works on music were translated into Persian during the medieval period.
Reason (R): The early Chishti Sufis were fond of musical assemblies called Sama.
Consider the above statements and select the correct answer from the codes given below.
Codes:
(a) Both (A) and (R) are true and (R) is the correct explanation of (A).
(b) Both (A) and (R) are true, but (R) is not the correct explanation of (A).
(c) (A) is true, but (R) is false.
(d) (A) is false, but (R) is true.

34. Given below are two statements, one is labelled as Assertion (A) and the other is labelled as Reason (R):
Assertion (A): It was in Shahjahan's reign that the arts of dance and music reached its highest watermark.
Reason (R): He was a patron of arts and literature.
Consider the above statements and select the correct answer from the codes given below.
Codes:
(a) Both (A) and (R) are true and (R) is the correct explanation of (A).
(b) Both (A) and (R) are true, but (R) is not the correct explanation of (A).
(c) (A) is true, but (R) is false.
(d) (A) is false, but (R) is true.

35. Which one of the following State was not a Nation State in the 17th century?
(a) France (b) Germany
(c) England (d) Spain

36. Given below are two statements, one is labelled as Assertion (A) and other is labelled as Reason (R):
Assertion (A): Assessment forever was the central point in the Permanent Settlement of Bengal introduced in 1793.
Reason (R): Cornwallis believed that the Zamindars will develop their lands.
Read the above statements and select the correct answer from the codes given below:
Codes:
(a) Both (A) and (R) are true, and (R) is the correct explanation of (A).
(b) Both (A) and (R) are true and (R) is not the correct explanation of (A).
(c) Both (A) and (R) are false.
(d) (A) is true, but (R) is false.

37. Who was the First President of Fort William of Calcutta?
(a) Charles Eyre
(b) John Child
(c) George Oxendan
(d) Gerald Aungier

38. Match List I with List II and select the correct answer from the codes given below:

List I	List II
A. Indian Mirror	i. M.N. Roy
B. Tribune	ii. G.A. Nateshan
C. Modern Review	iii. Debendranath Tagore
D. Independent India	iv. Dayal Singh

Codes:	A	B	C	D
(a)	iii	iv	ii	i
(b)	ii	iii	i	iv
(c)	iv	ii	iii	i
(d)	i	iii	iv	ii

39. Match List I with List II and select the correct answer from the codes given below:

List I	List II
A. Mahatma Gandhi	i. President of Surat Session
B. Ras Bihari Ghosh	ii. President of Calcutta Session
C. Dadabhai Naoroji	iii. President of Lahore Session
D. Jawaharlal Nehru	iv. President of Belgaum Session

Codes:	A	B	C	D
(a)	ii	i	iv	iii
(b)	iv	i	ii	iii
(c)	iii	ii	iv	i
(d)	i	iii	ii	iv

40. Match List I with List II and select the correct answer from the codes given below:

List I	List II
A. V.D. Savarkar	i. Gaddar Party
B. Lala Hardayal	ii. Curzon Wyllie
C. Tarakanath Das	iii. Abhinab Bharat
D. Madanlal Dhingra	iv. Free Hindustan

Codes:	A	B	C	D
(a)	ii	i	iv	iii
(b)	iii	ii	i	iv
(c)	i	ii	iv	iii
(d)	iii	i	iv	ii

41. Which of the following districts constituted as the Northern Circars in the Madras Presidency?
(a) Mustafanagar, Ellore, Kondaveedu, Rajahmundry
(b) Rajahmundry, Mustafanagar, Machilipatam, Ellore
(c) Mustafanagar, Ellore, Rajahmundry, Chicacole
(d) Chicacole, Mustafanagar, Ellore, Kondaveedu

42. The aim of the Cripps Mission was
(a) to prevent the Quit India Movement from being launched
(b) to persuade Indian leaders to support British war efforts
(c) to convince the Congress Ministries to withdraw their resignations
(d) to set up a Constitution making body immediately

43. Who wrote 'Planned Economy for India' (1936)?
(a) R.C. Dutt
(b) M. Visvesvarayya
(c) N.G. Ranga
(d) D.R. Gadgil

44. Given below are two statements, one labelled as Assertion (A) and other labelled as Reason (R):
Assertion (A): The English introduced Western Education in India.
Reason (R): They wanted to make Indians aware of scientific and national advancement.
Read the above statements and select the correct answer from the codes given below:
Codes:
(a) (A) is false, but (R) is true.
(b) Both (A) and (R) are false.
(c) (A) is true and (R) is the most correct explanation of (A).
(d) Both (A) and (R) are true, but (R) is not the correct explanation of (A).

45. Arrange the following in chronological order and select the correct answer from the codes given below:
(i) Second Anglo-Maratha War
(ii) Third Anglo-Mysore War
(iii) Second Carnatic War
(iv) First Anglo-Sikh War

Codes:
(a) (iii) (ii) (i) (iv)
(b) (ii) (iii) (iv) (i)
(c) (i) (iv) (iii) (ii)
(d) (iv) (iii) (i) (ii)

46. Arrange the following in chronological order and select the correct answer from the codes given below:
(i) Mundas Rebellion
(ii) Santhal Rebellion
(iii) Moplah Revolts
(iv) Deccan Riots

Codes:
(a) (iv) (i) (iii) (ii)
(b) (ii) (iii) (i) (iv)
(c) (i) (iv) (ii) (iii)
(d) (ii) (iv) (i) (iii)

47. Match List I with List II and select the correct answer from the codes given below:

List I	List II
A. Gou rakshini Sabha	i. Vivekananda
B. Rasta Goftar	ii. J.B. Wacha
C. Sadharan Brahmo Samaj	iii. Dayanand Saraswati
D. Prabuddha Bharatha	iv. Shivanath Sastri

Codes:	A	B	C	D
(a)	iii	ii	i	iv
(b)	ii	iv	iii	i
(c)	iii	ii	iv	i
(d)	i	iii	ii	iv

48. Arrange the following in chronological order and select the correct answer from the codes given below:
(i) Cripps Mission
(ii) Gandhi-Irwin Pact
(iii) Simon Commission
(iv) Partition of the Country

Codes:
(a) (i) (ii) (iii) (iv)
(b) (ii) (i) (iv) (iii)
(c) (ii) (i) (iii) (iv)
(d) (iii) (ii) (i) (iv)

49. Which law under the British regime allowed to imprison people without due trial?
(a) Rowlett Act
(b) Sedition Act of 1870
(c) Hindu Code Bill
(d) Ilbert Bill

50. The beginning of the Great Depression is related to
(a) The collapse of Prices in Japan
(b) The sudden rise of Price Index in Europe
(c) The collapse of Prices in Wall Street
(d) Depression in Pacific Ocean region

ANSWERS

1. (a)	2. (c)	3. (c)	4. (c)	5. (d)
6. (a)	7. (d)	8. (b)	9. (a)	10. (a)
11. (b)	12. (b)	13. (b)	14. (d)	15. (b)
16. (a)	17. (a)	18. (d)	19. (b)	20. (d)
21. (b)	22. (c)	23. (d)	24. (a)	25. (b)
26. (d)	27. (c)	28. (a)	29. (b)	30. (c)
31. (d)	32. (a)	33. (b)	34. (d)	35. (b)
36. (b)	37. (a)	38. (a)	39. (b)	40. (d)
41. (c)	42. (b)	43. (b)	44. (d)	45. (a)
46. (d)	47. (c)	48. (d)	49. (a)	50. (c)

PAPER–III

Note: This paper contains seventy five (75) objective type questions of two (2) marks each. All questions are compulsory.

1. Which one of the following is a Neolithic site in Vindhyan region?
   (a) Mahagara (b) Chirand
   (c) Bangarh (d) Khunti

2. Harappan sites have provided unique plan of settlement comprising of Citadel, Middle Town and Lower Town.
   (i) Kunal (ii) Lothal
   (iii) Rangpur (iv) Dholavira
   Select the correct answer by using the codes given below:
   Codes:
   (a) (i) and (ii) (b) (iii) and (iv)
   (c) (i), (ii) and (iii) (d) (iv) only

3. River Saraswati is known by which of the following names in Pakistan?
   (i) Nara (ii) Raini
   (iii) Hakra (iv) Wahinda
   Select your answer from the codes given below:
   Codes:
   (a) (i) and (iii)
   (b) (i) and (ii)
   (c) (i), (ii) and (iii)
   (d) (i), (ii), (iii) and (iv)

4. The Battle of Ten Kings was fought on the bank of which one of the following rivers?
   (a) Saraswati (b) Sindhu
   (c) Parushni (d) Beas

5. Given below are two statements, one is labelled as Assertion (A) and the other is labelled as Reason (R):
   Assertion (A): India had good contacts with Rome.
   Reason (R): The rouletted ware had been found at Brahmagiri, Sisupalgarh, Tamluk, Amaravati.
   Read the above statements and select the correct answers from the codes given below.
   Codes:
   (a) (A) and (R) are true and (R) is the full explanation of (A).
   (b) Both (A) and (R) are true, but (R) is not the correct explanation of (A).
   (c) (A) is true, but (R) is false.
   (d) (A) is false, but (R) is true.

6. The story of the migration of Videgha Mathava to the east accompanied by his priest Gotama Rahugana is mentioned in which of the following?
   (a) Gopatha Brahmana
   (b) Brihadaranyaka Upanishad
   (c) Satapatha Brahmana
   (d) Aitareya Brahmana

7. Match List I with List II and select the correct answer from the codes given below:

List I (Buddhist Councils)	List II (Places where held)
A. First	i. Pataliputra
B. Second	ii. Vaishali
C. Third	iii. Kashmir
D. Fourth	iv. Rajagriha

Codes:	A	B	C	D
(a)	iii	i	ii	iv
(b)	iv	ii	i	iii
(c)	ii	iii	iv	i
(d)	i	iv	iii	ii

8. Match List I with List II and select the correct answer from the codes given below:

List I	List II
A. Sakyas	i. Vaishali
B. Koliyas	ii. Pipphalivana
C. Moriyas	iii. Ramagrama
D. Lichchhavis	iv. Kapilavastu

Codes:	**A**	**B**	**C**	**D**
(a)	iii	i	iv	ii
(b)	iv	iii	ii	i
(c)	ii	iv	i	iii
(d)	i	ii	iii	iv

9. Arrange the following Pali canonical texts into chronological order and select the correct answer from the codes given below:
   (i) Samyukta Nikaya
   (ii) Chullavagga
   (iii) Sutta Nipata
   (iv) Buddhavamsa
   Codes:
   (a) (i), (iv), (iii), (ii) (b) (ii), (iii), (iv), (i)
   (c) (i), (ii), (iii), (iv) (d) (iv), (i), (iii), (ii)
10. The following were the leaders of the Ajivika Sect:
   (i) Makkhali Gosala
   (ii) Nanda Vachchha
   (iii) Kisa Samkichchha
   (iv) Bhadda
   Select the correct answer from the codes given below:
   Codes:
   (a) (i) and (ii)
   (b) (iii) and (iv)
   (c) (i), (ii) and (iii)
   (d) (iv) only
11. The stone portrait of Ashoka with his name inscribed on it has been found from the stupa remains of which one of the following sites?
   (a) Sanchi (b) Amaravati
   (c) Deur-Kuthar (d) Kanaganahalli
12. Given below are two statements, one labelled as Assertion (A) and the other labelled as Reason (R):
   Assertion (A): Inscriptions in Kharosthi have been found from Bengal.
   Reason (R): Kharosthi was widely in use in Bengal.
   Read the above statements and select the correct answer from the codes below:
   Codes:
   (a) Both (A) and (R) are true and (R) is the correct explanation of (A).
   (b) Both (A) and (R) are true and (R) is not the correct explanation of (A).
   (c) (A) is true, but (R) is false.
   (d) (A) is false, but (R) is true.
13. Dasaratha Jataka is found sculptured in stupa remains of the following South Indian sites:
   (i) Amaravati
   (ii) Nagarjunakonda
   (iii) Phanigiri
   (iv) Gummididurru
   Select the correct answer from the codes given below:
   Codes:
   (a) (i) and (iii) (b) (iii) and (ii)
   (c) (ii) only (d) (iv) only
14. Given below are two statements, one is labelled as Assertion (A) and the other is labelled as Reason (R):
   Assertion (A): As per the Mitakshara School, father could divide his property among his sons during his life time.
   Reason (R): The Mitakshara has recognised son's right of ownership by birth in ancestral property.
   In the context of the above two statements, which one of the following is correct? Give your answer from the codes given below:
   Codes:
   (a) Both (A) and (R) are true and (R) is the correct explanation of (A).
   (b) Both (A) and (R) are true, but (R) is not the correct explanation of (A).
   (c) (A) is true, but (R) is false.
   (d) (A) is false, but (R) is true.

15. Match List I with List II and select the correct answer from the codes given below:

List I	List II
A. Chandragupta	i. Tushaspha
B. Skandagupta	ii. Suvisakha
C. Rudradaman	iii. Parnadatta
D. Ashoka	iv. Pusyagupta

Codes:	A	B	C	D
(a)	i	ii	iii	iv
(b)	ii	iv	i	iii
(c)	iv	iii	ii	i
(d)	iii	i	iv	ii

16. Coins of Bhagilaya have been found from the following:
(i) Nasik
(ii) Kousambi
(iii) Narmada Valley
(iv) Godavari-Krishna Valley
Select the correct answer from the codes given below:
Codes:
(a) (i) and (ii) (b) (iii) and (iv)
(c) (iii) only (d) (iv) only

17. Shell Inscriptions have been discovered from the remains of Stupas at the following sites:
(i) Bharhut (ii) Amaravati
(iii) Deur-Kuthar (iv) Sanchi
Select the correct answer from the codes given below:
Codes:
(a) (ii) and (iii) (b) (i) and (iv)
(c) (i) and (iii) (d) (ii) and (iv)

18. Fragments of Devi-Chandragupta, a lost drama written by Vishakhadatta is preserved in the following:
(i) Katha-Saritsagara
(ii) Shringara-Prakasha
(iii) Viddhashalabhanjika
(iv) Harshacharita
Select the correct answer from the codes given below:
Codes:
(a) (i) and (iii) (b) (ii) and (iv)
(c) (ii) only (d) (iii) and (iv)

19. Carving of Naga-Shakha on doorjambs is a characteristic feature of the following regional styles of temple architecture:
(i) Chandella (ii) Pratihara
(iii) Solanki (iv) Paramara
Select the correct answer from the codes given below:
Codes:
(a) (i) and (iii) (b) (ii) only
(c) (i) and (iv) (d) (iii) and (iv)

20. Match List I with List II and select the correct answer from the codes given below:
List I
A. Narasimhavarman I
B. Shembiyan Mahadevi
C. Lokamahadevi
D. Kulottunga-I
List II
i. Rock-cut caves at Mamallapuram
ii. Agasteshvara temple at Anangapur
iii. Virupaksha temple at Pattadakal
iv. Shiva temple at Chidambaram

Codes:	A	B	C	D
(a)	ii	iii	iv	i
(b)	iv	i	ii	iii
(c)	iii	iv	i	ii
(d)	i	ii	iii	iv

21. Some Jaina Mahavidyas are sculptured with a snake mount:
(i) Kali (ii) Gauri
(iii) Vairotya (iv) Mahakali
Select the correct answer from the codes given below:
Codes:
(a) (i) and (iii) (b) (ii) and (iv)
(c) (iv) and (iii) (d) (iii) only

22. Which of the following Navagrahas is sculptured as the rio-anthropomorphic snake deity?

(a) Shani (b) Rahu
(c) Ketu (d) Mangal

23. Consider the following statements:
Assertion (A): Balban's Theory of Kingship was based on the policy of 'Blood and Iron'.
Reason (R): The prestige of the crown was undermined under the successors of Iltutmish.
Answer the question from the codes given below:
Codes:
(a) (A) is correct and (R) is wrong.
(b) Both (A) and (R) are correct. (R) is the correct explanation of (a).
(c) (A) is incorrect and (R) is correct. (R) is not the correct explanation of (A).
(d) (A) is correct and (R) is incorrect. (R) is the correct explanation of (A).

24. Who amongst the following legalised corruption in the land revenue department?
(a) Firozshah Tughlaq
(b) Sher Shah
(c) Malik Ambar
(d) None of the above

25. Who amongst the following by using 'Psycho-History' had proved that Muhammad-bin-Tughlaq was not 'mad' as commented for the first time by Elphinston?
(a) Agha Mahdi Hussain
(b) R.C. Jauhari
(c) Ishwari Prasad
(d) Shafat Ahmad Khan

26. *Abwab* refers to
(a) Land revenue claimed by the Muslim authorities.
(b) A system of revenue farming.
(c) A revenue paying State.
(d) Extra legal charges exacted by nobles.

27. What is the correct chronological sequence of the following Sufi Saints?
(i) Khwaja Ali Hujjwiri
(ii) Shaikh Badruddin Samarkhandi
(iii) Shah Nayamatullah Qadiri
(iv) Khwaja Baqi Billah
Select the correct answer from the codes given below:
Codes:
(a) (i), (ii), (iii), (iv) (b) (ii), (i), (iv), (iii)
(c) (iii), (ii), (i), (iv) (d) (iv), (i), (ii), (iii)

28. Consider the names of the following cities of Delhi:
(i) Jahanpanah (ii) Siri
(iii) Tughluqabad (iv) Khizarabad
Which among the following sequences represent the correct chronological order of foundation?
(a) (ii), (i), (iii), (iv) (b) (iii), (iv), (ii), (i)
(c) (iii), (ii), (iv), (i) (d) (ii), (iii), (i), (iv)

29. What is not to be considered as the nature of the Pre-Mughal Persian Historiography?
(a) Spiritual (b) Didactic
(c) Impressionistic (d) Provincial

30. Cannon and muskets in warfare in India were introduced by
(a) Balban (b) Alauddin Khalji
(c) Babur (d) Akbar

31. Find out the correct sequence of the rate of land revenue under Alauddin Khilji, Firoz Tughlaq, Akbar and Aurangzeb:
(a) $\frac{1}{2}, \frac{1}{2}, \frac{1}{3}, \frac{1}{2}$ (b) $\frac{1}{3}, \frac{1}{4}, \frac{1}{4}, \frac{1}{2}$
(c) $\frac{1}{4}, \frac{1}{3}, \frac{1}{2}, \frac{1}{2}$ (d) $\frac{1}{2}, \frac{1}{4}, \frac{1}{3}, \frac{1}{2}$

32. Match List I with List II and select the correct answer from the codes given below:
List I
A. Zabt B. Deshmukh
C. Vatan D. Ijaradari

List II

i. Mughal system of land measurement
ii. Hereditary land right
iii. Revenue officer
iv. Revenue farming system

Codes:	A	B	C	D
(a)	i	ii	iii	iv
(b)	i	iii	ii	iv
(c)	ii	i	iv	iii
(d)	ii	iv	iii	i

33. Which one of the following historical works of Amir Khusrau is in prose?
(a) Qiranussadain
(b) Nuh Sipihr
(c) Ashiqa
(d) Khazain-ul-Futuh

34. Babur assumed the title of "Ghazi" after the
(a) Battle of Panipat
(b) Battle of Khanwah
(c) Battle of Ghagra
(d) None of the above

35. Who amongst the following commented for the first time that Kabir tried to undermine the common people's pessimism in his Bhakti?
(a) Savitri Chandra (b) Yusuf Hussain
(c) J.N. Farquihar (d) Romilla Thapar

36. Given below are two statements, one is labelled as Assertion (A) and the other is labelled as Reason (R):
Assertion (A): There is no reliable chronology of events concerning the reign of Humayun, including his own movements.
Reason (R): The proper study of the chronology of events indicate that the so-called periods of Humayun's inactivity were much briefer than have been visualized.
Read the above statements and select the correct answer from the codes given below:
Codes:
(a) Both (A) and (R) are correct and (R) is the correct explanation of (A).
(b) (A) is correct, but (R) is false.
(c) Both (A) and (R) are correct and (R) is not the correct explanation of (A).
(d) Both (A) and (R) are false.

37. Why was the 'Double Dome' used in the Indo-Islamic architecture?
(a) To strengthen the buildings.
(b) To give cooling effect inside the building.
(c) To provide height to the buildings.
(d) For the purpose of beauty.

38. What is the main contribution of '*Tasawwuf*' in India?
(a) Service to Islam
(b) Service to humanity
(c) Influencing the Medieval Bhakti Movement
(d) Propagate the theory of '*Wahadat-ul-Wajud*'.

39. What was '*Shahrukhi*' coin in circulation during the Muslim period?
(a) A gold coin
(b) A silver coin
(c) A copper coin
(d) None of the above

40. Which one of the following is not the characteristic of Mughal painting?
(a) Inclusion of spiritual and mystic elements.
(b) Basically for the propagation of Islam.
(c) Portrait and miniature.
(d) Courtly and aristocratic

41. Find out the statement from below which is not correct?
(a) The Maratha polity under Peshwas got transformed into a close confederacy.
(b) The Peshwa created a new class of Sardars in the *Swaraj* area.

(c) The office of Peshwa became hereditary.
(d) Originally the Peshwa did not belong to the royal council.

42. In the context of the cultural and Ideological framework of the Mughal State which one of the following statements is not correct?
(a) Throughout the Mughal period there had been a constant process of reconciliation and adjustment between the central power and the regional elite.
(b) Because of decentralization during the 18th century a group of 'upstarts' came up to monopolize the resources of the empire.
(c) The Mughal process of centralisation left no space for existence of rival principles of organisation.
(d) Possibilities for diffusion of power had always been there in Mughal India.

43. Which one of the following statements regarding Abul Fazl's *Akbarnama* is not true?
(a) He usually does not refer to his sources.
(b) He makes some crude observations.
(c) He does not make generalizations.
(d) He is never secular.

44. What was the title of the British Museum *Baburnama* manuscript translated into English by Mrs. A.S. Beveridge?
(a) *Baburnama*
(b) *Waqyat-i-Baburi*
(c) *Tuzuk-i-Baburi*
(d) None of the above

45. The 'Black Hole' event was sensationalized by whom?
(a) Robert Clive (b) Verelest
(c) Holwell (d) Watson

46. The confederates against Tippu Sultan in the Third Mysore War included
(a) Travancore Raja, Nizam of Hyderabad and the English
(b) The English, Marathas and the Nawab of Carnatic
(c) The English, Marathas and the Nizam of Hyderabad
(d) The English, Nawab of Carnatic and the Nizam of Hyderabad

47. Which Princely State was not annexed under the Doctrine of Lapse in spite of not having natural heir?
(a) Satara (b) Karauli
(c) Pudukottai (d) Baroda

48. Legislative powers were restored back to the provinces in the Act of
(a) 1833 (b) 1853
(c) 1861 (d) 1892

49. The policy announcement regarding the 'progressive realization of responsible Government in India as an integral part of the British Empire' was made by
(a) Lord Morley (b) Lord Montague
(c) Lord Ripon (d) Lord Irwin

50. Paramountcy is paramount' was declared to define the relations of Indian States with British Government by which Commission?
(a) Hunter Commission
(b) Strachey Commission
(c) Butler Commission
(d) Campbell Commission

51. The Governor General who visited Allahabad to review the working of Mahalwari Land Revenue System was
(a) Lord William Bentinck
(b) Lord Auckland
(c) Lord Dalhousie
(d) Lord Canning

52. The land revenue demand under the Ryotwari in Madras was finally fixed to

fifty percent of the rental and the settlement was made for thirty years in the year

(a) 1820 (b) 1855
(c) 1864 (d) 1878

53. Policy of tariff holiday was practised by the British during

(a) 1858 to 1870 (b) 1870 to 1880
(c) 1882 to 1894 (d) 1898 to 1905

54. The worrisome aspect of the drain of wealth in the late nineteenth century according to Dadabhai Naoroji was

(a) transfer of India's accumulated gold
(b) unrequited exports
(c) depletion of urban wealth
(d) British investments in India

55. The Scheme of Local Finance was introduced by

(a) Lord Canning (b) Lord Mayo
(c) Lord Lytton (d) Lord Ripon

56. First factory legislation was passed to improve the working conditions of the labour in

(a) 1880 (b) 1881
(c) 1884 (d) 1893

57. Match List I with List II and select the correct answer from the codes given below:

List I	List II
A. B.P. Wadia	i. Trade Union Leader
B. Sri Narayana Guru	ii. Peasant Leader
C. S.N. Haldar	iii. Jamshedpur Labour Leader
D. Kunvarji Mehta	iv. South Indian Lower Caste Leader

Codes:	A	B	C	D
(a)	ii	iv	i	iii
(b)	iv	iii	ii	i
(c)	i	iv	iii	ii
(d)	iii	ii	iv	i

58. Match List I with List II and select the correct answer from the codes given below:

List I

A. Bihar Provincial Kisan Sabha
B. Ryat's Association in Guntur
C. Pratapgarh and Rae Bareli Peasant Leader
D. Rajasthan Peasant Leader

List II

i. Vijay Singh Pathik
ii. Sahajanand Saraswati
iii. N.G. Ranga
iv. Baba Ram Chandra

Codes:	A	B	C	D
(a)	ii	iii	iv	i
(b)	iv	ii	iii	i
(c)	iii	ii	iv	i
(d)	i	iv	ii	iii

59. Which Gandhian movement has been called a 'Spontaneous Revolution'?

(a) Champaran movement
(b) Non-cooperation movement
(c) Civil Disobedience movement
(d) Quit India movement

60. The inspirational leader behind the founding of the All India Women's Conference was

(a) Durga Bai Deshmukh
(b) Margaret Cousins
(c) Madam Cama
(d) Mutthulaxmi Reddy

61. Name the First Indian selected to Indian Civil Service.

(a) Surendranath Banerjee
(b) Anandamohan Bose
(c) Gurudas Banerjee
(d) Satyendra Nath Tagore

62. The Arya Samaj movement believed in:

(a) Idolatory (b) Polytheism
(c) Pantheism (d) Vedic ritualism

63. Which foreign journalist reported about the British brutality perpetrated against peaceful Satyagrahis at Dharasana Salt Depot during the Civil Disobedience Movement?
(a) Wels Miller (b) C.F. Andrews
(c) Palmer (d) Fischer

64. Who was the first President of All India Depressed Class Association?
(a) B.R. Ambedkar
(b) Shahu Maharaj
(c) E.V. Ramaswamy Naicker
(d) M.C. Rajah

65. The resignation by the Congress led ministries on 1st Nov. 1939 was celebrated by the Muslim League as
(a) Fulfilment Day
(b) Emancipation Day
(c) Deliverance Day
(d) Freedom Day

66. The First President of the All India Congress Socialist Party was
(a) Achyut Patwardhan
(b) Ram Manohar Lohia
(c) Jay Prakash Narayan
(d) Sampurnanand

67. Which Commission was entrusted the task of demarcating the line of India and Pakistan in 1947?
(a) Wavell (b) Redcliffe
(c) Alexander (d) Marshall

68. The First Indian Princely State which signed the Instrument of Accession to join the Indian Union was
(a) Jaipur (b) Patiala
(c) Bikaner (d) Bhopal

69. Match List I with List II and select the correct answer from the codes given below:

List I
A. Christian Historiography
B. Enlightenment Historiography
C. Romantic Historiography
D. Positivist Historiography

List II
i. The exposition of the Idea of Progress
ii. Attractive and Colourful Reconstruction of the Past
iii. Derivation of Historical Knowledge by applying Scientific Method of Inquiry
iv. Theorization of the Idea of Providentialism

Codes:	**A**	**B**	**C**	**D**
(a)	ii	iii	iv	i
(b)	i	iii	ii	iv
(c)	ii	iv	iii	i
(d)	iv	i	ii	iii

70. Who among the following historians is well known for his contributions to subaltern studies?
(a) Sumit Sarkar
(b) Bipin Chandra
(c) Ranjit Guha
(d) K.N. Panicker

Read the following passage and answer the following five questions (Nos. 71 to 75):

The most vicious system of racial oppression was set up in South Africa. The system of racial segregation, called apartheid, was enforced in the country by the Government of the White minority led by Daniel Malan, who came to power in 1948, and by the successive Governments. The non-Whites, over 80 per cent of the population, were denied the right to vote, strikes were banned, Africans were deported from some specified areas, education was segregated, mixed marriages were declared illegal (and immoral) and all dissent was banned under what was called the Suppression of Communism Act. Some of the greatest works of world literature, and not just political writings, were banned under the Suppression of Communism Act. Strict restrictions were imposed on the movement of Africans and they were required to carry a pass permitting them to do so. South Africa left the Commonwealth when the policy of apartheid came under attack at the conference of the Prime Ministers of Commonwealth countries.

71. Anti apartheid movement in South Africa was led by
   (a) African Peoples Party
   (b) African National Congress
   (c) Peoples Unity Front
   (d) National Congress of Africa

72. "The Freedom Charter" was adopted by the Congress of the People in the year
   (a) 1948 (b) 1954
   (c) 1955 (d) 1990

73. What was not the aim of the 'Suppression of Communism Act' passed by the Racist regime of South Africa?
   (a) To curb all dissent.
   (b) To placate the capitalist countries to support apartheid regime of South Africa.
   (c) To segregate the 'Black' and the 'White' population.
   (d) To put social restrictions on the 'Black' population.

74. First ever democratic elections in South Africa were won by Nelson Mandela in the year
   (a) 1989 (b) 1991
   (c) 1994 (d) 1996

75. The Government headed by Nelson Mandela was known as
   (a) Government of the African People
   (b) Government of National Unity
   (c) Government of the Black People
   (d) Government of Free People

ANSWERS

1. (a)	2. (d)	3. (d)	4. (c)	5. (b)
6. (c)	7. (b)	8. (b)	9. (c)	10. (c)
11. (d)	12. (c)	13. (c)	14. (b)	15. (c)
16. (c)	17. (b)	18. (c)	19. (b)	20. (d)
21. (d)	22. (c)	23. (b)	24. (b)	25. (c)
26. (d)	27. (a)	28. (d)	29. (d)	30. (c)
31. (a)	32. (b)	33. (d)	34. (b)	35. (d)
36. (a)	37. (b)	38. (b)	39. (b)	40. (b)
41. (d)	42. (c)	43. (d)	44. (d)	45. (c)
46. (c)	47. (b)	48. (c)	49. (b)	50. (c)
51. (a)	52. (c)	53. (c)	54. (b)	55. (b)
56. (b)	57. (c)	58. (a)	59. (d)	60. (b)
61. (d)	62. (d)	63. (a)	64. (d)	65. (c)
66. (d)	67. (b)	68. (c)	69. (d)	70. (c)
71. (b)	72. (c)	73. (b)	74. (c)	75. (b)

JUNE–2012

Note: This paper contains sixty (60) multiple choice questions, each question carrying two (2) marks. Candidate is expected to answer any fifty (50) questions. In case more than fifty (50) questions are attempted, only the first fifty (50) questions will be evaluated.

PAPER–I

1. Video-Conferencing can be classified as one of the following types of communication:
   (a) Visual one way
   (b) Audio-Visual one way
   (c) Audio-Visual two way
   (d) Visual two way

2. MC National University of Journalism and Communication is located at
   (a) Lucknow (b) Bhopal
   (c) Chennai (d) Mumbai

3. All India Radio (A.I.R.) for broadcasting was named in the year
   (a) 1926 (b) 1936
   (c) 1946 (d) 1956

4. In India for broadcasting TV programmes which system is followed?
   (a) NTCS (b) PAL
   (c) NTSE (d) SECAM

5. The term 'DAVP' stands for
   (a) Directorate of Advertising & Vocal Publicity
   (b) Division of Audio-Visual Publicity
   (c) Department of Audio-Visual Publicity
   (d) Directorate of Advertising & Visual Publicity

6. The term "TRP" is associated with TV shows stands for
   (a) Total Rating Points
   (b) Time Rating Points
   (c) Thematic Rating Points
   (d) Television Rating Points

7. Which is the number that comes next in the following sequence?
   2, 6, 12, 20, 30, 42, 56, ______
   (a) 60 (b) 64
   (c) 72 (d) 70

8. Find the next letter for the series YVSP ______ .
   (a) N (b) M
   (c) O (d) L

9. Given that in a code language, '645' means 'day is warm'; '42' means 'warm spring' and '634' means 'spring is sunny'; which digit represents 'sunny'?
   (a) 3 (b) 2
   (c) 4 (d) 5

10. The basis of the following classification is:
    'first President of India', 'author of Godan', 'books in my library', 'blue things' and 'students who work hard'
    (a) Common names
    (b) Proper names
    (c) Descriptive phrases
    (d) Indefinite description

11. In the expression 'Nothing is larger than itself' the relation 'is larger than' is
    (a) antisymmetric (b) asymmetrical
    (c) intransitive (d) irreflexive

12. **Assertion (A):** There are more laws on the books today than ever before, and

more crimes being committed than ever before.

Reason (R): Because to reduce crime we must eliminate the laws.

Choose the correct answer from below:

(a) (A) is true, (R) is doubtful and (R) is not the correct explanation of (A).
(b) (A) is false, (R) is true and (R) is the correct explanation of (A).
(c) (A) is doubtful, (R) is doubtful and (R) is not the correct explanation of (A).
(d) (A) is doubtful, (R) is true and (R) is not the correct explanation of (A).

13. If the proposition "All men are not mortal" is true then which of the following inferences is correct? Choose from the code given below:
1. "All men are mortal" is true.
2. "Some men are mortal" is false.
3. "No men are mortal" is doubtful.
4. "All men are mortal" is false.

Codes:

(a) 1, 2 and 3 (b) 2, 3 and 4
(c) 1, 3 and 4 (d) 1 and 3

14. Determine the nature of the following definition: "Abortion" means the ruthless murdering of innocent beings.
(a) Lexical (b) Persuasive
(c) Stipulative (d) Theoretical

15. Which one of the following is not an argument?
(a) Devadutt does not eat in the day so he must be eating at night.
(b) If Devadutt is growing fat and if he does not eat during the day, he will be eating at night.
(c) Devadutt eats in the night so he does not eat during the day.
(d) Since Devadutt does not eat in the day, he must be eating in the night.

16. Venn diagram is a kind of diagram to
(a) represent and assess the validity of elementary inferences of syllogistic form.
(b) represent but not assess the validity of elementary inferences of syllogistic form.
(c) represent and assess the truth of elementary inferences of syllogistic form.
(d) assess but not represent the truth of elementary inferences of syllogistic form.

17. Reasoning by analogy leads to
(a) certainty
(b) definite conclusion
(c) predictive conjecture
(d) surety

18. Which of the following statements are false? Choose from the code given below:
1. Inductive arguments always proceed from the particular to the general.
2. A cogent argument must be inductively strong.
3. A valid argument may have a false premise and a false conclusion.
4. An argument may legitimately be spoken of as 'true' or 'false'.

Codes:

(a) 2, 3 and 4 (b) 1 and 3
(c) 2 and 4 (d) 1 and 2

19. Six persons A, B, C, D, E and F are standing in a circle. B is between F and C, A is between E and D, F is to the left of D. Who is between A and F?
(a) B (b) C
(c) D (d) E

20. The price of petrol increases by 25%. By what percentage must a customer reduce the consumption so that the earlier bill on the petrol does not alter?

(a) 20% (b) 25%
(c) 30% (d) 33.33%

21. If Ram knows that y is an integer greater than 2 and less than 7 and Hari knows that y is an integer greater than 5 and less than 10, then they may correctly conclude that
(a) y can be exactly determined
(b) y may be either of two values
(c) y may be any of three values
(d) there is no value of y satisfying these conditions

22. Four pipes can fill a reservoir in 15, 20, 30 and 60 hours respectively. The first one was opened at 6 AM, second at 7 AM, third at 8 AM and the fourth at 9 AM. When will the reservoir be filled?
(a) 11 AM (b) 12 Noon
(c) 1 PM (d) 1:30 PM

The total electricity generation in a country is 97 GW. The contribution of various energy sources is indicated in percentage terms in the Pie Chart given below;

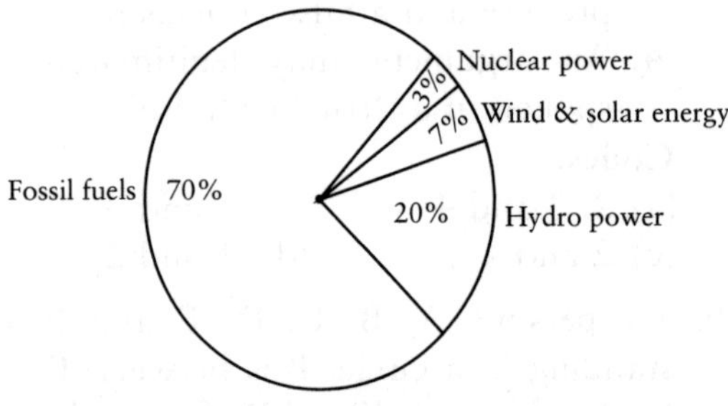

23. What is the contribution of wind and solar power in absolute terms in the electricity generation?
(a) 6.79 GW (b) 19.4 GW
(c) 9.7 GW (d) 29.1 GW

24. What is the contribution of renewable energy sources in absolute terms in the electricity generation?
(a) 29.1 GW (b) 26.19 GW
(c) 67.9 GW (d) 97 GW

25. TCP/IP is necessary if one is to connect to the
(a) Phone lines (b) LAN
(c) Internet (d) a Server

26. Each character on the keyboard of computer has an ASCII value which stands for
(a) American Stock Code for Information Interchange
(b) American Standard Code for Information Interchange
(c) African Standard Code for Information Interchange
(d) Adaptable Standard Code for Information Change

27. Which of the following is not a programming language?
(a) Pascal
(b) Microsoft Office
(c) Java
(d) C++

28. Minimum number of bits required to store any 3 digit decimal number is equal to
(a) 3 (b) 5
(c) 8 (d) 10

29. Internet explorer is a type of
(a) Operating System
(b) Compiler
(c) Browser
(d) IP address

30. POP3 and IMAP are e-mail accounts in which

(a) One automatically gets one's mail everyday
(b) One has to be connected to the server to read or write one's mail
(c) One only has to be connected to the server to send and receive email
(d) One does not need any telephone lines

31. Irritation in eyes is caused by the pollutant
(a) Sulphur di-oxide (b) Ozone
(c) PAN (d) Nitrous oxide

32. Which is the source of chlorofluorocarbons?
(a) Thermal power plants
(b) Automobiles
(c) Refrigeration and Airconditioning
(d) Fertilizers

33. Which of the following is not a renewable natural resource?
(a) Clean air (b) Fertile soil
(c) Fresh water (d) Salt

34. Which of the following parameters is not used as a pollution indicator in water?
(a) Total dissolved solids
(b) Coliform count
(c) Dissolved oxygen
(d) Density

35. S and P waves are associated with
(a) floods (b) wind energy
(c) earthquakes (d) tidal energy

36. Match List I and List II and select the correct answer from the codes given below:

List I	List II
(A) Ozone hole	(i) Tsunami
(B) Greenhouse effect	(ii) UV radiations
(C) Natural hazards	(iii) Methane
(D) Sustainable development	(iv) Eco-centrism

Codes:	A	B	C	D
(a)	(ii)	(iii)	(i)	(iv)
(b)	(iii)	(ii)	(i)	(iv)
(c)	(iv)	(iii)	(i)	(ii)
(d)	(iv)	(ii)	(iii)	(i)

37. Indian Institute of Advanced Study is located at
(a) Dharmshala (b) Shimla
(c) Solan (d) Chandigarh

38. Indicate the number of Regional Offices of National Council of Teacher Education.
(a) 04 (b) 05
(c) 06 (d) 08

39. Which of the following rights was considered the "Heart and Soul" of the Indian Constitution by Dr. B.R. Ambedkar?
(a) Freedom of Speech
(b) Right to Equality
(c) Right to Freedom of Religion
(d) Right to Constitutional Remedies

40. Who among the following created the office of the District Collector in India?
(a) Lord Cornwallis
(b) Warren Hastings
(c) The Royal Commission on Decentralisation
(d) Sir Charles Metcalfe

41. The Fundamental Duties of a citizen include
1. Respect for the Constitution, the National Flag and the National Anthem
2. To develop the scientific temper.
3. Respect for the Government.
4. To protect Wildlife.

Choose the correct answer from the codes given below:

Codes:
(a) 1, 2 and 3 (b) 1, 2 and 4
(c) 2, 3 and 4 (d) 1, 3, 4 and 2

42. The President of India takes oath
(a) to uphold the sovereignty and integrity of India.

(b) to bear true faith and allegiance to the Constitution of India.
(c) to uphold the Constitution and Laws of the country.
(d) to preserve, protect and defend the Constitution and the law of the country.

43. If you get an opportunity to teach a visually challenged student along with normal students, what type of treatment would you like to give him in the class?
(a) Not giving extra attention because majority may suffer.
(b) Take care of him sympathetically in the classroom.
(c) You will think that blindness is his destiny and hence you cannot do anything.
(d) Arrange a seat in the front row and try to teach at a pace convenient to him.

44. Which of the following is not a characteristic of a good achievement test?
(a) Reliability (b) Objectivity
(c) Ambiguity (d) Validity

45. Which of the following does not belong to a projected aid?
(a) Overhead projector(b) Blackboard
(c) Epidiascope (d) Slide projector

46. For a teacher, which of the following methods would be correct for writing on the blackboard?
(a) Writing fast and as clearly as possible.
(b) Writing the matter first and then asking students to read it.
(c) Asking a question to students and then writing the answer as stated by them.
(d) Writing the important points as clearly as possible.

47. A teacher can be successful if he/she
(a) helps students in becoming better citizens.
(b) imparts subject knowledge to students.
(c) prepares students to pass the examination.
(d) presents the subject matter in a well organized manner.

48. Dynamic approach to teaching means
(a) Teaching should be forceful and effective
(b) Teachers should be energetic and dynamic
(c) The topics of teaching should not be static, but dynamic
(d) The students should be required to learn through activities

49. The research that aims at immediate application is
(a) Action Research
(b) Empirical Research
(c) Conceptual Research
(d) Fundamental Research

50. When two or more successive footnotes refer to the same work which one of the following expressions is used?
(a) ibid. (b) et al.
(c) op. cit. (d) loc. cit.

51. Nine year olds are taller than seven year olds. This is an example of a reference drawn from
(a) Vertical study
(b) Cross-sectional study
(c) Time series study
(d) Experimental study

52. Conferences are meant for
(a) Multiple target groups
(b) Group discussions
(c) Show-casing new Research
(d) All of the above

53. Ex Post Facto research means
(a) The research is carried out after the incident
(b) The research is carried out prior to the incident

(c) The research is carried out along with the happening of an incident.
(d) The research is carried out keeping in mind the possibilities of an incident.

54. Research ethics do not include
(a) Honesty (b) Subjectivity
(c) Integrity (d) Objectivity

Read the following passage carefully and answer the questions 55 to 60:

James Madison said, "A people who mean to be their own governors must arm themselves with power that knowledge gives." In India, the Official Secrets Act, 1923 was a convenient smokescreen to deny members of the public access to information. Public functioning has traditionally been shrouded in secrecy. But in a democracy in which people govern themselves, it is necessary to have more openness. In the maturing of our democracy, right to information is a major step forward; it enables citizens to participate fully in the decision-making process that affects their lives so profoundly. It is in this context that the address of the Prime Minister in the Lok Sabha is significant. He said, "I would only like to see that everyone, particularly our civil servants, should see the Bill in a positive spirit; not as a draconian law for paralyzing Government, but as an instrument for improving Government-Citizen interface resulting in a friendly, caring and effective Government functioning for the good of our People." He further said, "This is an innovative Bill, where there will be scope to review its functioning as we gain experience. Therefore, this is a piece of legislation, whose working will be kept under constant reviews."

The Commission, in its Report, has dealt with the application of the Right to Information in Executive, Legislature and Judiciary. The judiciary could be a pioneer in implementing the Act in letter and spirit because much of the work that the Judiciary does is open to public scrutiny, Government of India has sanctioned an e-governance project in the Judiciary for about ₹700 crores which would bring about systematic classification, standardization and categorization of records. This would help the judiciary to fulfil its mandate under the Act. Similar capacity building would be required in all other public authorities. The transformation from non-transparency to transparency and public accountability is the responsibility of all three organs of State.

55. A person gets power
(a) by acquiring knowledge
(b) from the Official Secrets Act, 1923
(c) through openings
(d) by denying public information

56. Right to Information is a major step forward to
(a) enable citizens to participate fully in the decision making process
(b) to make the people aware of the Act
(c) to gain knowledge of administration
(d) to make the people Government friendly

57. The Prime Minister considered the Bill
(a) to provide power to the civil servants
(b) as an instrument for improving Government-citizen interface resulting in a friendly, caring and effective Government
(c) a draconian law against the officials
(d) to check the harassment of the people

58. The Commission made the Bill effective by
(a) extending power to the executive authorities
(b) combining the executive and legislative power

(c) recognizing Judiciary a pioneer in implementing the act in letter and spirit
(d) educating the people before its implementation

59. The Prime Minister considered the Bill innovative and hoped that
(a) It could be reviewed based on the experience gained on its functioning.
(b) The civil servants would see the Bill in a positive spirit.
(c) It would not be considered as a draconian law for paralyzing Government
(d) All of the above

60. The transparency and public accountability is the responsibility of three organs of the State. These three organs are
(a) Lok Sabha, Rajya Sabha and Judiciary
(b) Lok Sabha, Rajya Sabha and Executive
(c) Judiciary, Legislature and the Commission
(d) Legislature, Executive and Judiciary

ANSWERS

1. (c)	2. (b)	3. (b)	4. (b)	5. (d)
6. (a)	7. (c)	8. (b)	9. (a)	10. (c)
11. (d)	12. (a)	13. (b)	14. (b)	15. (b)
16. (a)	17. (c)	18. (c)	19. (c)	20. (a)
21. (a)	22. (c)	23. (a)	24. (b)	25. (c)
26. (b)	27. (b)	28. (d)	29. (c)	30. (c)
31. (c)	32. (c)	33. (d)	34. (d)	35. (c)
36. (a)	37. (b)	38. (a)	39. (d)	40. (b)
41. (b)	42. (d)	43. (d)	44. (c)	45. (b)
46. (d)	47. (a)	48. (d)	49. (a)	50. (a)
51. (b)	52. (d)	53. (a)	54. (b)	55. (a)
56. (a)	57. (b)	58. (c)	59. (d)	60. (d)

PAPER–II

Note: This paper contains fifty (50) objective type questions, each question carrying two (2) marks. Attempt all the questions.

1. Which one of the following pairs is not correct?
(a) Lower Palaeolithic : Hunting, gathering
(b) Upper Palaeolithic : Hunting, gathering
(c) Mesolithic : Hunting, gathering
(d) Neolithic : Food Production

2. Match the List I with List II and select the correct answer from the codes given below:

List I	List II
(A) Sarai Khola	(i) Haryana
(B) Tarkhanwaladera	(ii) Pakistan
(C) Kunal	(iii) Rajasthan
(D) Shikarpur	(iv) Gujarat

Codes:	A	B	C	D
(a)	(ii)	(iii)	(i)	(iv)
(b)	(i)	(ii)	(iii)	(iv)
(c)	(ii)	(iv)	(iii)	(i)
(d)	(i)	(ii)	(iv)	(iii)

3. Which one of the following pairs is correct?
(a) Rock shelter : Langhnaj
(b) Microlith : Mahadaha
(c) Site associated with butchering : Lekhakia
(d) Stone tool workshop : Isampur

4. Match List I with List II and select the correct answer from the codes given below:

List I
(A) Rigveda (B) Yajurveda
(C) Samaveda (D) Atharvaveda

List II

(i) Vajsaneye (ii) Shakala
(iii) Shaunaka (iv) Kauthum

Codes:	**A**	**B**	**C**	**D**
(a)	(i)	(iv)	(iii)	(ii)
(b)	(ii)	(i)	(iv)	(iii)
(c)	(i)	(iii)	(ii)	(iv)
(d)	(iii)	(iv)	(i)	(ii)

5. Match List I with List II and select the correct answer from the codes given below:

List I

(A) Digha Nikaya
(B) Khuddaka Nikaya
(C) Vinayapitaka
(D) Abhidhammapitaka

List II

(i) Dhammapada
(ii) Mahaparinibbana sutta
(iii) Kathavastu
(iv) Khandhaka

Codes:	**A**	**B**	**C**	**D**
(a)	(ii)	(i)	(iv)	(iii)
(b)	(iii)	(ii)	(iv)	(i)
(c)	(i)	(ii)	(iii)	(iv)
(d)	(iii)	(iv)	(ii)	(i)

6. 'Indica' of Megasthenes was preserved in later Greek accounts. Which one of the following Greek travellers' account is not associated with 'Indica'?
(a) Ktesius (b) Strabo
(c) Arrian (d) Pliny

7. Which one of the following pairs is not correct?
(a) Rock Edict : Sarnath
(b) Minor Rock Edict : Bahapur
(c) Pillar Edict : Rampurva
(d) Minor Pillar Edict : Sanchi

8. Which one of the following administrative structure in ascending order is correct?
(a) Dronamukha, Sthaniya, Samgrahana, Karvatika
(b) Sthaniya, Karvatika, Dronamukha, Samgrahana
(c) Sthaniya, Dronamukha, Karvatika, Samgrahana
(d) Sthaniya, Dronamukha, Samgrahana, Karvatika

9. What is the correct chronological order of the following?
(a) The Periplus of the Erythrean Sea
(b) Cosmos Indikopleustes
(c) Geography of Ptolemy
(d) Indica of Megasthenes
Choose the answer from the codes given below:
(a) (a) (b) (c) (d) (b) (a) (c) (d) (b)
(c) (d) (a) (c) (b) (d) (c) (d) (a) (b)

10. Match List I with List II and select the correct answer from the codes given below:

List I

(A) Agathocles (B) Kadphises I
(C) Vimakadphises (D) Kanishka I

List II

(i) Buddha (ii) Samkarshana
(iii) Atash (iv) Shiva

Codes:	**A**	**B**	**C**	**D**
(a)	(ii)	(i)	(iv)	(iii)
(b)	(i)	(iv)	(iii)	(ii)
(c)	(iii)	(i)	(ii)	(iv)
(d)	(iv)	(iii)	(ii)	(i)

11. Which one of the following evidence is not the correct evidence of Ramagupta in later period?
(a) Manasollasa of Someshwara
(b) Shankararya's commentary on Harshcharita
(c) Majmat-ul-Tawarikh of Abul Hasan Ali
(d) Sanjan Tamrapatra of Amoghvarsha

12. Given below are two statements, one is labelled as Assertion (A) and the other is labelled as Reason (R)

Assertion (A): The majority of peasants in the Post-Gupta Period were considered to belong to Sudra Varna.

Reason (R): A large scale incorporation of tribes into caste system started taking place from the Post-Gupta Period.

Read the above statements and select the correct answer from the codes given below:

Codes:

(a) Both (A) and (R) are correct and (R) is the correct explanation of (A)
(b) (A) is correct, but (R) is false
(c) (A) is false, but (R) is correct
(d) Both (A) and (R) are false

13. Which one of the following collection of hymns of Alvar poetry collected by Nathmuni?
(a) Periyapuranam
(b) Tirumurai
(c) Nalayira Divya Prabandhan
(d) Tiruttondal Tiruvantati

14. Identify the dynasty to which Queen Rudramadevi belonged to
(a) Chalukyas of Badami
(b) Pandyas of Madurai
(c) Kakatiyas of Warrangal
(d) Eastern Chalukyas of Vengi

15. Match List I with List II and select the correct answer from the codes given below:

List I

(A) Kirtivarman (B) Simhavishnu
(C) Dantivarman (D) Vijayalaya

List II

(i) Vatapi (ii) Tanjaur
(iii) Kanchipuram (iv) Manyekheta

Codes:	A	B	C	D
(a)	(iv)	(iii)	(ii)	(i)
(b)	(ii)	(iii)	(iv)	(i)
(c)	(iii)	(i)	(ii)	(iv)
(d)	(i)	(iii)	(iv)	(ii)

16. In which one of the following ancient literary works a separate section of painting is found?
(a) Panchasiddhantika
(b) Vishnudharmottara Purana
(c) Panchatantra
(d) Natyashastra

17. Which one of the following was the revenue officer of the Chola dynasty?
(a) Aulnayak
(b) Sherundaram
(c) Varitppottagakka
(d) Perumakkal

18. Which of the following statements are not correct?
(i) After Balban's death his son Bughra Khan assumed sovereignty in Lakhnauti
(ii) Alauddin Khalji extended his authority to Bengal
(iii) Ghiyasuddin Tughluq made Bengal part of the Delhi sultanate in 1324
(iv) Firuz Shah Tughluq invaded Bengal twice during the reign of Shamsuddin Iliyas Shah.

Select the correct answer from the codes given below:

Codes:

(a) (ii) (iii) (iv) (b) (ii) (iv)
(c) (ii) (iii) (d) (iii) (iv)

19. Match List I with List II and select the correct answer from the codes given below:

List I

(A) Shaikh Moinuddin Chishti
(B) Shaikh Bahauddin Zakariya
(C) Shaikh Farid-ud-din Masud Ganj-i-Shakar
(D) Shaikh Nizamuddin Auliya

List II

(i) Delhi (ii) Ajodhan
(iii) Multan (iv) Ajmer

Codes:	A	B	C	D
(a)	(iii)	(iv)	(ii)	(i)
(b)	(iii)	(ii)	(iv)	(i)
(c)	(iv)	(iii)	(ii)	(i)
(d)	(iv)	(ii)	(iii)	(i)

20. Who termed the dominion of Sultan Muhammad Tughlaq as 'Hind and Sind'?
   (a) Ziyauddin Barani
   (b) Abdal Malik Isami
   (c) Ibn Battuta
   (d) Yahia-bin Ahmad Sirhindi

21. What measures were adopted by Mahmud Gawan to curb the power of the Bahmani Nobles?
   (i) He reduced the size of their estate
   (ii) He increased the amount of land classified as royal domain
   (iii) He forbade governors from controlling more than a single fort
   (iv) He enhanced the rate of land revenue demand.

   Select the correct answer from the codes given below:

   Codes:
   (a) (i) (iv) (iii) (b) (i) (ii) (iii)
   (c) (iii) (iv) (ii) (d) (i) (iii) (iv)

22. Arrange the following in correct chronological order:
   (i) Chaitanya (ii) Eknath
   (iii) Surdas (iv) Tulsidas

   Codes:
   (a) (ii) (i) (iii) (iv)
   (b) (i) (ii) (iii) (iv)
   (c) (i) (ii) (iv) (iii)
   (d) (i) (iii) (ii) (iv)

23. Given below are two statements, one labelled Assertion (A) and other labelled Reason (R).

   Assertion (A): In military terms Firuz Shah Tughluq's reign was undistinguished.

   Reason (R): He could not subjugate the ruler of Nagarkot.

   In the context of the above two statements, which one of the following is correct?

   Codes:
   (a) Both (A) and (R) are true and (R) is the correct explanation of (A).
   (b) Both (A) and (R) are true, but (R) is not the correct explanation of (A).
   (c) (A) is true, but (R) is false
   (d) (A) is false, but (R) is true

24. Who described the Mughal imperial Harem as the 'Pavilion of chartity'?
   (a) Nizamuddin Ahmad
   (b) Abul Fazl
   (c) Gulbadan Begum
   (d) Abdul Hamid Lahori

25. In the Mughal System of administration, Mir Bakshi was
   (a) Commandar-in-chief of the Mughal army
   (b) Incharge of the imperial mint
   (c) Minister-in-charge of Treasury
   (d) Paymaster General

26. Which of the following social reforms was not introduced by Akbar?
   (a) Legalization of widows remarriage
   (b) Registration of marriage
   (c) Total ban on the practice of sati
   (d) The age of circumcision was raised to twelve

27. Which of the following statements is true?
   (a) In Mughal India, cultivation of indigo was confined to the provinces of Delhi and Agra
   (b) Madad-i-Maash grants were made hereditary by Aurangzeb
   (c) Altamgha Jagirs were made transferable by Jahangir
   (d) Kashmir was brought under the zabti system of land revenue assessment.

28. Match List I with List II and select the correct answer from the codes given below:

List I

(A) Maasir-i-Jahangiri
(B) Iqbalnama-i-Jahangiri
(C) Maasir-i- Alamgiri
(D) Futuhat-i-Alamgiri

List II

(i) Motmid Khan
(ii) Saqi Mustaid Khan
(iii) Khwaza Kamgar Ghairat Khan
(iv) Isardas Nagar

Codes:	A	B	C	D
(a)	(i)	(iii)	(ii)	(iv)
(b)	(iii)	(i)	(ii)	(iv)
(c)	(ii)	(iii)	(i)	(iv)
(d)	(i)	(ii)	(iii)	(iv)

29. Arrange the following events in chronological order:

(i) Mughal occupation of Balkh
(ii) Introduction of the system of month proportion
(iii) Extinction of Nizamshahi
(iv) Treaty of the Mughals with Bijapur and Golkunda

(a) (ii) (iii) (iv) (i) (b) (iii) (ii) (i) (iv)
(c) (iv) (iii) (ii) (i) (d) (ii) (iv) (i) (iii)

30. Arrange the following in chronological order:

(i) Prince Akbar's flight to the Deccan
(ii) Conquest of Golkunda by Aurangzeb
(iii) Capture of Chitagong by Shaista Khan
(iv) The institution of Khalsa by Guru Gobind Singh

Select the correct answer from the codes given below:

Codes:

(a) (i) (iii) (ii) (iv) (b) (iii) (i) (ii) (iv)
(c) (ii) (iv) (iii) (i) (d) (i) (iii) (iv) (ii)

31. Given below are two statements, one is labelled as Assertion (A) and the other is labelled as Reason (R):

Assertion (A): The English East India Company eliminated their Portuguese and Dutch trade rivals by the end of the Seventeenth century.

Reason (R): The English traders sold goods of superior quality at cheaper rates.

Read the above statements and select the correct answer from the codes given below:

Codes:

(a) Both (A) and (R) are true, and (R) is the correct explanation of (A)
(b) Both (A) and (R) are true but (R) is not the correct explanation of (A)
(c) (A) is true, but (R) is false
(d) (A) is false, but (R) is true

32. Given below are two statements, one is labelled as Assertion (A) and the other is labelled as Reason (R):

Assertion (A): The number of Rajput Mansabdars declined in the Mughal nobility during the second half of Aurangzeb's reign.

Reason (R): Aurangzeb assigned large number of Jagirs to nobles from the Deccan.

Read the above statements and select the correct answer from the codes given below:

Codes:

(a) Both (A) and (R) are true and (R) is the correct explanation of (A)
(b) Both (A) and (R) are true, but (R) is not the correct explanation of (A)
(c) (A) is true, but (R) is false
(d) (A) is false, but (R) is true

33. Match List I with List II and select the correct answer from the codes given below:

List I (Books)

(A) *Indian Painting under the Mughals*
(B) *Architecture of Mughal India*
(C) *The Technique of Mughal Painting*
(D) *Mughal Painting during Jahangir's Time*

List II (Authors)

(i) Ashok Kumar Das
(ii) Moti Chandra
(iii) Percy Brown
(iv) Catherine B. Asher

Codes:	A	B	C	D
(a)	(ii)	(i)	(iii)	(iv)
(b)	(iii)	(ii)	(iv)	(i)
(c)	(iv)	(ii)	(i)	(iii)
(d)	(iii)	(iv)	(ii)	(i)

34. Consider the names of the following Mughal Emperors of the Eighteenth century:

(i) Alamgir II
(ii) Ahmad Shah
(iii) Jahandar Shah
(iv) Muhammad Shah

Which among the following sequences represents the correct chronological order?

(a) (ii) (i) (iii) (iv) (b) (i) (ii) (iii) (iv)
(c) (iii) (iv) (ii) (i) (d) (iii) (iv) (i) (ii)

35. Given below are two statements, one is labelled as Assertion (A) and other is labelled as Reason (R).

Assertion (A): The 1857 Mutiny was suppressed by the British.

Reason (R): Except for a few like Rani of Jhansi, a very few Indian rulers participated in the mutiny.

Read the above statements and select the correct answer from the codes given below:

Codes:

(a) Both (A) and (R) are true and (R) is the correct explanation of (A)
(b) Both (A) and (R) are true, but (R) is not the correct explanation of (A)
(c) Both (A) and (R) are false
(d) (A) is true, but (R) is false

36. Given below are two statements, one labelled as Assertion (A) and other labelled as Reason (R).

Assertion (A): Dr. Annie Besant organised the Home Rule Movement against the British Rule.

Reason (R): She wanted to organise all sections of Indian people on the basis of a single political slogan above religious consideration.

Read the above statements and select the correct answer from the codes given below:

Codes:

(a) (A) is correct, but (R) is not correct
(b) (A) is not correct, but (R) is correct
(c) (A) and (R) both are not correct
(d) (A) is correct and (R) is the correct explanation of (A)

37. In which year did Robert Clive accept the Diwani of Bengal, Bihar and Orissa from the Mughal ruler.

(a) 1761 (b) 1765
(c) 1778 (d) 1781

38. The Treaty of Bassien (1802) was signed between:

(a) the English and Peshwa Baji Rao II
(b) the English and Tipu Sultan
(c) the English and Holkar
(d) the English and Gaikwad

39. The Home Rule Movement started by Annie Besant aimed at:

(a) boycotting foreign goods
(b) educating the Indian Masses
(c) attaining self-rule for India
(d) agitating against the British Monopoly in administration

40. Which of the following is the correct chronological order of the English East India Company factories established in India?
 (i) Surat (ii) Masulipatnam
 (iii) Hugli (iv) Balasore
 Codes:
 (a) (i) (ii) (iii) (iv) (b) (ii) (i) (iv) (iii)
 (c) (iii) (iv) (i) (ii) (d) (iv) (iii) (i) (ii)

41. Who was the first woman President of the Indian National Congress?
 (a) Sarojini Naidu
 (b) Annie Besant
 (c) Sucheta Kripalani
 (d) Madam Cama

42. Who wrote Poverty and Un-British Rule in India?
 (a) Dadabhai Naoroji
 (b) R.C. Dutt
 (c) Charles Wood
 (d) M.N. Roy

43. August 8, 1942 is important in Indian History for
 (a) Formation of Indian National Army by Subhash Chandra Bose at Singapore
 (b) Cripp's Proposals for Dominion status
 (c) Non-co-operation Movement launched by Mahatma Gandhi
 (d) Quit India Movement launched by Mahatma Gandhi

44. Which is correctly matched?
 (a) "Do or Die" – Jawaharlal Nehru
 (b) "Swaraj is my birth right" – Mahatma Gandhi
 (c) "Give me blood, I will give you freedom" – Subhash Chandra Bose
 (d) "Independence through non-violence must be our aim" – B.G. Tilak

45. Match List I with List II and select the correct answer from the codes given below:
 List I
 (A) Freedom at Midnight
 (B) The Story of the Integration of Indian States
 (C) Travancore Dewan
 (D) Secretary of State

 List II
 (i) Collins and Lapierre
 (ii) C. P. Ramaswami Iyar
 (iii) V. P. Menon
 (iv) Pethick-Lawrence

Codes:	A	B	C	D
(a)	(i)	(iii)	(ii)	(iv)
(b)	(iii)	(ii)	(i)	(iv)
(c)	(iv)	(iii)	(ii)	(i)
(d)	(ii)	(iv)	(iii)	(i)

46. Which of the following is the correct chronological order of the Viceroys?
 (i) North Brook (ii) Minto
 (iii) Linlithgow (iv) Mayo
 Codes:
 (a) (iv) (i) (ii) (iii) (b) (ii) (iii) (i) (iv)
 (c) (i) (ii) (iii) (iv) (d) (iii) (iv) (ii) (i)

47. Arrange the following into sequential order and select correct answer from the codes given below:
 (i) St. Thomae war
 (ii) The Pindari war
 (iii) Buxar war
 (iv) War of Chandurthi
 Codes:
 (a) (i) (iv) (iii) (ii)
 (b) (iv) (iii) (ii) (i)
 (c) (i) (ii) (iii) (iv)
 (d) (iv) (ii) (iii) (i)

48. Match List I with List II and select the correct answer from the codes given below:
 List I
 (A) Col. Tod (B) Johan Malcolm
 (C) C.R. Wilson (D) M. Wilks

List II

(i) Memoir of Central India
(ii) Annals and Antiquities of Rajasthan
(iii) Historical Sketches of South India
(iv) Early Annals of the English in Bengal

Codes:	A	B	C	D
(a)	(ii)	(i)	(iv)	(iii)
(b)	(ii)	(iii)	(iv)	(i)
(c)	(i)	(iv)	(iii)	(ii)
(d)	(iii)	(i)	(ii)	(iv)

49. Match List I with List II and select the correct answer from the codes given below:

List I

(A) Punjab Tenancy Act
(B) The Ilbert Bill
(C) Hunter Commission
(D) Chamber of Princes

List II

(i) 1883 (ii) 1868
(iii) 1921 (iv) 1882

Codes:	A	B	C	D
(a)	(ii)	(iii)	(i)	(iv)
(b)	(i)	(ii)	(iv)	(iii)
(c)	(iv)	(ii)	(iii)	(i)
(d)	(ii)	(i)	(iv)	(iii)

50. Chronologically arrange the following schools of historical thought as emerged at different points of time:

(i) Enlightenment Historiography
(ii) Church Historiography
(iii) Annals Historiography
(iv) Subaltern Historiography

Select the correct answer from the codes given below:

Codes:

(a) (i) (iii) (iv) (ii) (b) (ii) (iii) (i) (iv)
(c) (ii) (i) (iii) (iv) (d) (i) (ii) (iv) (iii)

ANSWERS

1. (c)	2. (a)	3. (d)	4. (b)	5. (a)
6. (a)	7. (a)	8. (c)	9. (c)	10. (a)
11. (a)	12. (a)	13. (c)	14. (c)	15. (d)
16. (b)	17. (c)	18. (b)	19. (c)	20. (c)
21. (b)	22. (a)	23. (c)	24. (a)	25. (d)
26. (c)	27. (b)	28. (b)	29. (a)	30. (b)
31. (c)	32. (b)	33. (d)	34. (c)	35. (a)
36. (d)	37. (b)	38. (a)	39. (c)	40. (b)
41. (b)	42. (a)	43. (d)	44. (c)	45. (a)
46. (a)	47. (a)	48. (a)	49. (d)	50. (c)

PAPER–III

Note: This paper contains seventy five (75) objective type questions, each question carrying two (2) marks. All questions are compulsory.

1. Match List I (Archaeological Site) with List II (Identification) and select the correct answer with the help of the code given below:

List I (Archaeological Site)

(A) Bagore (B) Brahmagiri
(C) Maheshwara (D) Tekkalakota

List II (Identification)

(i) Chalcolithic site of Madhya Pradesh
(ii) Megalithic site of Karnataka
(iii) Mesolithic site of Rajasthan
(iv) Neolithic site of Karnataka

Codes:	A	B	C	D
(a)	(i)	(iii)	(iv)	(ii)
(b)	(iii)	(ii)	(i)	(iv)
(c)	(iv)	(ii)	(iii)	(i)
(d)	(ii)	(i)	(iv)	(iii)

2. Which proto-historic site has yielded the evidence of threads of raw silk?

(a) Ahar (b) Inamgaon
(c) Navadatoli (d) Nevasa

3. Arrange the following Indologists in the chronological order and select the correct answer with the help of the code given below:

(i) William Jones
(ii) Alexander Cunningham
(iii) James Burgess
(iv) James Fergusson

Codes:

(a) (i) (ii) (iv) (iii) (b) (iv) (i) (ii) (iii)
(c) (i) (iv) (iii) (ii) (d) (ii) (iv) (i) (iii)

4. Match List I (Initiator/Writer) with List II (Journal/Book) and select the correct answer with the help of the code given below:

List I (Initiator/Writer)
(A) William Jones
(B) James Fergusson
(C) Alexander Cunningham
(D) James Burgess

List II (Journal/Book)
(i) Indian Antiquary
(ii) The Stupa of Bharhut
(iii) Asiatic Researches
(iv) Archaeology in India

Codes:	A	B	C	D
(a)	(iii)	(iv)	(ii)	(i)
(b)	(ii)	(i)	(iii)	(iv)
(c)	(iv)	(ii)	(i)	(iii)
(d)	(i)	(iii)	(iv)	(ii)

5. Match List I (Vedic rivers) with List II (Present counterparts) and select the correct answer with the help of the code given below:

List I (Vedic rivers)
(A) Vipas (B) Parusni
(C) Vitasta (D) Sutudri

List II (Present counterparts)
(i) Jhelum (ii) Ravi
(iii) Beas (iv) Sutlej

Codes:	A	B	C	D
(a)	(iii)	(ii)	(i)	(iv)
(b)	(ii)	(iv)	(iii)	(i)
(c)	(i)	(iii)	(iv)	(ii)
(d)	(iii)	(iv)	(ii)	(i)

6. The Boghaz Keui inscription from Asia Minor refers to the following Vedic deities:
(a) Indra, Varuna, Agni and Surya
(b) Indra, Varuna, Mitra and Agni
(c) Indra, Mitra, Varuna and Nasatyas
(d) Indra, Mitra, Dyuas and Nasatyas

7. To which of the following tribes did King Sudasa, described in the Rigveda as having defeated ten Kings, belong?
(a) Anu (b) Druhyu
(c) Tritsu (d) Yadu

8. Given below are two statements, one labelled as Assertion (A) and the other labelled as Reason (R):

Assertion (A): The Greek historian Herodotus tells us that 'India was the twentieth and most prosperous satrapy (province) of the Persian empire'.

Reason (R): By the time of Alexander's invasion (327-326 B.C.) all the Persian impact on India had become non-existent.

In the context of the above two statements, which one of the following is correct?
(a) Both (A) and (R) are true, and (R) is the correct explanation of (A).
(b) Both (A) and (R) are true, but (R) is not the correct explanation of (A).
(c) (A) is true, but (R) is false.
(d) (A) is false, but (R) is true.

9. Who had made the following statement? 'Bhagavapi Khatrio Ahampi Khatrio' (Bhagawan [Buddha] was a Kshatriya I too am a Kshatriya).
(a) Bimbisara (b) Prasenjit
(c) Ajatasatru (d) Sisunaga

10. Which one of the following Sangam poets has mentioned about the hoarded wealth of the rulers of the Nanda dynasty?
(a) Avvaiyar (b) Mamulanar
(c) Parnar (d) Ilango Adigal

11. Match List I (Officer) with List II (Department) and select the correct answer with the help of the codes given below:

List I (Officer)

(A) Sannidhata (B) Samaharta
(C) Panyadhaksa (D) Antaravamsika

List II (Department)

(i) Incharge of revenue collection
(ii) Incharge of commerce department
(iii) Incharge of the harem guards
(iv) Incharge of the treasury

Codes:	**A**	**B**	**C**	**D**
(a)	(ii)	(i)	(iv)	(iii)
(b)	(iv)	(i)	(iii)	(ii)
(c)	(iv)	(i)	(ii)	(iii)
(d)	(i)	(iii)	(iv)	(ii)

12. Match List I (Ruler) with List II (Associated person) and select the correct answer with the help of the codes given below:

List I (Ruler)	**List II (Associated person)**
(A) Bimbisara	(i) Deimachus
(B) Bindusara	(ii) St. Thomas
(C) Ajatasatru	(iii) Jivaka
(D) Gondopharnes	(iv) Vassakara

Codes:	**A**	**B**	**C**	**D**
(a)	(iii)	(i)	(iv)	(ii)
(b)	(ii)	(iii)	(i)	(iv)
(c)	(iv)	(ii)	(iii)	(i)
(d)	(iii)	(ii)	(iv)	(i)

13. It is generally accepted that a special feature of the period between 200 B.C. and 300 A.D. is the increase in external trade. Which of the following factors did not assist in the increase?

(a) From a political point of view India had become one.
(b) The Mauryas had constructed various roads and introduced uniform system of administration and this helped in increase in trade.
(c) Indo-Greek rulers helped by establishing close relations with countries of the Mediterranean and West Asia.
(d) The Saka, Parthian and Kusana rulers helped by establishing close ties with Central Asian rulers.

14. Match List I (Ancient Monument) with List II (Characteristic feature) and select the correct answer with the help of the codes given below:

List I (Ancient Monument)

(A) Sanchi Stupa (B) Nalanda
(C) Junnar (D) Ellora

List II (Characteristic feature)

(i) Tallest Buddhist structure
(ii) Represents Hindu, Buddhist and Jaina religions
(iii) Contained the relics of Sariputra and Maudgalyayana
(iv) Rock-cut Chaityahall with circular plan

Codes:	**A**	**B**	**C**	**D**
(a)	(iii)	(i)	(iv)	(ii)
(b)	(ii)	(iii)	(i)	(iv)
(c)	(iii)	(ii)	(iv)	(i)
(d)	(i)	(iv)	(iii)	(ii)

15. Which one of the following is not correctly matched?

(Ruler)		**(Figure shown on his coin)**
(a) Kumaragupta I	–	Chakrapurusa
(b) Kaniska	–	Ardokso
(c) Agatho cles	–	Balarama
(d) K. satrapa Rajuvula	–	Pallas

16. Match List I (Ancient City) with List II (Modern Representative) and select the correct answer with the help of the codes given below:

List I (Ancient City)
(A) Dasapura (B) Dvarasamudra
(C) Madhyamika (D) Samapa

List II (Modern Representative)
(i) Halebid (ii) Mandsor
(iii) Nagari (iv) Jaugada

Codes:	**A**	**B**	**C**	**D**
(a)	(ii)	(i)	(iii)	(iv)
(b)	(i)	(iv)	(ii)	(iii)
(c)	(iii)	(ii)	(i)	(iv)
(d)	(ii)	(iii)	(iv)	(i)

17. Who among the following assumed the title of 'Dharmamaharaja' which was justified by the performance of numerous Vedic sacrifices incuding the Asvamedha?
(a) Pusyamitra (b) Sarvatata
(c) Samudragupta (d) Pravarasena I

18. The seat of third Sangam of Tamil poets was located at
(a) Uraiyur (b) Madura
(c) Tanjore (d) Kanchi

19. Which one of the following Indian rulers had donated five villages to a Vihara built at Nalanda by Sailendra King Sri Balaputra?
(a) Kumaragupta I
(b) Harsa
(c) Devapala
(d) Bhaskaravarman

20. The rulers of which dynasty of the Deccan have been described by the Arab writers as the four great sovereigns of the world?
(a) Chalukyas of Vatapi
(b) Chalukyas of Kalyani
(c) Mauryas of Konkan
(d) Rastrakutas of Manyakheta

21. Which one of the following is not correctly matched?
(a) Rajasekhara – Viddhasalabhanjika
(b) Sri Harsa – Naisadhiya Charita
(c) Mahendravarman – Kavirajamarga
(d) Sudraka – Mrichchakatikam

22. Given below are two statements, one labelled as Assertion (A) and the other labelled as Reason (R):
Assertion (A): The growth of regional politics in early medieval India was accompanied by the composition of royal biographies by court poets.
Reason (R): Sandhyakaranandin's Ramacharita is written in slesa style and simultaneously tells the story of the epic hero Rama and the Pala King Ramapala.
In the context of the above two statements, which one of the following is correct?
(a) Both (A) and (R) are true and (R) is the correct explanation of (A).
(b) Both (A) and (R) are true, but (R) is not the correct explanation of (A).
(c) (A) is true, but (R) is false.
(d) (A) is false, but (R) is true.

23. Given below are two statements, one is labelled as Assertion (A) and the other is labelled as Reason (R):
Assertion (A): The Sultans of Delhi managed to consolidate an empire comprising a large part of India with their military power.
Reason (R): The main feature of the Delhi Sultanate was that the sultans based their military power with military elite bound together by Islam and certain tribal affinities.
Read the above statements and select the correct answer from the codes given below:
Codes:
(a) Both (A) and (R) are correct.
(b) Both (A) and (R) are false.
(c) (A) is incorrect, but (R) is true.
(d) (A) is correct, but (R) is false.

24. The first reference of 'Turkan-i-Chihalgani' has been made in

(a) Tabqat-i-Nasiri
(b) Futuh-us-Salatin
(c) Kitabur Rehla
(d) Khazain-ul-Futuh

25. Which Mongol general defeated Alauddin Khalji?
(a) Qadar
(b) Qutlugh Khwaja
(c) Targi
(d) Iqbalmand

26. Diwan-i-Khalsa was responsible to look after the
(a) Land under continuous cultivation
(b) Revenue free land granted as rewards
(c) Land under the direct control of the State
(d) Fallow land

27. Match List I with List II and select the correct answer from the codes given below:

List I
(A) Malgujar (B) Mufti
(C) Anjuman (D) Khanazad

List II
(i) Hereditary Muslim aristocrats
(ii) Local Muslim Association
(iii) Muslim learned person expert in religious law
(iv) Landholding primary zamindar

Codes:	A	B	C	D
(a)	(iv)	(iii)	(ii)	(i)
(b)	(iii)	(iv)	(i)	(ii)
(c)	(ii)	(iv)	(iii)	(i)
(d)	(i)	(iii)	(ii)	(iv)

28. Match List I with List II and select the correct answer from the codes given below:

List I
(A) Hundi (B) Dastak
(C) Sanad (D) Dadani

List II
(i) Mughal Imperial Order
(ii) Bill of Exchange
(iii) Advance paid to the primary producers
(iv) Permit issued to the European traders for the purpose of tax exemption

Codes:	A	B	C	D
(a)	(ii)	(iii)	(i)	(iv)
(b)	(iii)	(ii)	(iv)	(i)
(c)	(ii)	(iv)	(i)	(iii)
(d)	(iii)	(iv)	(i)	(ii)

29. When did the nine cusped arches were for the first time used in Muslim architecture in India?
(a) Buildings of Sikandar Lodi
(b) Buildings of Sher Shah
(c) Buildings of Nur Jahan
(d) Buildings of Shah Jahan

30. Who amongst the following commented on the rule of the First Afghan Empire in India that 'there was an opportunity to establish in India the constitutional monarchy but the dissensions amongst the Afghan nobles let the opportunity pass away'?
(a) K.A. Nizami
(b) Peter Jackson
(c) R.P. Tripathi
(d) John F. Richards

31. Which one of the following statements is not correct about Alauddin Khalji?
(a) He established the department called 'Diwan-i-Kohi'
(b) Ziyauddin Barni criticizes Alauddin's taxation policy
(c) Malik Fakhruddin, the Kotwal was loyal to him
(d) His son Qutbuddin Mubarak Khalji declared himself the 'Caliph'

32. The title of 'Mujaddid' was conferred to which Mughal Emperor by the contemporary historians?
(a) Humayun (b) Jahangir
(c) Shah Jahan (d) Aurangzeb

33. Match List I with List II and select the correct answer from the codes given below:
List I
(A) Ramanuja
(B) Chaitanya
(C) Vallabhacharya
(D) Nanak

List II
(i) Pushti Marg
(ii) Nirguna Bhakti
(iii) Vishitadvaita Philosophy
(iv) Gaudiya Vaishnavism

Codes:	A	B	C	D
(a)	(iii)	(ii)	(iv)	(i)
(b)	(ii)	(i)	(iv)	(iii)
(c)	(iv)	(ii)	(i)	(iii)
(d)	(iii)	(iv)	(i)	(ii)

34. Match List I with List II and select the correct answer from the codes given below:
List I
(A) Qadiriya Order
(B) Naqsbandiah Order
(C) Firdausi Order
(D) Shuttari Order

List II
(i) Shaikh Badruddin Samarkhandi
(ii) Shah Abdullah
(iii) Khwaja Baqi Billah
(iv) Shah Nayamatullah

Codes:	A	B	C	D
(a)	(i)	(ii)	(iii)	(iv)
(b)	(iv)	(iii)	(i)	(ii)
(c)	(iii)	(ii)	(iv)	(i)
(d)	(iv)	(i)	(ii)	(iii)

35. Match List I with List II and select the correct answer from the codes given below:
List I
(A) Masand (B) Sahajdari
(C) Sardeshmukhi (D) Dal Khalsa
List II
(i) A deputy of the Sikh Guru
(ii) Non-Khalsa Sikhs
(iii) A term for Maratha revenue demand
(iv) Sikh religious organization

Codes:	A	B	C	D
(a)	(i)	(ii)	(iii)	(iv)
(b)	(ii)	(i)	(iv)	(iii)
(c)	(ii)	(iv)	(i)	(iii)
(d)	(i)	(iii)	(ii)	(iv)

36. What new stylistic feature is found in the Tomb of Khan-i-Jahan Telangani built at Delhi under the Sultans of Delhi?
(a) Use of white marble against red sand stone
(b) True Arch
(c) Double Dome
(d) Octagonal in planning

37. Which styles of the Sultanate painting paved the way in the foundation of the Mughal style of painting?
(a) Chaurapanchasika, Laur Chanda and Indo-Persian
(b) Pala, Kashmiri and Laur Chanda
(c) Chaurpanchasika, Kashmiri and Indo-Persian
(d) Indo-Persian, Pala and Kashmiri

38. Consider the following statements and point out the incorrect one:
(a) Babur's Memoirs provide a flood of light on contemporary affairs.
(b) It exhibits Babur's interest in nature.
(c) It provides no information about Farghana, Samarqand and Kabul where he spent time.
(d) He throws light on his contemporaries, their good and bad points, including himself.

39. Tulsidas was the author of which book?
(a) Kavitawali
(b) Ramacharitamanas
(c) Gitawali
(d) All of the above

40. Who among the following is considered as the founder of 'Varkari' sect?
(a) Eknath (b) Tukaram
(c) Namdeva (d) Jnanesvara

41. Consider the following statements in the context of organization of Mughal ruling class during the 17th century and select the correct answer from the options given below:
(a) An aspect of the composite ruling class was the steady promotion of a small number of members belonging to the administrative services.
(b) These members were generally drawn from Khatri and Kayastha castes.
(c) A few Brahmins could also be found amongst this ruling class.
(d) All of the above.

42. Which one of the following Mughal painters was a caricaturist?
(a) Basawan (b) Manohar
(c) Miskin (d) Abul Hasan

43. Shah Jahan fought the Battle of Kartarpur against
(a) Guru Hargovind Singh
(b) Guru Har Kishan
(c) Guru Har Rai
(d) Guru Tegh Bahadur

44. Given below are two statements labelled as Assertion (A) and the other labelled as Reason (R):
Assertion (A): Recurring peasant revolts in the late 17th and early 18th centuries are believed to have been a major cause of the decline of Mughal Empire.
Reason (R): Regional sentiments against a centralized Mughal State had not been there.
In the context of the above two statements, which one of the following is correct?
Codes:
(a) Both (A) and (R) are true and (R) is the correct explanation of (A).
(b) Both (A) and (R) are true, but (R) is not the correct explanation of (A).
(c) (A) is true, but (R) is false.
(d) (A) is false, but (R) is true.

45. Which one of the following centre was not a Dutch commercial establishment in India?
(a) Masulipatam (b) Karikal
(c) Hugli (d) Balasore

46. Name the English Officer who obtained Madras on lease in 1639 from the ruler of Chandragiri.
(a) Sir Thomas Roe
(b) Francis Day
(c) Sir George Oxenden
(d) Sir John Child

47. Match List I with List II and select the correct answer from the codes given below the lists:
List I
(A) Second Carnatic War
(B) Third Anglo-Mysore War
(C) Second Anglo-Maratha War
(D) Third Carnatic War
List II
(i) Treaty of Paris
(ii) Treaty of Aixha Chapelle
(iii) Treaty of Srirangapatnam
(iv) Treaty of Bassein

Codes:	A	B	C	D
(a)	(iii)	(ii)	(iv)	(i)
(b)	(ii)	(i)	(iii)	(iv)
(c)	(i)	(iv)	(ii)	(iii)
(d)	(ii)	(iii)	(iv)	(i)

48. Which one of the following provisions was not part of the Subsidiary Alliance?

(a) The State has to keep British force under the command of English General.
(b) The State should take prior permission from the Company for waging of war or making peace with another State.
(c) The State should not have relation with any European power except English East India Company.
(d) The State can go for adoption in the case of not having natural heir.

49. Name the Governor General who adopted a policy of the Europeanisation of bureaucracy and an exclusion of Indians from higher posts.
(a) Warren Hastings (b) Cornwallis
(c) Wellesley (d) Dalhousie

50. Given below are two statements, one labelled as Assertion (A) and other labelled as Reason (R):
Assertion (A): The British introduced different land revenue tenures in different parts of India.
Reason (R): It led to the impoverishment of Indian peasantry.
In the context of above two statements, which one of the following is correct?
Codes:
(a) Both (A) and (R) are true, but (R) is not the correct explanation of (A).
(b) (A) is correct, but (R) is false.
(c) Both (A) and (R) are false.
(d) Both (A) and (R) are correct and (R) is the correct explanation of (A).

51. Curzon-Kitchner Controversy of 1904-05 is related to
(a) Partition of Bengal
(b) Abolition of military member in the Viceroy's Council
(c) Direct recruitment of police force
(d) Autonomy of the Calcutta University

52. Match List I with List II and select the correct answer from the codes given below the lists:
List I
(A) Punjab Land Alienation Act
(B) Central Provinces Land Alienation Act
(C) North West Provinces Land Alienation Act
(D) Deccan Agricultural Relief Act

List II
(i) 1900 (ii) 1879
(iii) 1904 (iv) 1916

Codes:	A	B	C	D
(a)	(i)	(iii)	(iv)	(ii)
(b)	(ii)	(i)	(iii)	(iv)
(c)	(iii)	(iv)	(ii)	(i)
(d)	(iv)	(ii)	(i)	(iii)

53. Name the ruler who was deposed in 1875 on charges of 'gross misrule'.
(a) Gangasingh of Bikaner
(b) Bupendranath Singh of Patiala
(c) Krishna Raja Wadiar of Mysore
(d) Malhar Rao Gaikwad of Baroda

54. The first English Evening Daily Newspaper from Madras was
(a) The Madras Mail
(b) The Madras Chronicle
(c) The Madras Herald
(d) The Madras Standard

55. "Forget not that the lower classes, the ignorant, the poor, the illiterate, the cobbler, the sweeper are thy flesh and blood, thy brothers"—These words are related to
(a) Jyotiba Phule
(b) Mahatma Gandhi
(c) B.R. Ambedkar
(d) Swami Vivekananda

56. "The Indian Rebellion of 1857 was not one movement .... it was many"—The above statement has been made by

(a) S.N. Sen (b) R.C. Majumdar
(c) C.A. Bayly (d) Eric Stokes

57. Match List I with List II and select the correct answer from the codes given below the lists:

List I
(A) Narayan Guru
(B) Tripuraneni Ramaswamy Choudary
(C) Venkataraylu Naidu
(D) Sridharula Naidu

List II
(i) Rising Sun
(ii) Jati Mimamsa
(iii) Shambuka Vadha
(iv) Veda Samaj

Codes:	**A**	**B**	**C**	**D**
(a)	(ii)	(i)	(iv)	(iii)
(b)	(ii)	(iii)	(i)	(iv)
(c)	(i)	(iv)	(iii)	(ii)
(d)	(iii)	(ii)	(i)	(iv)

58. Select the correct answer from the codes given below about the chronological sequence of the movements:
(i) Kuka Movement
(ii) Wahabi Movement
(iii) Mundas Revolt
(iv) Moplah Peasant Revolt

Codes:
(a) (ii) (i) (iii) (iv) (b) (i) (iii) (ii) (iv)
(c) (ii) (i) (iv) (iii) (d) (iii) (ii) (i) (iv)

59. Select the correct answer from the codes given below about the chronological sequence of the Act passed:
(i) Brahmo Marriage Act
(ii) Sarada Act
(iii) Hindu Widow's Re-marriage Act
(iv) Age of Consent Bill

Codes:
(a) (i) (iii) (iv) (ii) (b) (iii) (i) (ii) (iv)
(c) (iv) (i) (iii) (ii) (d) (iii) (i) (iv) (ii)

60. One of the following Congress leaders did not preside any Session of the Indian National Congress:
(a) Surendranath Bannerjee
(b) Gopala Krishna Gokhale
(c) Bala Gangadhar Tilak
(d) Mahatma Gandhi

61. The first Swadeshi dacoity or robbery was organised in the year 1906 in
(a) Maniktala (b) Rangapur
(c) Muzaffarpur (d) Midnapur

62. Who was called 'Morning Star' of Reformation?
(a) Martin Luther (b) John Calvin
(c) Zwingli (d) John Wycliffe

63. Who used the word 'Cold War' first?
(a) Winston Churchill
(b) Bernard Baruch
(c) Marshal
(d) Stressman

64. 'Pure Blood Aryan theory' is related to
(a) Fascism (b) Nihalism
(c) Syndicalism (d) Nazism

65. What position Nelson Mandela occupied in the African National Congress at the time of his release from jail after 26 years in 1990?
(a) President (b) Vice-President
(c) Secretary (d) Advisor

66. What was Marshal Plan?
(a) Control of European powers by military power.
(b) To spread American Dictatorship in Europe.
(c) Economic package of USA to control Communism.
(d) American Continent is meant for Americans only.

67. A concrete outcome of the Wavell Plan was the
(a) Constitution of the Constituent Assembly
(b) Complete independence for India gradually

(c) Hold a Referendum in the North-West Province
(d) Summoning of the Shimla Conference

68. Which one of the following Committees was appointed by the UPSC in 1974 to go into the issue of recruitment and selection methods?
(a) Bhagwati Committee
(b) D.S. Kothari Committee
(c) A.D. Gorwala Committee
(d) Santhanam Committee

69. Who among the following explicitly states that "History bases all its conclusions on rational evidence"?
(a) Herodotus (b) Thucydides
(c) Polybious (d) Tacitus

70. Which one of the following work was not authored by Leopol von Ranke?
(a) History of Rome
(b) History of France
(c) History of the Popes
(d) German History at the time of Reformation

Read the following passage carefully and choose the correct answer of the questions that follow (Q. No. 71 to 75):

Causation is a concept of such fundamental importance to historical understanding that E.H. Carr in his G.M. Trevelyan lectures (1961) declared the study of history to be the study of causes. But postmodernist thinking on the issue of historical causation is different. John Vincent would abandon the search for causes as futile and rather look for explanations. Writing in 1976, Theodore Zeldin thought of causation and chronology as the two tyrants to historians. Hayden White attacked the concept of causation as depriving people of both their freedom of action in the present and of control over the future by trapping them in an inescapable network of causation. Postmodernist theory installs interpretation in the place of empirical research into the causes of specific events.

Since the notion of cause depends on sequential time, some postmodernists attack the latter too. The cause of an occurrence must obviously come before it in time. But the postmodernist historian and philosopher, Ankersmit, says "Historical time is a recent and highly artificial invention of Western civilization," and the writing of historical narrative based on the concept of time, he has declared, is "building on quicksand." The postmodernists would prefer that the idea of sequential time be abandoned in the writing of history.

Richard Evans shows how the very idea of postmodern is paradoxical in that it is contrary to the assertion that there are no time periods in history. And the postmodernist statement that historical time is a thing of the past, itself uses the historical concept of time which the statement is intended to dismiss. The linear and sequential concept of time is far too powerful a principle to be dispensed with, for it is not an intellectual construct but a matter of everyday experience for people the world over. Time itself may be without boundaries, but in terms of human life it passes, and has limits.

71. What is the concept of causation by E.H. Carr?
(a) History cannot be understood devoid of cause-effect relationship.
(b) History depends on time and space.
(c) It is a matter of every day personal experience to inquire about the basis of an event.
(d) Causes should be undertaken in totality.

72. What does postmodernist think about the Historical causation?

(a) It is useless to search for it.
(b) It puts limitation on the Historian.
(c) Interpretation is necessary rather than the cause-effect relation.
(d) There are different opinions.

73. Which is not the concept of Time amongst the postmodernists?
(a) It should not be studied in the interpretation of History.
(b) It puts forth the theory that the interpretation of events be emphasized.
(c) Time deals with past.
(d) The factor of Time has not been thought of by the intellectuals.

74. Who amongst the following wrote that the cause-effect relationship is an obstacle for History?
(a) Richard Evans
(b) Ankersmit
(c) E.H. Carr
(d) Theodore Zeldin

75. Which one of the following said that the narrative History writing considering the Time is like constructing a building on a weak foundation?
(a) Ankersmit
(b) Theodore Zeldin
(c) Richard Evans
(d) E.H. Carr

ANSWERS

1. (b)	2. (d)	3. (c)	4. (a)	5. (a)
6. (c)	7. (c)	8. (c)	9. (c)	10. (b)
11. (c)	12. (a)	13. (a)	14. (a)	15. (a)
16. (a)	17. (d)	18. (b)	19. (c)	20. (d)
21. (c)	22. (a)	23. (c)	24. (b)	25. (c)
26. (c)	27. (a)	28. (c)	29. (d)	30. (c)
31. (a)	32. (c)	33. (d)	34. (b)	35. (a)
36. (d)	37. (a)	38. (c)	39. (d)	40. (c)
41. (d)	42. (c)	43. (a)	44. (b)	45. (c)
46. (b)	47. (d)	48. (d)	49. (b)	50. (d)
51. (b)	52. (a)	53. (d)	54. (a)	55. (d)
56. (c)	57. (b)	58. (a)	59. (d)	60. (c)
61. (b)	62. (d)	63. (a)	64. (d)	65. (b)
66. (c)	67. (d)	68. (b)	69. (b)	70. (a)
71. (a)	72. (d)	73. (d)	74. (d)	75. (a)

DECEMBER–2011

Note: This paper contains sixty (60) multiple choice questions, each question carrying two (2) marks. Candidate is expected to answer any fifty (50) questions. In case more than fifty (50) questions are attempted, only the first fifty (50) questions will be evaluated.

PAPER–I

1. Photo bleeding means
   (a) Photo cropping
   (b) Photo placement
   (c) Photo cutting
   (d) Photo colour adjustment

2. While designing communication strategy feed-forward studies are conducted by
   (a) Audience (b) Communicator
   (c) Satellite (d) Media

3. In which language the newspapers have highest circulation?
   (a) English (b) Hindi
   (c) Bengali (d) Tamil

4. Aspect ratio of TV Screen is
   (a) 4 : 3 (b) 3 : 4
   (c) 2 : 3 (d) 2 : 4

5. Communication with oneself is known as
   (a) Organisational Communication
   (b) Grapevine Communication
   (c) Interpersonal Communication
   (d) Intrapersonal Communication

6. The term 'SITE' stands for
   (a) Satellite Indian Television Experiment
   (b) Satellite International Television Experiment
   (c) Satellite Instructional Television Experiment
   (d) Satellite Instructional Teachers Education

7. What is the number that comes next in the sequence?

   2, 5, 9, 19, 37, ___
   (a) 76 (b) 74
   (c) 75 (d) 50

8. Find the next letter for the series MPSV.....
   (a) X (b) Y
   (c) Z (d) A

9. If '367' means 'I am happy'; '748' means 'you are sad' and '469' means 'happy and sad' in a given code, then which of the following represents 'and' in that code?
   (a) 3 (b) 6
   (c) 9 (d) 4

10. The basis of the following classification is 'animal', 'man', 'house', 'book', and 'student':
    (a) Definite descriptions
    (b) Proper names
    (c) Descriptive phrases
    (d) Common names

11. **Assertion (A):** The coin when flipped next time will come up tails.

    Reason (R): Because the coin was flipped five times in a row, and each time it came up heads.

    Choose the correct answer from below:
    (a) Both (A) and (R) are true, and (R) is the correct explanation of (A).

(b) Both (A) and (R) are false, and (R) is the correct explanation of (A).
(c) (A) is doubtful, (R) is true, and (R) is not the correct explanation of (A).
(d) (A) is doubtful, (R) is false, and (R) is the correct explanation of (A).

12. The relation 'is a sister of' is
(a) non-symmetrical (b) symmetrical
(c) asymmetrical (d) transitive

13. If the proposition "Vegetarians are not meat eaters" is false, then which of the following inferences is correct? Choose from the codes given below:
1. "Some vegetarians are meat eaters" is true.
2. "All vegetarians are meat eaters" is doubtful.
3. "Some vegetarians are not meat eaters" is true.
4. "Some vegetarians are not meat eaters" is doubtful.

Codes:
(a) 1, 2 and 3 (b) 2, 3 and 4
(c) 1, 3 and 4 (d) 1, 2 and 4

14. Determine the nature of the following definition:
'Poor' means having an annual income of ₹ 10,000.
(a) persuasive (b) precising
(c) lexical (d) stipulative

15. Which one of the following is not an argument?
(a) If today is Tuesday, tomorrow will be Wednesday.
(b) Since today is Tuesday, tomorrow will be Wednesday.
(c) Ram insulted me so I punched him in the nose.
(d) Ram is not at home, so he must have gone to town.

16. Venn diagram is a kind of diagram to
(a) represent and assess the truth of elementary inferences with the help of Boolean Algebra of classes.
(b) represent and assess the validity of elementary inferences with the help of Boolean Algebra of classes.
(c) represent but not assess the validity of elementary inferences with the help of Boolean Algebra of classes.
(d) assess but not represent the validity of elementary inferences with the help of Boolean Algebra of classes.

17. Inductive logic studies the way in which a premise may
(a) support and entail a conclusion
(b) not support but entail a conclusion
(c) neither support nor entail a conclusion
(d) support a conclusion without entailing it

18. Which of the following statements are true? Choose from the codes given below.
1. Some arguments, while not completely valid, are almost valid.
2. A sound argument may be invalid.
3. A cogent argument may have a probably false conclusion.
4. A statement may be true or false.

Codes:
(a) 1 and 2 (b) 1, 3 and 4
(c) Only 4 (d) 3 and 4

19. If the side of the square increases by 40%, then the area of the square increases by
(a) 60% (b) 40%
(c) 196% (d) 96%

20. There are 10 lamps in a hall. Each one of them can be switched on independently. The number of ways in which hall can be illuminated is
(a) 10^2 (b) 1023
(c) 2^{10} (d) 10!

21. How many numbers between 100 and 300 begin or end with 2?
    (a) 100 (b) 110
    (c) 120 (d) 180

22. In a college having 300 students, every student reads 5 newspapers and every newspaper is read by 60 students. The number of newspapers required is
    (a) at least 30 (b) at most 20
    (c) exactly 25 (d) exactly 5

The total CO_2 emissions from various sectors are 5 mmt. In the Pie Chart given below, the percentage contribution to CO_2 emissions from various sectors is indicated.

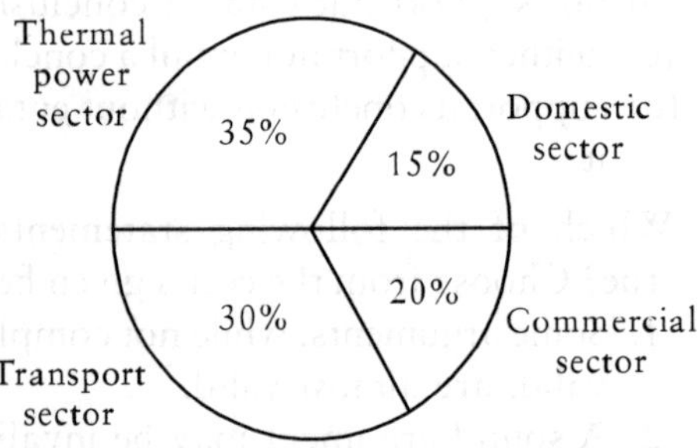

23. What is the absolute CO_2 emission from domestic sector?
    (a) 1.5 mmt (b) 2.5 mmt
    (c) 1.75 mmt (d) 0.75 mmt

24. What is the absolute CO_2 emission for combined thermal power and transport sectors?
    (a) 3.25 mmt (b) 1.5 mmt
    (c) 2.5 mmt (d) 4 mmt

25. Which of the following operating system is used on mobile phones?
    (a) Windows Vista
    (b) Android
    (c) Windows XP
    (d) All of the above

26. If $(y)_x$ represents a number y in base x, then which of the following numbers is smallest of all?
    (a) $(1111)_2$ (b) $(1111)_8$
    (c) $(1111)_{10}$ (d) $(1111)_{16}$

27. High level programming language can be converted to machine language using which of the following?
    (a) Oracle (b) Compiler
    (c) Mat lab (d) Assembler

28. HTML is used to create
    (a) machine language program
    (b) high level program
    (c) web page
    (d) web server

29. The term DNS stands for
    (a) Domain Name System
    (b) Defense Nuclear System
    (c) Downloadable New Software
    (d) Dependent Name Server

30. IPv4 and IPv6 are addresses used to identify computers on the internet. Find the correct statement out of the following:
    (a) Number of bits required for IPv4 address is more than number of bits required for IPv6 address.
    (b) Number of bits required for IPv4 address is same as number of bits required for IPv6 address.
    (c) Number of bits required for IPv4 address is less than number of bits required for IPv6 address.
    (d) Number of bits required for IPv4 address is 64.

31. Which of the following pollutants affects the respiratory tract in humans?
    (a) Carbon monoxide
    (b) Nitric oxide
    (c) Sulphur dioxide
    (d) Aerosols

32. Which of the following pollutants is not emitted from the transport sector?
    (a) Oxides of nitrogen
    (b) Chlorofluorocarbons
    (c) Carbon monoxide
    (d) Poly aromatic hydrocarbons

33. Which of the following sources of energy has the maximum potential in India?
    (a) Solar energy
    (b) Wind energy
    (c) Ocean thermal energy
    (d) Tidal energy

34. Which of the following is not a source of pollution in soil?
    (a) Transport sector
    (b) Agriculture sector
    (c) Thermal power plants
    (d) Hydropower plants

35. Which of the following is not a natural hazard?
    (a) Earthquake (b) Tsunami
    (c) Flash floods (d) Nuclear accident

36. Ecological footprint represents
    (a) area of productive land and water to meet the resources requirement
    (b) energy consumption
    (c) CO_2 emissions per person
    (d) forest cover

37. The aim of value education to inculcate in students is
    (a) the moral values
    (b) the social values
    (c) the political values
    (d) the economic values

38. Indicate the number of Regional Offices of University Grants Commission of India.
    (a) 10 (b) 07
    (c) 08 (d) 09

39. One-rupee currency note in India bears the signature of
    (a) The President of India
    (b) Finance Minister of India
    (c) Governor, Reserve Bank of India
    (d) Finance Secretary of Government of India

40. Match the List I with the List II and select the correct answer from the codes given below:

List I (Commissions and Committees)
A. First Administrative Reforms Commission
B. Paul H. Appleby Committee I
C. K. Santhanam Committee
D. Second Administrative Reforms Commission

List II (Year)
1. 2005
2. 1962
3. 1966
4. 1953

Codes:	A	B	C	D
(a)	1	3	2	4
(b)	3	4	2	1
(c)	4	2	3	1
(d)	2	1	4	3

41. Constitutionally the registration and recognition of political parties is the function performed by
    (a) The State Election Commission of respective States
    (b) The Law Ministry of Government of India
    (c) The Election Commission of India
    (d) Election Department of the State Governments

42. The members of Gram Sabha are
    (a) Sarpanch, Upsarpanch and all elected Panchas
    (b) Sarpanch, Upsarpanch and Village level worker
    (c) Sarpanch, Gram Sevak and elected Panchas
    (d) Registered voters of Village Panchayat

43. By which of the following methods the true evaluation of the students is possible?
(a) Evaluation at the end of the course
(b) Evaluation twice in a year
(c) Continuous evaluation
(d) Formative evaluation

44. Suppose a student wants to share his problems with his teacher and he visits the teacher's house for the purpose, the teacher should
(a) contact the student's parents and solve his problem
(b) suggest him that he should never visit his house
(c) suggest him to meet the principal and solve the problem
(d) extend reasonable help and boost his morale

45. When some students are deliberately attempting to disturb the discipline of the class by making mischief, what will be your role as a teacher?
(a) Expelling those students
(b) Isolate those students
(c) Reform the group with your authority
(d) Giving them an opportunity for introspection and improve their behaviour

46. Which of the following belongs to a projected aid?
(a) Blackboard (b) Diorama
(c) Epidiascope (d) Globe

47. A teacher is said to be fluent in asking questions, if he can ask
(a) meaningful questions
(b) as many questions as possible
(c) maximum number of questions in a fixed time
(d) many meaningful questions in a fixed time

48. Which of the following qualities is most essential for a teacher?
(a) He should be a learned person
(b) He should be a well dressed person
(c) He should have patience
(d) He should be an expert in his subject

49. A hypothesis is a
(a) law (b) canon
(c) postulate (d) supposition

50. Suppose you want to investigate the working efficiency of nationalised bank in India, which one of the following would you follow?
(a) Area Sampling
(b) Multi-stage Sampling
(c) Sequential Sampling
(d) Quota Sampling

51. Controlled group condition is applied in
(a) Survey Research
(b) Historical Research
(c) Experimental Research
(d) Descriptive Research

52. Workshops are meant for
(a) giving lectures
(b) multiple target groups
(c) showcase new theories
(d) hands on training/experience

53. Which one of the following is a research tool?
(a) Graph (b) Illustration
(c) Questionnaire (d) Diagram

54. Research is not considered ethical if it
(a) tries to prove a particular point.
(b) does not ensure privacy and anonymity of the respondent.
(c) does not investigate the data scientifically.
(d) is not of a very high standard.

Read the following passage carefully and answer the questions (55 to 60):

The catalytic fact of the twentieth century is uncontrollable development, consumerist society, political materialism, and spiritual devaluation. This inordinate development has led to the transcendental 'second reality' of sacred perception that biologically transcendence is a part of human life. As the century closes, it dawns with imperative vigour that the 'first reality' of enlightened rationalism and the 'second reality' of the Beyond have to be harmonised in a worthy state of man. The *de facto* values describe what we are, they portray the 'is' of our ethic, they are *est* values (Latin *est* means is). The ideal values tell us what we ought to be, they are *esto* values (Latin *esto* 'ought to be'). Both have to be in the ebb and flow of consciousness. The ever new science and technology and the ever-perennial faith are two modes of one certainty, that is the wholeness of man, his courage to be, his share in Being.

The materialistic foundations of science have crumbled down. Science itself has proved that matter is energy, processes are as valid as facts, and affirmed the non-materiality of the universe. The encounter of the 'two cultures', the scientific and the humane, will restore the normal vision, and will be the bedrock of a 'science of understanding' in the new century. It will give new meaning to the ancient perception that quantity (measure) and quality (value) coexist at the root of nature. Human endeavours cannot afford to be humanistically irresponsible.

55. The problem raised in the passage reflects overall on
   (a) Consumerism
   (b) Materialism
   (c) Spiritual devaluation
   (d) Inordinate development

56. The *de facto* values in the passage means
   (a) What is
   (b) What ought to be
   (c) What can be
   (d) Where it is

57. According to the passage, the 'first reality' constitutes
   (a) Economic prosperity
   (b) Political development
   (c) Sacred perception of life
   (d) Enlightened rationalism

58. Encounter of the 'two cultures', the scientific and the human implies
   (a) Restoration of normal vision
   (b) Universe is both material and non-material
   (c) Man is superior to nature
   (d) Co-existence of quantity and quality in nature

59. The contents of the passage are
   (a) Descriptive (b) Prescriptive
   (c) Axiomatic (d) Optional

60. The passage indicates that science has proved that
   (a) universe is material
   (b) matter is energy
   (c) nature has abundance
   (d) humans are irresponsible

ANSWERS

1. (a)	2. (b)	3. (a)	4. (a)	5. (d)
6. (c)	7. (c)	8. (b)	9. (c)	10. (d)
11. (c)	12. (b)	13. (a)	14. (b)	15. (a)
16. (b)	17. (d)	18. (d)	19. (d)	20. (b)
21. (b)	22. (c)	23. (d)	24. (a)	25. (b)
26. (a)	27. (b)	28. (c)	29. (a)	30. (c)
31. (a)	32. (b)	33. (b)	34. (d)	35. (d)
36. (a)	37. (a)	38. (b)	39. (d)	40. (b)
41. (c)	42. (d)	43. (d)	44. (d)	45. (d)
46. (c)	47. (d)	48. (c)	49. (d)	50. (b)
51. (c)	52. (d)	53. (c)	54. (b)	55. (c)
56. (a)	57. (d)	58. (a)	59. (a)	60. (b)

JUNE–2011

Note: This paper contains sixty (60) multiple choice questions, each question carrying two (2) marks. Candidate is expected to answer any fifty (50) questions. In case more than fifty (50) questions are attempted, only the first fifty (50) questions will be evaluated.

PAPER–I

1. A research paper is a brief report of research work based on
   (a) Primary Data only
   (b) Secondary Data only
   (c) Both Primary and Secondary Data
   (d) None of the above

2. Newton gave three basic laws of motion. This research is categorised as
   (a) Descriptive Research
   (b) Sample Survey
   (c) Fundamental Research
   (d) Applied Research

3. A group of experts in a specific area of knowledge assembled at a place and prepared a syllabus for a new course. The process may be termed as
   (a) Seminar (b) Workshop
   (c) Conference (d) Symposium

4. In the process of conducting research "Formulation of Hypothesis" is followed by
   (a) Statement of Objectives
   (b) Analysis of Data
   (c) Selection of Research Tools
   (d) Collection of Data

Read the following passage carefully and answer questions 5 to 10:

All historians are interpreters of text if they be private letters, Government records or parish birthlists or whatever. For most kinds of historians, these are only the necessary means to understanding something other than the texts themselves, such as a political action or a historical trend, whereas for the intellectual historian, a full understanding of his chosen texts is itself the aim of his enquiries. Of course, the intellectual history is particularly prone to draw on the focus of other disciplines that are habitually interpreting texts for purposes of their own, probing the reasoning that ostensibly connects premises and conclusions. Furthermore, the boundaries with adjacent subdisciplines are shifting and indistinct: the history of art and the history of science both claim a certain autonomy, partly just because they require specialised technical skills, but both can also be seen as part of a wider intellectual history, as is evident when one considers, for example, the common stock of knowledge about cosmological beliefs or moral ideals of a period.

Like all historians, the intellectual historian is a consumer rather than a producer of 'methods'. His distinctiveness lies in which aspect of the past he is trying to illuminate, not in having exclusive possession of either a corpus of evidence or a body of techniques. That being said, it does seem that the label 'intellectual history' attracts a disproportionate share of misunderstanding.

It is alleged that intellectual history is the history of something that never really mattered. The long dominance of the historical profession by political historians bred a kind of philistinism, an unspoken belief that power and its exercise was 'what mattered'. The prejudice was reinforced by the assertion that political action was never really the outcome of principles or ideas that were 'more flapdoodle'. The legacy of this precept is still discernible in the tendency to require ideas to have 'licensed' the political class before they can be deemed worthy of intellectual attention, as if there were some reasons why the history of art or science, of philosophy or literature, were somehow of interest and significance than the history of Parties or Parliaments. Perhaps in recent years the mirror-image of this philistinism has been more common in the claim that ideas of any one is of systematic expression or sophistication do not matter, as if they were only held by a minority.

Answer the following questions:

5. An intellectual historian aims to fully understand
   (a) the chosen texts of his own
   (b) political actions
   (c) historical trends
   (d) his enquiries
6. Intellectual historians do not claim exclusive possession of
   (a) conclusions
   (b) any corpus of evidence
   (c) distinctiveness
   (d) habitual interpretation
7. The misconceptions about intellectual history stem from
   (a) a body of techniques
   (b) the common stock of knowledge
   (c) the dominance of political historians
   (d) cosmological beliefs
8. What is philistinism?
   (a) Reinforcement of prejudice
   (b) Fabrication of reasons
   (c) The hold of land-owning classes
   (d) Belief that power and its exercise matter
9. Knowledge of cosmological beliefs or moral ideas of a period can be drawn as part of
   (a) literary criticism
   (b) history of science
   (c) history of philosophy
   (d) intellectual history
10. The claim that ideas of any one is of systematic expression do not matter, as if they were held by a minority, is
   (a) to have a licensed political class
   (b) a political action
   (c) a philosophy of literature
   (d) the mirror-image of philistinism
11. Public communication tends to occur within a more
   (a) complex structure
   (b) political structure
   (c) convenient structure
   (d) formal structure
12. Transforming thoughts, ideas and messages into verbal and non-verbal signs is referred to as
   (a) channelisation (b) mediation
   (c) encoding (d) decoding
13. Effective communication needs a supportive
   (a) economic environment
   (b) political environment
   (c) social environment
   (d) multi-cultural environment
14. A major barrier in the transmission of cognitive data in the process of communication is an individual's
   (a) personality (b) expectation
   (c) social status (d) coding ability
15. When communicated, institutionalised stereotypes become
   (a) myths (b) reasons
   (c) experiences (d) convictions

16. In mass communication, selective perception is dependent on the receiver's
(a) competence (b) pre-disposition
(c) receptivity (d) ethnicity

17. Determine the relationship between the pair of words NUMERATOR: DENOMINATOR and then select the pair of words from the following which have a similar relationship:
(a) fraction : decimal
(b) divisor : quotient
(c) top : bottom
(d) dividend : divisor

18. Find the wrong number in the sequence
125, 127, 130, 135, 142, 153, 165
(a) 130 (b) 142
(c) 153 (d) 165

19. If HOBBY is coded as IOBY and LOBBY is coded as MOBY; then BOBBY is coded as
(a) BOBY (b) COBY
(c) DOBY (d) OOBY

20. The letters in the first set have certain relationship. On the basis of this relationship, make the right choice for the second set

K/T : 11/20 :: J/R :?
(a) 10/8 (b) 10/18
(c) 11/19 (d) 10/19

21. If A = 5, B = 6, C = 7, D = 8 and so on, what do the following numbers stand for?
17, 19, 20, 9, 8
(a) Plane (b) Moped
(c) Motor (d) Tonga

22. The price of oil is increased by 25%. If the expenditure is not allowed to increase, the ratio between the reduction in consumption and the original consumption is
(a) 1:3 (b) 1:4
(c) 1:5 (d) 1:6

23. How many 8's are there in the following sequence which are preceded by 5 but not immediately followed by 3?
5 8 3 7 5 8 6 3 8 5 4 5 8 4 7 6
5 5 8 3 5 8 7 5 8 2 8 5
(a) 4 (b) 5
(c) 7 (d) 3

24. If a rectangle were called a circle, a circle a point, a point a triangle and a triangle a square, the shape of a wheel is
(a) Rectangle (b) Circle
(c) Point (d) Triangle

25. Which one of the following methods is best suited for mapping the distribution of different crops as provided in the standard classification of crops in India?
(a) Pie diagram
(b) Chorochromatic technique
(c) Isopleth technique
(d) Dot method

26. Which one of the following does not come under the methods of data classification?
(a) Qualitative (b) Normative
(c) Spatial (d) Quantitative

27. Which one of the following is not a source of data?
(a) Administrative records
(b) Population census
(c) GIS
(d) Sample survey

28. If the statement 'some men are cruel' is false, which of the following statements/ statement are/is true?
(i) All men are cruel.
(ii) No men are cruel.
(iii) Some men are not cruel.
(a) (i) and (iii) (b) (i) and (ii)
(c) (ii) and (iii) (d) Only (iii)

29. The octal number system consists of the following symbols

(a) 0 – 7
(b) 0 – 9
(c) 0 – 9, A – F
(d) None of the above

30. The binary equivalent of $(-19)_{10}$ in signed magnitude system is
(a) 11101100 (b) 11101101
(c) 10010011 (d) None of these

31. DNS in internet technology stands for
(a) Dynamic Name System
(b) Domain Name System
(c) Distributed Name System
(d) None of these

32. HTML stands for
(a) Hyper Text Markup Language
(b) Hyper Text Manipulation Language
(c) Hyper Text Managing Links
(d) Hyper Text Manipulating Links

33. Which of the following is type of LAN?
(a) Ethernet (b) Token Ring
(c) FDDI (d) All of the above

34. Which of the following statements is true?
(a) Smart cards do not require an operating system.
(b) Smart cards and PCs use some operating system.
(c) COS is smart card operating system.
(d) The communication between reader and card is in full duplex mode.

35. The Ganga Action Plan was initiated during the year
(a) 1986 (b) 1988
(c) 1990 (d) 1992

36. Identify the correct sequence of energy sources in order of their share in the power sector in India.
(a) Thermal > nuclear > hydro > wind
(b) Thermal > hydro > nuclear > wind
(c) Hydro > nuclear > thermal > wind
(d) Nuclear > hydro > wind > thermal

37. Chromium as a contaminant in drinking water in excess of permissible levels, causes
(a) Skeletal damage
(b) Gastrointestinal problem
(c) Dermal and nervous problems
(d) Liver/Kidney problems

38. The main precursors of winter smog are
(a) N_2O and hydrocarbons
(b) NO_x and hydrocarbons
(c) SO_2 and hydrocarbons
(d) SO_2 and ozone

39. Flash floods are caused when
(a) the atmosphere is convectively unstable and there is considerable vertical wind shear
(b) the atmosphere is stable
(c) the atmosphere is convectively unstable with no vertical windshear
(d) winds are catabatic

40. In mega cities of India, the dominant source of air pollution is
(a) transport sector
(b) thermal power
(c) municipal waste
(d) commercial sector

41. The first Open University in India was set up in the State of
(a) Andhra Pradesh
(b) Delhi
(c) Himachal Pradesh
(d) Tamil Nadu

42. Most of the Universities in India are funded by
(a) the Central Government
(b) the State Governments
(c) the University Grants Commission
(d) Private bodies and Individuals

43. Which of the following organisations looks after the quality of Technical and Management education in India?

(a) NCTE (b) MCI
(c) AICTE (d) CSIR

44. Consider the following statements: Identify the statement which implies natural justice.
    (a) The principle of natural justice is followed by the Courts.
    (b) Justice delayed is justice denied.
    (c) Natural justice is an inalienable right of a citizen.
    (d) A reasonable opportunity of being heard must be given.

45. The President of India is
    (a) the Head of State
    (b) the Head of Government
    (c) both Head of the State and the Head of the Government
    (d) None of the above

46. Who among the following holds office during the pleasure of the President of India?
    (a) Chief Election Commissioner
    (b) Comptroller and Auditor General of India
    (c) Chairman of the Union Public Service Commission
    (d) Governor of a State

Questions 47 to 49 are based upon the following diagram in which there are three interlocking circles A, P and S where A stands for Artists, circle P for Professors and circle S for Sportspersons. Different regions in the figure are lettered from a to f:

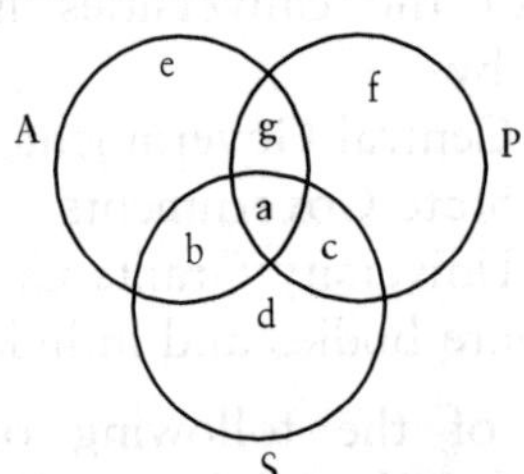

47. The region which represents artists who are neither sportsmen nor professors.
    (a) d (b) e
    (c) b (d) g

48. The region which represents professors, who are both artists and sportspersons.
    (a) a (b) c
    (c) d (d) g

49. The region which represents professors, who are also sportspersons, but not artists.
    (a) e (b) f
    (c) c (d) g

Questions 50 to 52 are based on the following data:

Measurements of some variable X were made at an interval of 1 minute from 10 A.M. to 10:20 A.M. The data, thus, obtained is as follows:

X: 60, 62, 65, 64, 63, 61, 66, 65, 70, 68
63, 62, 64, 69, 65, 64, 66, 67, 66, 64

50. The value of X, which is exceeded 10% of the time in the duration of measurement, is
    (a) 69 (b) 68
    (c) 67 (d) 66

51. The value of X, which is exceeded 90% of the time in the duration of measurement, is
    (a) 63 (b) 62
    (c) 61 (d) 60

52. The value of X, which is exceeded 50% of the time in the duration of measurement, is
    (a) 66 (b) 65
    (c) 64 (d) 63

53. For maintaining an effective discipline in the class, the teacher should
    (a) Allow students to do what they like.
    (b) Deal with the students strictly.
    (c) Give the students some problem to solve.
    (d) Deal with them politely and firmly.

54. An effective teaching aid is one which
(a) is colourful and good looking
(b) activates all faculties
(c) is visible to all students
(d) easy to prepare and use

55. Those teachers are popular among students who
(a) develop intimacy with them
(b) help them solve their problems
(c) award good grades
(d) take classes on extra tuition fee

56. The essence of an effective classroom environment is
(a) a variety of teaching aids
(b) lively student-teacher interaction
(c) pin-drop silence
(d) strict discipline

57. On the first day of his class, if a teacher is asked by the students to introduce himself, he should
(a) ask them to meet after the class
(b) tell them about himself in brief
(c) ignore the demand and start teaching
(d) scold the students for this unwanted demand

58. Moral values can be effectively inculcated among the students when the teacher
(a) frequently talks about values
(b) himself practices them
(c) tells stories of great persons
(d) talks of Gods and Goddesses

59. The essential qualities of a researcher are
(a) spirit of free enquiry
(b) reliance on observation and evidence
(c) systematisation or theorising of knowledge
(d) All of the above

60. Research is conducted to
1. Generate new knowledge
2. Not to develop a theory
3. Obtain research degree
4. Reinterpret existing knowledge

Which of the above are correct?
(a) 1, 3 & 2 (b) 3, 2 & 4
(c) 2, 1 & 3 (d) 1, 3 & 4

ANSWERS

1. (c)	2. (c)	3. (b)	4. (c)	5. (a)
6. (b)	7. (c)	8. (d)	9. (d)	10. (d)
11. (d)	12. (c)	13. (d)	14. (c)	15. (d)
16. (b)	17. (d)	18. (d)	19. (b)	20. (b)
21. (b)	22. (c)	23. (a)	24. (c)	25. (a)
26. (b)	27. (a)	28. (b)	29. (a)	30. (d)
31. (b)	32. (a)	33. (d)	34. (c)	35. (a)
36. (b)	37. (d)	38. (c)	39. (a)	40. (a)
41. (a)	42. (c)	43. (c)	44. (d)	45. (b)
46. (d)	47. (b)	48. (a)	49. (c)	50. (c)
51. (b)	52. (d)	53. (d)	54. (b)	55. (b)
56. (b)	57. (b)	58. (b)	59. (d)	60. (d)

DECEMBER–2010

Note: This paper contains sixty (60) multiple choice questions, each question carrying two (2) marks. Candidate is expected to answer any fifty (50) questions. In case more than fifty (50) questions are attempted, only the first fifty (50) questions will be evaluated.

PAPER–I

1. Which of the following variables cannot be expressed in quantitative terms?
   (a) Socio-economic Status
   (b) Marital Status
   (c) Numerical Aptitude
   (d) Professional Attitude
2. A doctor studies the relative effectiveness of two drugs of dengue fever. His research would be classified as
   (a) Descriptive Survey
   (b) Experimental Research
   (c) Case Study
   (d) Ethnography
3. The term 'phenomenology' is associated with the process of
   (a) Qualitative Research
   (b) Analysis of Variance
   (c) Correlational Study
   (d) Probability Sampling
4. The 'Sociogram' technique is used to study
   (a) Vocational Interest
   (b) Professional Competence
   (c) Human Relations
   (d) Achievement Motivation

Read the following passage carefully and answer questions from 5 to 10.

It should be remembered that the nationalist movement in India, like all nationalist movements, was essentially a bourgeois movement. It represented the natural historical stage of development, and to consider it or to criticise it as a working-class movement is wrong. Gandhi represented that movement and the Indian masses in relation to that movement to a supreme degree, and he became the voice of Indian people to that extent. The main contribution of Gandhi to India and the Indian masses has been through the powerful movements which he launched through the National Congress. Through nation-wide action he sought to mould the millions, and largely succeeded in doing so, and changing them from a demoralised, timid and hopeless mass, bullied and crushed by every dominant interest, and incapable of resistance, into a people with self-respect and self-reliance, resisting tyranny, and capable of united action and sacrifice for a larger cause.

Gandhi made people think of political and economic issues and every village and every bazaar hummed with argument and debate on the new ideas and hopes that filled the people. That was an amazing psychological change. The time was ripe for it, of course, and circumstances and world conditions worked for this change. But a great leader is necessary to take advantage of circumstances and conditions. Gandhi was that leader, and he released many of the bonds that imprisoned and disabled our minds, and none of us who experienced it can ever forget that great feeling of release and exhilaration that came over the Indian people.

Gandhi has played a revolutionary role in India of the greatest importance because he knew how to make the most of the objective conditions and could reach the heart of the masses, while groups with a more advanced ideology functioned largely in the air because they did not fit in with those conditions and could therefore not evoke any substantial response from the masses.

It is perfectly true that Gandhi, functioning in the nationalist plane, does not think in terms of the conflict of classes, and tries to compose their differences. But the action he has indulged and taught the people has inevitably raised mass consciousness tremendously and made social issues vital. Gandhi and the Congress must be judged by the policies they pursue and the action they indulge in. But behind this, personality counts and colours those policies and activities. In the case of very exceptional person like Gandhi the question of personality becomes especially important in order to understand and appraise him. To us he has represented the spirit and honour of India, the yearning of her sorrowing millions to be rid of their innumerable burdens, and an insult to him by the British Government or others has been an insult to India and her people.

5. Which one of the following is true of the given passage?
   (a) The passage is a critique of Gandhi's role in Indian movement for independence
   (b) The passage hails the role of Gandhi in India's freedom movement
   (c) The author is neutral on Gandhi's role in India's freedom movement
   (d) It is an account of Indian National Congress's support to the working-class movement

6. The change that the Gandhian movement brought among the Indian masses was
   (a) Physical (b) Cultural
   (c) Technological (d) Psychological

7. To consider the nationalist movement or to criticise it as a working-class movement was wrong because it was a
   (a) historical movement
   (b) voice of the Indian people
   (c) bourgeois movement
   (d) movement represented by Gandhi

8. Gandhi played a revolutionary role in India because he could
   (a) preach morality
   (b) reach the heart of Indians
   (c) see the conflict of classes
   (d) lead the Indian National Congress

9. Groups with advanced ideology functioned in the air as they did not fit in with
   (a) objective conditions of masses
   (b) the Gandhian ideology
   (c) the class consciousness of the people
   (d) the differences among masses

10. The author concludes the passage by
   (a) criticising the Indian masses
   (b) the Gandhian movement
   (c) pointing out the importance of the personality of Gandhi
   (d) identifying the sorrows of millions of Indians

11. Media that exist in an interconnected series of communication—points are referred to as
   (a) Networked media
   (b) Connective media
   (c) Nodal media
   (d) Multimedia

12. The information function of mass communication is described as

(a) diffusion (b) publicity
(c) surveillance (d) diversion

13. An example of asynchronous medium is
(a) Radio (b) Television
(c) Film (d) Newspaper

14. In communication, connotative words are
(a) explicit (c) abstract
(b) simple (d) cultural

15. A message beneath a message is labelled as
(a) embedded text (b) internal text
(c) inter-text (d) sub-text

16. In analog mass communication, stories are
(a) static (b) dynamic
(c) interactive (d) exploratory

17. Determine the relationship between the pair of words ALWAYS : NEVER and then select from the following pair of words which have a similar relationship
(a) often : rarely
(b) frequently : occasionally
(c) constantly : frequently
(d) intermittently : casually

18. Find the wrong number in the sequence
52, 51, 48, 43, 34, 27, 16
(a) 27 (b) 34
(c) 43 (d) 48

19. In a certain code, PAN is written as 31 and PAR as 35, then PAT is written in the same code as
(a) 30 (b) 37
(c) 39 (d) 41

20. The letters in the first set have certain relationship. On the basis of this relationship, make the right choice for the second set:
AF : IK : : LQ :?
(a) MO (b) NP
(c) OR (d) TV

21. If 5472 = 9, 6342 = 6, 7584 = 6, what is 9236?
(a) 2 (b) 3
(c) 4 (d) 5

22. In an examination, 35% of the total students failed in Hindi, 45% failed in English and 20% in both. The percentage of those who passed in both subjects is
(a) 10 (b) 20
(c) 30 (d) 40

23. Two statements I and II given below are followed by two conclusions (a) and (b). Supposing the statements are true, which of the following conclusions can logically follow?

Statements:
I. Some flowers are red.
II. Some flowers are blue.

Conclusions:
(A) Some flowers are neither red nor blue.
(B) Some flowers are both red and blue.
(a) Only (A) follows
(b) Only (B) follows
(c) Both (A) and (B) follows
(d) Neither (A) nor (B) follows

24. If the statement 'all students are intelligent' is true, which of the following statements are false?
(i) No students are intelligent.
(ii) Some students are intelligent.
(iii) Some students are not intelligent.
(a) (i) and (ii) (b) (i) and (iii)
(c) (ii) and (iii) (d) (i) Only

25. A reasoning where we start with certain particular statements and conclude with a universal statement is called
(a) Deductive Reasoning
(b) Inductive Reasoning
(c) Abnormal Reasoning
(d) Transcendental Reasoning

26. What is the smallest number of ducks that could swim in this formation—two ducks in front of a duck, two ducks behind a duck and a duck between two ducks?
(a) 5 (b) 7
(c) 4 (d) 3

27. Mr. A, Miss B, Mr. C and Miss D are sitting around a table and discussing their trades.
(i) Mr. A sits opposite to the cook.
(ii) Miss B sits right to the barber.
(iii) The washerman sits right to the barber.
(iv) Miss D sits opposite to Mr. C.

What are the trades of A and B?
(a) Tailor and barber
(b) Barber and cook
(c) Tailor and cook
(d) Tailor and washerman

28. Which one of the following methods serve to measure correlation between two variables?
(a) Scatter Diagram
(b) Frequency Distrubution
(c) Two-way table
(d) Coefficient of Rank Correlation

29. Which one of the following is not an Internet Service Provider (ISP)?
(a) MTNL
(b) BSNL
(c) ERNET India
(d) Infotech India Ltd.

30. The hexadecimal number system consists of the symbols
(a) 0 - 7 (b) 0 - 9, A - F
(c) 0 - 7, A - F (d) None of these

31. The binary equivalent of $(-15)_{10}$ is (2's complement system is used)
(a) 11110001 (b) 11110000
(c) 10001111 (d) None of these

32. 1 GB is equal to
(a) 2^{30} bits (b) 2^{30} bytes
(c) 2^{20} bits (d) 2^{20} bytes

33. The set of computer programs that manage the hardware/software of a computer is called
(a) Compiler system
(b) Operation system
(c) Operating system
(d) None of these

34. SMIME in Internet technology stands for
(a) Secure Multipurpose Internet Mail Extension
(b) Secure Multimedia Internet Mail Extension
(c) Simple Multipurpose Internet Mail Extension
(d) Simple Multimedia Internet Mail Extension

35. Which of the following is not covered in 8 missions under the Climate Action Plan of Government of India?
(a) Solar power
(b) Waste to energy conversion
(c) Afforestation
(d) Nuclear energy

36. The concentration of Total Dissolved Solids (TDS) in drinking water should not exceed
(a) 500 mg/L (b) 400 mg/L
(c) 300 mg/L (d) 200 mg/L

37. 'Chipko' movement was first started by
(a) Arundhati Roy
(b) Medha Patkar
(c) Ila Bhatt
(d) Sunderlal Bahuguna

38. The constituents of photochemical smog responsible for eye irritation are
(a) SO_2 and O_3 (b) SO_2 and NO_2
(c) HCHO and PAN (d) SO_2 and SPM

39. **Assertion (A):** Some carbonaceous aerosols may be carcinogenic.
Reason (R): They may contain polycyclic aromatic hydrocarbons (PAHs).
(a) Both (A) and (R) are correct and (R) is the correct explanation of (A).
(b) Both (A) and (R) are correct but (R) is not the correct explanation of (A).
(c) (A) is correct, but (R) is false.
(d) (A) is false, but (R) is correct.

40. Volcanic eruptions affect
(a) atmosphere and hydrosphere
(b) hydrosphere and biosphere
(c) lithosphere, biosphere and atmosphere
(d) lithosphere, hydrosphere and atmosphere

41. India's first Defence University is in the State of
(a) Haryana (b) Andhra Pradesh
(c) Uttar Pradesh (d) Punjab

42. Most of the Universities in India
(a) conduct teaching and research only
(b) affiliate colleges and conduct examinations
(c) conduct teaching/research and examinations
(d) promote research only

43. Which one of the following is not a Constitutional Body?
(a) Election Commission
(b) Finance Commission
(c) Union Public Service Commission
(d) Planning Commission

44. Which one of the following statements is not correct?
(a) Indian Parliament is supreme.
(b) The Supreme Court of India has the power of judicial review.
(c) There is a division of powers between the Centre and the States.
(d) There is a Council of Ministers to aid and advise the President.

45. Which one of the following statements reflects the republic character of Indian democracy?
(a) Written constitution
(b) No State religion
(c) Devolution of power to local Government institutions
(d) Elected President and directly or indirectly elected Parliament

46. Who among the following appointed by the Governor can be removed by only the President of India?
(a) Chief Minister of a State
(b) A member of the State Public Service Commission
(c) Advocate-General
(d) Vice-Chancellor of a State University

47. If two small circles represent the class of the 'men' and the class of the 'plants' and the big circle represents 'mortality', which one of the following figures represent the proposition 'All men are mortal?.'

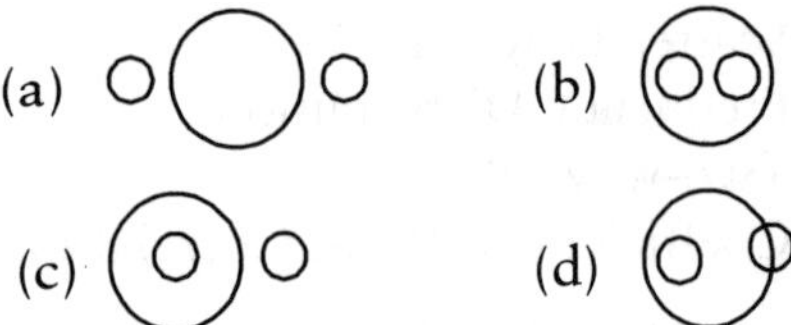

The following table presents the production of electronic items (TVs and LCDs) in a factory during the period from 2006 to 2010. Study the table carefully and answer the questions from 48 to 52:

Year	2006	2007	2008	2009	2010
TVs	6000	9000	13000	11000	8000
LCDs	7000	9400	9000	10000	12000

48. In which year, the total production of electronic items is maximum?
(a) 2006 (b) 2007
(c) 2008 (d) 2010

49. What is the difference between averages of production of LCDs and TVs from 2006 to 2008?
(a) 3000 (b) 2867
(c) 3015 (d) None of these

50. What is the year in which production of TVs is half the production of LCDs in the year 2010?
(a) 2007 (b) 2006
(c) 2009 (d) 2008

51. What is the ratio of production of LCDs in the years 2008 and 2010?
(a) 4:3 (b) 3:4
(c) 1:3 (d) 2:3

52. What is the ratio of production of TVs in the years 2006 and 2007?
(a) 6:7 (b) 7:6
(c) 2:3 (d) 3:2

53. Some students in a class exhibit great curiosity for learning. It may be because such children
(a) Are gifted
(b) Come from rich families
(c) Show artificial behaviour
(d) Create indiscipline in the class

54. The most important quality of a good teacher is
(a) Sound knowledge of subject matter
(b) Good communication skills
(c) Concern for students' welfare
(d) Effective leadership qualities

55. Which one of the following is appropriate in respect of teacher-student relationship?
(a) Very informal and intimate
(b) Limited to classroom only
(c) Cordial and respectful
(d) Indifferent

56. The academic performance of students can be improved if parents are encouraged to
(a) supervise the work of their wards
(b) arrange for extra tuition
(c) remain unconcerned about it
(d) interact with teachers frequently

57. In a lively classroom situation, there is likely to be
(a) occasional roars of laughter
(b) complete silence
(c) frequent teacher-student dialogue
(d) loud discussion among students

58. If a parent approaches the teacher to do some favour to his/her ward in the examination, the teacher should
(a) try to help him
(b) ask him not to talk in those terms
(c) refuse politely and firmly
(d) ask him rudely to go away

59. Which of the following phrases is not relevant to describe the meaning of research as a process?
(a) Systematic Activity
(b) Objective Observation
(c) Trial and Error
(d) Problem Solving

60. Which of the following is not an example of a continuous variable?
(a) Family size (b) Intelligence
(c) Height (d) Altitude

ANSWERS

1. (d)	2. (b)	3. (a)	4. (c)	5. (b)
6. (d)	7. (c)	8. (b)	9. (a)	10. (c)
11. (a)	12. (c)	13. (d)	14. (d)	15. (d)
16. (a)	17. (a)	18. (b)	19. (b)	20. (d)
21. (a)	22. (b)	23. (c)	24. (d)	25. (b)
26. (a)	27. (c)	28. (d)	29. (d)	30. (b)
31. (d)	32. (b)	33. (c)	34. (a)	35. (d)
36. (a)	37. (d)	38. (b)	39. (a)	40. (d)
41. (a)	42. (d)	43. (b)	44. (a)	45. (d)
46. (b)	47. (c)	48. (c)	49. (d)	50. (b)
51. (b)	52. (c)	53. (a)	54. (b)	55. (c)
56. (d)	57. (c)	58. (c)	59. (c)	60. (c)

PAPER–II

Note: This paper contains fifty (50) objective type questions, each question carrying two (2) marks. All questions are compulsory.

1. The eulogies or "prashasti" among the following inscriptions:
   I. Aihole Inscription of Pulakesin II.
   II. Allahabad Pillar Inscription of Samudra Gupta.
   III. Junagarh Inscription of Rudradaman.
   IV. Hathigumpha Inscription of Kharavela.

   Codes:
   (a) I, II and III are correct.
   (b) I and II are only correct.
   (c) II and III are only correct.
   (d) I, III and IV are correct.

2. Match List I with List II and select the correct answer from the codes given below:

   List I (Indus Valley Town)
   (A) Mohenjodaro (B) Ropar
   (C) Banawali (D) Harappa

   List II (River Bank)
   1. Ghaggar 2. Ravi
   3. Sutlej 4. Indus

Codes:	A	B	C	D
(a)	2	3	4	1
(b)	2	3	1	4
(c)	4	2	1	3
(d)	4	3	1	2

3. Given below are two statements, one labelled as Assertion (A) and the other labelled as Reason (R):

   Assertion (A): The Varna system existed during the Rigvedic period.

   Reason (R): Mandala X of Rigveda mentions Chaturvarna system.

   Codes:
   (a) Both (A) and (R) are true and (R) is the correct explanation of (A).
   (b) Both (A) and (R) are true, but (R) is not a correct explanation of (A).
   (c) (A) is true, but (R) is false.
   (d) (A) is false, but (R) is true.

4. Arrange the following dynasties in chronological order by using the codes given below:
   I. Shunga dynasty
   II. Haryanka dynasty
   III. Nanda dynasty
   IV. Mauryan dynasty

   Codes:
   (a) II, I, III, IV (b) I, II, III, IV
   (c) III, I, II, IV (d) IV, II, I, III

5. Match the following with reference to the Buddha's life:

   List I (Symbol)
   (A) Lotus (B) Horse
   (C) Wheel (D) Stupa

   List II (Buddha's event)
   1. Renunciation 2. Birth
   3. Mahaparinirvana 4. First Sermon

Codes:	A	B	C	D
(a)	1	2	4	3
(b)	2	1	4	3
(c)	2	1	3	4
(d)	4	1	2	3

6. The Bodhisatva Doctrine is associated with
   (a) Mahayana Buddhism
   (b) Hinayana Buddhism
   (c) Vajrayana Buddhism
   (d) Theravada Buddhism

7. Four Buddhist Councils were held in the following places. Arrange them in chronological order by using the codes given below:

I. Vaishali II. Rajagriha
III. Kundala Vana IV. Pataliputra

Codes:

(a) I, III, IV, II (b) II, IV, III, I
(c) III, I, IV, II (d) II, I, IV, III

8. Given below are two statements, one labelled as Assertion (A) and the other labelled as Reason (R):

Assertion (A): Satavahana society shows traces of matrilineal elements.

Reason (R): Queens and not Kings were the real rulers during Satavahana period.

Codes:

(a) Both (A) and (R) are true and (R) is the correct explanation of (A).
(b) Both (A) and (R) are true, but (R) is not a correct explanation of (A).
(c) (A) is true, but (R) is false.
(d) (A) is false, but (R) is true.

9. Ashoka carved out rock-cut caves at Barabar and Nagarjun hills in Bihar for one of the following:
(a) Hinayana (b) Digambara
(c) Mahayana (d) Ajivika

10. The chief port for trade with Burma and Ceylon during the Mauryan period was
(a) Arikamedu
(b) Tamralipti
(c) Barukaccha (Broach)
(d) Sopara

11. Buddha image appeared with Halo (Prabha Mandala) around the head and adorned with flying Gandharva Figures and Lotus designs in the following School of Art:
(a) Gandhara School of Art
(b) Gupta School of Art
(c) Mathura School of Art
(d) Amaravati School of Art

12. In which of the following crafts did India benefit most technologically under the influence of Rome?
(a) Glass making
(b) Ship building
(c) Gem-cutting
(d) Manufacture of arms

13. Ujjain was made the second capital of Guptas during the reign of
(a) Kumara Gupta
(b) Chandra Gupta II
(c) Samudra Gupta
(d) Skanda Gupta

14. Which of the following were the Buddhist seats of learning?

I. Nalanda II. Vikramasila
III. Kanchipuram IV. Varanasi

Codes:

(a) I, II and IV are correct.
(b) I, III and IV are correct.
(c) I and IV are only correct.
(d) I and II are only correct.

15. Which of the following were the principal crops of Agriculture during the Sangam period?
(a) Rice and Sugarcane
(b) Wheat and Rice
(c) Wheat and Barley
(d) Rice and Cotton

16. Mifta-ul-Futuh composed by Amir Khusrau describes
(a) The military campaigns of Jalal-ud-Din Khalji
(b) The meeting between Bughra Khan and Kaikubad
(c) Ala-ud-Din Khalji's conquest of Chittor
(d) Ghyas-ud-Din Tughlaq's achievements

17. Which of the following statements is/are true?
(i) Ala-ud-Din Khalji instructed Malik Kafur to annex the Kakatiya State.
(ii) Kakatiya ruler Pratap Rudra was to be made a tributary King to Ala-ud-Din Khalji.

(iii) Pratap Rudra regularly sent annual tribute to the Delhi Sultans.

(iv) Pratap Rudra was escorted to Delhi by Khusro Shah.

Select your answer from the codes given below:

Codes:

(a) (i) only (b) (ii) only
(c) (i), (ii) and (iii) (d) (ii), (iii) and (iv)

18. Given below are two statements, one labelled as Assertion (A) and the other labelled as Reason (R):

Assertion (A): Sheikh Nizamuddin Aulia saw the reign of seven Sultans, succeeding one after another, on the throne of Delhi, but he never visited the court of any of them.

Reason (R): He disliked the State Patronage to the Suhrawardi Sufi Saints.

In the context of the above two statements, which one of the following is correct?

Codes:

(a) Both (A) and (R) are true and (R) is the correct explanation of (A).
(b) Both (A) and (R) are true, but (R) is not the correct explanation of (A).
(c) (A) is true, but (R) is false.
(d) (A) is false, but (R) is true.

19. Who stated that "although only a tenth of the (Muslim) population of Delhi reached Deogir (Daulatabad) yet they were able to turn the city into a fertile and prosperous land?"

(a) Ibn Battuta
(b) Shams-i-Siraj Afif
(c) Abd-al-Malik Isami
(d) Zia-ud-Din Barani

20. Match List I with List II and select the correct answer from the codes given below:

List I

(A) Wakil-i-dar (B) Amir-i-hajib
(C) Ariz-i-mumalik (D) Barid-i-mumalik

List II

1. Controller general of the military department
2. Head of the State news agency
3. Master of Ceremonies at the Court
4. Officer incharge of royal household

Codes:	**A**	**B**	**C**	**D**
(a)	4	3	1	2
(b)	2	1	4	3
(c)	4	1	2	3
(d)	2	3	4	1

21. Which of the following statement is not true about Kabir?

(a) He rejected differences based on caste, race and religion.
(b) He was opposed to scriptural knowledge.
(c) He rejected adherence to empty rituals.
(d) He advocated a philosophy of devotion and labour.

22. Which of the following measures were taken by Mahmud Gawan to curb the power of the Bahmani nobles?

(i) He reduced the size of their estates.
(ii) He increased the amount of land classified as royal domain.
(iii) He lowered the rate of land revenue demand.
(iv) He forbade governors from controlling more than a single fort.

Select the correct answer from the codes given below:

(a) (i), (ii), (iii) (b) (i), (ii), (iv)
(c) (ii) and (iii) (d) (ii) and (iv)

23. Who is the author of 'Archaeology, Art and Religion: New Perspectives on Vijayanagara'?

(a) Noburu Karashima
(b) Anila Verghese
(c) Kathleen D. Morrison
(d) Carla M. Sinopoli

24. Arrange the following into correct chronological order:
(i) Creation of twelve Subahs by Akbar
(ii) Introduction of the Dahsala system.
(iii) Introduction of the dagh system.
(iv) Introduction of the dual rank (the zat and the sawar).
Select your answer from the codes given below:
Codes:
(a) (iii) (ii) (i) (iv) (b) (iv) (i) (ii) (iii)
(c) (iii) (iv) (ii) (i) (d) (i) (ii) (iii) (iv)

25. Match List I with List II and select the correct answer from the codes given below:
List I
(A) Introduction of the practice of *Jhroka darshan*
(B) Recovery of Qandahar from the Safavids
(C) Mughal occupation of Balkh
(D) Conquest of Kangra
List II
1. 1620 2. 1646
3. 1638 4. 1580

Codes:	A	B	C	D
(a)	4	3	2	1
(b)	1	2	4	3
(c)	4	2	3	1
(d)	1	4	2	3

26. Given below are two statements, one labelled as Assertion (A) and the other labelled as Reason (R):
Assertion (A): It was in Jahangir's reign that the art of painting reached its highest water mark.
Reason (R): He was against architectural decoration.
In the context of the above two statements, which one of the following is correct?
Codes:
(a) Both (A) and (R) are true and (R) is the correct explanation of (A).
(b) Both (A) and (R) are true, but (R) is not the correct explanation of (A).
(c) (A) is true, but (R) is false.
(d) (A) is false, but (R) is true.

27. Match List I with List II and select the correct answer from the codes given below:
List I
(A) Iqbalnama-i-Jahangiri
(B) Tarikh-i-Rashidi
(C) Shahjahannama
(D) Fatuhat-i-Alamgiri
List II
1. Inayat Khan
2. Mutmad Khan
3. Isar Das Nagar
4. Mirza Haider Doghlat

Codes:	A	B	C	D
(a)	1	2	4	3
(b)	4	2	3	1
(c)	2	1	4	3
(d)	2	4	1	3

28. Match List I with List II and select the correct answer from the codes given below:
List I (Monument)
(A) Jame Masjid (Char Minar)
(B) Hira Masjid
(C) Moti Masjid
(D) Gol Gumbaz
List II (Ruler who built it)
1. Abdullah Qutub Shah
2. Shahjahan
3. Mohammad Quli Qutub Shah
4. Ali Adil Shah

Codes:	A	B	C	D
(a)	1	4	3	2
(b)	3	1	2	4
(c)	2	1	4	3
(d)	2	4	3	1

29. Who among the following historians looks upon Shivaji as the 'most constructive genius of medieval times'?
(a) Vincent A. Smith
(b) M.G. Ranade
(c) Jadunath Sarkar
(d) A.R. Kulkarni

30. Who applied the 'Great Firm' theory to explain the decline of the Mughal Empire?
(a) W.C. Smith (b) C.A. Bayly
(c) J.F. Richards (d) Karen Leonard

31. Arrange in chronological order the Indian initiative in education.
(i) Bethune School, Calcutta
(ii) Banaras Hindu University
(iii) M.A.O. College, Aligarh
(iv) Hindu College, Calcutta
Codes:
(a) (iv) (i) (iii) (ii) (b) (iii) (iv) (ii) (i)
(c) (i) (ii) (iii) (iv) (d) (ii) (iii) (iv) (i)

32. The author of Tuhfut-ul-Muwahidin was
(a) Sir Syed Ahmad Khan
(b) Raja Rammohan Roy
(c) Maulana Abul Kalam Azad
(d) Altaf Husain Hali

33. Who denounced Congress as a 'microscopic minority'?
(a) Sir Syed Ahmad Khan
(b) Lord Dufferin
(c) Lord Curzon
(d) Theodore Beck

34. Since when Income Tax was permanently imposed in India?
(a) 1860 (b) 1869
(c) 1878 (d) 1886

35. Under the 'Guarantee System' the British companies investing in railways were assured a guaranteed dividend of
(a) 3 % (b) 5 %
(c) 8 % (d) 10 %

36. Maulana Abdul Bari belonged to the
(a) Aligarh School
(b) Deoband Madarsa
(c) Firangi Mahal School
(d) Nadwat-ul-Ulema

37. Who argued the Khilafat Movement was the result of the emergence of a 'Middle Class' among Indian Muslims?
(a) Peter Hardy
(b) Francis Robinson
(c) W.C. Smith
(d) Mohd. Mujeeb

38. Arrange the following events into correct chronological order:
(i) Cabinet Mission Plan
(ii) Bombay Plan
(iii) Wavell Plan
(iv) Mountbatten Plan
Codes:
(a) (ii) (i) (iii) (iv) (b) (ii) (i) (iv) (iii)
(c) (i) (ii) (iii) (iv) (d) (iv) (iii) (ii) (i)

39. Who opened a widow home at Pune, formed a widow remarriage association, married to a widow in 1893 and in 1916 founded a Women's University in Bombay?
(a) M.G. Ranade
(b) Prof. D.K. Karve
(c) Bal Gangadhar Tilak
(d) G.V. Joshi

40. Match List I with List II and select the correct answer from the codes given below:
List I
(A) Vanchi Iyer
(B) T.K. Madhavan
(C) Srinivas Pillay
(D) E.V. Ramaswami Naiker

List II

1. Tinnevelli Conspiracy Case
2. Vaikom Satyagraha
3. The Hindu Progressive Improvement Society
4. Self Respect Movement

Codes:	A	B	C	D
(a)	2	1	3	4
(b)	3	4	2	1
(c)	4	3	1	2
(d)	1	2	3	4

41. The Subaltern Interpretation of Indian history is not shared by
(a) Ranjit Guha (b) Shahid Amin
(c) Bipan Chandra (d) Gyan Pandey

42. Match List I with List II and select the correct answer from the codes given below:

List I

(A) Mahatma Gandhi
(B) Bal Gangadhar Tilak
(C) Maulana Mohd Ali
(D) Maulana Abul Kalam Azad

List II

1. Al-Hilal 2. Harijan
3. Kesari 4. Hamdard

Codes:	A	B	C	D
(a)	2	3	4	1
(b)	1	2	3	4
(c)	4	3	2	1
(d)	3	2	4	1

43. Who amongst the following was the author of the 'Silk Letter Conspiracy'?
(a) Maulana Abdul Bari
(b) Maulana Abul Kalam Azad
(c) Zafar Ali Khan
(d) Obeidullah Sindhi

44. Arrange the following events into correct chronological order:
(i) Chittagong Armoury Raid Case
(ii) Bomb Blast in Muzaffarpur
(iii) Lahore Conspiracy Case
(iv) Kakori Case

Codes:
(a) (ii) (iii) (iv) (i) (b) (iv) (ii) (iii) (i)
(c) (i) (iv) (ii) (iii) (d) (iii) (i) (ii) (iv)

45. Bhudan Movement was started by
(a) Mahatma Gandhi
(b) Jai Prakash Narayan
(c) Vinoba Bhave
(d) Kaka Kalelkar

46. Who was known as the 'Prince of Humanists'?
(a) Francisco Petrarch
(b) Dante
(c) Boccacio
(d) Erasmus

47. Which country could not develop into a Nation State in the sixteenth century?
(a) England (b) France
(c) Germany (d) Spain

48. Match List I with List II and select the correct answer from the codes given below the lists:

List I

(A) Napoleon Bonaparte
(B) Jean Jacques Rousseau
(C) Croce
(D) Madame Roland

List II

1. 'A history is contemporary history'
2. 'Liberty what crimes are committed in thy name'
3. 'Man is born free but everywhere he is in chains'
4. 'I am the Child of Revolution'

Codes:	A	B	C	D
(a)	1	2	3	4
(b)	3	4	1	2
(c)	3	4	2	1
(d)	4	3	1	2

49. Who propounded the Theory of Utilitarianism?
(a) David Hume
(b) John Stuart Mill
(c) Jeremy Bentham
(d) Eric Stokes

50. The 'Great Depression' (1929) economic crisis was met by adopting the policy of
(a) Stimulus
(b) Marshall Plan
(c) New Deal
(d) Open Door

ANSWERS

1. (c)	2. (c)	3. (b)	4. (d)	5. (d)
6. (d)	7. (c)	8. (a)	9. (a)	10. (b)
11. (a)	12. (a)	13. (a)	14. (b)	15. (d)
16. (d)	17. (a)	18. (a)	19. (b)	20. (c)
21. (d)	22. (d)	23. (b)	24. (c)	25. (b)
26. (a)	27. (a)	28. (b)	29. (c)	30. (d)
31. (c)	32. (c)	33. (b)	34. (a)	35. (a)
36. (a)	37. (c)	38. (b)	39. (c)	40. (d)
41. (b)	42. (c)	43. (c)	44. (b)	45. (d)
46. (d)	47. (c)	48. (a)	49. (b)	50. (a)

JUNE–2010

Note: This paper contains sixty (60) multiple choice questions, each question carrying two (2) marks. Candidate is expected to answer any fifty (50) questions. In case more than fifty (50) questions are attempted, only the first fifty (50) questions will be evaluated.

PAPER–I

1. Which one of the following is the most important quality of a good teacher?
   (a) Punctuality and sincerity
   (b) Content mastery
   (c) Content mastery and reactive
   (d) Content mastery and sociable
2. The primary responsibility for the teacher's adjustment lies with
   (a) The children
   (b) The principal
   (c) The teacher himself
   (d) The community
3. As per the NCTE norms, what should be the staff strength for a unit of 100 students at B.Ed. level?
   (a) 1 + 7 (b) 1 + 9
   (c) 1 + 10 (d) 1 + 5
4. Research has shown that the most frequent symptom of nervous instability among teachers is
   (a) Digestive upsets
   (b) Explosive behaviour
   (c) Fatigue
   (d) Worry
5. Which one of the following statements is correct?
   (a) Syllabus is an annexure to the curriculum.
   (b) Curriculum is the same in all educational institutions.
   (c) Curriculum includes both formal and informal education.
   (d) Curriculum does not include methods of evaluation.
6. A successful teacher is one who is
   (a) Compassionate and disciplinarian
   (b) Quite and reactive
   (c) Tolerant and dominating
   (d) Passive and active

Read the following passage carefully and answer the questions 7 to 12.

The phrase "What is it like?" stands for a fundamental thought process. How does one go about observing and reporting on things and events that occupy segments of earth space? Of all the infinite variety of phenomena on the face of the earth, how does one decide what phenomena to observe? There is no such thing as a complete description of the earth or any part of it, for every microscopic point on the earth's surface differs from every other such point. Experience shows that the things observed are already familiar, because they are like phenomena that occur at home or because they resemble the abstract images and models developed in the human mind.

How are abstract images formed? Humans alone among the animals possess language; their words symbolise not only specific things but also mental images of classes of things. People can remember what they have seen or experienced because they attach a word symbol to them.

During the long record of our efforts to gain more and more knowledge about the face of the earth as the human habitat, there has been a continuing interplay between things and events. The direct observation through the senses is described as a percept; the mental image is described as a concept. Percepts are what some people describe as reality, in contrast to mental images, which are theoretical, implying that they are not real.

The relation of Percept to Concept is not as simple as the definition implies. It is now quite clear that people of different cultures or even individuals in the same culture develop different mental images of reality and what they perceive is a reflection of these preconceptions. The direct observation of things and events on the face of the earth is so clearly a function of the mental images of the mind of the observer that the whole idea of reality must be reconsidered.

Concepts determine what the observer perceives, yet concepts are derived from the generalisations of previous percepts. What happens is that the educated observer is taught to accept a set of concepts and then sharpens or changes these concepts during a professional career. In any one field of scholarship, professional opinion at one time determines what concepts and procedures are acceptable, and these form a kind of model of scholarly behaviour.

7. The problem raised in the passage reflects on
   (a) thought process
   (b) human behaviour
   (c) cultural perceptions
   (d) professional opinion
8. According to the passage, human beings have mostly in mind
   (a) Observation of things
   (b) Preparation of mental images
   (c) Expression through language
   (d) To gain knowledge
9. Concept means
   (a) A mental image
   (b) A reality
   (c) An idea expressed in language form
   (d) All the above
10. The relation of Percept to Concept is
    (a) Positive (b) Negative
    (c) Reflective (d) Absolute
11. In the passage, the earth is taken as
    (a) The Globe
    (b) The Human Habitat
    (c) A Celestial Body
    (d) A Planet
12. Percept means
    (a) Direct observation through the senses
    (b) A conceived idea
    (c) Ends of a spectrum
    (d) An abstract image
13. Action research means
    (a) A longitudinal research
    (b) An applied research
    (c) A research initiated to solve an immediate problem
    (d) A research with socio-economic objective
14. Research is
    (a) Searching again and again
    (b) Finding solution to any problem
    (c) Working in a scientific way to search for truth of any problem
    (d) None of the above
15. A common test in research demands much priority on
    (a) Reliability (b) Usability
    (c) Objectivity (d) All of the above
16. Which of the following is the first step in starting the research process?

(a) Searching sources of information to locate problem
(b) Survey of related literature
(c) Identification of problem
(d) Searching for solutions to the problem

17. If a researcher conducts a research on finding out which administrative style contributes more to institutional effectiveness? This will be an example of
(a) Basic Research
(b) Action Research
(c) Applied Research
(d) None of the above

18. Normal Probability Curve should be
(a) Positively skewed
(b) Negatively skewed
(c) Leptokurtic skewed
(d) Zero skewed

19. In communication, a major barrier to reception of messages is
(a) audience attitude
(b) audience knowledge
(c) audience education
(d) audience income

20. Post-modernism is associated with
(a) Newspapers (b) Magazines
(c) Radio (d) Television

21. Didactic communication is
(a) intra-porsonal (b) inter-personal
(c) organisational (d) relational

22. In communication, the language is
(a) the non-verbal code
(b) the verbal code
(c) the symbolic code
(d) the iconic code

23. Identify the correct sequence of the following:
(a) Source, channel, message, receiver
(b) Source, receiver, channel, message
(c) Source, message, receiver, channel
(d) Source, message, channel, receiver

24. **Assertion (A):** Mass media promote a culture of violence in the society.

Reason (R): Because violence sells in the market as people themselves are violent in character.
(a) Both (A) and (R) are true and (R) is the correct explanation of (A).
(b) Both (A) and (R) are true, but (R) is not the correct explanation of (A).
(c) (A) is true, but (R) is false.
(d) Both (A) and (R) are false.

25. When an error of 1% is made in the length of a square, the percentage error in the area of a square will be
(a) 0 (b) 1/2
(c) 1 (d) 2

26. On January 12, 1980, it was a Saturday. The day of the week on January 12, 1979 was
(a) Thursday (b) Friday
(c) Saturday (d) Sunday

27. If water is called food, food is called tree, tree is called earth, earth is called world, which of the following grows a fruit?
(a) Water (b) Tree
(c) World (d) Earth

28. E is the son of A, D is the son of B, E is married to C, C is the daughter of B. How is D related to E?
(a) Brother (b) Uncle
(c) Father-in-law (d) Brother-in-law

29. If INSURANCE is coded as ECNARUSNI, how HINDRANCE will be coded?
(a) CADNIHWCE (b) HANODEINR
(c) AENIRHDCN (d) ECNARDNIH

30. Find the next number in the following series: 2, 5, 10, 17, 26, 37, 50, ?
(a) 63 (b) 65
(c) 67 (d) 69

31. Which of the following is an example of circular argument?
    (a) God created man in his image and man created God in his own image.
    (b) God is the source of a scripture and the scripture is the source of our knowledge of God.
    (c) Some of the Indians are great because India is great.
    (d) Rama is great because he is Rama.

32. Lakshmana is a morally good person because
    (a) he is religious (b) he is educated
    (c) he is rich (d) he is rational

33. Two statements I and II given below are followed by two conclusions (a) and (b). Supposing the statements are true, which of the following conclusions can logically follow?

    Statements:

    I. Some religious people are morally good.

    II. Some religious people are rational.

    Conclusion:

    (A) Rationally religious people are good morally.

    (B) Non-rational religious persons are not morally good.

    (a) Only (A) follows
    (b) Only (B) follows
    (c) Both (A) and (B) follow
    (d) Neither (A) nor (B) follows

34. Certainty is
    (a) an objective fact
    (b) emotionally satisfying
    (c) logical
    (d) ontological

Questions from 35 to 36 are based on the following diagram in which there are three intersecting circles I, S and P where circle I stands for Indians, circle S stands for Scientists and circle P for Politicians. Different regions of the figure are lettered from a to g.

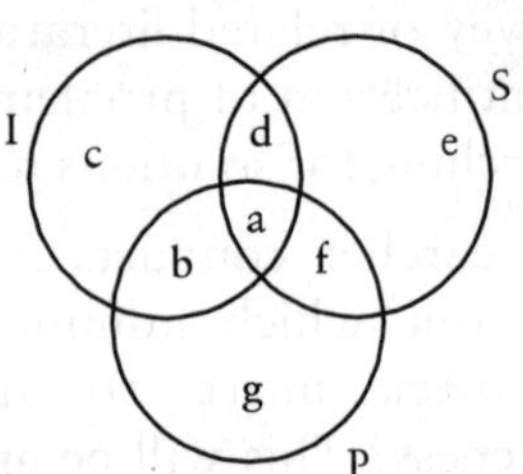

35. The region which represents non-scientists who are politicians.
    (a) f (b) d
    (c) a (d) c

36. The region which represents politicians who are Indians as well as scientists.
    (a) b (b) c
    (c) a (d) d

37. The population of a city is plotted as a function of time (years) in graphic form below:

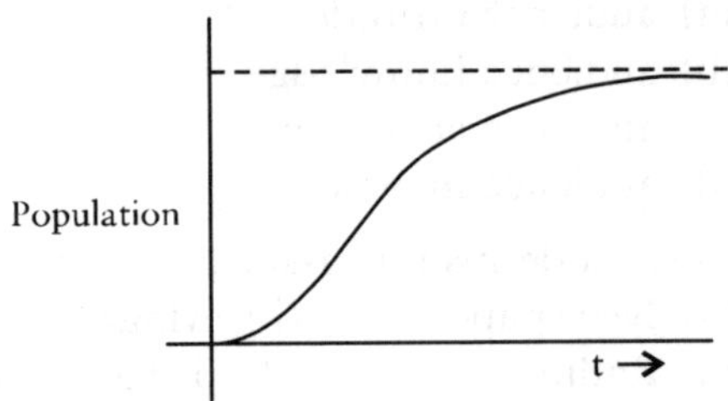

Which of the following inference can be drawn from the above plot?
    (a) The population increases exponentially.
    (b) The population increases in parabolic fashion.
    (c) The population initially increases in a linear fashion and then stabilises.
    (d) The population initially increases exponentially and then stabilises.

In the following chart, the price of logs is shown in per cubic metre and that of Plywood and Saw Timber in per tonnes. Study the chart and answer the following questions 38 to 40.

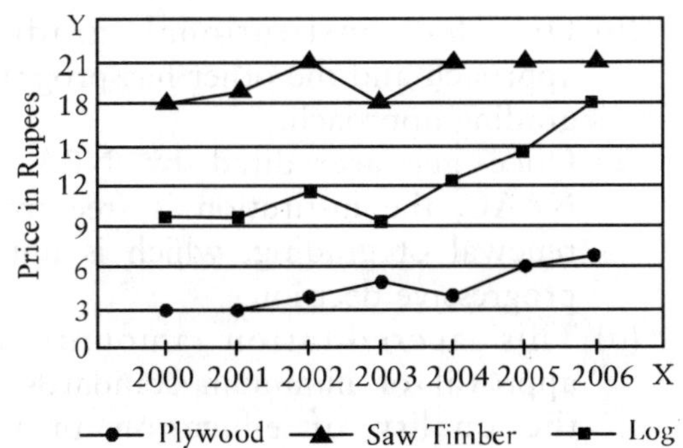

38. Which product shows the maximum percentage increase in price over the period?
(a) Saw timber (b) Plywood
(c) Log (d) None of these

39. What is the maximum percentage increase in price per cubic metre of log?
(a) 6 (b) 12
(c) 18 (d) None of these

40. In which year the prices of two products increased and that of the third increased?
(a) 2000 (b) 2002
(c) 2003 (d) 2006

41. Which one of the following is the oldest Archival source of data in India?
(a) National Sample Surveys
(b) Agricultural Statistics
(c) Census
(d) Vital Statistics

42. In a large random data set following normal distribution, the ratio (%) of number of data points which are in the range of (mean ± standard deviation) to the total number of data points, is
(a) ~ 50% (b) ~ 67%
(c) ~ 97% (d) ~ 47%

43. Which number system is usually followed in a typical 32-bit computer?
(a) 2 (b) 8
(c) 10 (d) 16

44. Which one of the following is an example of Operating System?
(a) Microsoft Word
(b) Microsoft Excel
(c) Microsoft Access
(d) Microsoft Windows

45. Which one of the following represent the binary equivalent of the decimal number 23?
(a) 01011 (b) 10111
(c) 10011 (d) None of these

46. Which one of the following is different from other members?
(a) Google (b) Windows
(c) Linux (d) Mac

47. Where does a computer add and compare its data?
(a) CPU (b) Memory
(c) Hard disk (d) Floppy disk

48. Computers on an internet are identified by
(a) e-mail address
(b) street address
(c) IP address
(d) None of the above

49. The Right to Information Act, 2005 makes the provision of
(a) Dissemination of all types of information by all Public authorities to any person
(b) Establishment of Central, State and District Level Information Commissions as an appellate body
(c) Transparency and accountability in Public authorities
(d) All of the above

50. Which type of natural hazards cause maximum damage to property and lives?
(a) Hydrological
(b) Hydro-meteorological
(c) Geological
(d) Geo-chemical

51. Dioxins are produced from
(a) Wastelands
(b) Power plants
(c) Sugar factories
(d) Combustion of plastics

52. The slogan "A tree for each child" was coined for
(a) Social forestry program
(b) Clean Air program
(c) Soil conservation program
(d) Environmental protection program

53. The main constituents of biogas are
(a) Methane and Carbon dioxide
(b) Methane and Nitric oxide
(c) Methane, Hydrogen and Nitric oxide
(d) Methane and Sulphur dioxide

54. **Assertion (A):** In the world as a whole, the environment has degraded during past several decades.

Reason (R): The population of the world has been growing significantly.
(a) (A) is correct, (R) is correct and (R) is the correct explanation of (A).
(b) (A) is correct, (R) is correct and (R) is not the correct explanation of (A).
(c) (A) is correct, but (R) is false.
(d) (A) is false, but (R) is correct.

55. Climate change has implications for
1. soil moisture 2. forest fires
3. biodiversity 4. groundwater

Identify the correct combination according to the code:

Codes:
(a) 1 and 3 (b) 1, 2 and 3
(c) 1, 3 and 4 (d) 1, 2, 3 and 4

56. The accreditation process by National Assessment and Accreditation Council (NAAC) differs from that of National Board of Accreditation (NBA) in terms of
(a) Disciplines covered by both being the same, there is duplication of efforts.
(b) One has institutional grading approach and the other has program grading approach.
(c) Once get accredited by NBA or NAAC, the institution is free from renewal of grading, which is not a progressive decision.
(d) This accreditation amounts to approval of minimum standards in the quality of education in the institution concerned.

57. Which option is not correct?
(a) Most of the educational institutions of National repute in scientific and technical sphere fall under 64th entry of Union list.
(b) Education, in general, is the subject of concurrent list since 42nd Constitutional Amendment Act 1976.
(c) Central Advisory Board on Education (CABE) was first established in 1920.
(d) India had implemented the right to Free and Compulsory Primary Education in 2002 through 86th Constitutional Amendment.

58. Which statement is not correct about the "National Education Day" of India?
(a) It is celebrated on 5th September every year.
(b) It is celebrated on 11th November every year.
(c) It is celebrated in the memory of India's first Union Minister of Education, Dr. Abul Kalam Azad.
(d) It is being celebrated since 2008.

59. Match List I with List II and select the correct answer from the codes given below:

List I
(Articles of the Constitution)
A. Article 280 B. Article 324
C. Article 323 D. Article 315

List II (Institutions)
1. Administrative Tribunals
2. Election Commission of India
3. Finance Commission at Union level
4. Union Public Service Commission

Codes:	A	B	C	D
(a)	1	2	3	4
(b)	3	2	1	4
(c)	2	3	4	1
(d)	2	4	3	1

60. Deemed Universities declared by UGC under Section 3 of the UGC Act 1956, are not permitted to
(a) offer programs in higher education and issue degrees
(b) give affiliation to any institute of higher education
(c) open off-campus and off-shore campus anywhere in the country and overseas respectively without the permission of the UGC
(d) offer distance education programs without the approval of the Distance Education Council

ANSWERS

1. (b)	2. (c)	3. (c)	4. (b)	5. (c)
6. (a)	7. (c)	8. (a)	9. (a)	10. (c)
11. (b)	12. (a)	13. (c)	14. (c)	15. (d)
16. (c)	17. (c)	18. (d)	19. (c)	20. (d)
21. (b)	22. (b)	23. (d)	24. (d)	25. (d)
26. (b)	27. (c)	28. (d)	29. (d)	30. (b)
31. (b)	32. (a)	33. (d)	34. (c)	35. (a)
36. (c)	37. (d)	38. (c)	39. (d)	40. (b)
41. (c)	42. (b)	43. (a)	44. (d)	45. (b)
46. (b)	47. (a)	48. (c)	49. (d)	50. (c)
51. (d)	52. (d)	53. (a)	54. (b)	55. (d)
56. (c)	57. (a)	58. (a)	59. (b)	60. (b)

PAPER–II

Note: This paper contains fifty (50) multiple choice questions, each question carrying two (2) marks. All questions are compulsory.

1. Which of the following is associated with the lower Palaeolithic period?
(a) Homo erectus
(b) Neanderthal
(c) Homo sapience
(d) Homo sapience sapience

2. Which among the following represents the Mesolithic period?
(a) Olduwan tools (b) Hand axe
(c) Triangle tools (d) Polished tools

3. Which among the following denotes the Neolithic period?
(a) Kunal (b) Lothal
(c) Daimabad (d) Chirand

4. Given below are two statements, one is labelled as Assertion (A) and the other is labelled as Reason (R):
Assertion (A): Harappa civilization was developed with the application of copper tools.
Reason (R): This enabled people to make better use of the available natural resources.
Read the above statements and select the correct answer from the codes below:
Codes:
(a) (A) is incorrect, but (R) is true.
(b) Both (A) and (R) are incorrect.
(c) Both (A) and (R) are true.
(d) (A) is correct, but (R) is false.

5. Given below are two statements, one is labelled as Assertion (A) and the other is labelled as Reason (R):

Assertion (A): During the Rig Vedic period the society was pastoral.

Reason (R): The mode of subsistence was primarily based on pastoralism.

Read the above statements and select the correct answer from the codes below:

Codes:

(a) (A) is correct, but (R) is false.
(b) (A) is untrue, but (R) is true.
(c) Both (A) and (R) are false.
(d) Both (A) and (R) are correct.

6. Given below are two statements, one is labelled as Assertion (A) and the other is labelled as Reason (R):

Assertion (A): The rise of religious movements in the 6th century BC was an outcome of prevalent social and economic unrest.

Reason (R): The improved economic condition of the deprived sections of the society embolden them to seek their rightful place.

Read the above statements and select the correct answer from the codes given below:

Codes:

(a) (A) is correct, but (R) is false.
(b) (A) is incorrect, but (R) is true.
(c) Both (A) and (R) are correct.
(d) Both (A) and (R) are incorrect.

7. Given below are two statements, one is labelled as Assertion (A) and the other is labelled as Reason (R):

Assertion (A): Kushana period witnessed large scale cultural integration.

Reason (R): Kushana Kings advocated themselves it by example.

Read the above statements and select the correct answer from the codes given below:

Codes:

(a) (A) is correct, but (R) is incorrect.
(b) (A) is false, but (R) is true.
(c) Both (A) and (R) are false.
(d) Both (A) and (R) are true.

8. Arrange the following into sequential order and select the correct answer from the codes given below:

(i) Megalithic period
(ii) Chalcolithic period
(iii) Northern Black Polished Ware
(iv) Black and Red Ware

Codes:

(a) (iii), (iv), (i), (ii) (b) (ii), (iv), (i), (iii)
(c) (iv), (ii), (iii), (i) (d) (i), (iii), (iv), (ii)

9. Arrange the following into sequential order and select the correct answer from the codes given below:

(i) Janapada (ii) Mahajanapada
(iii) Empire (iv) Jana

Codes:

(a) (ii), (iii), (i), (iv) (b) (iii), (iv), (ii), (i)
(c) (iv), (i), (ii), (iii) (d) (iv), (ii), (i), (iii)

10. Arrange the following into sequential order and select the correct answer from the codes given below:

(i) Malvikagnimitra
(ii) Harshacharita
(iii) Ashtadhyayi
(iv) Rajatarangini

Codes:

(a) (ii), (iii), (iv), (i) (b) (iii), (ii), (i), (iv)
(c) (iv), (ii), (i), (iii) (d) (iii), (i), (ii), (iv)

11. Arrange the following into sequential order and select the correct answer from the codes given below:

(i) Pulkeshin–II
(ii) Pushyamitra Shunga
(iii) Shankaracharya
(iv) Chandabaradai

Codes:

(a) (ii), (i), (iii), (iv) (b) (i), (iii), (ii), (iv)
(c) (iii), (iv), (ii), (i) (d) (iv), (i), (iii), (ii)

12. Match List I with List II and select the correct answer from the codes given below:

List I
(A) Levirate
(B) Punchmarked coins
(C) Varmanas
(D) Nalanda

List II
(i) Kamrup
(ii) Rig Veda
(iii) Bihar
(iv) Early Historical Period

Codes:	A	B	C	D
(a)	(ii)	(iii)	(i)	(iv)
(b)	(ii)	(iv)	(i)	(iii)
(c)	(iii)	(ii)	(iv)	(i)
(d)	(iv)	(iii)	(ii)	(i)

13. Match List I with List II and select the correct answer from the codes given below:

List I
(A) Second Urbanization
(B) Kharavela
(C) Gautamiputra
(D) Vikramadeva Charita

List II
(i) Satavahana Dynasty
(ii) Bilhana
(iii) Orissa
(iv) Iron

Codes:	A	B	C	D
(a)	(iv)	(i)	(ii)	(iii)
(b)	(iii)	(ii)	(iv)	(i)
(c)	(ii)	(iv)	(iii)	(i)
(d)	(iv)	(iii)	(i)	(ii)

14. Match List I with List II and select the correct answer from the codes given below:

List I
(A) Nagar style of architecture
(B) Shravanbelagola
(C) Tantrayan
(D) Mahenderaverman Shailey

List II
(i) Buddhism (ii) Pallava dynasty
(iii) North India (iv) Karnataka

Codes:	A	B	C	D
(a)	(iii)	(iv)	(i)	(ii)
(b)	(iv)	(i)	(ii)	(iii)
(c)	(ii)	(iv)	(iii)	(i)
(d)	(iv)	(iii)	(i)	(ii)

15. Match List I with List II and select the correct answer from the codes given below:

List I	List II
(A) Kalibanga	(i) R.C. Gaur
(B) Mitathal	(ii) M.D.N. Sahi
(C) Atranjikhera	(iii) Suraj Bhan
(D) Jakhera	(iv) B.B. Lal

Codes:	A	B	C	D
(a)	(ii)	(iii)	(i)	(iv)
(b)	(iv)	(iii)	(i)	(ii)
(c)	(iii)	(iv)	(ii)	(i)
(d)	(i)	(iii)	(iv)	(ii)

16. In which of the following sources it is stated that Prithviraj III entertained the ambition of conquering the whole world?
(a) Taj-ul-Maasir
(b) Prithviraj Prabandha
(c) Tabqat-i-Nasiri
(d) Prithviraj Raso

17. Who among the following Delhi Sultans enlarged the Quwwat-ul-Islam mosque?
(i) Iltut Mish
(ii) Balban
(iii) Alaud-Din Khalji
(iv) Firozshah Tughlaq

Select your answer from the codes given below:
Codes:
(a) (i), (ii), (iv) (b) (i) and (iii)
(c) (ii) and (iv) (d) (i), (ii), (iii)

18. Who among the following Sultans of Delhi advocated the policy that "follow the middle course in realizing the Kharaj"?

(a) Balban
(b) Jalalud-Din Khalji
(c) Ghyasuddin Tughlaq
(d) Firoj Tughlaq

19. Which of the following statements are not true about Sultan Ghyasud-Din Tughlaq?
(i) He befriended Shaikh Nizamuddin Aulia.
(ii) He gave certain concessions to Khots and Muqaddams.
(iii) He sent his son Ulugh Khan to recover arrears of tribute from Pratapa Rudra.
(iv) He levied a tax termed haqq-i-shurb.
Select the correct answer from the codes given below:
Codes:
(a) (i), (ii) and (iii) (b) (i) and (iii)
(c) (ii) and (iii) (d) (ii) and (iv)

20. Who put forth the hypothesis of 'Urban revolution' in northern India during the thirteenth and fourteenth centuries?
(a) K.M. Ashraf
(b) Moreland
(c) Mohammad Habib
(d) K.S. Lal

21. Given below are two statements, one labelled as Assertion (A) and the other labelled as Reason (R):
Assertion (A): The arrival of north Indian Sufis in the Deccan during the fourteenth and fifteenth centuries brought deep changes in the region's political and religious fabric.
Reason (R): They came to the Deccan to justify Khalji and early Tughlaq invasions of the Deccan plateau.
In the context of the above two statements, which one of the following is correct?
Codes:
(a) Both (A) and (R) are true and (R) is the correct explanation of (A).
(b) Both (A) and (R) are true, but (R) is not the correct explanation of (A).
(c) (A) is true, but (R) is false.
(d) (A) is false, but (R) is true.

22. Which of the following is the correct chronological order of the Vijayanagara ruling dynasties?
(a) Saluva, Tuluva, Sangama, Aravidu
(b) Sangama, Saluva, Tuluva, Aravidu
(c) Sangama, Tuluva, Saluva, Aravidu
(d) Sangama, Aravidu, Saluva, Tuluva

23. The Portuguese captured Goa in the year
(a) 1496 (b) 1510
(c) 1524 (d) 1556

24. Arrange the following events into correct chronological order:
(i) Propagation of Vaishnavite Bhakti by Ramananda
(ii) Compilation of Adigrantha
(iii) Close of the Ibadatkhana
(iv) Foundation of the Chishti order in the Deccan
Select the correct answer from the codes given below:
Codes:
(a) (i), (iv), (iii), (ii) (b) (i), (iii), (ii), (iv)
(c) (ii), (iv), (i), (iii) (d) (iv), (i), (iii), (ii)

25. Given below are two statements, one labelled as Assertion (A) and the other labelled as Reason (R):
Assertion (A): Akbar proclaimed Dahsala in the twenty-fourth year of his reign.
Reason (R): He decided to abolish all other existing methods of land revenue assessment in the Mughal empire.
In the context of the above two statements, which one of the following is correct?
Codes:
(a) Both (A) and (R) are true and (R) is the correct explanation of (A).
(b) Both (A) and (R) are true, but (R) is not the correct explanation of (A).

(c) (A) is true, but (R) is false.
(d) (A) is false, but (R) is true.

26. Match List I with List II and select the correct answer from the codes given below:

List I (Event)
(A) The Mughal conquest of Malwa
(B) Introduction of the *Ilahi* Era
(C) Annexation of Kashmir in Mughal empire
(D) Conquest of Orissa

List II (Year)
(i) 1584 (ii) 1592
(iii) 1585 (iv) 1561

Codes:	**A**	**B**	**C**	**D**
(a)	(iii)	(ii)	(i)	(iv)
(b)	(iv)	(i)	(iii)	(ii)
(c)	(i)	(iii)	(iv)	(ii)
(d)	(iii)	(i)	(ii)	(iv)

27. Which of the following illustrated manuscripts were prepared during Akbar's time?
(i) The *Diwan-i-Amir Hasan Dihlavi*
(ii) The *Raj Kanwar*
(iii) The *Tutinama*
(iv) The *Yoga Vashista*
Select your answer from the codes given below:
Codes:
(a) (i), (ii) and (iv) (b) (ii) and (iv)
(c) (i), (iii) and (iv) (d) (iii) and (iv)

28. Who among the following foreign travellers described the manufacture of indigo in India?
(a) Ibn Battuta
(b) Nicolo De Conti
(c) William Finch
(d) Peter Mundi

29. Match List I with List II and select the correct answer from the codes given below:

List I
(A) Ahmad Yadgar
(B) Sujan Rai
(C) Khwaja Kamghar Ghairat Khan
(D) Shah Nawaz Khan

List II
(i) *Maasir-i-Jahangiri*
(ii) *Maasir-ul-Umara*
(iii) *Tarikh-i-Salatin-i-Afghaniah*
(iv) *Khulast-ut-Twarikh*

Codes:	**A**	**B**	**C**	**D**
(a)	(iii)	(iv)	(i)	(ii)
(b)	(ii)	(i)	(iii)	(iv)
(c)	(iii)	(ii)	(i)	(iv)
(d)	(i)	(iv)	(iii)	(ii)

30. Shahu was set free from the Mughal captivity by
(a) Aurangzeb
(b) Prince Azam
(c) Prince Kam Bakhsh
(d) Jahandar Shah

31. By which act the British Parliament had abolished the monopoly of East India Company's trade in India?
(a) Regulating Act, 1773
(b) Charter Act, 1813
(c) Charter Act, 1833
(d) Government of India Act, 1858

32. Arrange the following British Legislations concerning women in chronological order:
(i) Hindu Widow Remarriage Act
(ii) The Native Marriage Act (Civil Marriage Act)
(iii) Abolition of Sati in Bengal Province
(iv) The Age of Consent Act
Codes:
(a) (iii), (i), (ii), (iv) (b) (i), (ii), (iii), (iv)
(c) (iv), (ii), (i), (iii) (d) (ii), (iii), (iv), (i)

33. Arrange in chronological order the Famine Commissions formed by the Government of British India:

(i) Macdowell Commission
(ii) Lyall Commission
(iii) Campbell Commission
(iv) Strachey Commission

Codes:

(a) (iv), (iii), (ii), (i) (b) (iii), (iv), (i), (ii)
(c) (i), (ii), (iii), (iv) (d) (ii), (iii), (i), (iv)

34. Maulana Shibli Nomani belonged to the
(a) Aligarh School
(b) Deoband Madarsa
(c) Firangi Mahal
(d) Nadwat-ul-ulema

35. Gandhiji's intervention in the Ahmedabad Mill Strike of 1917 led to the enhancement of wages of the workers by
(a) 25 % (b) 30 %
(c) 35 % (d) 40 %

36. The chief grievance of the peasants in Champaran Satyagraha (1917) was against the
(a) awabs or illegal cesses
(b) oppression of the landlords
(c) land revenue demand
(d) tinkathia system

37. In which Session the Indian National Congress adopted the resolution on Fundamental Rights?
(a) Madras (1927) (b) Lahore (1929)
(c) Karachi (1931) (d) Faizpur (1936)

38. Who argued that de-industrialization did not take place in India under the colonial rule?
(a) Amiyo Baghchi (b) Bipan Chandra
(c) Morris D Morris (d) Toru Matsui

39. Who founded the Hindu College of Calcutta in 1817?
(a) David Hare
(b) William Jones
(c) H.T. Princep
(d) Henry Vivian Derozio

40. Match List I with List II and select the correct answer.

List I
(A) Maulana Abul Kalam Azad
(B) Dadabhai Naoroji
(C) Sir Syed Ahmad Khan
(D) Subhash Chandra Bose

List II
(i) The Indian Struggle
(ii) Asbab-i-Baghawat-i-Hind
(iii) Poverty and Un-British Rule in India
(iv) India Wins Freedom

Codes:	**A**	**B**	**C**	**D**
(a)	(iv)	(iii)	(ii)	(i)
(b)	(iii)	(ii)	(i)	(iv)
(c)	(ii)	(iv)	(iii)	(i)
(d)	(i)	(ii)	(iii)	(iv)

41. Match List I with List II and select the correct answer.

List I
(A) Chinnava
(B) Haji Shariat Ullah
(C) Alluri Sitaram Raju
(D) Krishna Daji Pandit

List II
(i) Rampa Uprising 1922
(ii) Gadkari Revolt 1944
(iii) Faraizi Movement 1838
(iv) Kittur Uprising 1924

Codes:	**A**	**B**	**C**	**D**
(a)	(iv)	(iii)	(i)	(ii)
(b)	(iii)	(iv)	(i)	(ii)
(c)	(i)	(ii)	(iii)	(iv)
(d)	(ii)	(i)	(iv)	(iii)

42. Paramountcy is the position of permanent power enjoyed by the British Government in relation to the
(a) Zamindars
(b) Princely states
(c) Peasants
(d) Christian Missionaries

43. The Congress Ministry in Madras during 1937-39 was headed by

(a) T. Prakasham
(b) Subramanium Bharti
(c) C. Rajgopalachari
(d) K. Kamraj

44. Who was the Chairman of the Drafting Committee of the Indian Constitution?
(a) Dr. Rajendra Prasad
(b) Dr. B.R. Ambedkar
(c) B.N. Rau
(d) Jawaharlal Nehru

45. Arrange the following events in their chronological order:
(i) Cripps Mission
(ii) Quit India Movement
(iii) Individual Satyagraha
(iv) August Offer
Codes:
(a) (i), (ii), (iii), (iv) (b) (iv), (iii), (i), (ii)
(c) (iii), (iv), (ii), (i) (d) (ii), (i), (iv), (iii)

46. Who was known as the father of 'Humanism'?
(a) Dante (b) Erasmus
(c) Machiavelli (d) Petrarch

47. The fee paid to the Lord for the use of the mill, brewery and bakery was known as
(a) Banalité (b) Corveé
(c) Gabélle (d) Taille

48. The theory of 'General Will' was put forward by
(a) Diderot (b) Montesquieu
(c) Rousseau (d) Voltaire

49. Bullionism and the favourable balance of trade were the basic features of
(a) Colonialism
(b) Commercialism
(c) Free Trade
(d) Mercantilism

50. Match List I with List II and select the correct answer from the codes given below the lists:

List I
(A) Erasmus (B) Machiavelli
(C) Thomas More (D) Dante

List II
(i) Divine Comedy
(ii) Utopia
(iii) The Prince
(iv) Praise of Folly

Codes:	A	B	C	D
(a)	(iii)	(ii)	(i)	(iv)
(b)	(ii)	(i)	(iii)	(iv)
(c)	(i)	(ii)	(iii)	(iv)
(d)	(iv)	(iii)	(ii)	(i)

ANSWERS

1. (a)	2. (c)	3. (d)	4. (b)	5. (d)
6. (c)	7. (d)	8. (b)	9. (c)	10. (d)
11. (a)	12. (b)	13. (d)	14. (a)	15. (b)
16. (d)	17. (b)	18. (d)	19. (d)	20. (c)
21. (c)	22. (b)	23. (b)	24. (d)	25. (c)
26. (b)	27. (c)	28. (c)	29. (a)	30. (b)
31. (b)	32. (a)	33. (b)	34. (a)	35. (c)
36. (d)	37. (c)	38. (c)	39. (a)	40. (a)
41. (a)	42. (b)	43. (c)	44. (b)	45. (b)
46. (d)	47. (b)	48. (b)	49. (b)	50. (d)

DECEMBER–2009

Note: This paper contains sixty (60) multiple choice questions, each question carrying two (2) marks. Candidate is expected to answer any fifty (50) questions. In case more than fifty (50) questions are attempted, only the first fifty (50) questions will be evaluated.

PAPER–I

1. The University which telecasts interaction educational programs through its own channel is
   (a) Osmania University
   (b) University of Pune
   (c) Annamalai University
   (d) Indira Gandhi National University (IGNOU)

2. Which of the following skills are needed for present day teacher to adjust effectively with the classroom teaching?
   1. Knowledge of technology
   2. Use of technology in teaching learning
   3. Knowledge of students' needs
   4. Content mastery

   (a) 1 and 3 (b) 2 and 3
   (c) 2, 3 and 4 (d) 2 and 4

3. Who has signed as MoU for Accreditation of Teacher Education Institutions in India?
   (a) NAAC and UGC
   (b) NCTE and NAAC
   (c) UGC and NCTE
   (d) NCTE and IGNOU

4. The primary duty of the teacher is to
   (a) raise the intellectual standard of the students
   (b) improve the physical standard of the students
   (c) help all-round development of the students
   (d) imbibe value system in the students

5. Micro teaching is more effective
   (a) during the preparation for teaching-practice
   (b) during the teaching-practice
   (c) after the teaching-practice
   (d) always

6. What quality the students like the most in a teacher?
   (a) Idealist philosophy
   (b) Compassion
   (c) Discipline
   (d) Entertaining

7. A null hypothesis is
   (a) when there is no difference between the variables
   (b) the same as research hypothesis
   (c) subjective in nature
   (d) when there is difference between the variables

8. The research which is exploring new facts through the study of the past is called
   (a) Philosophical research
   (b) Historical research
   (c) Mythological research
   (d) Content analysis

9. Action research is
   (a) An applied research
   (b) A research carried out to solve immediate problems
   (c) A longitudinal research
   (d) Simulative research

10. The process not needed in Experimental Researches is
    (a) Observation (b) Manipulation
    (c) Controlling (d) Content Analysis
11. Manipulation is always a part of
    (a) Historical research
    (b) Fundamental research
    (c) Descriptive research
    (d) Experimental research
12. Which correlation co-efficient best explains the relationship between creativity and intelligence?
    (a) 1.00 (b) 0.6
    (c) 0.5 (d) 0.3

Read the following passage and answer the Question Nos. 13 to 18:

The decisive shift in British Policy really came about under mass pressure in the autumn and winter of 1945 to 46—the months which Penderel Moon while editing Wavell's Journal has perceptively described as 'The Edge of a Volcano'. Very foolishly, the British initially decided to hold public trials of several hundreds of the 20,000 I.N.A. prisoners (as well as dismissing from service and detaining without trial no less than 7,000). They compounded the folly by holding the first trial in the Red Fort, Delhi in November 1945, and putting on the dock together a Hindu, a Muslim and a Sikh (P.K. Sehgal, Shah Nawaz, Gurbaksh Singh Dhillon). Bhulabhai Desai, Tejbahadur Sapru and Nehru appeared for the defence (the latter putting on his barrister's gown after 25 years), and the Muslim League also joined the countrywide protest. On 20 November, an Intelligence Bureau note admitted that "there has seldom been a matter which has attracted so much Indian public interest and, it is safe to say, sympathy...this particular brand of sympathy cuts across communal barriers". A journalist (B. Shiva Rao) visiting the Red Fort prisoners on the same day reported that 'There is not the slightest feeling among them of Hindu and Muslim.... A majority of the men now awaiting trial in the Red Fort is Muslim. Some of these men are bitter that Mr. Jinnah is keeping alive a controversy about Pakistan.' The British became extremely nervous about the I.N.A. spirit spreading to the Indian Army, and in January the Punjab Governor reported that a Lahore reception for released I.N.A. prisoners had been attended by Indian soldiers in uniform.

13. Which heading is more appropriate to assign to the above passage?
    (a) Wavell's Journal
    (b) Role of Muslim League
    (c) I.N.A. Trials
    (d) Red Fort Prisoners
14. The trial of P.K. Sehgal, Shah Nawaz and Gurbaksh Singh Dhillon symbolises
    (a) communal harmony
    (b) threat to all religious persons
    (c) threat to persons fighting for the freedom
    (d) British reaction against the natives
15. I.N.A. stands for
    (a) Indian National Assembly
    (b) Indian National Association
    (c) Inter-national Association
    (d) Indian National Army
16. 'There has seldom been a matter which has attracted so much Indian Public Interest and, it is safe to say, sympathy... this particular brand of sympathy cuts across communal barriers.' Who sympathises to whom and against whom?
    (a) Muslims sympathised with Shah Nawaz against the British
    (b) Hindus sympathised with P.K. Sehgal against the British
    (c) Sikhs sympathised with Gurbaksh Singh Dhillon against the British
    (d) Indians sympathised with the persons who were to be trialled

17. The majority of people waiting for trial outside the Red Fort and criticising Jinnah were the
(a) Hindus
(b) Muslims
(c) Sikhs
(d) Hindus and Muslims both

18. The sympathy of Indian soldiers in uniform with the released I.N.A. prisoners at Lahore indicates
(a) Feeling of Nationalism and Fraternity
(b) Rebellion nature of Indian soldiers
(c) Simply to participate in the reception party
(d) None of the above

19. The country which has the distinction of having the two largest circulated newspapers in the world is
(a) Great Britain
(b) The United States
(c) Japan
(d) China

20. The chronological order of non-verbal communication is
(a) Signs, symbols, codes, colours
(b) Symbols, codes, signs, colours
(c) Colours, signs, codes, symbols
(d) Codes, colours, symbols, signs

21. Which of the following statements is not connected with communication?
(a) Medium is the message.
(b) The world is an electronic cocoon.
(c) Information is power.
(d) Telepathy is technological.

22. Communication becomes circular when
(a) the decoder becomes an encoder
(b) the feedback is absent
(c) the source is credible
(d) the channel is clear

23. The site that played a major role during the terrorist attack on Mumbai (26/11) in 2008 was
(a) Orkut (b) Facebook
(c) Amazon.com (d) Twitter

24. **Assertion (A):** For an effective classroom communication at times it is desirable to use the projection technology.
Reason (R): Using the projection technology facilitates extensive coverage of course contents.
(a) Both (A) and (R) are true, and (R) is the correct explanation.
(b) Both (A) and (R) are true, but (R) is not the correct explanation.
(c) (A) is true, but (R) is false.
(d) (A) is false, but (R) is true.

25. January 1, 1995 was a Sunday. What day of the week lies on January 1, 1996?
(a) Sunday (b) Monday
(c) Wednesday (d) Saturday

26. When an error of 1% is made in the length and breadth of a rectangle, the percentage error (%) in the area of a rectangle will be
(a) 0 (b) 1
(c) 2 (d) 4

27. The next number in the series 2, 5, 9, 19, 37, ? will be
(a) 74 (b) 75
(c) 76 (d) None of these

28. There are 10 true-false questions in an examination. Then these questions can be answered in
(a) 20 ways (b) 100 ways
(c) 240 ways (d) 1024 ways

29. What will be the next term in the following?
DCXW, FEVU, HGTS, ?
(a) AKPO (b) ABYZ
(c) JIRQ (d) LMRS

30. Three individuals X, Y, Z hired a car on a sharing basis and paid ₹ 1,040. They used it for 7, 8, 11 hours, respectively.

What are the charges paid by Y?
(a) ₹ 290 (b) ₹ 320
(c) ₹ 360 (d) ₹ 440

31. Deductive argument involves
(a) sufficient evidence
(b) critical thinking
(c) seeing logical relations
(d) repeated observation

32. Inductive reasoning is based on or presupposes
(a) uniformity of nature
(b) God created the world
(c) unity of nature
(d) laws of nature

33. To be critical, thinking must be
(a) practical
(b) socially relevant
(c) individually satisfying
(d) analytical

34. Which of the following is an analogous statement?
(a) Man is like God
(b) God is great
(c) Gandhiji is the Father of the Nation
(d) Man is a rational being

Questions from 35-36 are based on the following diagram in which there are three intersecting circles. H representing The Hindu, I representing Indian Express and T representing The Times of India. A total of 50 persons were surveyed and the number in the Venn diagram indicates the number of persons reading the newspapers.

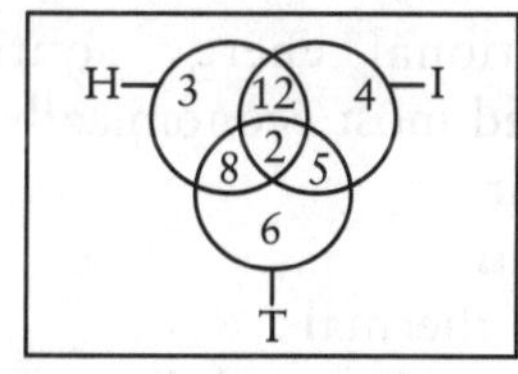

35. How many persons would be reading at least two newspapers?
(a) 23 (b) 25
(c) 27 (d) 29

36. How many persons would be reading almost two newspapers?
(a) 23 (b) 25
(c) 27 (d) 48

37. Which of the following graphs does not represent regular (periodic) behaviour of the variable f(t)?

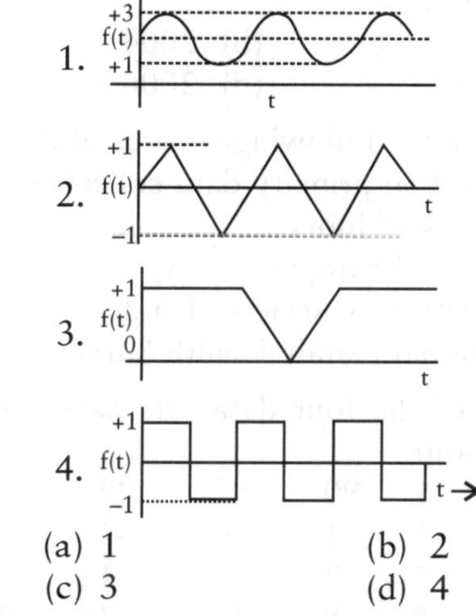

(a) 1 (b) 2
(c) 3 (d) 4

Study the following graph and answer the questions 38 to 40.

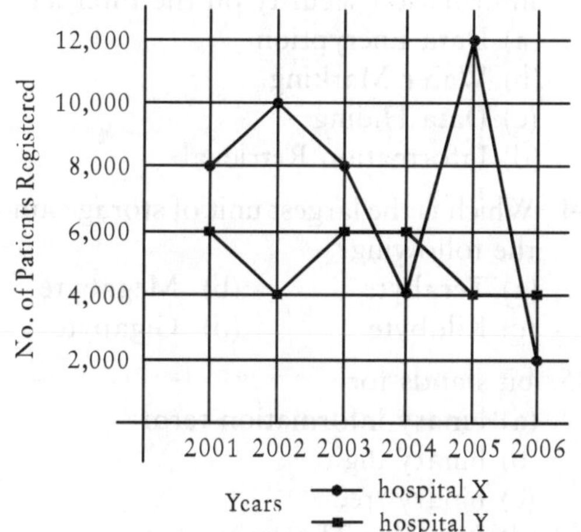

38. In which year total number of patients registered in hospital X and hospital Y was the maximum?

(a) 2003 (b) 2004
(c) 2005 (d) 2006

39. What is the maximum dispersion in the registration of patients in the two hospitals in a year?
(a) 8000 (b) 6000
(c) 4000 (d) 2000

40. In which year there was maximum decrease in registration of patients in hospital X?
(a) 2003 (b) 2004
(c) 2005 (d) 2006

41. Which of the following sources of data is not based on primary data collection?
(a) Census of India
(b) National Sample Survey
(c) Statistical Abstracts of India
(d) National Family Health Survey

42. Which of the four data sets have more dispersion?

(a) 88	91	90	92	89	91
(b) 0	1	1	0	–1	–2
(c) 3	5	2	4	1	5
(d) 0	5	8	10	–2	–8

43. Which of the following is not related to information security on the Internet?
(a) Data Encryption
(b) Water Marking
(c) Data Hiding
(d) Information Retrieval

44. Which is the largest unit of storage among the following?
(a) Terabyte (b) Megabyte
(c) Kilobyte (d) Gigabyte

45. bit stands for
(a) binary information term
(b) binary digit
(c) binary tree
(d) Bivariate Theory

46. Which one of the following is not a linear data structure?
(a) Array (b) Binary Tree
(c) Queue (d) Stack

47. Which one of the following is not a network device?
(a) Router (b) Switch
(c) Hub (d) CPU

48. A compiler is used to convert the following to object code which can be executed
(a) High-level language
(b) Low-level language
(c) Assembly language
(d) Natural language

49. The great Indian Bustard bird is found in
(a) Thar Desert of Rajasthan
(b) Malabar Coast
(c) Coastal regions of India
(d) Delta regions

50. The Sagarmanthan National Park has been established to preserve the eco-system of which mountain peak?
(a) Kanchenjunga (b) Mount Everest
(c) Annapurna (d) Dhaulavira

51. Maximum soot is released from
(a) Petrol vehicles
(b) CNG vehicles
(c) Diesel vehicles
(d) Thermal Power Plants

52. Surface Ozone is produced from
(a) Transport sector
(b) Cement plants
(c) Textile industry
(d) Chemical industry

53. Which one of the following non-conventional energy sources can be exploited most economically?
(a) Solar
(b) Wind
(c) Geo-thermal
(d) Ocean Thermal Energy Conversion (OTEC)

54. The most recurring natural hazard in India is
(a) Earthquakes (b) Floods
(c) Landslides (d) Volcanoes

55. The recommendation of National Knowledge Commission for the establishment of 1500 Universities is to
(a) create more teaching jobs
(b) ensure increase in student enrolment in higher education
(c) replace or substitute the privately managed higher education institutions by public institutions
(d) enable increased movement of students from rural areas to urban areas

56. According to Article 120 of the Constitution of India, the business in Parliament shall be transacted in
(a) Only English
(b) Only Hindi
(c) Both English and Hindi
(d) All the languages included in Eighth Schedule of the Constitution

57. Which of the following is more interactive and student centric?
(a) Seminar
(b) Workshop
(c) Lecture
(d) Group Discussion

58. The Parliament in India is composed of
(a) Lok Sabha and Rajya Sabha
(b) Lok Sabha, Rajya Sabha and Vice President
(c) Lok Sabha, Rajya Sabha and President
(d) Lok Sabha, Rajya Sabha with their Secretariats

59. The enrolment in higher education in India is contributed both by Formal System of Education and by System of Distance Education. Distance education contributes
(a) 50% of formal system
(b) 25% of formal system
(c) 10% of the formal system
(d) Distance education system's contribution is not taken into account while considering the figures of enrolment in higher education

60. **Assertion (A):** The UGC Academic Staff Colleges came into existence to improve the quality of teachers.
Reason (R): University and college teachers have to undergo both orientation and refresher courses.
(a) Both (A) and (R) are true and (R) is the correct explanation.
(b) Both (A) and (R) are correct but (R) is not the correct explanation of (A).
(c) (A) is correct and (R) is false.
(d) (A) is false and (R) is correct.

ANSWERS

1. (d)	2. (c)	3. (b)	4. (c)	5. (b)
6. (c)	7. (a)	8. (b)	9. (b)	10. (b)
11. (c)	12. (b)	13. (c)	14. (a)	15. (d)
16. (d)	17. (b)	18. (a)	19. (c)	20. (a)
21. (d)	22. (a)	23. (a)	24. (a)	25. (b)
26. (c)	27. (b)	28. (d)	29. (c)	30. (b)
31. (c)	32. (a)	33. (b)	34. (a)	35. (c)
36. (d)	37. (c)	38. (c)	39. (a)	40. (d)
41. (c)	42. (d)	43. (d)	44. (a)	45. (b)
46. (b)	47. (d)	48. (a)	49. (a)	50. (b)
51. (d)	52. (a)	53. (a)	54. (b)	55. (b)
56. (c)	57. (d)	58. (c)	59. (b)	60. (a)

PAPER–II

Note: This paper contains fifty (50) objective type questions, each question carrying two (2) marks. Attempt all the questions.

1. Which of the following stands for Lower Palaeolithic period?
   (a) Homo Habilis
   (b) Homo Sapiens
   (c) Homo Sapiens Sapiens
   (d) Australoid
2. Which of the following is associated with Palaeolithic period?
   (a) Crescent
   (b) Triangle
   (c) Polished Hand Axe
   (d) Acheulian Hand Axe
3. Which of the following represents Mesolithic period?
   (a) Ground tools (b) Olduwan
   (c) Clactonian (d) Microliths
4. Which of the following stands for Neolithic?
   (a) Scavenging
   (b) Gathering-Hunting
   (c) Food production
   (d) Pastoralism
5. Which of the following denotes permanent living?
   (a) Nomadism (b) Transhumance
   (c) Semi-sedentism (d) Sedentism
6. Match List I with List II and choose your answer from the codes given below:

   List I
   (A) Harappa Civilization
   (B) Aryans
   (C) Gautami Putra
   (D) Shravanabelgola

   List II
   (i) Spoked wheel
   (ii) Copper technology
   (iii) Jainism
   (iv) Satavahana

Codes:	A	B	C	D
(a)	(ii)	(iv)	(iii)	(i)
(b)	(iii)	(ii)	(iv)	(i)
(c)	(ii)	(i)	(iv)	(iii)
(d)	(iv)	(iii)	(i)	(ii)

7. Match List I with List II and choose your answer from the codes given below:

List I	List II
(A) Ayas	(i) Latin
(B) Aes	(ii) Sanskrit
(C) Ayari	(iii) English
(D) Iron	(iv) Avesta

Codes:	A	B	C	D
(a)	(ii)	(i)	(iv)	(iii)
(b)	(i)	(ii)	(iv)	(iii)
(c)	(ii)	(i)	(iii)	(iv)
(d)	(iii)	(ii)	(i)	(iv)

8. Match List I with List II and choose your answer from the codes given below:

List I	List II
(A) Vajji	(i) Indraprastha
(B) Chedi	(ii) Kausambi
(C) Vats	(iii) Vaishali
(D) Kuru	(iv) Shaktimati

Codes:	A	B	C	D
(a)	(iv)	(i)	(iii)	(ii)
(b)	(iii)	(iv)	(ii)	(i)
(c)	(i)	(iii)	(ii)	(iv)
(d)	(ii)	(iv)	(i)	(iii)

9. Match List I with List II and choose your answer from the codes given below:

   List I
   (A) Thirthankar
   (B) Kathasaritasagar
   (C) Bodhisatva
   (D) Brihtakathamanjri

List II

(i) Buddhism (ii) Jainism
(iii) Somadeva (iv) Ksheminder

Codes:	**A**	**B**	**C**	**D**
(a)	(ii)	(iii)	(i)	(iv)
(b)	(i)	(iv)	(iii)	(ii)
(c)	(iii)	(ii)	(iv)	(i)
(d)	(iv)	(i)	(ii)	(iii)

10. Match List I with List II and choose your answer from the codes given below:

List I

(A) Triratna
(B) Jataka
(C) Mudrarakshas
(D) Kathasaritasagar

List II

(i) Buddhism (ii) Jainism
(iii) Somadeva (iv) Vishakhadatt

Codes:	**A**	**B**	**C**	**D**
(a)	(ii)	(iii)	(iv)	(i)
(b)	(ii)	(i)	(iii)	(iv)
(c)	(iv)	(ii)	(i)	(iii)
(d)	(ii)	(i)	(iv)	(iii)

11. Given below are two statements, one labelled as Assertion (A) and the other labelled as Reason (R):

Assertion (A): The concept of 'Sarve Hitai and Sarve Sukhai' in Vedic Philosophy is for the upliftment of all the people.

Reason (R): It aims to work for the betterment of all human beings.

In the context of the above two statements, which of the following is correct?

(a) Both (A) and (R) are true.
(b) (A) is true but (R) is untrue.
(c) (A) is false but (R) is true.
(d) Both (A) and (R) are untrue.

12. Given below are two statements, one labelled as Assertion (A) and the other labelled as Reason (R):

Assertion (A): The concept of 'Bahujan Hitai and Bahujan Sukhai' in Buddhism is for the upliftment of the majority of the people.

Reason (R): It aims to relieve the majority of the population of its problems.

In the context of the above two statements, which of the following is correct?

(a) (A) is true but (R) is untrue.
(b) (R) is true but (A) is untrue.
(c) Both (A) and (R) are true.
(d) Both (R) and (A) are untrue.

13. Given below are two statements, one labelled as Assertion (A) and the other labelled as Reason (R):

Assertion (A): Kushana period was the golden age in ancient Indian history.

Reason (R): This period witnessed all round development.

In the context of the above two statements, which of the following is correct?

(a) (A) is true but (R) is false.
(b) (R) is true but (A) is false.
(c) Both (A) and (R) are false.
(d) Both (A) and (R) are true.

14. Given below are two statements, one labelled as Assertion (A) and the other labelled as Reason (R):

Assertion (A): Indian feudal system discouraged agriculture production.

Reason (R): It was enemical to agricultural growth.

In view of the above two statements, which of the following is correct?

(a) (A) is true but (R) is false.
(b) (R) is true but (A) is false.
(c) Both (A) and (R) are true.
(d) Both (A) and (R) are false.

15. Given below are two statements, one labelled as Assertion (A) and the other labelled as Reason (R):

Assertion (A): Pulkeshin-II defeated Harshvardhana.

Reason (R): He wanted to expand his empire in north India.

In the context of the above two statements, which of the following is correct?

(a) (A) is true but (R) is false.
(b) (R) is true but (A) is false.
(c) Both (A) and (R) are true.
(d) Both (A) and (R) are false.

16. Given below are two statements, one labelled as Assertion (A) and the other labelled as Reason (R):

Assertion (A): In spite of large and efficient army, Balban did not think of territorial expansion of his Sultanate.

Reason (R): Tughril's Revolt completely diverted his attention towards its suppression.

In the context of the above two statements, which one of the following is correct?

(a) Both (A) and (R) are true and (R) is the correct explanation of (A).
(b) Both (A) and (R) are true, but (R) is not the correct explanation of (A).
(c) (A) is true, but (R) is false.
(d) (R) is true, but (A) is false.

17. Which one of the following Sultans brought the Ashokan Pillar to Delhi?

(a) Giasuddin Tughlaq
(b) Muhammad-bin-Tughlaq
(c) Firoz Tughlaq
(d) Sikander Lodi

18. Who among the following in South India did not accept the sovereignty of Alauddin?

(a) Pandyas (b) Hoysalas
(c) Yadavas (d) Kakatiyas

19. Title of the book in which Amir Khusrau describes the political and social conditions of the reign of Qutubuddin Mubrak Shah is

(a) Kharzain-ul-Futuh
(b) Nuh-i-Siphar
(c) Mifta-ul-Futuh
(d) Tughlaq Nama

20. In Bahamani Kingdom, 'Sadre-i-Jahan' was the chief of which department?

(a) Religious and judicial
(b) Military
(c) Foreign
(d) Revenue including land revenue

21. What is the correct sequence of the following?

(i) Muntakhab-ul-Tawarikh
(ii) Kitab-ul-Hind
(iii) Muntakhab-ul-Lubab
(iv) Tabqat-i-Nasiri

Codes:

(a) i, iii, iv, ii (b) ii, iv, i, iii
(c) iv, iii, i, ii (d) iii, iv, ii, i

22. Vascodagama visited which one of the following ports?

(a) Goa (b) Madgoan
(c) Mangalore (d) Calicut

23. Given below are two statements, one labelled as Assertion (A) and the other labelled as Reason (R):

Assertion (A): The Chishti Silsila was the most prominent amongst the Sufi orders.

Reason (R): The Silsila had its sphere of influence in Rajasthan, Punjab, Bihar, Bengal, Orissa and the Deccan.

In the context of the above two statements, which one of the following is correct?

(a) Both (A) and (R) are true and (R) is the correct explanation of (A).
(b) Both (A) and (R) are true, but (R) is not the correct explanation of (A).
(c) (A) is true, but (R) is false.
(d) (R) is true, but (A) is false.

24. Struggle between Mughal forces with Maharana Pratap of Mewar which took place in June, 1576, has been described by Abul Fazal as the Battle of
(a) Haldighati (b) Gogunda
(c) Khamnor (d) Kumbhalgarh

25. Given below are two statements, one labelled as Assertion (A) and the other labelled as Reason (R):
Assertion (A): After five years of direct administration and experimentation, Akbar placed the lands of North India with the Mansabdars.
Reason (R): Akbar's treasuries obtained and augmented revenue from the new system.
In the context of the above two statements, which one of the following is correct?
(a) Both (A) and (R) are true and (R) is the correct explanation of (A).
(b) (A) is false but (R) is correct.
(c) (A) is correct but (R) is false.
(d) Both (A) and (R) are false.

26. The 'du-aspa' and 'Seh-aspa' rank was first introduced during the reign of
(a) Akbar (b) Jahangir
(c) Shajahan (d) Aurangzeb

27. 'Pietra-dura' technique of surface ornamentation was first adopted in
(a) Itimad-ud-Daula's Tomb
(b) Taj Mahal
(c) Diwan-e-Am (Red Fort, Delhi)
(d) Moti Masjid (Agra Fort)

28. On whom Jahangir conferred the title of Nadir-ul-Jama?
(a) Abul Hassan (b) Mansur
(c) Basant (d) Giasuddin Beg

29. Which was the most important commodity exported from India in the 17th Century?
(a) Spices (b) Cotton textile
(c) Indigo (d) Saltpetre

30. Given below are two statements, one labelled as Assertion (A) and the other labelled as Reason (R):
Assertion (A): By 1750 A.D., Peshwa became all powerful in Maratha Kingdom.
Reason (R): Peshwas shifted their head-quarter from Satara to Pune.
In the context of the above two statements, which one of the following is correct?
Codes:
(a) (A) is correct, but (R) is wrong.
(b) Both (A) and (R) are correct, but (R) is not the correct explanation of (A).
(c) (A) is wrong, but (R) is correct.
(d) Both (A) and (R) are wrong.

31. The Permanent Settlement was made with the
(a) Zamindars
(b) Peasant Cultivators
(c) Village Communities
(d) Muqaddams

32. Parsi Social Reformer Behramji M. Malabari carried on his campaign against
(a) Infant and Child Marriage
(b) Polygamy
(c) Female Infanticide
(d) Widow remarriage

33. Which tribal leader was regarded as an incarnation of God and Father of the World (Dharti Aba)?
(a) Kanhu Santha (b) Rupa Naik
(c) Birsa Munda (d) Joria Bhagat

34. Who said "The British rule was a bleeding drain from India"?
(a) Dadabhai Naoroji
(b) M.G. Ranade
(c) R.C. Dutt
(d) Bal Gangadhar Tilak

35. A leading British Parliamentarian and Politician admitted that the Revolt of 1857 was a 'National Revolt' not a 'Military Mutiny'.
(a) Lord Dalhousie
(b) Lord Canning
(c) William Gladstone
(d) Benjamin Disraeli

36. Which social reformer of Maharashtra became famous by the name of 'Lokhitwadi'?
(a) Atmaram Pandurang
(b) Bal Gangadhar Tilak
(c) Gopal Hari Deshmukh
(d) Gopal Krishna Gokhale

37. Raja Ram Mohan Roy raised his voice and agitated against which evil custom and practice?
(a) Caste Custom
(b) Kulinism
(c) Sati Pratha
(d) Widow remarriage

38. Who was not associated with the Aligarh Movement?
(a) Altaf Hussain Hali
(b) Nazir Ahmad
(c) Maulana Abul Kalam Azad
(d) Chiragh Ali

39. The Journal *Bahishkrit Bharat* was started by
(a) Jyotiba Phule
(b) Dr. B.R. Ambedkar
(c) M.K. Gandhi
(d) Karsandas Mulji

40. Who took over the leadership of the Brahmo Samaj after the death of Raja Ram Mohan Roy?
(a) Dwarka Nath Tagore
(b) Keshav Chandra Sen
(c) Devendra Nath Tagore
(d) Ram Chandra Vidya Vagish

41. Who made the greatest contribution in organizing the Kisan Sabha Movement?
(a) N.G. Ranga
(b) Vallabh Bhai Patel
(c) Jawaharlal Nehru
(d) Swami Sahjanand Saraswati

42. An Indian revolutionary who was a Professor of Sanskrit and Philosophy in the Universities of Berkeley and Stanford died in Philadelphia
(a) Shyamji Krishna Verma
(b) Lala Har Dayal
(c) Tarak Nath Das
(d) Bhai Parmanand

43. Under the 'Old Guarantee System' the British Companies investing in railways were assured a guarantee of
(a) 3 % (b) 5 %
(c) 8 % (d) 10 %

44. Who argued that de-industrialization did not take place in India in the colonial period?
(a) Bipan Chandra
(b) Amiyo Baghchi
(c) Anil Seal
(d) Morris D. Morris

45. Which Princely State resembled 'Ramrajya' according to Gandhiji?
(a) Baroda (b) Gwalior
(c) Mysore (d) Patiala

46. Arrange the following events in chronological order:
I. Indian States Commission
II. Round Table Conference
III. Establishment of All India States People's Conference
IV. First Justice Party Government
(a) IV, III, I, II
(b) III, I, IV, II
(c) I, IV, III, II
(d) II, III, IV, I

47. During Renaissance the interest in the study of Graeco-Roman Classics came to be known as
(a) Individualism (b) Hedonism
(c) Romanticism (d) Humanism

48. Bandung Conference relates to
(a) Nazism (b) Non-alignment
(c) Apartheid (d) Imperialism

49. Calvinists in France were known as
(a) Puritans (b) Presbyterians
(c) Huguenots (d) Catholics

50. Who was the first Greek Historian?
(a) Thucydides (b) Herodotus
(c) Homer (d) Megasthenes

ANSWERS

1. (c)	2. (b)	3. (d)	4. (c)	5. (d)
6. (c)	7. (a)	8. (b)	9. (a)	10. (d)
11. (a)	12. (c)	13. (b)	14. (a)	15. (a)
16. (b)	17. (c)	18. (c)	19. (b)	20. (a)
21. (b)	22. (d)	23. (a)	24. (b)	25. (d)
26. (b)	27. (a)	28. (a)	29. (b)	30. (c)
31. (a)	32. (a)	33. (c)	34. (a)	35. (d)
36. (c)	37. (c)	38. (c)	39. (b)	40. (c)
41. (d)	42. (b)	43. (b)	44. (d)	45. (a)
46. (a)	47. (d)	48. (d)	49. (c)	50. (b)

JUNE–2009

Note: This paper contains fifty (50) objective type questions, each question carrying two (2) marks. Attempt all the questions.

PAPER–I

1. Good evaluation of written material should not be based on
   (a) Linguistic expression
   (b) Logical presentation
   (c) Ability to reproduce whatever is read
   (d) Comprehension of subject

2. Why do teachers use teaching aid?
   (a) To make teaching fun-filled
   (b) To teach within understanding level of students
   (c) For students' attention
   (d) To make students attentive

3. Attitudes, concepts, skills and knowledge are products of
   (a) Learning (b) Research
   (c) Heredity (d) Explanation

4. Which among the following gives more freedom to the learner to interact?
   (a) Use of film
   (b) Small group discussion
   (c) Lectures by experts
   (d) Viewing country-wide classroom program on TV

5. Which of the following is not a product of learning?
   (a) Attitudes (b) Concepts
   (c) Knowledge (d) Maturation

6. How can the objectivity of the research be enhanced?
   (a) Through its impartiality
   (b) Through its reliability
   (c) Through its validity
   (d) All of these

7. Action-research is
   (a) An applied research
   (b) A research carried out to solve immediate problems
   (c) A longitudinal research
   (d) All the above

8. The basis on which assumptions are formulated
   (a) Cultural background of the country
   (b) Universities
   (c) Specific characteristics of the castes
   (d) All of these

9. Which of the following is classified in the category of the developmental research?
   (a) Philosophical research
   (b) Action research
   (c) Descriptive research
   (d) All the above

10. We use Factorial Analysis
    (a) To know the relationship between two variables
    (b) To test the Hypothesis
    (c) To know the difference between two variables
    (d) To know the difference among the many variables

Read the following passage and answer the questions 11 to 15:

While the British rule in India was detrimental to the economic development of the country, it did help in starting of the process of modernising Indian society and formed several progressive institutions during that process. One of the most beneficial institutions, which were initiated by the British, was democracy. Nobody can dispute that despite its many shortcomings, democracy was and is far better alternative to the arbitrary rule of the rajas and nawabs, which prevailed in India in the pre-British days.

However, one of the harmful traditions of British democracy inherited by India was that of conflict instead of cooperation between elected members. This was its essential feature. The party, which got the support of the majority of elected members, formed the Government while the others constituted a standing opposition. The existence of the opposition to those in power was and is regarded as a hallmark of democracy.

In principle, democracy consists of rule by the people; but where direct rule is not possible, it's rule by persons elected by the people. It is natural that there would be some differences of opinion among the elected members as in the rest of the society.

Normally, members of any organisations have differences of opinion between themselves on different issues but they manage to work on the basis of a consensus and they do not normally form a division between some who are in majority and are placed in power, while treating the others as in opposition.

The members of an organisation usually work on consensus. Consensus simply means that after an adequate discussion, members agree that the majority opinion may prevail for the time being. Thus persons who form a majority on one issue and whose opinion is allowed to prevail may not be on the same side if there is a difference on some other issue.

It was largely by accident that instead of this normal procedure, a two-party system came to prevail in Britain and that is now being generally taken as the best method of democratic rule.

Many democratically inclined persons in India regret that such a two-party system was not brought about in the country. It appears that to have two parties in India—of more or less equal strength—is a virtual impossibility. Those who regret the absence of a two-party system should take the reasons into consideration.

When the two-party system got established in Britain, there were two groups among the rules (consisting of a limited electorate) who had the same economic interests among themselves and who therefore formed two groups within the selected members of Parliament.

There were members of the British aristocracy (which landed interests and consisting of lord, barons, etc.) and members of the new commercial class consisting of merchants and artisans. These groups were more or less of equal strength and they were able to establish their separate rule at different times.

Answer the following questions:

11. In pre-British period, when India was ruled by the independent rulers
    (a) Peace and prosperity prevailed in the society
    (b) People were isolated from political affairs
    (c) Public opinion was inevitable for policy making
    (d) Law was equal for one and all

12. What is the distinguishing feature of the democracy practised in Britain?
    (a) End to the rule of might is right.
    (b) Rule of the people, by the people and for the people.
    (c) It has stood the test of time.
    (d) Cooperation between elected members.

13. Democracy is practised where
    (a) Elected members form a uniform opinion regarding policy matter.
    (b) Opposition is more powerful than the ruling combine.
    (c) Representatives of masses.
    (d) None of these.
14. Which of the following is true about the British rule in India?
    (a) It was behind the modernisation of the Indian society.
    (b) India gained economically during that period.
    (c) Various establishments were formed for the purpose of progress.
    (d) None of these.
15. Who became the members of the new commercial class during that time?
    (a) British Aristocrats
    (b) Lord and Barons
    (c) Political Persons
    (d) Merchants and Artisans
16. Which one of the following Telephonic Conferencing with a radio link is very popular throughout the world?
    (a) TPS (b) Telepresence
    (c) Video conference (d) Video teletext
17. Which is not 24 hours news channel?
    (a) NDTV 24×7
    (b) ZEE News
    (c) Aajtak
    (d) Lok Sabha Channel
18. The main objective of FM station in radio is
    (a) Information, Entertainment and Tourism
    (b) Entertainment, Information and Interaction
    (c) Tourism, Interaction and Entertainment
    (d) Entertainment only
19. In communication chatting on internet is
    (a) Verbal communication
    (b) Non-verbal communication
    (c) Parallel communication
    (d) Grapevine communication
20. Match List I with List II and select the correct answer using the codes given below:

    List I (Artists)

    A. Pandit Jasraj B. Kishan Maharaj
    C. Ravi Shankar D. Udai Shankar

    List II (Art)

    1. Hindustani vocalist
    2. Sitar
    3. Tabla
    4. Dance

Codes:	A	B	C	D
(a)	1	2	3	4
(b)	1	3	4	2
(c)	1	3	2	4
(d)	3	2	1	4

21. Insert the missing number in the following.
    3, 8, 18, 23, 33, ?, 48
    (a) 37 (b) 40
    (c) 38 (d) 45
22. In a certain code, CLOCK is written as KCOLC. How would STEPS be written in that code?
    (a) SPEST (b) SPSET
    (c) SPETS (d) SEPTS
23. The letters in the first set have a certain relationship. On the basis of this relationship mark the right choice for the second set
    BDFH : OMKI :: GHIK : ?
    (a) FHJL (b) RPNL
    (c) LNPR (d) LJHF
24. What was the day of the week on 1st January 2001?
    (a) Friday (b) Monday
    (c) Sunday (d) Wednesday

25. Find out the wrong number in the sequence.
52, 51, 48, 43, 34, 27, 16
(a) 27 (b) 34
(c) 43 (d) 48

26. In a deductive argument conclusion is
(a) Summing up of the premises
(b) Not necessarily based on premises
(c) Entailed by the premises
(d) Additional to the premises

27. 'No man are mortal' is contradictory of
(a) Some man are mortal
(b) Some man are not mortal
(c) All men are mortal
(d) No mortal is man

28. A deductive argument is valid if
(a) premises are false and conclusion is true
(b) premises are false and conclusion is also false
(c) premises are true and conclusion is false
(d) premises are true and conclusion is true

29. Structure of logical argument is based on
(a) Formal validity
(b) Material truth
(c) Linguistic expression
(d) Aptness of examples

30. Two ladies and two men are playing bridge and seated at North, East, South and West of a table. No lady is facing East. Persons sitting opposite to each other are not of the same sex. One man is facing South. Which direction are the ladies facing to?
(a) East and West
(b) North and West
(c) South and East
(d) None of these

Questions 31 and 32 are based on the following venn diagram in which there are three intersecting circles representing Hindi knowing persons, English knowing persons and persons who are working as teachers. Different regions so obtained in the figure are marked as a, b, c, d, e, f and g.

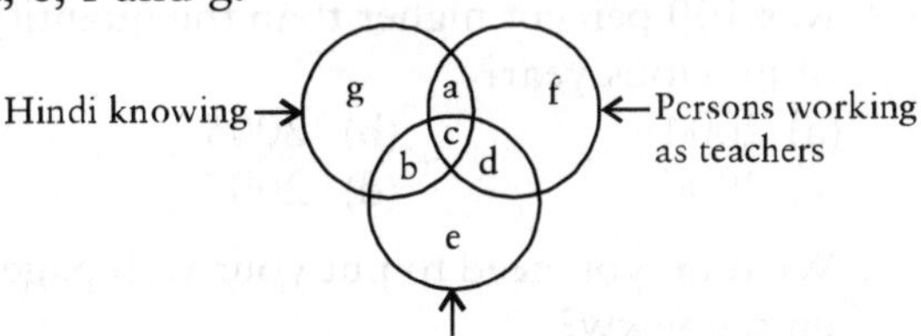

31. If you want to select Hindi and English knowing teachers, which of the following is to be selected?
(a) g (b) b
(c) c (d) e

32. If you want to select persons, who do not know English and are not teachers, which of the region is to be selected?
(a) e (b) g
(c) b (d) a

Study the following graph carefully and answer questions 33 to 35.

Export of Engineering Goods

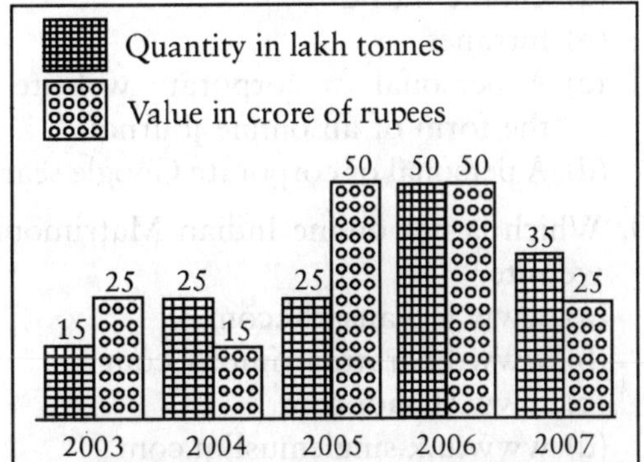

33. In which year the quantity of engineering goods' exports was maximum?
(a) 2005 (b) 2006
(c) 2004 (d) 2007

34. In which year the value of engineering goods decreased by 50 percent compared to the previous year?
(a) 2004 (b) 2007
(c) 2005 (d) 2006

35. In which year the quantity of exports was 100 percent higher than the quantity of previous year?
(a) 2004 (b) 2005
(c) 2006 (d) 2007

36. What do you need to put your web pages on the www?
(a) a connection to internet
(b) a web browser
(c) a web server
(d) All of the above

37. Which was the first company to launch mobile phone services in India?
(a) Essar (b) BPL
(c) Hutchison (d) Airtel

38. Chandrayan I was launched on 22nd October, 2008 in India from
(a) Bangalore (b) Sri Harikota
(c) Chennai (d) Ahmedabad

39. What is blog?
(a) Online music
(b) Intranet
(c) A personal or corporate website in the form of an online journal
(d) A personal or corporate Google search

40. Which is not online Indian Matrimonial website?
(a) www.jeevansathi.com
(b) www.bharatmatrimony.com
(c) www.shaadi.com
(d) www.u.k.singlemuslim.com

41. Environmental impact assessment is an objective analysis of the probable changes in
(a) physical characteristics of the environment
(b) biophysical characteristics of the environment
(c) socio-economic characteristics of the environment
(d) All the above

42. Bog is a wetland that receives water from
(a) nearby water bodies
(b) melting
(c) Only rainfall
(d) Only sea

43. Which of the following region is in the very high risk zone of earthquakes?
(a) Central Indian Highland
(b) Coastal region
(c) Himalayan region
(d) Indian desert

44. Match List I with List II and select the correct answer using the codes given below.

List I (Institutes)
A. Central Arid Zone Institute
B. Space Application Centre
C. Indian Institute of Public Administration
D. Headquarters of Indian Science Congress

List II (Cities)
1. Kolkata 2. New Delhi
3. Ahmedabad 4. Jodhpur

Codes:	A	B	C	D
(a)	4	3	2	1
(b)	4	2	1	3
(c)	3	1	2	4
(d)	1	2	4	3

45. Indian coastal areas experienced Tsunami disaster in the year
(a) 2005 (b) 2004
(c) 2006 (d) 2007

46. The Kothari Commission's report was entitled on
(a) Education and National Development
(b) Learning to be adventure

(c) Diversification of Education
(d) Education and socialisation in democracy

47. Which of the following is not a Dualmode University?
(a) Delhi University
(b) Bangalore University
(c) Madras University
(d) Indira Gandhi National Open University

48. Which part of the Constitution of India is known as "Code of Administrators"?
(a) Part I (b) Part II
(c) Part III (d) Part IV

49. Which article of the constitution provides safeguards to Naga Customary and their social practices against any act of Parliament?
(a) Article 371 A (b) Article 371 B
(c) Article 371 C (d) Article 263

50. Which one of the following is not the tool of good governance?
(a) Right to Information
(b) Citizens' Charter
(c) Social Auditing
(d) Judicial Activism

ANSWERS

1. (a)	2. (a)	3. (a)	4. (b)	5. (d)
6. (d)	7. (b)	8. (a)	9. (d)	10. (d)
11. (b)	12. (d)	13. (a)	14. (c)	15. (a)
16. (b)	17. (d)	18. (b)	19. (b)	20. (c)
21. (c)	22. (c)	23. (b)	24. (b)	25. (b)
26. (c)	27. (c)	28. (d)	29. (b)	30. (b)
31. (c)	32. (b)	33. (b)	34. (b)	35. (c)
36. (d)	37. (d)	38. (b)	39. (c)	40. (d)
41. (d)	42. (a)	43. (b)	44. (a)	45. (b)
46. (a)	47. (d)	48. (d)	49. (a)	50. (d)

PAPER-II

Note: This paper contains fifty (50) multiple-choice questions, each question carrying two (2) marks. Attempt all of them.

1. Which of the following is not associated with Palaeolithic?
(a) Mongoloid
(b) Homo sapiens
(c) Homo sapiens sapiens
(d) Homo erectus

2. Which of the following is not associated with Mesolithic?
(a) Hunting - gathering
(b) Domestication of animals
(c) Domestication of plants
(d) Horticulture

3. Which of the following is not associated with New Stone age?
(a) Domestication of plants
(b) Iron
(c) Sedentary life
(d) Early village settlements

4. Which of the following is not associated with the first Urbanization?
(a) Town Planning (b) Citadel
(c) Defence wall (d) Coins

5. Which of the following is not associated with Megaliths?
(a) Pastoralism
(b) Ash mounds
(c) Iron tools
(d) Institutional trade

6. Match List I with List II and choose your answer from the codes given below:

List I	List II
(A) Uttarapath	(i) Pratisthan
(B) Kalinga	(ii) Taxila
(C) Satavahana	(iii) Mahismati
(D) Avanti	(iv) Tosali

Codes:	A	B	C	D
(a)	(ii)	(iv)	(i)	(iii)
(b)	(iii)	(ii)	(iv)	(i)
(c)	(iv)	(iii)	(ii)	(i)
(d)	(i)	(iv)	(iii)	(ii)

7. Match List I with List II and choose your answer from the codes given below:

List I

(A) Indika (B) Harshacharita
(C) Prithwiraj Raso (D) Rajatarangini

List II

(i) Banabhatta (ii) Chandbardai
(iii) Megasthanese (iv) Kalhana

Codes:	A	B	C	D
(a)	(iv)	(iii)	(i)	(ii)
(b)	(iii)	(i)	(ii)	(iv)
(c)	(ii)	(iv)	(iii)	(i)
(d)	(i)	(ii)	(iv)	(iii)

8. Match List I with List II and choose your answer from the codes given below:

List I

(A) Junagarh Inscription
(B) Iron pillar Inscription
(C) Banskhera Inscription
(D) Aihole Inscription

List II

(i) Harshavardhana
(ii) Pushyagupta
(iii) Chandergupta–II
(iv) Pulkeshin–II

Codes:	A	B	C	D
(a)	(ii)	(iii)	(i)	(iv)
(b)	(i)	(ii)	(iv)	(iii)
(c)	(iii)	(iv)	(ii)	(i)
(d)	(iv)	(i)	(ii)	(iii)

9. Match List I with List II and choose your answer from the codes given below:

List I	List II
(A) Anga	(i) Giribraj
(B) Magadha	(ii) Champa
(C) Kosal	(iii) Vaishali
(D) Vajji	(iv) Shravasti

Codes:	A	B	C	D
(a)	(ii)	(i)	(iv)	(iii)
(b)	(i)	(iii)	(ii)	(iv)
(c)	(iii)	(iv)	(i)	(ii)
(d)	(iv)	(ii)	(iii)	(i)

10. Match List I with List II and choose your answer from the codes given below:

List I	List II
(A) Pallava	(i) Praversen
(B) Ikshavaku	(ii) Ishwardatt
(C) Abhir	(iii) Dhanyakatak
(D) Vakataka	(iv) Kanchipuram

Codes:	A	B	C	D
(a)	(iv)	(iii)	(ii)	(i)
(b)	(iii)	(ii)	(i)	(iv)
(c)	(iv)	(ii)	(iii)	(i)
(d)	(ii)	(i)	(iv)	(iii)

11. Given below are two statements, one labelled as Assertion (A) and the other labelled as Reason (R):

Assertion (A): Second urbanisation in India was caused by the use of iron technology.

Reason (R): Iron technology was the moving force.

In the context of the above two statements which of the following is correct?

(a) (A) is true but (R) is untrue
(b) (R) is true but (A) is untrue
(c) Both (A) and (R) are true
(d) Both (A) and (R) are untrue

12. Given below are two statements, one labelled as Assertion (A) and the other labelled as Reason (R):

Assertion (A): The punch marked coins were inscribed in Brahami Script.

Reason (R): It facilitated trade.

In context of the above two statements which of the following is correct?

(a) (A) is true but (R) is false
(b) (R) is true but (A) is false
(c) Both (A) and (R) are true
(d) Both (A) and (R) are false

13. Given below are two statements, one labelled as Assertion (A) and the other labelled as Reason (R):
Assertion (A): Sangam literature is a 'Sanskrit Kavya'.
Reason (R): It offers information on the social conditions.
In view of the above two statements which of the following is correct?
(a) (A) is true but (R) is false
(b) (A) is false but (R) is true
(c) Both (A) and (R) are false
(d) Both (A) and (R) are true

14. Given below are two statements, one labelled as Assertion (A) and the other labelled as Reason (R):
Assertion (A): Gupta period witnessed growth of literary writings.
Reason (R): Overall conditions were conducive to such a development.
In the context of the above two statements which of the following is true?
(a) (A) is true but (R) is false
(b) (R) is true but (A) is false
(c) Both (A) and (R) are false
(d) Both (A) and (R) are true

15. Given below are two statements, one labelled as Assertion (A) and the other labelled as Reason (R):
Assertion (A): Tripartite struggle was the political struggle for the Supremacy of north India.
Reason (R): This was essential.
In the context of the above two statements which of the following is correct?
(a) (A) is true but (R) is false
(b) (A) is false but (R) is true
(c) Both (A) and (R) are false
(d) Both (A) and (R) are true

16. Given below are two statements, one labelled as Assertion (A) and the other labelled as Reason (R):
Assertion (A): Iltutmish was not a usurper.
Reason (R): There was nothing to be usurped.
In the context of the above two statements, which of the following is correct?
(a) Both (A) and (R) are true and (R) is the correct explanation of (A)
(b) Both (A) and (R) are true but (R) is not the correct explanation of (A)
(c) (A) is true, but (R) is false
(d) (A) is false, but (R) is true

17. The post of Diwan-i-Mustkharaj was created by which of the following Sultans?
(a) Alauddin Khalji
(b) Ghiyasuddin Balban
(c) Razia
(d) Ibrahim Lodi

18. 'Pushti Marg' was founded by:
(a) Chaitanya
(b) Vallabhacharya
(c) Ramanand
(d) Nimabark

19. Match List I of rulers with List II of travellers and choose your answer from the code below:
List I (Rulers)
(A) Devaraya I
(B) Devaraya II
(C) Krishna Devaraya
(D) Achyuta Devarayalu

List II (Travellers)
(i) Domingo Paes
(ii) Abdul Razak
(iii) Nichlo-De-Conti
(iv) Ferno Nuniz

Codes:	**A**	**B**	**C**	**D**
(a)	(iii)	(ii)	(i)	(iv)
(b)	(ii)	(iv)	(iii)	(i)
(c)	(iii)	(i)	(ii)	(iv)
(d)	(i)	(iii)	(ii)	(iv)

20. Given below are two statements, one labelled as Assertion (A) and the other labelled as Reason (R):

Assertion (A): Mughals failed to reconstitute the agrarain system of Western Deccan.

Reason (R): Decades of Mughal campaign on Ahmadnagar, Khandesh and Bijapur weakened their authority on Western Deccan.

In the context of the above two statements which one of the following is correct?

(a) Both (A) and (R) are true and (R) is the correct explanation of (A)
(b) Both (A) and (R) are true, but (R) is not the correct explanation of (A)
(c) (A) is true, but (R) is false
(d) (R) is true, but (A) is false

21. In 1595–96 the Mughal Mansabdars were classified into:

(a) 6 groups (b) 5 groups
(c) 4 groups (d) 3 groups

22. Match List I with List II and choose your answer from the code below:

List I (Battles)
(A) Battle of Rajmahal
(B) Second Battle of Panipat
(C) Battle of Khanwa
(D) Battle of Ghagara

List II (Year of the Battles)
(i) 1527 A.D. (ii) 1529 A.D.
(iii) 1556 A.D. (iv) 1576 A.D.

Codes:	**A**	**B**	**C**	**D**
(a)	(ii)	(iii)	(i)	(iv)
(b)	(iv)	(i)	(ii)	(iii)
(c)	(iii)	(iv)	(i)	(ii)
(d)	(iv)	(iii)	(i)	(ii)

23. Match List I with List II and choose your answer from the code below:

List I (Writers)
(A) Nizamuddin Ahmad
(B) Ali Muhammad Khan
(C) Gul Badan Begam
(D) Ibn Batuta

List II (Works)
(i) Humayun Nama
(ii) Mirat-i-Ahmadi
(iii) Tabqat-i-Akbari
(iv) Rahela

Codes:	**A**	**B**	**C**	**D**
(a)	(iii)	(ii)	(i)	(iv)
(b)	(iv)	(i)	(ii)	(iii)
(c)	(i)	(iv)	(iii)	(ii)
(d)	(iii)	(ii)	(iv)	(i)

24. Who was the ruler of Mewar at the time of Akbar's attack on Chittor in 1567-1568 A.D.?

(a) Rana Sanga
(b) Rana Udai Singh
(c) Maharana Pratap
(d) Rana Amar Singh

25. Match List I with List II and select the correct answer from the code given below:

List I
(A) R.P. Tripathi
(B) Ishwari Prasad
(C) K.S. Lal
(D) Agha Mehdi Husain

List II
(i) Tughlaq Dynasty
(ii) Twilight of the Delhi Sultanate
(iii) Some Aspects of Muslim Administration
(iv) History of Qarauna Turks

Codes:	A	B	C	D
(a)	(iii)	(iv)	(ii)	(i)
(b)	(ii)	(i)	(iii)	(iv)
(c)	(iv)	(ii)	(i)	(iii)
(d)	(i)	(iii)	(ii)	(iv)

26. Main export commodity of Vijayanagar Kingdom was....
(a) Black pepper (b) Textiles
(c) Salt (d) Silk

27. What is the correct chronological sequence of the following Peshwas?
(i) Bajirao I
(ii) Balaji Vishwanath
(iii) Balaji Bajirao
(iv) Madhavarao

Codes:
(a) (i) (iii) (ii) (iv)
(b) (iv) (ii) (i) (iii)
(c) (ii) (i) (iii) (iv)
(c) (iii) (iv) (i) (ii)

28. The south Indian city famous for Inlay work during medieval period was:
(a) Tanjore (b) Bidar
(c) Bijapur (d) Hampi

29. What was the sequence of the establishment of factories in India by the following European powers? Choose your answer from the code given below:
(i) English (ii) French
(iii) Dutch (iv) Portuguese

Codes:
(a) (iv) (iii) (i) (ii)
(b) (i) (iii) (ii) (iv)
(c) (ii) (iv) (i) (iii)
(d) (iii) (i) (iv) (ii)

30. 'Nishan' documents are defined as:
(a) Letters written in the name of Mughal princes
(b) Letters written in the name of Mughal Emperor
(c) Letters sent by the Mughal officials
(d) Letters sent by the ruler to another ruler

31. The Ryotwari settlement was made with the:
(a) Zamindars
(b) Cultivators
(c) Village communities
(d) Muqaddams

32. Who remarked in 1834 that "The bones of the cotton weavers are bleaching the plains of India"?
(a) Lord Macaulay
(b) Lord William Bentinck
(c) Dadabhai Naoroji
(d) Raja Ram Mohan Ray

33. The highest British Capital Investment in India was made in the:
(a) Tea, Coffee and the Indigo Plantation.
(b) Railways, Banking, Insurance and Shipping
(c) Cotton Textile Industry.
(d) Jute Mills.

34. Who was the first to formulate theory of three successive phases of British Colonialism in India namely, Mercantilist, Free Trade, Mercantile Capitalism and Finance Imperialism?
(a) Dadabhai Naoroji
(b) R.C. Dutt
(c) R.P. Dutt
(d) Karl Marx

35. In 1920 the All India Trade Union Congress was organized by:
(a) B.P. Wadia
(b) Mahatma Gandhi
(c) N.M. Joshi
(d) Jawaharlal Nehru

36. Who was the greatest Parsi Social Reformer of the 19th century?
(a) Jamsetji Tata
(b) Rustom Behramji
(c) Behramji M. Malabari
(d) Pheroz Shah Mehta

37. Which modern historian opined that the "so called first national war of independence was neither first, nor national, nor a war of independence"?
(a) S.N. Sen (b) Tarachand
(c) R.C. Majumdar (d) K.K. Dutta

38. Who gave the call—"One religion, one caste and one God for mankind"?
(a) Jyotiba Phule
(b) Swami Vivekanand
(c) Shri Narayana Guru
(d) Periyar Ramaswami Naikar

39. Who was a bitter critic of Sir Syed Ahmad Khan's ideas and the Aligarh movement?
(a) Chiragh Ali
(b) Altaf Hussain Hali
(c) Nazir Ahmad
(d) Jamaluddin Afghani

40. The two greatest pioneers in the cause of widow's education were:
(a) D.K. Karve and Pandita Ramabai
(b) M.G. Ranade and R.G. Bhandarkar
(c) Ishwar Chandra Vidya Sagar and Keshav Chandrasen
(d) B.M. Malabari and K. Sridharlu Naidu

41. Who argued that the Khilafat Movement was a result of the emergence of a 'middle class' among Indian Muslims?
(a) Francis Robinson
(b) W.C. Smith
(c) Mushirul Hasan
(d) Mohd. Mujeeb

42. In the Ahemdabad Mill strike of 1917 Mahatma Gandhi's intervention resulted in the enhancement of wages for the workers by:
(a) 25% (b) 35%
(c) 45% (d) 55%

43. Chittagong Armoury Raid was Organized under the leadership of:
(a) Jatin Das
(b) Surya Sen
(c) Ganesh Ghosh
(d) Khudiram Bose

44. Who was the first President of the Harijan Sevak Sangha founded by Mahatma Gandhi?
(a) G.D. Birla
(b) Mahadev Desai
(c) Amritlal Thakkar
(d) Dr. B.R. Ambedkar

45. Who amongst the following was chosen as Dewan of three princely states - Mysore, Jaipur and Hyderabad?
(a) M. Vishweshraya
(b) C.P. Ramaswami Iyer
(c) V.P. Madhava Rao
(d) Mirza Ismail

46. Adyar was the famous centre and headquarter of the:
(a) Aurobindo Ashram
(b) Madras Mahajan Sabha
(c) Theosophical Society
(d) Ramakrishna Mission

47. Who called commerce is a perpetual war of wit and energy among all nations?
(a) Jean Bodin
(b) Jean Baptist Colbert
(c) Thomas Mun
(d) Thomas Hobbes

48. Whiteman's burden was theory of:
(a) Humanism
(b) Imperialism
(c) Non-alignment
(d) Socialism

49. Who amongst the following belongs to the sub-altern school of historiography?
(a) Bipan Chandra
(b) Romila Thapar
(c) Ranjit Guha
(d) Ramchandra Guha

50. Who was universally acclaimed as the Prince of the Humanists?
(a) Erasmus
(b) John Colet
(c) Thomas More
(d) Francisco Petrarch

ANSWERS

1. (d)	2. (d)	3. (b)	4. (d)	5. (d)
6. (a)	7. (b)	8. (a)	9. (a)	10. (a)
11. (c)	12. (b)	13. (b)	14. (d)	15. (a)
16. (b)	17. (a)	18. (b)	19. (a)	20. (d)
21. (d)	22. (d)	23. (a)	24. (b)	25. (a)
26. (b)	27. (c)	28. (a)	29. (a)	30. (a)
31. (b)	32. (b)	33. (a)	34. (d)	35. (c)
36. (c)	37. (c)	38. (c)	39. (d)	40. (a)
41. (c)	42. (b)	43. (b)	44. (a)	45. (b)
46. (c)	47. (b)	48. (b)	49. (c)	50. (a)

DECEMBER–2008

Note: This paper contains fifty (50) objective type questions, each question carrying two (2) marks. Attempt all the questions.

PAPER–I

1. According to Swami Vivekananda, teacher's success depends on
   (a) His renunciation of personal gain and service to others
   (b) His professional training and creativity
   (c) His concentration on his work and duties with a spirit of obedience to God
   (d) His mastery on the subject and capacity in controlling the students
2. Which of the following teacher will be liked most?
   (a) A teacher of high idealistic attitude
   (b) A loving teacher
   (c) A teacher who is disciplined
   (d) A teacher who often amuses his students
3. A teacher's most important challenge is
   (a) To make students do their home work
   (b) To make teaching-learning process enjoyable
   (c) To maintain discipline in the class-room
   (d) To prepare the question paper
4. Value-education stands for
   (a) making a student healthy
   (b) making a student to get a job
   (c) inculcation of virtues
   (d) all-round development of personality
5. When a normal student behaves in an erratic manner in the class, you would
   (a) pull up the student then and there
   (b) talk to the student after the class
   (c) ask the student to leave the class
   (d) ignore the student
6. The research is always
   (a) verifying the old knowledge
   (b) exploring new knowledge
   (c) filling the gap between knowledge
   (d) All of these
7. The research that applies the laws at the time of field study to draw more and more clear ideas about the problem is
   (a) Applied research
   (b) Action research
   (c) Experimental research
   (d) None of these
8. When a research problem is related to heterogeneous population, the most suitable sampling method is
   (a) Cluster Sampling
   (b) Stratified Sampling
   (c) Convenient Sampling
   (d) Lottery Method
9. The process not needed in experimental research is:
   (a) Observation
   (b) Manipulation and replication
   (c) Controlling
   (d) Reference collection
10. A research problem is not feasible only when

(a) it is researchable
(b) it is new and adds something to knowledge
(c) it consists of independent and dependent variables
(d) it has utility and relevance

Read the following passage carefully and answer the questions 11 to 15:

Radically changing monsoon patterns, reduction in the winter rice harvest and a quantum increase in respiratory diseases all part of the environmental doomsday scenario which is reportedly playing out in South Asia. According to a United Nations Environment Program report, a deadly three-kilometer deep blanket of pollution comprising a fearsome, cocktail of ash, acids, aerosols and other particles has enveloped in this region. For India, already struggling to cope with a drought, the implication of this are devastating and further crop failure will amount to a life and death question for many Indians. The increase in premature deaths will have adverse social and economic consequences and a rise in morbidities will place an unbearable burden on our crumbling health system. And there is no one to blame but ourselves. Both official and corporate India has always been allergic to any mention of clean technology. Most mechanical two wheelers roll of the assembly line without proper pollution control system. Little effort is made for R&D on simple technologies, which could make a vital difference to people's lives and the environment.

However, while there is no denying that South Asia must clean up its act, skeptics might question the timing of the haze report. The Kyoto meet on climate change is just two weeks away and the stage is set for the usual battle between the developing world and the West, particularly the United States of America. President Mr. Bush has adamantly refused to sign any protocol, which would mean a change in American consumption level. U.N. environment report will likely find a place in the U.S. arsenal as it plants an accusing finger towards controls like India and China. Yet the U.S.A. can hardly deny its own dubious role in the matter of erasing trading quotas.

Richer countries can simply buy up excess credits from poorer countries and continue to pollute. Rather than try to get the better of developing countries, who undoubtedly have taken up environmental shortcuts in their bid to catch up with the West, the U.S.A. should take a look at the environmental profigacy, which is going on within. From opening up virgin territories for oil exploration to relaxing the standards for drinking water, Mr. Bush's policies are not exactly beneficial, not even to America's interests. We realise that we are all in this together and that pollution anywhere should be a global concern otherwise there will only be more tunnels at the end of the tunnel.

11. Both official and corporate India is allergic to
    (a) Failure of Monsoon
    (b) Poverty and Inequality
    (c) Slowdown in Industrial Production
    (d) Mention of Clean Technology

12. If the rate of premature death increases it will
    (a) Exert added burden on the crumbling economy
    (b) Have adverse social and economic consequences
    (c) Make positive effect on our effort to control population
    (d) Have less job aspirants in the society

13. According to the passage, the two-wheeler industry is not adequately concerned about
    (a) Passenger safety on the roads
    (b) Life cover insurance of the vehicle owner

(c) Pollution control system in the vehicle
(d) Rising cost of the two wheelers

14. What could be the reason behind timing of the haze report just before the Kyoto meet?
(a) United Nations is working hand-in-glove with U.S.A.
(b) Organisers of the forthcoming meet to teach a lesson to the U.S.A.
(c) Drawing attention of the world towards devastating effects of environment degradation.
(d) U.S.A. wants to use it as a handle against the developing countries in the forthcoming meet.

15. Which of the following is the indication of environmental degradation in South Asia?
(a) Social and economic inequality
(b) Crumbling health care system
(c) Inadequate pollution control system
(d) Radically changing monsoon pattern

16. Community Radio is a type of radio service that caters to the interest of
(a) Local audience (b) Education
(c) Entertainment (d) News

17. Orcut is a part of
(a) Intrapersonal Communication
(b) Mass Communication
(c) Group Communication
(d) Interpersonal Communication

18. Match List I with List II and select the correct answer using the codes given below.

List I (Artists)
(A) Amrita Shergill
(B) T. Swaminathan Pillai
(C) Bhimsen Joshi
(D) Padma Subramaniyam

List II (Art)
1. Flute 2. Classical Song
3. Painting 4. Bharat Natyam

Codes:	A	B	C	D
(a)	3	1	2	4
(b)	2	3	1	4
(c)	4	2	3	1
(d)	1	4	2	3

19. Which is not correct in latest communication award?
(a) Salman Rushdie - Booker's Prize—July 20, 2008
(b) Dilip Sanghavi - Business Standard CEO Award, July 22, 2008
(c) Tapan Sinha - Dada Saheb Falke Award, July 21, 2008
(d) Gautam Ghosh - Osians Lifetime Achievement Award, July 11, 2008

20. Firewalls are used to protect a communication network system against
(a) Unauthorised attacks
(b) Virus attacks
(c) Data-driven attacks
(d) Fire-attacks

21. Insert the missing number in the following
$\frac{2}{3}, \frac{4}{7}, ?, \frac{11}{21}, \frac{16}{31},$
(a) $\frac{10}{8}$ (b) $\frac{6}{10}$
(c) $\frac{5}{10}$ (d) $\frac{7}{13}$

22. In a certain code, GAMESMAN is written as AGMEMSAN. How would DISCLOSE be written in that code?
(a) IDSCOLSE (b) IDCSOLES
(c) IDSCOLES (d) IDSCLOSE

23. The letters in the first set have a certain relationship. On the basis of this relationship mark the right choice for the second set : AST : BRU :: NQV: ?

(a) ORW (b) MPU
(c) MRW (d) OPW

24. On what dates of April, 1994 did Sunday fall?
(a) 2, 9, 16, 23, 30
(b) 3, 10, 17, 24
(c) 4, 11, 18, 25
(d) 1, 8, 15, 22, 29

25. Find out the wrong number in the sequence
125, 127, 130, 135, 142, 153, 165
(a) 130 (b) 142
(c) 153 (d) 165

26. There are five books A, B, C, D and E. The book C lies above D, the book E is below A and B is below E. Which is at the bottom?
(a) E (b) B
(c) A (d) C

27. Logical reasoning is based on
(a) Truth of involved propositions
(b) Valid relation among the involved propositions
(c) Employment of symbolic language
(d) Employment of ordinary language

28. Two propositions with the same subject and predicate terms but different in quality are
(a) Contradictory (b) Contrary
(c) Subaltern (d) Identical

29. The premises of a valid deductive argument
(a) Provide some evidence for its conclusion
(b) Provide no evidence for its conclusion
(c) Are irrelevant for its conclusion
(d) Provide conclusive evidence for its conclusion

30. Syllogistic reasoning is
(a) Deductive (b) Inductive
(c) Experimental (d) Hypothetical

Study the following Venn diagram and answer questions nos. 31 to 33.

Three circles representing GRADUATES, CLERKS and GOVERNMENT EMPLOYEES are intersecting. The intersections are marked A, B, C, e, f, g and h. Which part best represents the statements in questions 31 to 33?

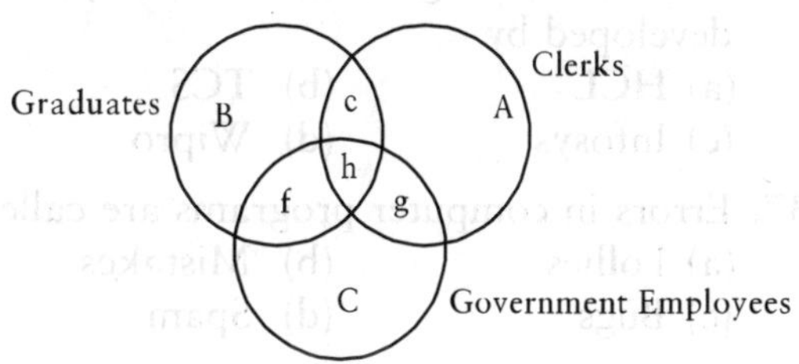

31. Some Graduates are Government employees but not as Clerks.
(a) h (b) g
(c) f (d) e

32. Clerks who are graduates as well as government employees.
(a) e (b) f
(c) g (d) h

33. Some graduates are Clerks but not Government employees.
(a) f (b) g
(c) h (d) e

Study the following graph and answer questions numbers from 34 to 35

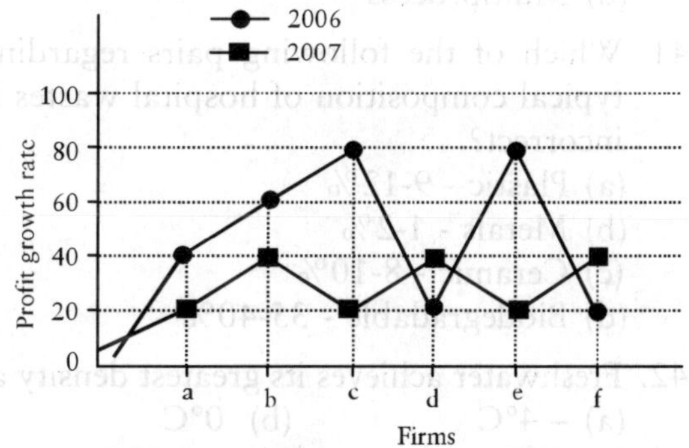

34. Which of the firms got maximum profit growth rate in the year 2006.

(a) ab (b) ce
(c) cd (d) ef

35. Which of the firms got maximum profit growth rate in the year 2007.
(a) bdf (b) acf
(c) bed (d) ace

36. The accounting software 'Tally' was developed by
(a) HCL (b) TCS
(c) Infosys (d) Wipro

37. Errors in computer programs are called
(a) Follies (b) Mistakes
(c) Bugs (d) Spam

38. HTML is basically used to design
(a) Webpage
(b) Website
(c) Graphics
(d) Tables and Frames

39. 'Micro Processing' is made for
(a) Computer
(b) Digital System
(c) Calculator
(d) Electronic Goods

40. Information, a combination of graphics, text, sound, video and animation is called
(a) Multiprogram
(b) Multifacet
(c) Multimedia
(d) Multiprocess

41. Which of the following pairs regarding typical composition of hospital wastes is incorrect?
(a) Plastic - 9-12%
(b) Metals - 1-2%
(c) Ceramic - 8-10%
(d) Biodegradable - 35-40%

42. Freshwater achieves its greatest density at
(a) – 4°C (b) 0°C
(c) 4°C (d) – 2.5°C

43. Which one of the following is not associated with earthquakes?
(a) Focus (b) Epicenter
(c) Seismograph (d) Swells

44. The tallest trees in the world are found in the region
(a) Equatorial region
(b) Temperate region
(c) Monsoon region
(d) Mediterranean region

45. Match List I with List II and select the correct answer from the codes given below.

List I (National Parks)
(A) Periyar
(B) Nandan Kanan
(C) Corbett National Park
(D) Sariska Tiger Reserve

List II (States)
1. Orissa
2. Kerala
3. Rajasthan
4. Uttarakhand

Codes:	A	B	C	D
(a)	2	1	4	3
(b)	1	2	4	3
(c)	3	2	1	4
(d)	1	2	3	4

46. According to Radhakrishnan Commission, the aim of Higher Education is
(a) To develop the democratic values, peace and harmony
(b) To develop great personalities who can give their contributions in politics, administration, industry and commerce
(c) Both (a) and (b)
(d) None of these

47. The National Museum at New Delhi is attached to
(a) Delhi University
(b) a Deemed University

(c) a Subordinate Office of the JNU
(d) Part of Ministry of Tourism and Culture

48. Match List I with List II and select the correct answer from the code given below.

List I (Institutions)	List II (Locations)
(A) National Law Institute	1. Shimla
(B) Indian Institute of Advanced Studies	2. Bhopal
(C) National Judicial Academy	3. Hyderabad
(D) National Savings Institute	4. Nagpur

Codes:	A	B	C	D
(a)	3	2	4	1
(b)	1	2	3	4
(c)	4	3	1	2
(d)	3	1	2	4

49. Election of Rural and Urban local bodies are conducted and ultimately supervised by
(a) Election Commission of India
(b) State Election Commission
(c) District Collector and District Magistrate
(d) Concerned Returning Officer

50. Which opinion is not correct?
(a) Education is a subject of concurrent list of VII schedule of Constitution of India
(b) University Grants Commission is a statutory body
(c) Patent, inventions, design, copyright and trade marks are the subject of concurrent list
(d) Indian Council of Social Science Research is a statutory body related to research in social sciences

ANSWERS

1. (d)	2. (c)	3. (b)	4. (c)	5. (b)
6. (d)	7. (a)	8. (b)	9. (d)	10. (b)
11. (d)	12. (b)	13. (c)	14. (c)	15. (d)
16. (a)	17. (d)	18. (a)	19. (b)	20. (a)
21. (d)	22. (a)	23. (d)	24. (b)	25. (d)
26. (b)	27. (b)	28. (a)	29. (d)	30. (a)
31. (c)	32. (d)	33. (d)	34. (b)	35. (a)
36. (b)	37. (c)	38. (a)	39. (a)	40. (c)
41. (d)	42. (c)	43. (d)	44. (b)	45. (a)
46. (c)	47. (d)	48. (d)	49. (b)	50. (c)

PAPER–II

Note: This paper contains fifty (50) objective type questions, each question carrying two (2) marks. Attempt all the questions.

Read the passage given below and answer the questions that follow, based on the passage you understand:

India's underdevelopment was not traditional or inherited from the precolonial past. India of the eighteenth century was undeveloped and not underdeveloped. On a world scale, it was not less but perhaps more developed than many other national economies, as most of the world development has occurred after the eighteenth century and basically after 1850. In fact, there was not much of a gap between the economic condition of Mughal India and that of pre-industrial Europe and Japan. The basic feature of colonialism in India in its long history since the 1750s was the appropriation by Britain of the social surplus produced in India. Also while the forms of surplus appropriation underwent changes through different stages of colonialism direct appropriation of surplus, employment of our boys, unequal exchange, profits of industrial capitalism and interest on public debt, the fact of surplus appropriation remained constant and basic. There were of course, many changes and some of them were positive for example, the development of the railways- when seen in isolation. But these changes came within and as part of the colonial framework and became, therefore, part of the process of underdevelopment. Colonialism is best seen as a totality or a unified structure. The newly developed institutions and evolving structures formed an interconnected and mutually reinforcing network, which survived and brought into being the colonial structure.

1. Why was India's underdevelopment not traditional?
   (a) India in the 18th century was undeveloped
   (b) India did not inherit underdevelopment from the past
   (c) India in the 18th century was not underdeveloped
   (d) India was not a poor nation
2. Why eighteenth century India could not be called underdeveloped?
   (a) World development occured after 18th century
   (b) India did not lag behind other nations
   (c) Most other nations developed after 1850
   (d) Indian economy was comparable with contemporary Europe and Japan
3. Which of the following is the basic feature of colonialism?
   (a) unequal exchange
   (b) appropriation of social surplus
   (c) interest on public debt
   (d) expropriation of the industrial profit
4. Why the railways could not alter the course of development in India?
   (a) Railways were only superficial
   (b) Railways were positive changes
   (c) Railways were often neglected
   (d) Railways formed only a part of the colonial framework
5. Colonialism should be seen by:
   (a) its networks (b) its institutions
   (c) its totality (d) its changes
6. Which of the following represents Palaeolithic?
   (a) Microliths
   (b) Madras industry
   (c) Neoliths
   (d) Megaliths
7. Which among the following is associated with Mesolithic?
   (a) Sohan (b) Burzahom
   (c) Bhimbitaka (d) Shortughai
8. Which of the following stands for New Stone age?
   (a) Hunting
   (b) Pastoralism
   (c) Scavenging
   (d) Food production
9. Which among the following denotes Harappa Civilization?
   (a) Malwa Culture
   (b) Gandhar Grave Culture
   (c) Megalithic Culture
   (d) Sothi Culture
10. Given below are two statements, one labelled Assertion (A) and the other labelled Reason (R):
    Assertion (A): Kushan period in ancient Indian history is the most prosperous period.
    Reason (R): We witness all round development during this period.
    Read the above statements and select the correct answer from the codes below:
    Codes:
    (a) (A) is correct, but (R) false
    (b) (A) is false, but (R) true
    (c) Both (A) and (R) are incorrect
    (d) Both (A) and (R) are correct

11. Given below are two statements, one labelled Assertion (A) and the other labelled Reason (R):
Assertion (A): Beginning of landgrants in Gupta period is associated with the inception of feudalism.
Reason (R): This was imperative for economic development.
Read the above statements and select the correct answer from the codes below:
Codes:
(a) (A) is correct, but (R) is incorrect
(b) (A) is false, but (R) true
(c) Both (A) and (R) are incorrect
(d) Both (A) and (R) are true

12. Given below are two statements, one labelled Assertion (A) and the other labelled Reason (R):
Assertion (A): Arabs invaded India in the first half of the 8th century A.D.
Reason (R): They were inspired by the imperialistic considerations.
Read the above statements and select the correct answer from the codes below:
Codes:
(a) Both (A) and (R) are true
(b) Both (A) and (R) are incorrect
(c) (A) is true, but (R) is False
(d) (A) is untrue, but (R) is true

13. Arrange the following into sequential order and select the correct answer from the codes given below:
(i) Chalcolithic age (ii) Iron age
(iii) Bronze age (iv) Stone age
Codes:
(a) (iii), (ii), (i), (iv) (b) (ii), (i), (iv), (iii)
(c) (iv), (iii), (i), (ii) (d) (i), (iv), (ii), (iii)

14. Arrange the following into sequential order and select the correct answer from the codes given below:
(i) Rajatarangini
(ii) Harsh Charit
(iii) Prithvi Raj Raso
(iv) Sangam literature
Codes:
(a) (iv), (iii), (ii), (i) (b) (iii), (iv), (i), (ii)
(c) (i), (iii), (ii), (iv) (d) (iv), (ii), (i), (iii)

15. Arrange the following in chronological sequence and select the correct answer from the codes given below:
(i) Chakravartin (ii) Maharaja
(iii) Maharajadhiraj (iv) Rajan
Codes:
(a) (iii), (ii), (i), (iv) (b) (iv), (iii), (ii), (i)
(c) (ii), (i), (iii), (iv) (d) (iv), (ii), (iii), (i)

16. Which of the order below is correct? Select the correct answer from the codes given below:
(i) Ganga kingdom
(ii) Arab invasion
(iii) Mahender Pallava
(iv) Rise of Hoysala power
Codes:
(a) (iii), (ii), (i), (iv) (b) (iv), (iii), (ii), (i)
(c) (ii), (i), (iv), (iii) (d) (i), (ii), (iii), (iv)

17. Match List I with List II and select the correct answer from the codes given below:
List I
(A) Sabha and Samiti
(B) Northern Black Polished Ware
(C) Girnar inscription
(D) Devanam Piyon
List II
(i) Rudradaman (ii) Vedic period
(iii) Ashoka (iv) Gangetic plain

Codes:	A	B	C	D
(a)	(ii)	(iv)	(iii)	(i)
(b)	(ii)	(iv)	(i)	(iii)
(c)	(iv)	(ii)	(i)	(iii)
(d)	(ii)	(i)	(iv)	(iii)

18. Match List I with List II and select the correct answer from the codes below:

List I
(A) Bodhisattva
(B) Dravid Style of architecture
(C) Mihirkula
(D) Chandella

List II
(i) Jejakbhukti (ii) Huna
(iii) South India (iv) Buddhism

Codes:	**A**	**B**	**C**	**D**
(a)	(iv)	(iii)	(i)	(ii)
(b)	(i)	(iii)	(ii)	(iv)
(c)	(iv)	(iii)	(ii)	(i)
(d)	(i)	(iv)	(ii)	(iii)

19. Match List I with List II and select the correct answer from the codes given below:

List I
(A) Etched Carnelian bead
(B) Copper
(C) Bary gaza
(D) Tamralipti

List II
(i) Bengal (ii) Port
(iii) Harappa (iv) Rajasthan

Codes:	**A**	**B**	**C**	**D**
(a)	(iv)	(ii)	(iii)	(i)
(b)	(iv)	(i)	(ii)	(iii)
(c)	(iv)	(iii)	(ii)	(i)
(d)	(iii)	(iv)	(ii)	(i)

20. When did Sher Shah Suri annex Malwa?
(a) 1540 (b) 1541
(c) 1542 (d) 1543

21. Who was awarded the title of Mirza Raja?
(a) Bhar Mai (b) Jai Singh
(c) Jaswant Singh (d) Raj Singh

22. In Maratha administration, Majumdar was?
(a) Accountant
(b) Secretary
(c) Government Official
(d) Cashier

23. Battle of Haldighati was fought between:
(a) Mughals and Amber
(b) Mughals and Kota
(c) Mughals and Mewar
(d) Mughals and Marwar

24. Arrange the following in correct sequence:
(a) Alauddin Masud Shah, Razia Sultan, Moizuddin Bahramshah, Ruknuddin Firuzshah
(b) Ruknuddin Firuzshah, Razia Sultan, Moizuddin Bahramshah, Alauddin Masud Shah
(c) Razia Sutlan, Alauddin Masud Shah, Ruknuddin Firuzshah, Moizuddin Bahramshah
(d) Moizuddin Bahramshah, Alauddin Masud Shah, Ruknuddin Firuzshah, Razia Sultan

25. Arrange the following in correct sequence:
(a) Nasiruddin Qubacha, Zafar Khan, Ghazi Malik, Islam Shah.
(b) Nasiruddin Qubacha, Islam Shah, Ghazi Malik, Zafar Khan.
(c) Nasiruddin Qubacha, Ghazi Malik, Islam Shah, Zafar Khan.
(d) Ghazi Malik, Nasiruddin Qubacha, Islam Shah, Zafar Khan.

26. Arrange the following in correct chronological order:
(a) Devgiri, Ranthambore, Malwa, Gujarat
(b) Malwa, Ranthambore, Gujarat, Devgiri
(c) Gujarat, Ranthambore, Malwa, Devgiri
(d) Ranthambore, Malwa, Gujarat, Devgiri

27. Match List I with List II and select the correct answer form the codes given below:

List I
(A) Ali Muhammad Khan
(B) Zia-ud-din Barani

(C) Bhim Sen
(D) Inayat Khan

List II
(i) Nuskha-i-Dilkusha
(ii) Mirat-i-Ahmadi
(iii) Shahjahan Nama
(iv) Fatawa-i-Jahandari

Codes:	**A**	**B**	**C**	**D**
(a)	(ii)	(iv)	(i)	(iii)
(b)	(i)	(iii)	(iv)	(ii)
(c)	(iv)	(ii)	(i)	(iii)
(d)	(iii)	(iv)	(ii)	(i)

28. Match List I with List II and select the correct answer form the codes given below:

List I	**List II**
(A) Shah Mir	(i) Jajnagar
(B) Zafar Khan	(ii) Khandesh
(C) Malik Raja	(iii) Kashmir
(D) Jauna Khan	(iv) Gujarat

Codes:	**A**	**B**	**C**	**D**
(a)	(i)	(iv)	(ii)	(iii)
(b)	(ii)	(i)	(iii)	(iv)
(c)	(iii)	(iv)	(ii)	(i)
(d)	(iv)	(ii)	(iii)	(i)

29. Match List I with List II and select the correct answer form the codes given below:

List I
(A) Lambardar (B) Barid
(C) Waqia Nawis (D) Jawabit

List II
(i) State Laws
(ii) News Reporter
(iii) Village Headman
(iv) Intelligence Officer

Codes:	**A**	**B**	**C**	**D**
(a)	(iv)	(i)	(ii)	(iii)
(b)	(ii)	(iii)	(iv)	(i)
(c)	(iii)	(iv)	(ii)	(i)
(d)	(i)	(iii)	(iv)	(ii)

30. Given below are two statements, one labelled as Assertion (A), and the other labelled as Reason (R):
Assertion (A): During the seventeenth century India, the economic growth stimulated by the growing importance of a new external connection: the link between Mughal India and early modern Europe.
Reason (R): Each trading concern in Mughal India operated under a Royal Charter which granted it exclusive national rights to carry out the India trade.
In the context of the above two statements, which one of the following is correct?
Codes:
(a) (A) is correct, but (R) is wrong
(b) Both (A) and (R) are correct
(c) (A) is wrong, but (R) is correct
(d) Both (A) and (R) are wrong

31. Given below are two statements, one labelled as Assertion (A), and the other labelled as Reason (R):
Assertion (A): Khan Jahan enjoyed more extensive powers than had been vouchsafed to any previous Wazir .
Reason (R): Firoz Shah Tughlaq capitulated and gave Kahn Jahan, his Wazir, permission to employ and dismiss whomsoever he wished.
In the context of the above two statements, which one of the following is correct?
Codes:
(a) (A) is correct, but (R) is wrong
(b) Both (A) and (R) are correct
(c) (A) is wrong, but (R) is correct
(d) Both (A) and (R) are wrong

32. Given below are two statements, one labelled as Assertion (A), and the other labelled as Reason (R):

Assertion (A): The Mughal empire was connected by a surprisingly rapid information loop for public news.

Reason (R): The Mughal emperors did not receive news reports from distant provincial capitals within a few days which could be read out daily in the public audience hall.

In the context of the above two statements, which one of the following is correct?

Codes:

(a) (A) is correct, but (R) is wrong
(b) Both (A) and (R) are correct
(c) (A) is wrong, but (R) is correct
(d) Both (A) and (R) are wrong

33. The Act of 1919 provided for:
   (a) a separate and simultaneous ICS examination to be held in India.
   (b) a separate, but not simultaneous, ICS examination to be held in India.
   (c) reservation for Indians in the ICS examination.
   (d) holding of the ICS examination in Bombay, Calcutta and Madras.

34. Which of the following concepts is not associated with the non-cooperation movement?
   (a) Atmasakti (b) Non-violence
   (c) Boycott (d) Charka

35. The filature is a system related to:
   (a) cotton weaving (b) iron-smelting
   (c) silk-reeling (d) copper working

36. Who had evolved the concept of the drain of wealth?
   (a) Bankim Chandra Chatterjee
   (b) Romesh Dutt
   (c) Dadabhai Naoroji
   (d) Bipan Chandra

37. Given below are two statements, one labelled Assertion (A) and the other labelled Reason (R):

Assertion (A): The Revolt of 1857 marked an important watershed in the evolution of British policies towards the Indian states.

Reason (R): The Revolt of 1857 ended the rule of the East India Company.

In the context of the above two statements, which one of the following is correct?

(a) Both (A) and (R) are true and (R) is the correct explanation of (A).
(b) Both (A) and (R) are true but (R) does not explain (A).
(c) (A) is true and (R) is false.
(d) (A) is false and (R) is true.

38. Given below are two statements, one labelled Assertion (A) and the other labelled Reason (R).

Assertion (A): Gandhi for the first time had made untouchability an issue of public concern.

Reason (R): He wanted to broaden the social base of the Congress.

In the context of the above two statements, which one of the following is correct?

(a) Both the statements are false.
(b) (A) is true and (R) is false.
(c) Both (A) and (R) are true but (R) does not explain (A).
(d) Both (A) and (R) are true and (R) explains (A).

39. Given below are two statements, one labelled Assertion (A) and the other labelled Reason (R):

Assertion (A): What occured in India under British rule was at the most aborted modernization, typical of modern colonial economic structure.

Reason (R): British persistently followed the policy of turning India into an agriculture country.

In the context of the above two statements, which one of the following is correct?

(a) Both (A) and (R) are true and (R) is only the partial explanation of (A).
(b) Both (A) and (R) are true and (R) fully explains (A).
(c) (A) is true and (R) is false.
(d) Both (A) and (R) are false.

40. Arrange the following in chronological order:
(i) Simon Commission
(ii) Indian Industrial Commission
(iii) Indian Financial Commission
(iv) Indian Education Commission
Options:
(a) (i) (ii) (iv) (iii) (b) (i) (iii) (iv) (ii)
(c) (iv) (ii) (iii) (i) (d) (i) (iii) (ii) (iv)

41. Arrange the following in chronological order:
(i) Praja Mandal (ii) Hool
(iii) Ulgulan (iv) Marias
Options:
(a) (ii) (iii) (iv) (i) (b) (i) (ii) (iv) (iii)
(c) (iv) (i) (ii) (iii) (d) (ii) (iii) (iv) (i)

42. Arrange the following in chronological order:
(i) Age of Consent Act
(ii) Deccan Agricultural Relief Act
(iii) Police Act
(iv) Universities Act
Options:
(a) (i) (iii) (ii) (iv) (b) (iii) (ii) (i) (iv)
(c) (iii) (i) (ii) (iv) (d) (iii) (ii) (iv) (i)

43. Match the List I with List II using the code:
List I
(A) Prosperous British India
(B) The History of British India
(C) The Economic History of India
(D) Origins of Nationality in South Asia

List II
(i) C.A. Bayly (ii) R.C. Dutt
(iii) William Digley (iv) James Mill

Codes:	A	B	C	D
(a)	(ii)	(iii)	(i)	(iv)
(b)	(iii)	(iv)	(ii)	(i)
(c)	(iii)	(i)	(ii)	(iv)
(d)	(iv)	(iii)	(ii)	(i)

44. Match the List I with List II using the code:
List I
(A) Permanent Settlement
(B) Ryotwari Settlement
(C) Mahalwari Settlement
(D) Bombay Survey System

List II
(i) Alexander Reed
(ii) Thomas Law
(iii) G. Wingate
(iv) Holt Mackenzie.

Codes:	A	B	C	D
(a)	(ii)	(i)	(iv)	(iii)
(b)	(ii)	(i)	(iii)	(iv)
(c)	(iii)	(iv)	(ii)	(i)
(d)	(iv)	(iii)	(ii)	(i)

45. Match the List I with List II using the code:
List I
(A) William Jones
(B) Charles Grant
(C) Thomas Macaulay
(D) Thomas Munro

List II
(i) Evangelicalism
(ii) Utilitarianism
(iii) Orientalism
(iv) Liberalism

Codes:	A	B	C	D
(a)	(iv)	(ii)	(iii)	(i)
(b)	(iii)	(i)	(iv)	(ii)
(c)	(iii)	(ii)	(i)	(iv)
(d)	(iii)	(iv)	(ii)	(i)

46. The Nazi Soviet Pact was signed in:
    (a) 1937 (b) 1938
    (c) 1939 (d) 1940
47. Which country disagreed with England and France over colonial issues in 1940s?
    (a) America (b) Russia
    (c) Germany (d) Italy
48. Identify the non-commonwealth country from the following:
    (a) Pakistan (b) Nepal
    (c) Sri Lanka (d) Myanmar
49. Research is a studious search for:
    (a) Identification
    (b) Facts
    (c) Hunt for material
    (d) Hypothesis
50. Who among the following was worried against entry of value judgements in Social Science Research?
    (a) T.W. Hutchison
    (b) M.J. Ulmer
    (c) Louis Dumont
    (d) John Stuart Mill

ANSWERS

1. (a)	2. (c)	3. (b)	4. (d)	5. (c)
6. (a)	7. (a)	8. (d)	9. (d)	10. (d)
11. (a)	12. (c)	13. (c)	14. (d)	15. (d)
16. (c)	17. (b)	18. (c)	19. (d)	20. (c)
21. (b)	22. (a)	23. (c)	24. (b)	25. (b)
26. (c)	27. (a)	28. (c)	29. (c)	30. (d)
31. (a)	32. (a)	33. (a)	34. (a)	35. (b)
36. (c)	37. (a)	38. (d)	39. (b)	40. (c)
41. (d)	42. (c)	43. (b)	44. (a)	45. (b)
46. (c)	47. (b)	48. (d)	49. (b)	50. (a)

JUNE–2008

Note: This paper contains fifty (50) objective type questions, each question carrying two (2) marks. Attempt all the questions.

PAPER–I

1. The teacher has been glorified by the phrase "Friend, philosopher and guide" because:
   (a) He has to play all vital roles in the context of society
   (b) He transmits the high value of humanity to students
   (c) He is the great reformer of the society
   (d) He is a great patriot
2. The most important cause of failure for teacher lies in the area of
   (a) interpersonal relationship
   (b) lack of command over the knowledge of the subject
   (c) verbal ability
   (d) strict handling of the students
3. A teacher can establish rapport with his students by
   (a) becoming a figure of authority
   (b) impressing students with knowledge and skill
   (c) playing the role of a guide
   (d) becoming a friend to the students
4. Education is a powerful instrument of
   (a) Social transformation
   (b) Personal transformation
   (c) Cultural transformation
   (d) All the above
5. A teacher's major contribution towards the maximum self-realisation of the student is affected through
   (a) Constant fulfilment of the students' needs
   (b) Strict control of classroom activities
   (c) Sensitivity to students' needs, goals and purposes
   (d) Strict reinforcement of academic standards
6. Research problem is selected from the stand point of
   (a) Researcher's interest
   (b) Financial support
   (c) Social relevance
   (d) Availability of relevant literature
7. Which one is called non-probability sampling?
   (a) Cluster sampling
   (b) Quota sampling
   (c) Systematic sampling
   (d) Stratified random sampling
8. Formulation of hypothesis may not be required in
   (a) Survey method
   (b) Historical studies
   (c) Experimental studies
   (d) Normative studies
9. Field-work based research is classified as
   (a) Empirical (b) Historical
   (c) Experimental (d) Biographical
10. Which of the following sampling method is appropriate to study the prevalence of AIDS amongst male and female in India in 1976, 1986, 1996 and 2006?

(a) Cluster sampling
(b) Systematic sampling
(c) Quota sampling
(d) Stratified random sampling

Read the following passage and answer the questions 11 to 15:

The fundamental principle is that Article 14 forbids class legislation but permits reasonable classification for the purpose of legislation which classification must satisfy the twin tests of classification being founded on an intelligible differentia which distinguishes persons or things that are grouped together from those that are left out of the group and that differentia must have a rational nexus to the object sought to be achieved by the Statute in question. The thrust of Article 14 is that the citizen is entitled to equality before law and equal protection of laws. In the very nature of things the society being composed of unequals a welfare State will have to strive by both executive and legislative action to help the less fortunate in society to ameliorate their condition so that the social and economic inequality in the society may be bridged. This would necessitate a legislative application to a group of citizens otherwise unequal and amelioration of whose lot is the object of state affirmative action. In the absence of the doctrine of classification such legislation is likely to flounder on the bedrock of equality enshrined in Article 14. The Court realistically appraising the social and economic inequality and keeping in view the guidelines on which the State action must move as constitutionally laid down in Part IV of the Constitution evolved the doctrine of classification. The doctrine was evolved to sustain a legislation or State action designed to help weaker sections of the society or some such segments of the society in need of succour. Legislative and executive action may accordingly be sustained if it satisfies the twin tests of reasonable classification and the rational principle correlated to the object sought to be achieved.

The concept of equality before the law does not involve the idea of absolute equality among human beings which is a physical impossibility. All that Article 14 guarantees is a similarity of treatment contra-distinguished from identical treatment. Equality before law means that among equals the law should be equal and should be equally administered and that the likes should be treated alike. Equality before the law does not mean that things which are different shall be as though they are the same. It of course means denial of any special privilege by reason of birth, creed or the like. The legislation as well as the executive government, while dealing with diverse problems arising out of an infinite variety of human relations must of necessity have the power of making special laws, to attain any particular object and to achieve that object it must have the power of selection or classification of persons and things upon which such laws are to operate.

11. Right to equality, one of the fundamental rights, is enunciated in the constitution under Part III, Article
    (a) 12 (b) 13
    (c) 14 (d) 15

12. The main thrust of Right to equality is that it permits
    (a) class legislation
    (b) equality before law and equal protection under the law
    (c) absolute equality
    (d) special privilege by reason of birth

13. The social and economic inequality in the society can be bridged by
    (a) executive and legislative action
    (b) universal suffrage
    (c) identical treatment
    (d) None of the above

14. The doctrine of classification is evolved to
(a) Help weaker sections of the society
(b) Provide absolute equality
(c) Provide identical treatment
(d) None of the above

15. While dealing with diverse problems arising out of an infinite variety of human relations, the government
(a) must have the power of making special laws
(b) must not have any power to make special laws
(c) must have power to withdraw equal rights
(d) None of the above

16. Communication with oneself is known as
(a) Group communication
(b) Grapevine communication
(c) Interpersonal communication
(d) Intrapersonal communication

17. Which broadcasting system for TV is followed in India?
(a) NTSE (b) PAL
(c) SECAM (d) NTCS

18. All India Radio before 1936 was known as
(a) Indian Radio Broadcasting
(b) Broadcasting Service of India
(c) Indian State Broadcasting Service
(d) All India Broadcasting Service

19. The biggest news agency of India is
(a) PTI
(b) UNI
(c) NANAP
(d) Samachar Bharati

20. Prasar Bharati was launched in the year
(a) 1995 (b) 1997
(c) 1999 (d) 2001

21. A statistical measure based upon the entire population is called parameter while measure based upon a sample is known as
(a) Sample parameter
(b) Inference
(c) Statistics
(d) None of these

22. The importance of the correlation co-efficient lies in the fact that
(a) There is a linear relationship between the correlated variables
(b) It is one of the most valid measure of statistics
(c) It allows one to determine the degree or strength of the association between two variables
(d) It is a non-parametric method of statistical analysis

23. The F-test
(a) is essentially a two tailed test
(b) is essentially a one tailed test
(c) can be one tailed as well as two tailed depending on the hypothesis
(d) can never be a one tailed test

24. What will be the next letter in the following series
DCXW, FEVU, HGTS, ____
(a) AKPO (b) JBYZ
(c) JIRQ (d) LMRS

25. The following question is based on the diagram given below. If the two small circles represent formal classroom education and distance education and the big circle stands for university system of education, which figure represents the university systems.

(a) (b)

(c) (d)

26. The statement, '*To be non-violent is good*' is a

(a) Moral judgement
(b) Factual judgement
(c) Religious judgement
(d) Value judgement

27. **Assertion (A):** Man is a rational being.

Reason (R): Man is a social being.
(a) Both (A) and (R) are true and (R) is the correct explanation of (A)
(b) Both (A) and (R) are true but (R) is not the correct explanation of (A)
(c) (A) is true but (R) is false
(d) (A) is false but (R) is true

28. Value Judgements are
(a) Factual Judgements
(b) Ordinary Judgements
(c) Normative Judgements
(d) Expression of public opinion

29. Deductive reasoning proceeds from
(a) general to particular
(b) particular to general
(c) one general conclusion to another general conclusion
(d) one particular conclusion to another particular conclusion

30. AGARTALA is written in code as 14168171, the code for AGRA is
(a) 1641 (b) 1416
(c) 1441 (d) 1461

31. Which one of the following is the most comprehensive source of population data?
(a) National Family Health Surveys
(b) National Sample Surveys
(c) Census
(d) Demographic Health Surveys

32. Which one of the following principles is not applicable to sampling?
(a) Sample units must be clearly defined
(b) Sample units must be dependent on each other
(c) Same units of sample should be used throughout the study
(d) Sample units must be chosen in a systematic and objective manner

33. If January 1st, 2007 is Monday, what was the day on 1st January 1995?
(a) Sunday (b) Monday
(c) Friday (d) Saturday

34. Insert the missing number in the following series
4 16 8 64 ? 256
(a) 16 (b) 24
(c) 32 (d) 20

35. If an article is sold for ₹ 178 at a loss of 11%; what would be its selling price in order to earn a profit of 11%?
(a) ₹ 222.50 (b) ₹ 267
(c) ₹ 222 (d) ₹ 220

36. WYSIWYG—describes the display of a document on screen as it will actually print
(a) What you state is what you get
(b) What you see is what you get
(c) What you save is what you get
(d) What you suggest is what you get

37. Which of the following is not a Computer language?
(a) PASCAL (b) UNIX
(c) FORTRAN (d) COBOL

38. A keyboard has at least
(a) 91 keys (b) 101 keys
(c) 111 keys (d) 121 keys

39. An E-mail address is composed of
(a) two parts (b) three parts
(c) four parts (d) five parts

40. Corel Draw is a popular
(a) Illustration program
(b) Programming language
(c) Text program
(d) None of the above

41. Human ear is most sensitive to noise in which of the following ranges
(a) 1-2 KHz (b) 100-500 Hz
(c) 10-12 KHz (d) 13-16 KHz

42. Which one of the following units is used to measure intensity of noise?

(a) decible (b) Hz
(c) Phon (d) Watts/m^2

43. If the population growth follows a logistic curve, the maximum sustainable yield
(a) is equal to half the carrying capacity
(b) is equal to the carrying capacity
(c) depends on growth rates
(d) depends on the initial population

44. Chemical weathering of rocks is largely dependent upon
(a) high temperature
(b) strong wind action
(c) heavy rainfall
(d) glaciation

45. Structure of earth's system consists of the following: Match List I with List II and give the correct answer.

List I (Zone)
A. Atmosphere B. Biosphere
C. Hydrosphere D. Lithosphere

List II (Chemical Character)
1. Inert gases
2. Salt, freshwater, snow and ice
3. Organic substances, skeleton matter
4. Light silicates

Codes:	A	B	C	D
(a)	2	3	1	4
(b)	1	3	2	4
(c)	2	1	3	4
(d)	3	1	2	4

46. NAAC is an autonomous institution under the aegis of
(a) ICSSR (b) CSIR
(c) AICTE (d) UGC

47. National Council for Women's Education was established in
(a) 1958 (b) 1976
(c) 1989 (d) 2000

48. Which one of the following is not situated in New Delhi?
(a) Indian Council of Cultural Relations
(b) Indian Council of Scientific Research
(c) National Council of Educational Research and Training
(d) Indian Institute of Advanced Studies

49. Autonomy in higher education implies freedom in
(a) Administration
(b) Policy-making
(c) Finance
(d) Curriculum development

50. Match List I with List II and select the correct answer from the code given below

List I (Institutions)
A. Dr. Hari Singh Gour University
B. S.N.D.T. University
C. M.S. University
D. J.N. Vyas University

List II (Locations)
1. Mumbai 2. Baroda
3. Jodhpur 4. Sagar

Codes:	A	B	C	D
(a)	4	1	2	3
(b)	1	2	3	4
(c)	3	1	2	4
(d)	2	4	1	3

ANSWERS

1. (b)	2. (b)	3. (b)	4. (d)	5. (c)
6. (c)	7. (b)	8. (b)	9. (a)	10. (d)
11. (c)	12. (b)	13. (a)	14. (a)	15. (a)
16. (d)	17. (b)	18. (c)	19. (a)	20. (b)
21. (a)	22. (c)	23. (c)	24. (c)	25. (b)
26. (a)	27. (b)	28. (c)	29. (a)	30. (d)
31. (c)	32. (b)	33. (d)	34. (a)	35. (c)
36. (b)	37. (b)	38. (b)	39. (a)	40. (a)
41. (b)	42. (a)	43. (a)	44. (c)	45. (b)
46. (d)	47. (a)	48. (d)	49. (c)	50. (a)

PAPER–II

Note: This paper contains fifty (50) objective type questions, each question carrying two (2) marks. Attempt all the questions.

Indian nationalism emanated from 'traditional patriotism', a socially active sentiment of attachment to land, language and cult, that developed in the subcontinent long before the process of Westernisation had begun. In India of the eighteenth and early nineteenth centuries, such sentiments were emerging on a regional basis as homeland was being defined by various terms like *desh*, *vatan* or *nadu*, where identities were gradually taking shape with the development of regional languages and religions affiliations. But although regionally centred at Bengal, Maharashtra, Awadh or Mysore, their isolation broke down through various means of communication, the political legitimacy of the Mughal empire was recognised throughout Hindustan, which was thought to be the abode of both Hindus and Muslims; and cultural barriers melted down through commercialisation and regular pilgrimages. As the East India company established its hegemony, this traditional patriotism manifested itself through various indigenous critiques of foreign rule deviating from the established ethical traditions of good government and through irate reactions to Christian missionary propaganda. Finally, it burst forth through numerous acts of resistance, participated by both princes and the commoners, culminating in the revolt of 1857. After the revolt, a modern sector of politics gradually evolved in India, through rapid spread of education, development of communication systems, such as the railways and telegraph, and the emergence of a new public space created by the colonial institutions.

1. The 'nationalism' in pre-colonial India meant:
   (a) Patriotism
   (b) Linguistic affinity
   (c) Cultural construction of homeland
   (d) Social activism
2. What contributed most to the dissolution of cultural barriers?
   (a) Commercialization
   (b) Creation of mughal empire
   (c) Pilgrimage
   (d) Communication networks
3. The East India Company's rule resulted in:
   (a) Evangelicalism
   (b) Good Government
   (c) New Ethical Tradition
   (d) Consolidation of patriotic sentiments
4. The revolt of 1857 was:
   (a) an aristocratic revolt
   (b) a revolt of the common people
   (c) a reactionary upsurge
   (d) the culmination of the early resistance
5. What was the most important outcome of the direct administration?
   (a) growth of education
   (b) development of railways and telegraph
   (c) evolution of a modern sector of politics
   (d) growth of colonial institutions
6. Which among the following is associated with Palaeolithic:
   (a) Chopper-Chopping tools
   (b) Geometric tools
   (c) Pecking tools
   (d) Polished tools
7. Which among the following represents Mesolithic:
   (a) Gathering
   (b) Hunting
   (c) Food production
   (d) Domestication of animals

8. Which among the following stands for Neolithic:
   (a) Nomadism (b) Transhumance
   (c) Sedentism (d) Urbanism
9. Which of the following is associated with the Harappa Civilization?
   (a) Chauntra (b) Langhnaj
   (c) Mehrgarh (d) Ahar
10. Given below are two statements one labelled Assertion (A) and the other labelled Reason (R):
   Assertion (A): The pace of human development was very slow during the stone age.
   Reason (R): Primarily because humans were dependent on hit and trial method of learning.
   Read the above statements and select the correct answer from the codes below:
   Codes:
   (a) (A) is correct, but (R) is wrong
   (b) Both (A) and (R) are correct
   (c) (A) is wrong, but (R) is correct
   (d) Both (A) and (R) are incorrect
11. Given below are two statements one labelled Assertion (A) and the other labelled Reason (R):
   Assertion (A): The first urbanization in India decayed by the end of 3rd millennium BC.
   Reason (R): This was caused primarily by the changes in climatic conditions.
   Read the above statements and select the correct code below:
   Codes:
   (a) (A) is correct, but (R) is wrong
   (b) (A) is incorrect, but (R) is true
   (c) Both (A) and (R) are correct
   (d) Both (A) and (R) are wrong
12. Given below are two statements one labelled Assertion (A) and the other labelled Reason (R):
   Assertion (A): The second urbanization occurred in the Gangetic plains during the second half of the first millennium BC.
   Reason (R): This was effected by the favorable climatic conditions.
   Read the above statements and select the correct answer from the codes below:
   Codes:
   (a) Both (A) and (R) are incorrect
   (b) Both (A) and (R) are true
   (c) (A) is correct, but (R) is false
   (d) (A) is untrue, but (R) is true
13. Arrange the following into sequential order and select the correct answer from the following codes:
   (i) Janapada (ii) Mahajanapada
   (iii) Jana (iv) Empire
   Codes:
   (a) (ii), (iii), (i), (iv) (b) (iii), (iv), (ii), (i)
   (c) (iv), (ii), (i), (iii) (d) (iii), (i), (ii), (iv)
14. Arrange the following into sequential order and select the correct answer from the following codes:
   (i) Junagarh inscription
   (ii) Allahabad pillar inscription
   (iii) Aihole inscription
   (iv) Pathari Stamb inscription
   Codes:
   (a) (iv), (i), (iii), (ii) (b) (i), (ii), (iii), (iv)
   (c) (ii), (iii), (iv), (i) (d) (iii), (iv), (i), (ii)
15. Arrange the following into sequential order and select the correct answer from the following codes:
   (i) Ramayana
   (ii) Samved
   (iii) Mahabharata
   (iv) Ashtadhyayi
   Codes:
   (a) (i), (iv), (iii), (ii) (b) (ii), (iii), (i), (iv)
   (c) (iii), (i), (ii), (iv) (d) (iv), (ii), (i), (iii)

16. Organise the following into chronological order and select the correct answer from the following codes:
   (i) Fa-Hien (ii) Megasthenes
   (iii) Hiuen-Tsang (iv) Alberuni
   Codes:
   (a) (ii), (i), (iii), (iv) (b) (iii), (ii), (iv), (i)
   (c) (iv), (iii), (ii), (i) (d) (i), (iv), (ii), (iii)

17. Match List I with List II and select the correct answer from the codes below:
   List I
   (A) Twin Mound System
   (B) Vidath
   (C) Doctrine of Karma
   (D) Saptang Theory

   List II
   (i) Rig Veda
   (ii) Harappa Civilization
   (iii) Arthashastra
   (iv) Brahmanism

Codes:	**A**	**B**	**C**	**D**
(a)	(ii)	(i)	(iv)	(iii)
(b)	(iv)	(i)	(ii)	(iii)
(c)	(iii)	(iv)	(ii)	(i)
(d)	(iv)	(iii)	(ii)	(i)

18. Match List I with List II and select the correct answer from the codes below:
   List I
   (A) Dhamma Vijay
   (B) Kanyopayadan
   (C) Poet king
   (D) Sarthavaha

   List II
   (i) Samundragupta
   (ii) Caravan traders
   (iii) Harsh Vardhan
   (iv) Ashoka

Codes:	**A**	**B**	**C**	**D**
(a)	(iii)	(iv)	(i)	(ii)
(b)	(iv)	(i)	(iii)	(ii)
(c)	(iv)	(i)	(ii)	(iii)
(d)	(i)	(iv)	(ii)	(iii)

19. Match List I with List II and select the correct answer from the codes below:

List I	**List II**
(A) Varnashrama	(i) Buddhism
(B) Tirthankara	(ii) Brahmanism
(C) Shaivism	(iii) Jainism
(D) Vajrayana	(iv) Vedic

Codes:	**A**	**B**	**C**	**D**
(a)	(iv)	(iii)	(ii)	(i)
(b)	(ii)	(i)	(iv)	(iii)
(c)	(iii)	(iv)	(ii)	(i)
(d)	(iv)	(ii)	(iii)	(i)

20. *Chahlghani* was dominant during the reign of:
   (a) Qutbuddin Aibak
   (b) Iltutmish
   (c) Balban
   (d) Alauddin Khalji

21. When did Babur adopt the title of *Ghazi*?
   (a) 1525 (b) 1526
   (c) 1527 (d) 1528

22. The Rishi *Silsilah* refers to an order of sufi saints in:
   (a) Kashmir (b) Ajmer
   (c) Hyderabad (d) Agra

23. Who was the writer of *Safinat-ul Auliya*?
   (a) Mian Mir
   (b) Mulla Shah Badakhshi
   (c) Nizam-ud-din Ahmad
   (d) Dara Shikoh

24. Name the two Delhi Sultanate historians whose works bear the same title "Tarikh-i Firuzshahi":
   (a) Zia-ud-din Barani and Amir Khusrau
   (b) Shams Siraj Afif and Minhaj Siraj
   (c) Hasan Nizami and Amir Khusrau
   (d) Zia-ud-din Barani and Shams Siraj Afif

25. Given below are two statements one labelled as Assertion (A) and the other labelled as Reason (R):

Assertion (A): *Zat* denotes the number of troopers held by the mansabdars

Reason (R): *Sawar* denotes the personal status and standing in the Mughal administrative hierarchy.

In the context of the above two statements, which one of the following is correct.

Codes:

(a) (A) is correct, but (R) is wrong
(b) Both (A) and (R) are correct
(c) (A) is wrong, but (R) is correct
(d) Both (A) and (R) are wrong

26. Given below are two statements one labelled as Assertion (A) and the other labelled as Reason (R):

Assertion (A): Invading of Balkh and Badakhshan and three closely spaced sieges of Qandahar by Shahjahan resulted in nothing except the shedding of blood, the killing of thirty to forty thousand of people, and the expenditure of thirty five million rupees.

Reason (R): It did not have any effect on Mughal resources.

In the context of the above two statements, which one of the following is correct?

Codes:

(a) (A) is correct, but (R) is wrong
(b) Both (A) and (R) are correct
(c) (A) is wrong, but (R) is correct
(d) Both (A) and (R) are wrong

27. Given below are two statements one labelled as Assertion (A) and the other labelled as Reason (R):

Assertion (A): Alauddin khalji was involved in major changes in the taxation system and collection of grain. He also undertook certain measures to ensure low prices.

Reason (R): In the interests of expanding his forces and of maintaining them on low pay.

In the context of the above two statements, which one of the following is correct?

Codes:

(a) (A) is correct, but (R) is wrong
(b) Both (A) and (R) are correct
(c) (A) is wrong, but (R) is correct
(d) Both (A) and (R) are wrong

28. Which of the following is chronologically correct?

(a) Sangama, Saluva, Tuluva, Aravidu
(b) Saluva, Tuluva, Aravidu, Sangama
(c) Tuluva, Aravidu, Sangama, Saluva
(d) Aravidu, Sangama, Saluva, Tuluva

29. Arrange the following in correct sequence:

(a) Shams Siraj Afif, Abbas Khan Sarwani, Hasan Nizami, Minhaj Siraj
(b) Hasan Nizami, Minhaj Siraj, Shams Siraj Afif, Abbas Khan Sarwani
(c) Abbas Khan Sarwani, Hasan Nizami, Shams Siraj Afif, Minhaj Siraj
(d) Minhaj Siraj, Abbas Khan Sarwani, Hasan Nizami, Shams Siraj Afif

30. Arrange the following in correct sequence:

(a) Battle of Ghagra, Battle of Kalinjar, Second Battle of Panipat, Battle of Talikota
(b) Second Battle of Panipat, Battle of Kalinjar, Battle of Talikota, Battle of Ghagra
(c) Battle of Kalinjar, Battle of Ghagra, Second Battle of Panipat, Battle of Talikota
(d) Battle of Talikota, Battle of Kalinjar, Second Battle of Panipat, Battle of Ghagra

31. Match List I with List II and select the correct answer from the codes given below:

List I	List II
(A) Nicolo De Conti	(i) Russia
(B) Athanasius	(ii) Italy
(C) Abdur Razzaq	(iii) Portugal
(D) Domingo Paes	(iv) Iran

Codes:	A	B	C	D
(a)	(i)	(ii)	(iii)	(iv)
(b)	(iii)	(iv)	(ii)	(i)
(c)	(ii)	(i)	(iv)	(iii)
(d)	(iv)	(iii)	(ii)	(i)

32. Match List I with List II and select the correct answer from the codes given below:

List I

(A) Mutamid Khan (B) Lahori
(C) Badaoni (D) Khafi Khan

List II

(i) Padshahnama
(ii) Muntkhab-ut-Tawarikh
(iii) Iqbalnamd-i-Tahangiri
(iv) Muntkhab-ul-Lubab

Codes:	A	B	C	D
(a)	(i)	(ii)	(iii)	(iv)
(b)	(iv)	(iii)	(ii)	(i)
(c)	(iii)	(i)	(ii)	(iv)
(d)	(ii)	(iv)	(iii)	(i)

33. Match List I with List II and select the correct answer from the codes given below:

List I

(A) Quwwat-ul Islam mosque
(B) Alai Darwaza
(C) Atala mosque
(D) Rohtasgarh Fort

List II

(i) Shershah Suri
(ii) Qutbuddin Aibek
(iii) Alauddin Khalji
(iv) Ibrahim Shah Sharqi

Codes:	A	B	C	D
(a)	(ii)	(iii)	(iv)	(i)
(b)	(i)	(ii)	(iii)	(iv)
(c)	(iv)	(iii)	(ii)	(i)
(d)	(iii)	(iv)	(i)	(ii)

34. Cornwallis code of 1793 separated:
(a) Civil from judicial administration
(b) Revenue collection from administration of civil justice
(c) The Bengal from central administration
(d) The civil from military administration

35. The Ulgulan (ULGULAN) was a movement of the:
(a) Agarias (b) Juangs
(c) Hos (d) Mundas

36. Identify the person not favouring the idea of land tax being permanently fixed:
(a) Alexander Dow
(b) Henri Patullo
(c) Philip Francis
(d) Warren Hastings

37. Given below are two statements one labelled as Assertion (A) and the other labelled as Reason (R):
Assertion (A): The Roytwari system did not eliminate village elites as intermediaries between the government and the peasantry.
Reason (R): The village power structure was hardly altered and even more strengthened by the new system
In the context of the above two statements, which one of the following is correct?
Codes:
(a) (A) is true and (R) is false
(b) (A) is false and (R) is true
(c) Both (A) and (R) are true
(d) Both (A) and (R) are false

38. Given below are two statements one labelled as Assertion (A) and the other labelled as Reason (R):
Assertion (A): The goal of the extremists was swaraj, which different leaders interpreted differently.

Reason (R): The leaders coming from different linguistic zones understood it differently.

In the context of the above statements, which one of the following is correct.

Codes:

(a) Both (A) and (R) are true
(b) (A) is true and (R) is false
(c) (A) is false and (R) is true
(d) Both (A) and (R) are false

39. Given below are two statements, one labelled as Assertion (A) and the other labelled as Reason (R):

Assertion (A): The Morley-Minto Reforms satisfied both the contending factions of Indian National Congress

Reason (R): The Morley-Minto Reforms addressed all their concerns.

In the context of the above two statements, which one of the following is correct.

Codes:

(a) (A) is true but (R) is false
(b) (A) is false but (R) is true
(c) Both (A) and (R) are false
(d) (A) is true but (R) does not explain (A)

40. Which of the following is chronologically correct?

(a) Parthana Samaj – Brahmo Samaj – Arya Samaj – Poona Sarvajanik Sabha – Atmiya Sabha
(b) Atmiya Sabha – Brahmo Samaj – Parthana Samaj – Arya Samaj – Poona Sarvajanik Sabha
(c) Atmiya Sabha – Parthana Samaj – Brahmo Samaj – Arya Samaj – Poona Sarvajanik Sabha
(d) Atmiya Sabha – Brahmo Samaj – Parthana Samaj – Poona Sarvajanik Sabha – Arya Samaj

41. Arrange the following in chronological order:

(i) The Indian Penal Code
(ii) The code of Civil Procedure
(iii) The Criminal Procedure Code
(iv) Police Act

Options:

(a) (i) (iii) (iv) (ii) (b) (ii) (iii) (i) (iv)
(c) (ii) (i) (iv) (iii) (d) (i) (iv) (ii) (iii)

42. Arrange the following in chronological order:

(i) Satara Prati Sarkar
(ii) Mopalah
(iii) Tamralipta Jatiya Sarkar
(iv) Hool

Options:

(a) (i) (iii) (ii) (iv) (b) (ii) (iv) (i) (iii)
(c) (iv) (ii) (iii) (i) (d) (iii) (i) (ii) (iv)

43. Match the List I with List II using the code:

List I

(A) The Emergence of Indian Nationalism
(B) Nationalism and Colonialism in Modern India
(C) The Nation and its Fragments
(D) Nationalism wihout a Nation in India

List II

(i) Partha Chatterjee
(ii) Anil seal
(iii) G. Alloysius
(iv) Rajnarain Chandavarkar

Codes:	**A**	**B**	**C**	**D**
(a)	(ii)	(iii)	(iv)	(i)
(b)	(ii)	(i)	(iii)	(iv)
(c)	(ii)	(iv)	(i)	(iii)
(d)	(iii)	(iv)	(ii)	(i)

44. Match List I with List II using codes:

List I

(A) Bengalee
(B) Bande Mataram
(C) Amrita Bazar Patrika
(D) Bangabasi

List II
(i) Aurobindo Ghosh
(ii) Bankim Chandra Chatterjee
(iii) Surendranath Banerjee
(iv) Motilal Ghosh

Codes:	A	B	C	D
(a)	(ii)	(iii)	(iv)	(i)
(b)	(iii)	(ii)	(i)	(iv)
(c)	(iii)	(iv)	(ii)	(i)
(d)	(iii)	(i)	(iv)	(ii)

45. Match List I with List II using the codes:

List I	List II
(A) Anjuman	(i) Polygamy
(B) Kulin	(ii) Cultivator
(C) Kanakkaram	(iii) Association
(D) Mitakshara	(iv) Inheritance

Codes:	A	B	C	D
(a)	(i)	(iii)	(iv)	(ii)
(b)	(iii)	(i)	(ii)	(iv)
(c)	(iii)	(i)	(iv)	(ii)
(d)	(iv)	(iii)	(ii)	(i)

46. During second world war, who said, "I have not become the King's First Minister to preside over the liquidation of the British Empire".
(a) Lord Beaconsfield
(b) John Lloyd
(c) Winston Churchill
(d) Benjamin Disraeli

47. Where was the first socialist group formed?
(a) Great Britain (b) Russia
(c) Germany (d) France

48. What was most obvious expression of imperialism?
(a) Superior technology
(b) Colonies
(c) Communication network
(d) Cultural supremacy

49. Research in observation process has to be:
(a) continuous and persistent
(b) occasional and general
(c) hurriedly carried proposition
(d) none of the above

50. Who warns against defining 'behaviour' as 'rationality'?
(a) Milton Friedman
(b) Vincent J. Tarascio
(c) Werner Hochwald
(d) Stark Werner

ANSWERS

1. (a)	2. (a)	3. (d)	4. (b)	5. (c)
6. (a)	7. (b)	8. (c)	9. (c)	10. (a)
11. (b)	12. (b)	13. (d)	14. (b)	15. (b)
16. (a)	17. (a)	18. (b)	19. (a)	20. (b)
21. (c)	22. (a)	23. (d)	24. (d)	25. (d)
26. (a)	27. (b)	28. (a)	29. (b)	30. (a)
31. (c)	32. (c)	33. (a)	34. (a)	35. (d)
36. (c)	37. (a)	38. (b)	39. (c)	40. (b)
41. (d)	42. (c)	43. (c)	44. (d)	45. (b)
46. (c)	47. (b)	48. (b)	49. (a)	50. (c)

DECEMBER–2007

Note: This paper contains fifty (50) objective type questions, each question carrying two (2) marks. Attempt all the questions.

PAPER–I

1. Verbal guidance is least effective in the learning of
   (a) Aptitudes (b) Skills
   (c) Attitudes (d) Relationship
2. Which is the most important aspect of the teacher's role in learning?
   (a) The development of insight into what consititutes an adequate performance
   (b) The development of insight into what consititutes the pitfalls and dangers to be avoided
   (c) The provision of encouragement and moral support
   (d) The provision of continuous diagnostic and remedial help
3. The most appropriate purpose of learning is
   (a) personal adjustment
   (b) modification of behaviour
   (c) social and political awarness
   (d) preparing oneself for employment
4. The students who keep on asking questions in the class should be
   (a) encouraged to find answer independently
   (b) advised to meet the teacher after the class
   (c) encouraged to continue questioning
   (d) advised not to disturb during the lecture
5. Maximum participation of students is possible in teaching through
   (a) discussion method
   (b) lecture method
   (c) audio-visual aids
   (d) textbook method
6. Generalised conclusion on the basis of a sample is technically known as
   (a) Data analysis and interpretation
   (b) Parameter inference
   (c) Statistical inference
   (d) All of the above
7. The experimental study is based on
   (a) The manipulation of variables
   (b) Conceptual parameters
   (c) Replication of research
   (d) Survey of literature
8. The main characteristic of scientific research is
   (a) empirical (b) theoretical
   (c) experimental (d) All of the above
9. Authenticity of a research finding is its
   (a) Originality (b) Validity
   (c) Objectivity (d) All of the above
10. Which technique is generally followed when the population is finite?
    (a) Area Sampling Technique
    (b) Purposive Sampling Technique
    (c) Systematic Sampling Technique
    (d) None of the above

Read the following passage and answer the questions 11 to 15:

Gandhi's overall social and environmental philosophy is based on what human beings need rather than what they want. His early introduction to the teachings of Jains, Theosophists, Christian sermons, Ruskin and Tolstoy, and most significantly the *Bhagavad Gita*, were to have profound impact on the development of Gandhi's holistic thinking on humanity, nature and their ecological interrelation. His deep concern for the disadvantaged, the poor and rural population created an ambience for an alternative social thinking that was at once far-sighted, local and immediate. For Gandhi was acutely aware that the demands generated by the need to feed and sustain human life, compounded by the growing industrialisation of India, far outstripped the finite resources of nature. This might nowadays appear naive or commonplace, but such pronouncements were as rare as they were heretical a century ago. Gandhi was also concerned about the destruction, under colonial and modernist designs, of the existing infrastructures which had more potential for keeping a community flourishing within ecologically-sensitive traditional patterns of subsistence, especially in the rural areas, than did the incoming Western alternatives based on nature-blind technology and the enslavement of human spirit and energies.

Perhaps the moral principle for which Gandhi is best known is that of active non-violence, derived from the traditional moral restraint of not injuring another being. The most refined expression of this value is in the great epic of the *Mahabharata*, (c. 100 BCE to 200 CE), where moral development proceeds through placing constraints on the liberties, desires and acquisitiveness endemic to human life. One's action is judged in terms of consequences and the impact it is likely to have on another. Jainas had generalised this principle to include all sentient creatures and biocommunities alike. Advanced Jaina monks and nuns will sweep their path to avoid harming insects and even bacteria. Non-injury is a non-negotiable universal prescription.

11. Which one of the following have a profound impact on the development of Gandhi's holistic thinking on humanity, nature and their ecological interrelations?
    (a) Jain teachings
    (b) Christian sermons
    (c) *Bhagavad Gita*
    (d) Ruskin and Tolstoy
12. Gandhi's overall social and environmental philosophy is based on human beings'
    (a) need (b) desire
    (c) wealth (d) welfare
13. Gandhiji's deep concern for the disadvantaged, the poor and rural population created an ambience for an alternative
    (a) rural policy
    (b) social thinking
    (c) urban policy
    (d) economic thinking
14. Colonial policy and modernisation led to the destruction of
    (a) major industrial infrastructure
    (b) irrigation infrastructure
    (c) urban infrastructure
    (d) rural infrastructure
15. Gandhi's active non-violence is derived from
    (a) Moral restraint of not injuring another being
    (b) Having liberties, desires and acquisitiveness
    (c) Freedom of action
    (d) Nature-blind technology and enslavement of human spirit and energies
16. DTH service was started in the year
    (a) 2000 (b) 2002
    (c) 2004 (d) 2006
17. National Press day is celebrated on
    (a) 16th November (b) 19th November
    (c) 21st November (d) 30th November

18. The total number of members in the Press Council of India are
(a) 28 (b) 14
(c) 17 (d) 20

19. The right to impart and receive information is guaranteed in the Constitution of India by Article
(a) 19(2)(a) (b) 19(16)
(c) 19(2) (d) 19(1)(a)

20. Use of radio for higher education is based on the presumption of
(a) Enriching curriculum based instruction
(b) Replacing teacher in the long run
(c) Everybody having access to a radio set
(d) Other means of instruction getting outdated

21. Find out the number which should come at the place of question mark which will complete the following series.
5, 4, 9, 17, 35, ? = 139
(a) 149 (b) 79
(c) 49 (d) 69

Questions 22 to 24 are based on the following diagram in which there are three interlocking circles I, S and P, where circle I stands for Indians, circle S for Scientists and circle P for Politicians. Different regions in the figure are lettered from a to f.

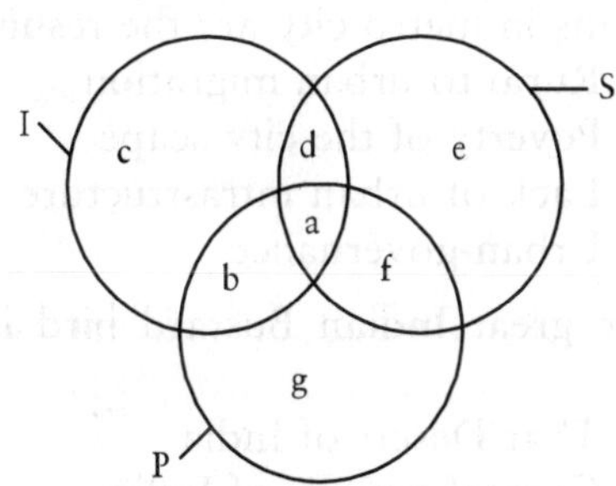

22. The region which represents Non-Indian Scientists who are Politicians.
(a) f (b) d
(c) a (d) c

23. The region which represents Indians who are neither Scientists nor Politicians.
(a) g (b) c
(c) f (d) a

24. The region which represents Politicians who are Indians as well as Scientists.
(a) b (b) c
(c) a (d) d

25. Which number is missing in the following series?
2, 5, 10, 17, 26, 37, 50, ?
(a) 63 (b) 65
(c) 67 (d) 69

26. The function of measurement includes.
(a) Prognosis (b) Diagnosis
(c) Prediction (d) All of the above

27. Logical arguments are based on.
(a) Scientific reasoning
(b) Customary reasoning
(c) Mathematical reasoning
(d) Syllogistic reasoning

28. Insert the missing number 4 : 17 : : 7 : ?
(a) 48 (b) 49
(c) 50 (d) 51

29. Choose the odd word.
(a) Nun (b) Knight
(c) Monk (d) Priest

30. Choose the number which is different from others in the group.
(a) 49 (b) 63
(c) 77 (d) 81

31. Probability sampling implies.
(a) Stratified Random Sampling
(b) Systematic Random Sampling
(c) Simple Random Sampling
(d) All of the above

32. Insert the missing number.
$\frac{36}{62}, \frac{39}{63}, \frac{43}{61}, \frac{48}{64}, ?$

(a) $\frac{51}{65}$ (b) $\frac{56}{60}$

(c) $\frac{54}{65}$ (d) $\frac{33}{60}$

33. At what time between 3 and 4 o'clock will the hands of a watch point in opposite directions?
(a) 40 minutes past three
(b) 45 minutes past three
(c) 50 minutes past three
(d) 55 minutes past three

34. Mary has three children. What is the probability that none of the three children is a boy?

(a) $\frac{1}{2}$ (b) $\frac{1}{3}$

(c) $\frac{3}{4}$ (d) 1

35. If the radius of a circle is increased by 50 percent. Its area is increased by
(a) 125 percent (b) 100 percent
(c) 75 percent (d) 50 percent

36. CD ROM stands for
(a) Computer Disk Read Only Memory
(b) Compact Disk Read Over Memory
(c) Compact Disk Read Only Memory
(d) Computer Disk Read Over Memory

37. The 'brain' of a computer which keeps peripherals under its control is called
(a) Common Power Unit
(b) Common Processing Unit
(c) Central Power Unit
(d) Central Processing Unit

38. Data can be saved on backing storage medium known as
(a) Compact Disk Recordable
(b) Computer Disk Rewritable
(c) Compact Disk Rewritable
(d) Computer Data Rewritable

39. RAM means
(a) Random Access Memory
(b) Rigid Access Memory
(c) Rapid Access Memory
(d) Revolving Access Memory

40. www represents
(a) who what and where
(b) weird wide web
(c) word wide web
(d) world wide web

41. Deforestation during the recent decades has led to
(a) Soil erosion
(b) Landslides
(c) Loss of bio-diversity
(d) All of the above

42. Which one of the following natural hazards is responsible for causing highest human disaster?
(a) Earthquakes
(b) Volcanic eruptions
(c) Snowstorms
(d) Tsunami

43. Which one of the following is appropriate for natural hazard mitigation?
(a) International AID
(b) Timely Warning System
(c) Rehabilitation
(d) Community Participation

44. Slums in metro city are the result of
(a) Rural to urban migration
(b) Poverty of the city-scape
(c) Lack of urban infrastructure
(d) Urban-governance

45. The great Indian Bustard bird is found in
(a) Thar Desert of India
(b) Coastal regions of India
(c) Temperate Forests in the Himalaya
(d) Tarai zones of the Himalayan Foot

46. The first Indian Satellite for serving the educational sector is known as
(a) SATEDU (b) INSAT-B
(c) EDUSAT (d) DMSAT-C

47. Exclusive educational channel of IGNOU is known as
(a) Gyan Darshan (b) Gyan Vani
(c) Door Darshan (d) Prasar Bharati

48. The headquarter of Mahatma Gandhi Antarrashtriya Hindi Vishwavidyalaya is situated in
(a) Sevagram (b) New Delhi
(c) Wardha (d) Ahmedabad

49. Match List I with List II and select the correct answer using the codes given below.

List I (Institutes)
A. Central Institute of English and Foreign Languages
B. Gramodaya Vishwavidyalaya
C. Central Institute of Higher Tibetan Studies
D. IGNOU

List II (Locations)
1. Chitrakoot 2. Hyderabad
3. New Delhi 4. Dharmasala

Codes:	A	B	C	D
(a)	2	1	4	3
(b)	4	3	2	1
(c)	3	4	1	2
(d)	1	2	4	3

50. The aim of vocationalisation of education is
(a) preparing students for a vocation along with knowledge
(b) converting liberal education into vocational education
(c) giving more importance to vocational than general education
(d) making liberal education job-oriented

ANSWERS

1. (b)	2. (a)	3. (b)	4. (a)	5. (a)
6. (c)	7. (c)	8. (c)	9. (d)	10. (c)
11. (c)	12. (a)	13. (b)	14. (c)	15. (a)
16. (d)	17. (a)	18. (a)	19. (d)	20. (b)
21. (d)	22. (a)	23. (b)	24. (c)	25. (b)
26. (d)	27. (d)	28. (c)	29. (b)	30. (c)
31. (d)	32. (c)	33. (c)	34. (d)	35. (a)
36. (c)	37. (d)	38. (c)	39. (a)	40. (d)
41. (d)	42. (a)	43. (b)	44. (a)	45. (a)
46. (c)	47. (a)	48. (c)	49. (a)	50. (d)

PAPER–II

Note: This paper contains fifty (50) objective type questions, each question carrying two (2) marks. All questions are compulsory.

Read the passage given below and answer the questions (1-5) that follow, based on your understanding of the passage:

Northwards Indian cultural influence spread through Central Asia to China. Faint and weak contact between China and India was probably made in Mauryan times, if not before, but only when, some 2,000 years ago, the Han Empire began to drive its frontiers towards the Caspian did India and China really meet. Unlike South-East Asia, China did not assimilate Indian ideas in every aspect of her culture, but the whole of the Far East is in India's debt for Buddhism, which helped to mould the distinctive civilizations of China, Korea, Japan and Tibet.

As well as her special gifts to Asia, India has conferred many practical blessings on the world at large; notably rice, cotton, the sugar cane, many spices, the domestic fowl, the game of chess and, most important of all, the decimal system of numeral notation, the invention of an unknown Indian mathematician early in the Christian era. The extent of the spiritual influence of India on the ancient West is much disputed. The heterodox Jewish sect of the Essenes, which probably influenced early Christianity, followed monastic practices in some respects similar to those of Buddhism. Parallels may be traced between a few passages in the New Testament and the Pali scriptures. Similarities between the teachings of western philosophers and mystics from Pythagoras to Plotinus and those of the Upanisads have frequently been noticed. None of these similarities, however, is close enough to give certainty, especially as we have no evidence that any classical writer had a deep knowledge of Indian religion. We can only say that there was always some contact between the Hellenic world and India, mediated first by the Achaemenid Empire, then by that of the Seleucids, and finally, under the Romans, by the traders of the Indian ocean. Christianity began to spread at the time when this contact was closest. We know that Indian ascetics occasionally visited the West, and that there was a colony of Indian merchants at Alexandria. The possibility of Indian influence on Neo-platonism and early Christianity cannot be ruled out.

1. Which country did not assimilate Indian ideas in every aspect?
   (a) South-East Asia (b) Tibet
   (c) Japan (d) China
2. How the Indian cultural influence spread to the China?
   (a) through Central Asia to China
   (b) during Mauryan times
   (c) through Buddhism
   (d) due to Han empire
3. The Jewish sect of the Essenes had borrowed from India:
   (a) the decimal system in maths
   (b) the chess game
   (c) the food-grains
   (d) the monastic system
4. How the Indian influence penetrated in the Western World?
   (a) Through contact between Hellenic World and India
   (b) By Indian monks
   (c) By Indian traders
   (d) By Itinerants
5. The Romans finally were influenced by India:
   (a) through monks
   (b) through traders
   (c) through Itinerants
   (d) through teachers
6. Which one of the following prehistoric sites has provided evidence for cultivation of Wild and Sown variety of Paddy:
   (a) Belan (b) Bagor
   (c) Adamgarh (d) Burzahom
7. What is the main achievement of the Neolithic revolution?
   (a) Animal husbandry
   (b) Agriculture
   (c) Nomadic life
   (d) Painting
8. Consider the following statements:
   (1) In Rig Vedic time the King was the absolute monarch.
   (2) Feudalism originated during the Rig Vedic period.
   (3) Purohita was the foremost among the functionaries of the King during the Rig Vedic time.

   Which of the statements given above is/are correct?
   (a) (1) and (2) (b) (2) and (3)
   (c) (1), (2) and (3) (d) (3) only
9. Given below are two statements, one labelled as Assertion (A) and the other labelled as Reason (R):

Assertion (A): The concept of middle path in Buddhism is to destroy all pains in human's life.

Reason (R): It ends the extreme views.

In the context of the above two statements which one of the following is correct?

(a) (A) is true, but (R) is false
(b) (R) is true, but (A) is false
(c) Both (A) and (R) are true
(d) Both (A) and (R) are false

10. What was upavasatha (uposatha) in Buddhist order?
(a) It was an act of general confession of Buddhist monks when they assembled every fortnight on the evenings of full and new moons
(b) It was the vow taken by the newly admitted monks
(c) It was staying in the Viharas during rains
(d) It was an act of fasting by the monks as punishment

11. Who got excavated the rock-cut caves on Nagarjuni hills?
(a) Chandragupta Maurya
(b) Ashoka
(c) Dasharatha
(d) Samprati

12. Given below are two statements, one labelled as Assertion (A) and the other labelled as Reason (R):

Assertion (A): Under Ashoka Mauryan monarchy had taken the shape of military despotism.

Reason (R): Rock Edicts of Ashoka show him as remarking—"All men are my children"

In the context of the above two statements which one of the following is correct?

(a) (A) is correct, but (R) is wrong
(b) Both (A) and (R) are correct
(c) (A) is wrong, but (R) is correct
(d) Both (A) and (R) are wrong

13. Given below are two statements, one labelled as Assertion (A) and the other labelled as Reason (R):

Assertion (A): Some Yavanas (Greeks) were converted to Vaishnava faith during the reign of the Sungas.

Reason (R): Bhagavata erected a Garuda pillar at Besnagar.

In the context of the above two statements which one of the following is correct?

(a) (A) is correct, but (R) is wrong
(b) Both (A) and (R) are correct, but (R) is not the correct explanation of (A)
(c) (A) is wrong, but (R) is correct
(d) Both (A) and (R) are wrong

14. The earliest Hindu temple is carved at:
(a) Sonkha (b) Aihole
(c) Deogarh (d) Vidisha

15. Hiuen Tsang visited Kanchi during the rule of which one of the following rulers of Pallava dynasty?
(a) Mahendra Varman–I
(b) Paramesvara Varman–I
(c) Narasimha Varman–I
(d) Narasimha Varman–II

16. Match List I with List II and choose your answer from the codes given below:

List I (Inscriptions)
(A) Bilahari Stone Inscription
(B) Mehrauli Pillar Inscription
(C) Mandsaur Pillar Inscription
(D) Hathigumpha Inscription

List II (Rulers)
(i) Yasodharman (ii) Kharavela
(iii) Yuvarajadeva (iv) Chandra

Codes:	A	B	C	D
(a)	(iv)	(ii)	(iii)	(i)
(b)	(ii)	(iii)	(i)	(iv)
(c)	(i)	(iv)	(iii)	(ii)
(d)	(iii)	(iv)	(i)	(ii)

17. Match List I with List II and select the correct answer from the codes given below:

List I (Authors)

(A) Bharavi (B) Ashvaghosha
(C) Varahamihira (D) Kalhana

List II (Works)

(i) Buddha charita (ii) Kiratarjuniyam
(iii) Rajatarangini (iv) Brihatsamhita

Codes:	A	B	C	D
(a)	(i)	(ii)	(iv)	(iii)
(b)	(ii)	(i)	(iv)	(iii)
(c)	(iii)	(iv)	(ii)	(i)
(d)	(iv)	(iii)	(i)	(ii)

18. Given below are two statements, one labelled as Assertion (A) and the other labelled as Reason (R):

    Assertion (A): The Cholas followed the Pallava traditions in temple construction.

    Reason (R): They built a number of monolithic temples throughout their kingdom following the Pallava style.

    In the context of the above two statements, which one of the following is correct?

    Codes:

    (a) (A) is correct, but (R) is wrong
    (b) Both (A) and (R) are correct
    (c) (A) is wrong, but (R) is correct
    (d) Both (A) and (R) are wrong

19. Match List I with List II and select the correct answer from the codes given below:

    List I

    (A) Prithviraja II
    (B) Jayasimha Siddharaja
    (C) Govindachandra
    (D) Gangeyadeva

    List II (Period)

    (i) 1110 – 1155 A.D.
    (ii) 1165 – 1169 A.D.
    (iii) 1094 – 1143 A.D.
    (iv) 1015 – 1041 A.D.

Codes:	A	B	C	D
(a)	(iv)	(iii)	(i)	(ii)
(b)	(i)	(iii)	(ii)	(iv)
(c)	(ii)	(iii)	(i)	(iv)
(d)	(iv)	(ii)	(iii)	(i)

20. Dhoyi was the court poet of which one of the following rulers of the Sena dynasty of Bengal?

    (a) Hemantasena (b) Vijayasena
    (c) Vallalasena (d) Lakshmanasena

21. Who among the following organized the Chishti Silsilah in Bengal?

    (a) Shaikh Hamid-ud-din
    (b) Shaikh Qutub-ud-din Munawwar
    (c) Shaikh Siraj-ud-din Usman
    (d) Shaikh Shah Wilayat

22. Consider the following group of Bhakti saints who flourished at different points of time in various parts of the country:

    (i) The Varkari saints of Maharashtra
    (ii) The Virashaiva saints of Karnataka
    (iii) The Alwars and Nayanars of the Tamil country
    (iv) The Dadupanthis of Rajasthan

    Which of the following sequence is chronologically correct?

    (a) (i) (ii) (iii) (iv)
    (b) (iii) (i) (ii) (iv)
    (c) (iii) (iv) (i) (ii)
    (d) (iii) (ii) (i) (iv)

23. Mifta-ul-futuh composed by Amir Khusrav describes:

    (a) The meeting between Bughra Khan and Kaikubad
    (b) The military campaigns of Jalal-ud-din Khalji
    (d) The conquest of Gujrat by Ala-ud-din Khalji
    (d) The military campaigns during the reigns of Mubarak Shah

24. Under which Sultan of Delhi the Mongol threat in the North-west reached at its threatening climax?
(a) Balban
(b) Jalaluddin Khalji
(c) Alauddin Khalji
(d) Muhammad bin Tughluq

25. Who among the following described Delhi as the largest city in the entire 'Islamic East'?
(a) Alberuni (b) Amir Khusrav
(c) Ibn Battuta (d) Shms Siraj Afif

26. Given below are two statements, one labelled as Assertion (A) and the other labelled as Reason (R):
Assertion (A): From the very beginning of the Bahmani kingdom the foreigners wielded considerable influence in the politics of the kingdom.
Reason (R): Bahman Shah did not trust the Deccanis.
In the context of the above two statements, which one of the following is correct?
Codes:
(a) Both (A) and (R) are true and (R) is the correct explanation of (A)
(b) Both (A) and (R) are true, but (R) is not the correct explanation of (A)
(c) (A) is true, but (R) is false
(d) (R) is true, but (A) is false

27. Which of the following foreigners, who visited Vijayanagara, have described Sahgamana (sati)?
(1) Nicolo Conti (2) Domingo Paes
(3) Fernao Nuniz (4) Varthema
Codes:
(a) (2) and (4) (b) (1) and (3)
(c) (1), (2) and (4) (d) (2) and (3)

28. The Portuguese captured Goa from the Sultan of Bijapur in:
(a) 1496 (b) 1510
(c) 1524 (d) 1558

29. Given below are two statements, one labelled as Assertion (A) and the other labelled as Reason (R):
Assertion (A): Akbar proclaimed Dahsala in the twenty-fourth year of his reign (1579).
Reason (R): He decided to abolish the practice of annual measurement of land.
In the context of the above two statements, which one of the following is correct?
Codes:
(a) Both (A) and (R) are true, and (R) is the correct explanation of (A)
(b) Both (A) and (R) are true, but (R) is not the correct explanation of (A)
(c) (A) is true, but (R) is false
(d) (R) is true, but (A) is false

30. Which of the following works deal with music?
(1) Man-kutuhal
(2) Tuhfat-ul Hind
(3) Madhavanala-Kamkandala
(4) Kitab-i Nauras
Codes:
(a) (1), (2), (3) (b) (1), (3), (4)
(c) (2), (3), (4) (d) (1), (2), (4)

31. Match List I with List II and select the correct answer from the codes given below:
List I (Monuments)
(A) Atala Masjid
(B) Bara Sona Masjid
(C) Gol Gumbaz
(D) Charminar
List II (Builders)
(i) Ali Adil Shah
(ii) Ibrahim Shah Sharqi
(iii) Nusrat Shah
(iv) Muhammad Quli Qutub Shah

Codes:	**A**	**B**	**C**	**D**
(a)	(ii)	(iii)	(iv)	(i)
(b)	(iii)	(ii)	(iv)	(i)

(c)	(ii)	(iii)	(i)	(iv)
(d)	(iii)	(ii)	(i)	(iv)

32. Which of the following manuscripts were illustrated during Akbar's time?
(1) The Diwan-i-Amir Hasan Dihilavi
(2) The Raj Kunwar
(3) The Tutinama
(4) The Yoga Vashishta
Codes:
(a) (1), (2) and (3) (b) (3) and (4)
(c) (1) and (2) (d) (2), (3) and (4)

33. Which of the following was not a Mughul coin?
(a) Muzaffari (b) Muhar
(c) Anna (d) Do Dami

34. Match List I with List II and select the correct answer from the codes given below:
List I (Term)
(A) *Sair-hasil Jagir* (B) *Pai baqi*
(C) *Al-tamgah* (D) *Arazi*
List II (Meaning)
(i) Permanent revenue assignment
(ii) Measured area figures
(iii) Most paying jagir
(iv) Land reserved for allotment in jagir

Codes:	**A**	**B**	**C**	**D**
(a)	(iv)	(ii)	(i)	(iii)
(b)	(iii)	(iv)	(i)	(ii)
(c)	(ii)	(iii)	(i)	(iv)
(d)	(iv)	(ii)	(iii)	(i)

35. Which of the following is not correctly matched?
(a) Treaty of Purandar – 1664 A.D.
(b) Reimposition of Jaziya – 1679 A.D.
(c) Conquest of Golconda – 1686 A.D.
(d) Capture and execution of Shambhaji – 1689 A.D.

36. Who founded the Hindu college of Calcutta in 1817?
(a) David Hare
(b) William Jones
(c) H.T. Princep
(d) Henry Vivian Derozio

37. Under the 'Guarantee System' the British companies investing in railways were assured a guaranteed dividend of:
(a) 3% (b) 5%
(c) 8% (d) 10%

38. The Famine commission in 1880 was set up by the Government of India under:
(a) H.T. Princep
(b) H.H. Wilson
(c) Sir John Strachey
(d) Sir John McPherson

39. Maulana Abdul Bari belonged to the:
(a) Aligarh School
(b) Deoband Madarsa
(c) Firangi Mahal
(d) Nadwat-ul-ulema

40. Who drafted the address presented to Lord Minto in October 1906 at Shimla led by theAga Khan?
(a) Aga Khan
(b) Syed Husain Bilgrami
(c) M.A. Jinnah
(d) Mohisun-ul-Mulk

41. Eka movement was started by the:
(a) Peasants of Hardoi and Barabanki etc.,
(b) Revolutionary terrorists in Bengal
(c) Workers in South India
(d) Zamindars of Oudh

42. Which aspect of Indian Society have been highlighted by Prem Chand in his novel Nirmala?
(a) Class conflict between landlords and peasants
(b) Dowry and marriage of young girl with an old widower
(c) The problem of middle class life and prostitution in society
(d) Racial discrimination by Europeans

43. The first session of All India Kisan Sabha was presided by:
(a) N.G. Ranga
(b) Narendra Dev
(c) Sahjanand Saraswati
(d) Raghva Das

44. The Indian National Congress passed a resolution on the Fundamental Rights at its:
(a) Lucknow Session, 1916
(b) Madras Session, 1927
(c) Lahore Session, 1929
(d) Karachi Session, 1931

45. Match the personalities in the List I with the cases in List II and select the correct answer from the codes given below:

List I (Personality)
(A) Ashfaqullah Khan
(B) Prafulla Chaki
(C) Sukhdev
(D) Ganesh Ghosh

List II (Case)
(i) Lahore conspiracy case
(ii) Kakori case
(iii) Chittagong Armoury case
(iv) Bomb assault in Muzaffarpur in 1908

Codes:	**A**	**B**	**C**	**D**
(a)	(iii)	(i)	(ii)	(iv)
(b)	(i)	(iii)	(iv)	(ii)
(c)	(ii)	(iv)	(i)	(iii)
(d)	(iv)	(iii)	(ii)	(i)

46. The theory of 'General Will' was propounded by:
(a) Montesquieu (b) Karl Marx
(c) Rousseau (d) Voltaire

47. Who wrote the book entitled 'Imperialism is the Highest Stage of Capitalism'?
(a) Karl Marx
(b) V.I. Lenin
(c) J.V. Stalin
(d) Rosa Luxemburg

48. Which country could not develop into a nation state in the sixteenth century?
(a) France (b) Great Britain
(c) Italy (d) Spain

49. Apartheid policy was followed by:
(a) Great Britain
(b) France
(c) South Africa
(d) United States of America

50. Renaissance paintings known as the 'Last supper' and 'Mona Lisa' were the famous works of:
(a) Fra Lippo Lippi
(b) Leonardo da Vinci
(c) Michel Angelo
(d) Raphael

ANSWERS

1. (d)	2. (b)	3. (d)	4. (a)	5. (b)
6. (a)	7. (b)	8. (d)	9. (c)	10. (b)
11. (c)	12. (c)	13. (c)	14. (c)	15. (c)
16. (c)	17. (a)	18. (b)	19. (c)	20. (d)
21. (b)	22. (d)	23. (b)	24. (c)	25. (c)
26. (b)	27. (b)	28. (b)	29. (c)	30. (d)
31. (c)	32. (b)	33. (a)	34. (b)	35. (c)
36. (a)	37. (b)	38. (c)	39. (c)	40. (d)
41. (a)	42. (c)	43. (c)	44. (d)	45. (c)
46. (a)	47. (b)	48. (d)	49. (a)	50. (b)

JUNE–2007

Note: This paper contains fifty (50) objective type questions, each question carrying two (2) marks. Attempt all the questions.

PAPER–I

1. Teacher uses visual-aids to make learning
   (a) simple
   (b) more knowledgeable
   (c) quicker
   (d) interesting

2. The teacher's role at the higher educational level is to
   (a) provide information to students
   (b) promote self-learning in students
   (c) encourage healthy competition among students
   (d) help students to solve their personal problems

3. Which one of the following teachers would you like the most?
   (a) Punctual
   (b) Having research aptitude
   (c) Loving and having high idealistic philosophy
   (d) Who often amuses his students

4. Micro teaching is most effective for the student-teacher
   (a) during the practice-teaching
   (b) after the practice-teaching
   (c) before the practice-teaching
   (d) None of the above

5. Which is the least important factor in teaching?
   (a) Punishing the students
   (b) Maintaining discipline in the class
   (c) Lecturing in impressive way
   (d) Drawing sketches and diagrams on the blackboard

6. To test null hypothesis, a researcher uses
   (a) t test (b) ANOVA
   (c) x^2 (d) factorial analysis

7. A research problem is feasible only when
   (a) it has utility and relevance
   (b) it is researchable
   (c) it is new and adds something to knowledge
   (d) All of the above

8. Bibliography given in a research report
   (a) shows vast knowledge of the researcher
   (b) helps those interested in further research
   (c) has no relevance to research
   (d) All of the above

9. Fundamental research reflects the ability to
   (a) Synthesise new ideals
   (b) Expound new principles
   (c) Evaluate the existing material concerning research
   (d) Study the existing literature regarding various topics

10. The study in which the investigators attempt to trace an effect is known as
    (a) Survey Research
    (b) *Ex-post Facto* Research

(c) Historical Research
(d) Summative Research

Read the following passage and answer the questions 11 to 15:

All political systems need to mediate the relationship between private wealth and public power. Those that fail risk a dysfunctional government captured by wealthy interests. Corruption is one symptom of such failure with private willingness-to-pay trumping public goals. Private individuals and business firms pay to get routine services and to get to the head of the bureaucratic queue. They pay to limit their taxes, avoid costly regulations, obtain contracts at inflated prices and get concessions and privatised firms at low prices. If corruption is endemic, public officials—both bureaucrats and elected officials—may redesign programs and propose public projects with few public benefits and many opportunities for private profit. Of course, corruption, in the sense of bribes, pay-offs and kickbacks, is only one type of government failure. Efforts to promote 'good governance' must be broader than anti-corruption campaigns. Governments may be honest but inefficient because no one has an incentive to work productively, and narrow elites may capture the state and exert excess influence on policy. Bribery may induce the lazy to work hard and permit those not in the inner circle of cronies to obtain benefits. However, even in such cases, corruption cannot be confined to 'functional' areas. It will be a temptation whenever private benefits are positive. It may be a reasonable response to a harsh reality but, over time, it can facilitate a spiral into an even worse situation.

11. The governments which fail to focus on the relationship between private wealth and public power are likely to become
(a) Functional
(b) Dysfunctional
(c) Normal functioning
(d) Good governance

12. One important symptom of bad governance is
(a) Corruption
(b) High taxes
(c) Complicated rules and regulations
(d) High prices

13. When corruption is rampant, public officials always aim at many opportunities for:
(a) Public benefits (b) Public profit
(c) Private profit (d) Corporate gains

14. Productivity linked incentives to public/private officials is one of the indicatives for
(a) Efficient government
(b) Bad governance
(c) Inefficient government
(d) Corruption

15. The spiralling corruption can only be contained by promoting
(a) Private profit
(b) Anti-corruption campaign
(c) Good governance
(d) Pay-offs and kickbacks

16. Press Council of India is located at
(a) Chennai (b) Mumbai
(c) Kolkata (d) Delhi

17. Adjusting the photo for publication by cutting is technically known as
(a) Photo cutting
(b) Photo bleeding
(c) Photo cropping
(d) Photo adjustment

18. Feedback of a message comes from
(a) Satellite (b) Media
(c) Audience (d) Communicator

19. Collection of information in advance before designing communication strategy is known as

(a) Feedback (b) Feed-forward
(c) Research study (d) Opinion poll

20. The aspect ratio of TV screen is
(a) 4:3 (b) 4:2
(c) 3:5 (d) 2:3

21. Which is the number that comes next in the sequence?
9, 8, 8, 8, 7, 8, 6, __
(a) 5 (b) 6
(c) 8 (d) 4

22. If in a certain language PUNCTUAL is coded as 16598623, how would ACTUPULN be coded?
(a) 834536 (b) 29861635
(c) 834530 (d) 834539

23. The question to be answered by factorial analysis of the quantitative data does not explain one of the following
(a) Is 'X' related to 'Y'?
(b) How is 'X' related to 'Y'?
(c) How does 'X' affect the dependent variable 'Y' at different levels of another independent variable 'K' or 'M'?
(d) How is 'X' by 'K' related to 'M'?

24. January 12, 1980 was Saturday, what day was January 12, 1979?
(a) Saturday (b) Friday
(c) Sunday (d) Thursday

25. How many Mondays are there in a particular month of a particular year, if the month ends on Wednesday?
(a) 5 (b) 4
(c) 3 (d) None of these

26. From the given four statements, select the two which cannot be true but yet both can be false. Choose the right pair.
1. All men are mortal
2. Some men are mortal
3. No man is mortal
4. Some men are not mortal
(a) 1 and 2 (b) 3 and 4
(c) 1 and 3 (d) 2 and 4

27. A Syllogism must have
(a) Three terms (b) Four terms
(c) Six terms (d) Five terms

28. Copula is that part of proposition which denotes the relationship between
(a) Subject and predicate
(b) Known and unknown
(c) Major premise and minor premise
(d) Subject and object

29. "E" denotes
(a) Universal Negative Proposition
(b) Particular Affirmative Proposition
(c) Universal Affirmative Proposition
(d) Particular Negative Proposition

30. 'A' is the father of 'C' and 'D' is the son of 'B'. 'E' is the brother of 'A'. If 'C' is the sister of 'D' how is 'B' related to 'E'?
(a) Daughter (b) Husband
(c) Sister-in-law (d) Brother-in-law

31. Which of the following methods will you choose to prepare choropleth map of India showing urban density of population?
(a) Quartiles (b) Quintiles
(c) Mean and SD (d) Break-point

32. Which of the following methods is best suited to show on a map the types of crops being grown in a region?
(a) Choropleth (b) Chorochromatic
(c) Choroschematic (d) Isopleth

33. A ratio represents the relation between
(a) Part and Part
(b) Part and Whole
(c) Whole and Whole
(d) All of the above

34. Out of four numbers, the average of the first three numbers is thrice the fourth number. If the average of the four numbers is 5, the fourth number is

(a) 4.5 (b) 5
(c) 2 (d) 4

35. Circle graphs are used to show
(a) How various sections share in the whole
(b) How various parts are related to the whole
(c) How one whole is related to other wholes
(d) How one part is related to other parts

36. On the keyboard of computer each character has an "ASCII" value which stands for
(a) American Stock Code for Information Interchange
(b) American Standard Code for Information Interchange
(c) African Standard Code for Information Interchange
(d) Adaptable Standard Code for Information Change

37. Which part of the Central Processing Unit (CPU) performs calculation and makes decisions
(a) Arithmetic Logic Unit
(b) Alternating Logic Unit
(c) Alternate Local Unit
(d) American Logic Unit

38. "Dpi" stands for
(a) Dots per inch
(b) Digits per unit
(c) Dots pixel inch
(d) Diagrams per inch

39. The process of laying out a document with text, graphics, headlines and photographs is involved in
(a) Deck Top Publishing
(b) Desk Top Printing
(c) Desk Top Publishing
(d) Deck Top Printing

40. Transfer of data from one application to another line is known as
(a) Dynamic Disk Exchange
(b) Dodgy Data Exchange
(c) Dogmatic Data Exchange
(d) Dynamic Data Exchange

41. Tsunami occurs due to
(a) Mild earthquakes and landslides in the oceans
(b) Strong earthquakes and landslides in the oceans
(c) Strong earthquakes and landslides in mountains
(d) Strong earthquakes and landslides in deserts

42. Which of the natural hazards have big effect on Indian people each year?
(a) Cyclones (b) Floods
(c) Earthquakes (d) Landslides

43. Comparative Environment Impact Assessment study is to be conducted for
(a) the whole year
(b) three seasons excluding monsoon
(c) any three seasons
(d) the worst season

44. Sea level rise results primarily due to
(a) Heavy rainfall
(b) Melting of glaciers
(c) Submarine volcanism
(d) Seafloor spreading

45. The plume rise in a coal based power plant depends on
1. Buoyancy
2. Atmospheric stability
3. Momentum of exhaust gases identify

Codes:
(a) Both (1) and (2)
(b) Both (2) and (3)
(c) Both (1) and (3)
(d) (1), (2) and (3)

46. Value education makes a student
(a) Good citizen
(b) Successful businessman

(c) Popular teacher
(d) Efficient manager

47. Networking of libraries through electronic media is known as
(a) Inflibnet (b) Libinfnet
(c) Internet (d) HTML

48. The University which telecasts interactive educational programs through its own channel is
(a) B.R. Ambedkar Open University, Hyderabad
(b) I.G.N.O.U.
(c) University of Pune
(d) Annamalai University

49. The Government established the University Grants Commission by an Act of Parliament in the year
(a) 1980 (b) 1948
(c) 1950 (d) 1956

50. Universities having central campus for imparting education are called
(a) Central Universities
(b) Deemed Universities
(c) Residential Universities
(d) Open Universities

ANSWERS

1. (d)	2. (a)	3. (a)	4. (b)	5. (a)
6. (c)	7. (d)	8. (b)	9. (b)	10. (b)
11. (b)	12. (a)	13. (c)	14. (a)	15. (c)
16. (d)	17. (c)	18. (c)	19. (d)	20. (a)
21. (c)	22. (b)	23. (c)	24. (b)	25. (d)
26. (b)	27. (a)	28. (b)	29. (a)	30. (d)
31. (b)	32. (c)	33. (b)	34. (c)	35. (a)
36. (a)	37. (a)	38. (a)	39. (c)	40. (d)
41. (b)	42. (b)	43. (a)	44. (b)	45. (d)
46. (a)	47. (a)	48. (b)	49. (d)	50. (b)

PAPER–II

Note: This paper contains fifty (50) objective type questions, each question carrying two (2) marks. Attempt all the questions.

Read the passage given below and answer the questions that follow, based on your understanding of the passage:

Many authorities may doubt that Indian thought had any effect on that of the ancient West, but there can be no doubt of its direct and indirect influence on the thought of Europe and America in the last century and a half, though this has not received adequate recognition. This influence has not come by way of organized neo-Hindu missions. The last eighty years have seen the foundation of the Theosophical Society, of various Buddhist societies, and of societies in Europe and America looking for inspiration to the saintly 19th-century Bengali mystic, Paramahamsa Ramakrishna, and to his equally saintly disciple, Swami Vivekananda. Lesser organizations and groups have been founded in the West by other Indian mystics and their disciples, some of them noble, earnest and spiritual, others of more dubious character. Here and there Westerners themselves, sometimes armed with a working knowledge of Sanskrit and first-hand Indian experience, have tried to convert the West to a streamlined Yoga or Vedanta. We would in no way disparage these teachers or their followers, many of whom are of great intellectual and spiritual calibre; but whatever we may think of the Western propagators of Indian mysticism, we cannot claim that they have had any great effect on our civilization. More subtle, but more powerful, has been the influence of Mahatma Gandhi, through the many friends of India in the West who were impressed by his burning sincerity and energy, and by the ultimate success of his policy of non-violence in achieving India's independence. Greater than any of these influences, however, has been the influence of ancient Indian religious literature through philosophy.

The pioneers of the Asiatic Society of Bengal quickly gained a small but enthusiastic following in Europe, and Goethe and many other writers of the early 19th century read all they could of ancient Indian literature in translation. We know that Goethe borrowed a device of Indian dramaturgy for the prologue to "Faust", and who can say that the triumphant final chorus of the second part of that work was not in part inspired by the monism of Indian thought as he understood it? From Goethe onwards most of the great German philosophers knew something of Indian philosophy. Schopenhauer, whose influence on literature and psychology has been so considerable, indeed openly admitted his debt, and his outlook was virtually that of Buddhism. The monisms of Fichte and Hegel might never have taken the forms they did if it had not been for Anquetil-Duperron's translation of the Upanisads and the work of other pioneer Indologists. In the English-speaking world the strongest Indian influence was felt in America, where Emerson, Thoreau and other New England writers avidly studied much Indian religious literature in translation, and exerted immense influence on their contemporaries and successors, notably Walt Whitman. Through Carlyle and others the German philosophers in their turn made their mark on England, as did the Americans through many late 19th-century writers such as Richard Jeffries and Edward Carpenter.

Though in the contemporary philosophical schools of Europe and America the monistic and idealist philosophies of the last century carry little weight, their influence has been considerable, and all of them owe something at least to ancient India. The sages who meditated in the jungles of the Ganga Valley six hundred years or more before Christ are still forces in the world.

1. The objectives of the author is to:
   (a) Describe the effect of Indian thought on the thought of the western world
   (b) Describe the influence of Neo-Hindu missions in Europe and America
   (c) Describe the influence of Gandhian thought on the west
   (d) Describe the spread of Yoga and Vedanta in the west
2. According to the author, during recent times, the more subtle and powerful impact was that of the thoughts of:
   (a) Swami Vivekananda
   (b) Theosophical Society
   (c) Mahatma Gandhi
   (d) Paramahamsa Ramakrishna
3. Who among the following was a German philosopher to openly admit his debt to Indian thoughts?
   (a) Emerson (b) Walt Whitman
   (c) Schopenhauer (d) Thoreau
4. Where in the English speaking world was the influence of Indian thought felt strongest?
   (a) Europe (b) England
   (c) Canada (d) America
5. The approach of the author to develop the theme of the passage is:
   (a) Analytical (b) Descriptive
   (c) Laudatory (d) Biased
6. 'Man like creature', which racially differed from 'Homo Sapiens' is designated as:
   (a) Neanderthal
   (b) Pithecanthropus
   (c) Sinanthropus
   (d) Hominid
7. Match List I with List II and select the correct answer from the code given below:

List I (Harappan site)
(A) Satka-Kh
(B) Shortughai
(C) Kotlanihangakhan
(D) Deshalpur

List II (Geographical Location)
(i) Punjab (ii) Afghanistan
(iii) Baluchistan (iv) Gujarat

Codes:	A	B	C	D
(a)	(ii)	(i)	(iv)	(iii)
(b)	(iii)	(ii)	(i)	(iv)
(c)	(iv)	(iii)	(i)	(ii)
(d)	(i)	(iii)	(ii)	(iv)

8. Which of the following weapons of war have not been found in the Harappan culture? Select the correct answer from the code given below:
(i) Bows and Arrows
(ii) Swords
(iii) Shields
(iv) Helmets
Codes:
(a) (i) only (b) (ii) and (iii)
(c) (i), (iii) and (iv) (d) (ii), (iii) and (iv)

9. Which Harappan site has yielded the evidence of stone-architecture in the form of a big gate, circular pillar etc.?
(a) Dhaulavira (b) Banawali
(c) Rakhigarhi (d) Bhagawanpura

10. Which features help us in identifying with Śiva the figure occurring on Harappan seals? Select the correct answer from the code given below:
(i) It is represented with a trident
(ii) It is seated in the yogic posture
(iii) It is surrounded by animals
(iv) It is accompanied by a Parvati like female figure
Codes:
(a) (i) and (ii) (b) (ii) and (iii)
(c) (i), (ii) and (iii) (d) (ii), (iii) and (iv)

11. Given below are two statements, one labelled as Assertion (A) and the other labelled as Reason (R):
Assertion (A): The importance of irrigation to Indian agricultural conditions was fully recognized.
Reason (R): The Arthasastra refers to a water tax which was regularly collected wherever the state assisted in providing irrigation.
In the context of the above two statements, which one of the following is correct?
(a) Both (A) and (R) are true and (R) is the correct explanation of (A)
(b) Both (A) and (R) are true but (R) is not the correct explanation of (A)
(c) (A) is true, but (R) is false
(d) (A) is false, but (R) is true

12. Arrange the following Greco-Roman authors in the chronological sequence. Select the correct answer from the code given below:
(1) Ktesias (2) Pliny
(3) Strabo (4) Ptolemy
Codes:
(a) (1) (3) (2) (4)
(b) (1) (4) (3) (2)
(c) (4) (1) (2) (3)
(d) (4) (3) (2) (1)

13. Arrange the following inscriptions in the chronological sequence. Select the correct answer from the code given below:
(1) Separate Kalinga Edict
(2) Besnagar Garuda Pillar Inscription
(3) Sohgaura Copper-plate Inscription
(4) Nasik cave Inscription of Nahapana
Codes:
(a) (1) (4) (2) (3)
(b) (2) (3) (1) (4)
(c) (3) (1) (2) (4)
(d) (4) (2) (3) (1)

14. Which of the following pairs is not correctly matched?
   (a) Junagarh Inscription of Rudradaman : Tuśāshpha
   (b) Hathigumpha Inscription of Kharavela : Parśvanātha
   (c) Udaigiri Cave Inscription of Chandragupta II : Virasena Śāba
   (d) Mandasor Stone Inscription of Kumaragupta and Bandhuvarman : Vatsabhatti

15. Match List I with List II and select the correct answer from the code given below:

List I (Ruler)
(A) Chandragupta II
(B) Agathokles
(C) Kshatrapa Rajuvula
(D) Kanishka

List II (Figure on the Coin)
(i) Pallas
(ii) Ardoksho
(iii) Balarama
(iv) Chakra-Purusha

Codes:	**A**	**B**	**C**	**D**
(a)	(iv)	(iii)	(i)	(ii)
(b)	(ii)	(iii)	(iv)	(i)
(c)	(i)	(ii)	(iv)	(iii)
(d)	(iv)	(i)	(iii)	(ii)

16. Which one of the following inscriptions throws a significant light on the Pasupata sect of Saivism?
   (a) Taxila Silver Scroll Inscription of the Kushana King
   (b) Mathura Pillar Inscription of Chandragupta II
   (c) Karamdandā Śivalinga Inscription of Kumāragupta I
   (d) Harhā Inscription of Maukharai King Iśānavarman

17. The Paditrupputtu is a collection of poems in the praise of which of the following Kings?
   (a) Chola (b) Chera
   (c) Pandya (d) None of these

18. Which one of the following is correctly matched?
   (a) Kural : Kamban
   (b) Ahanānūru : Paranar
   (c) Puranānūru : Mamulanar
   (d) Śilappadigāram : Ilangovadigal

19. Given below are two statements, one labelled as Assertion (A) and the other labelled as Reason (R):

Assertion (A): From a Nalanda copper-plate we learn that the Pala King Devapala donated five villages for the upkeep of a Buddhist monastery at Nalanda built by Balputradeva, King of Suvarnadvipa and yava-bhumi.

Reason (R): The Pala Kings are chiefly notable for their patronage of Buddhism.

In the context of the above two statements, which one of the following is correct?
   (a) Both (A) and (R) are true and (R) is the correct explanation of (A)
   (b) Both (A) and (R) are true but (R) is not the correct explanation of (A)
   (c) (A) is true, but (R) is false
   (d) (A) is false, but (R) is true

20. Match List I with List II and select the correct answer from the code given below the lists:

List I (Thinker)
(A) Spengler (B) Travelyan
(C) Oakshot (D) Collingwood

List II (View about history)
(i) "The fact is....that past in history varies with the present."
(ii) "History ends not in future but in present."

(iii) "History is a re-enactment of the past experiences."

(iv) "The value of history is not scientific. Its true value is educational."

Codes:	A	B	C	D
(a)	(ii)	(iv)	(i)	(iii)
(b)	(iv)	(i)	(iii)	(ii)
(c)	(iii)	(iv)	(ii)	(i)
(d)	(iv)	(ii)	(i)	(iii)

21. Given below are two statements, one labelled as Assertion (A) and the other labelled as Reason (R):

Assertion (A): Balban sought to increase the prestige and power of the monarchy, and to centralize all authority in the hands of the Sultan.

Reason (R): He wanted to induct the Mongols into the nobility.

In the context of the above two statements, which one of the following is correct?

Codes:

(a) Both (A) and (R) are true and (R) is the correct explanation of (A)
(b) Both (A) and (R) are true, but (R) is not the correct explanation of (A)
(c) (A) is true, but (R) is false
(d) (R) is true, but (A) is false

22. Various Sufi orders were introduced in India at different points of time.

Which one of the following represents the correct chronological sequence of the introduction of these Orders?

(a) The Chishtis - The Suhrawardis - The Qadiris - The Naqshbandis
(b) The Chishtis - The Suhrawardis - The Naqshbandis - The Qadiris
(c) The Suhrawardis - The Chishtis - The Qadiris - The Naqshbandis
(d) The Suhrawardis - The Chishtis - The Naqshbandis - The Qadiris

23. Match List I with List II and select the correct answer from the code given below:

List I (Women Bhakti saints)

(A) Akkamahadevi (B) Lai Ded
(C) Bahinabai (D) Sahjo bai

List II (Sectarian Association)

(i) Saint-Poetess belonging to the Charandasi sect
(ii) Belonging to the Varkari sect
(iii) Virashaiva Saint
(iv) Shaivite Bhakti poetess

Codes:	A	B	C	D
(a)	(iii)	(ii)	(i)	(iv)
(b)	(iii)	(i)	(iv)	(ii)
(c)	(iii)	(iv)	(i)	(ii)
(d)	(iii)	(iv)	(ii)	(i)

24. The contemporary chronicle of the Sayyid period is:

(a) Tarikh-i-Mubarakshahi
(b) Waqiat-i-Mushtaqi
(c) Futub-us-Salatin
(d) Masalik-ul-Absar

25. Taraf in the Bahmani Kingdom signified:

(a) Province (b) Lard grant
(c) Transit Tax (d) Gold Coin

26. Which of the following pairs of authors and their works is not correctly matched?

(a) Shaikh Quthan – Mirgavati
(b) Manjhan – Madhumalti
(c) Kesavdas – Ramchandrika
(d) Nanddas – Dyan-Manjari

27. Which of the following temples of Vijayanagara was substantially rebuilt in Krishnadevaraya's time?

(a) Nagendrasayana temple
(b) Virupaksha temple
(c) Pattabhirama temple
(d) Ganigitti Jaina temple

28. Match List I with List II and select the correct answer from the code given below:

List I (Event)	List II (Year)
(A) Conquest of Malwa	(i) 1561
(B) Closure of the Ibadatkhana	(ii) 1584
(C) Introduction of Ilahi era	(iii) 1592
(D) Conquest of Orissa	(iv) 1582

Codes:	A	B	C	D
(a)	(i)	(iv)	(ii)	(iii)
(b)	(ii)	(i)	(iv)	(iii)
(c)	(i)	(iii)	(ii)	(iv)
(d)	(i)	(ii)	(iii)	(iv)

29. Which of the following Mughal painters according to Abul Fazl-was excellent in drawing of features?
(a) Abdus Samad (b) Daswant
(c) Mir Saiyid Ali (d) Basawan

30. Given below are two statements, one labelled as Assertion (A), and the other labelled as Reason (R):
Assertion (A): Jahangir estabilished the tradition that the Rana of Mewar would be exempted from personal attendance and service at the Mughal Court.
Reason (R): He wanted to humiliate Raja Man Singh of Amber.
Codes:
(a) Both (A) and (R) are true and (R) is the correct explanation of (A)
(b) Both (A) and (R) are true, but (R) is not the correct explanation of (A)
(c) (A) is true, but (R) is false
(d) (A) is false, but (R) is true

31. Who described Mughal cities as 'Camp Cities'?
(a) Manucci (b) Bernier
(c) Tavernier (d) Peter Mundi

32. Who among the following estimated the total population of India in 1600 at about hundred million?
(a) Morland (b) Kingsley Davis
(c) Irfan Habib (d) Ashok V. Desai

33. The English East India company founded a permanent factory at Surat in the year:
(a) 1611 (b) 1613
(c) 1621 (d) 1626

34. Arrange the following in chronological order and select the correct answer from the code given below:
(1) Mughal occupation of Balkh
(2) Khan Jahan Lodi's rebellion
(3) Treaties with Golconda and Bijapur
(4) End of Nizamshahi

Codes:
(a) (1), (4), (3), (2) (b) (2), (1), (4), (3)
(c) (2), (4), (3), (1) (d) (3), (2), (1), (4)

35. Given below are two statements, one labelled as Assertion (A), and the other labelled as Reason (R):
Assertion (A): In 1690, Aurangzeb issued a farman, which made the madad-i-maash completely hereditary.
Reason (R): Aurangzeb wanted to bring the Marathas under the control of the Mughals.
Codes:
(a) Both (A) and (R) are true, and (R) is the correct explanation of (A)
(b) Both (A) and (R) are true, but (R) is not the correct explanation of (A)
(c) (A) is true, but (R) is false
(d) (A) is false, but (R) is true

36. What was the major change effected by the Act of 1858?
(a) The Indian army was reorganized
(b) The Indians were given more representation into the Legislative Council
(c) The power transferred from the East India Company to the British Crown
(d) The East India Company took over direct control over the affairs in India

37. Who founded the Bethune college in Calcutta?
   (a) Ishwar Chandra Vidyasagar
   (b) Raja Ram Mohan Roy
   (c) Rabindra Nath Tagore
   (d) Surendra Nath Banerji
38. The partition of Bengal (1905) was annulled by the:
   (a) Indian Councils Act of 1909
   (b) Chelmsford Montague Report
   (c) Proclamation of Delhi Durbar in 1911
   (d) Government of India Act of 1935
39. Who argued that the theory of de-industrialization was a myth?
   (a) Amiyo Baghchi
   (b) Daniel Thorner
   (c) Morris D. Morris
   (d) Toru Matsui
40. When was the first Industrial Commission set up in India?
   (a) 1916 (b) 1936
   (c) 1947 (d) 1950
41. In the second half of the 19th Century, British capital was mainly invested in:
   (a) Iron and Steel
   (b) Textile Industry
   (c) Plantation Industry
   (d) Railways
42. Gandhi's intervention in the Ahemdabad Mill strike in 1917 resulted in the enhancement of wages for the workers by:
   (a) 10% (b) 15%
   (c) 25% (d) 35%
43. 'Dyarchy' in the Provincial government was established by the:
   (a) Act of 1892 (b) Act of 1909
   (c) Act of 1919 (d) Act of 1935
44. The main grievance of the peasants in the Champaran Satyagraha (1917) was regarding the:
   (a) abwabs or illegal causes
   (b) oppression of the landlords
   (c) tinkathia system
   (d) land revenue demands
45. Match the List I with List II and select the correct answer:

   List I
   (A) Chaudhry Khaliquzzaman
   (B) Jawaharlal Nehru
   (C) Maulana Abul Kalam Azad
   (D) Dr. Rajendra Prasad

   List II
   (i) India Wins Freedom
   (ii) Pathway to Pakistan
   (iii) India Divided
   (iv) Discovery of India

Codes:	**A**	**B**	**C**	**D**
(a)	(iv)	(ii)	(i)	(iii)
(b)	(iii)	(i)	(iv)	(ii)
(c)	(i)	(iii)	(iv)	(ii)
(d)	(ii)	(iv)	(i)	(iii)

46. The Silk Letter conspiracy was organized by:
   (a) Maulana Abdul Bari and Maulana Mohammad Ali
   (b) Maulana Obeidullah Sindhi and Maulana Barkatullah
   (c) Maulana Abul Kalam Azad and Maulana Mahmud Hasan
   (d) Raja Mahendra Pratap and Von Hentig
47. During Renaissance the study of Greco-Roman classics came to be known as:
   (a) Individualism
   (b) Hedonism
   (c) Humanism
   (d) Scholasticism
48. Who called commerce as 'a perpetual war of wit and energy among all nations'?
   (a) Jean Bodin
   (b) Jean Baptiste Colbert

(c) Thomas Mun
(d) Thomas Hobbes

49. Calvinists in France were called:
(a) Catholics
(b) Huguenots
(c) Presbyterians
(d) Puritans

50. Who amongst the following was known as the Prince of humanists?
(a) Desidarius Erasmus
(b) John Colet
(c) Thomas More
(d) Francesco Petrarch

ANSWERS

1. (a)	2. (c)	3. (c)	4. (d)	5. (a)
6. (a)	7. (b)	8. (d)	9. (a)	10. (b)
11. (a)	12. (a)	13. (a)	14. (b)	15. (a)
16. (d)	17. (b)	18. (d)	19. (a)	20. (c)
21. (c)	22. (b)	23. (c)	24. (a)	25. (a)
26. (d)	27. (b)	28. (a)	29. (d)	30. (c)
31. (a)	32. (a)	33. (b)	34. (c)	35. (c)
36. (c)	37. (a)	38. (c)	39. (c)	40. (a)
41. (d)	42. (d)	43. (d)	44. (c)	45. (d)
46. (b)	47. (c)	48. (b)	49. (b)	50. (a)

DECEMBER–2006

Note: This paper contains fifty (50) objective type questions, each question carrying two (2) marks. Attempt all the questions.

PAPER–I

1. Which of the following is *not* instructional material?
   (a) Over Head Projector
   (b) Audio Casset
   (c) Printed Material
   (d) Transparency

2. Which of the following statement is *not* correct?
   (a) Lecture Method can develop reasoning
   (b) Lecture Method can develop knowledge
   (c) Lecture Method is one way process
   (d) During Lecture Method students are passive

3. The main objective of teaching at Higher Education Level is:
   (a) To prepare students to pass examination
   (b) To develop the capacity to take decisions
   (c) To give new information
   (d) To motivate students to ask questions during lecture

4. Which of the following statement is correct?
   (a) Reliability ensures validity
   (b) Validity ensures reliability
   (c) Reliability and validity are independent of each other
   (d) Reliability does not depend on objectivity

5. Which of the following indicates evaluation?
   (a) Ram got 45 marks out of 200
   (b) Mohan got 38 percent marks in English
   (c) Shyam got First Division in final examination
   (d) All the above

6. Research can be conducted by a person who:
   (a) has studied research methodology
   (b) holds a postgraduate degree
   (c) possesses thinking and reasoning ability
   (d) is a hard worker

7. Which of the following statements is correct?
   (a) Objectives of research are stated in first chapter of the thesis
   (b) Researcher must possess analytical ability
   (c) Variability is the source of problem
   (d) All the above

8. Which of the following is *not* the Method of Research?
   (a) Observation (b) Historical
   (c) Survey (d) Philosophical

9. Research can be classified as:
   (a) Basic, Applied and Action Research
   (b) Quantitative and Qualitative Research
   (c) Philosophical, Historical, Survey and Experimental Research
   (d) All the above

10. The first step of research is:
    (a) Selecting a problem
    (b) Searching a problem
    (c) Finding a problem
    (d) Identifying a problem

Read the following passage and answer the question nos. 11 to 15:

After almost three decades of contemplating Swarovski-encrusted navels on increasing flat abs, the Mumbai film industry is on a discovery of India and itself. With budgets of over 30 crore each, four soon to be released movies by premier directors are exploring the idea of who we are and redefining who the other is. It is a fundamental question which the bling-bling, glam-sham and disham-disham tends to avoid. It is also a question which binds an audience when the lights go dim and the projector rolls: as a nation, who are we? As a people, where are we going?

The Germans coined a word for it, zeitgeist, which perhaps Yash Chopra would not care to pronounce. But at 72, he remains the person who can best capture it. After being the first to project the diasporic Indian on screen in Lamhe in 1991, he has returned to his roots in a new movie. Veer Zaara, set in 1986, where Pakistan, the traditional other, the part that got away, is the lover and the saviour. In Subhash Ghai's Kisna, set in 1947, the other is the English woman. She is not a memsahib, but a mehbooba. In Ketan Mehta's The Rising, the East India Englishman is not the evil oppressor of countless cardboard characterisations, which span the spectrum from Jewel in the Crown to Kranti, but an honourable friend.

This is Manoj Kumar's Desh Ki Dharti with a difference : there is culture, not contentious politics; balle balle, not bombs : no dooriyan (distance), only nazdeekiyan (closeness).

All four films are heralding a new hero and heroine. The new hero is fallible and vulnerable, committed to his dharma, but also not afraid of failure—less of a boy and more of a man. He even has a grown up name : Veer Pratap Singh in Veer-Zaara and Mohan Bhargav in Swades. The new heroine is not a babe, but often a bebe, dressed in traditional Punjabi clothes, often with the stereotypical body type as well, as in Bride and Prejudice of Gurinder Chadha.

11. Which word Yash Chopra would not be able to pronounce?
    (a) Bling + bling (b) Zeitgeist
    (c) Montaz (d) Dooriyan

12. Who made Lamhe in 1991?
    (a) Subhash Ghai (b) Yash Chopra
    (c) Aditya Chopra (d) Sakti Samanta

13. Which movie is associated with Manoj Kumar?
    (a) Jewel in the Crown
    (b) Kisna
    (c) Zaara
    (d) Desh Ki Dharti

14. Which is the latest film by Yash Chopra?
    (a) Deewar
    (b) Kabhi Kabhi
    (c) Dilwale Dulhaniya Le Jayenge
    (d) Veer Zaara

15. Which is the dress of the heroine in Veer-Zaara?
    (a) Traditional Gujarati Clothes
    (b) Traditional Bengali Clothes
    (c) Traditional Punjabi Clothes
    (d) Traditional Madrasi Clothes

16. Which one of the following can be termed as verbal communication?
    (a) Prof. Sharma delivered the lecture in the class room.
    (b) Signal at the cross-road changed from green to orange.
    (c) The child was crying to attract the attention of the mother.
    (d) Dipak wrote a letter for leave application.

17. Which is the 24 hours English Business news channel in India?
(a) Zee News (b) NDTV 24×7
(c) CNBC (d) India News

18. Consider the following statements in communication:
(i) Hema Malini is the Chairperson of the Children's Film Society, India.
(ii) Yash Chopra is the Chairman of the Central Board of Film Certification of India.
(iii) Sharmila Tagore is the Chairperson of National Film Development Corporation.
(iv) Dilip Kumar, Raj Kapoor and Preeti Zinta have all been recipients of Dada Saheb Phalke Award.

Which of the statements given above is/are correct?
(a) (i) and (iii) (b) (ii) and (iii)
(c) (iv) only (d) (iii) only

19. Which of the following pair is *not* correctly matched?
(a) N. Ram : The Hindu
(b) Barkha Dutt : Zee News
(c) Pranay Roy : NDTV 24×7
(d) Prabhu Chawla : Aaj taak

20. "Because you deserve to know" is the punchline used by:
(a) The Times of India
(b) The Hindu
(c) Indian Express
(d) Hindustan Times

21. In the sequence of numbers 8, 24, 12, X, 18, 54 the missing number X is:
(a) 26 (b) 24
(c) 36 (d) 32

22. If A stands for 5, B for 6, C for 7, D for 8 and so on, then the following numbers stand for 17, 19, 20, 9 and 8:
(a) PLANE (b) MOPED
(c) MOTOR (d) TONGA

23. The letters in the first set have certain relationship. On the basis of this relationship what is the right choice for the second set?

AST : BRU : : NQV : ?
(a) ORW (b) MPU
(c) MRW (d) OPW

24. In a certain code, PAN is written as 31 and PAR as 35. In this code PAT is written as:
(a) 30 (b) 37
(c) 38 (d) 39

25. The sides of a triangle are in the ratio of $\frac{1}{2}:\frac{1}{3}:\frac{1}{4}$. If its perimeter is 52 cm, the length of the smallest side is:
(a) 9 cm (b) 10 cm
(c) 11 cm (d) 12 cm

26. Which one of the following statements is completely non-sensical?
(a) He was a bachelor, but he married recently.
(b) He is a bachelor, but he married recently.
(c) When he married, he was not a bachelor.
(d) When he was a bachelor, he was not married.

27. Which of the following statements are mutually contradictory?
(i) All flowers are not fragrant.
(ii) Most flowers are not fragrant.
(iii) None of the flowers is fragrant.
(iv) Most flowers are fragrant.

Choose the correct answer from the code given below:
Codes:
(a) (i) and (ii) (b) (i) and (iii)
(c) (ii) and (iii) (d) (iii) and (iv)

28. Which of the following statements say the same thing?

(i) "I am a teacher" (said by Arvind)
(ii) "I am a teacher" (said by Binod)
(iii) "My son is a teacher" (said by Binod's father)
(iv) "My brother is a teacher" (said by Binod's sister)
(v) "My brother is a teacher" (said by Binod's only sister)
(vi) "My sole enemy is a teacher" (said by Binod's only enemy)

Choose the correct answer from the code given below:

Codes:
(a) (i) and (ii)
(b) (ii), (iii), (iv) and (v)
(c) (ii) and (vi)
(d) (v) and (vi)

29. Which of the following are correct ways of arguing?
(i) There can be no second husband without a second wife.
(ii) Anil is a friend of Bob, Bob is a friend of Raj, hence Anil is a friend of Raj.
(iii) A is equal to B, B is equal to C, hence A is equal to C.
(iv) If everyone is a liar, then we cannot prove it.

Choose the correct answer from the code given below:

Codes:
(a) (iii) and (iv)
(b) (i), (iii) and (iv)
(c) (ii), (iii) and (iv)
(d) (i), (ii), (iii) and (iv)

30. Which of the following statement/s are ALWAYS FALSE?
(i) The sun will not rise in the East some day.
(ii) A wooden table is not a table.
(iii) Delhi city will be drowned under water.
(iv) Cars run on water as fuel.

Choose the correct answer from the code given below:

Codes:
(a) (i), (iii) and (iv) (b) Only (iii)
(c) (i), (ii) and (iii) (d) (ii) alone

Study the following graph and answer question numbers 31 to 33:

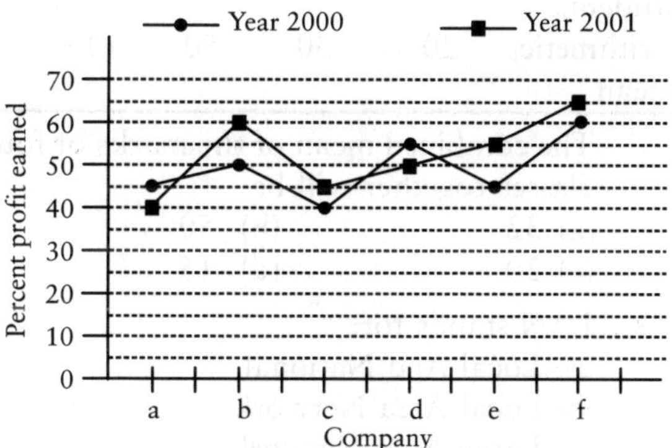

31. In the year 2000, which of the following Companies earned maximum percent profit?
(a) a (b) b
(c) d (d) f

32. In the year 2001, which of the following Companies earned minimum percent profit?
(a) a (b) c
(c) d (d) e

33. In the years 2000 and 2001, which of the following Companies earned maximum average percent profit?
(a) f (b) e
(c) d (d) b

34. Human Development Report for 'each' of the year at global level has been published by:
(a) UNDP (b) WTO
(c) IMF (d) World Bank

35. The number of students in four classes A, B, C, D and their respective mean marks obtained by each of the class are given below:

	Class A	Class B	Class C	Class D
Number of students	10	40	30	20
Arithmetic mean	20	30	50	15

The combined mean of the marks of four classes together will be:
(a) 32 (b) 50
(c) 20 (d) 15

36. LAN stands for:
(a) Local And National
(b) Local Area Network
(c) Large Area Network
(d) Live Area Network

37. Which of the following statement is correct?
(a) Modem is a software
(b) Modem helps in stabilizing the voltage
(c) Modem is the operating system
(d) Modem converts the analog signal into digital signal and vice-versa

38. Which of the following is the appropriate definition of a computer?
(a) Computer is a machine that can process information.
(b) Computer is an electronic device that can store, retrieve and process both qualitative and quantitative data quickly and accurately.
(c) Computer is an electronic device that can store, retrieve and quickly process only quantitative data.
(d) Computer is a machine that can store, retrieve and process quickly and accurately only qualitative information

39. Information and Communication Technology includes:
(a) On line learning
(b) Learning through the use of EDUSAT
(c) Web Based Learning
(d) All the above

40. Which of the following is the appropriate format of URL of e-mail?
(a) www_mail.com
(b) www@mail.com
(c) WWW@mail.com
(d) www.mail.com

41. The most significant impact of volcanic erouption has been felt in the form of:
(a) change in weather
(b) sinking of islands
(c) loss of vegetation
(d) extinction of animals

42. With absorption and decomposition of CO_2 in ocean water beyond desired level, there will be:
(a) decrease in temperature
(b) increase in salinity
(c) growth of phyto plankton
(d) rise in sea level

43. Arrange column II in proper sequence so as to match it with column I and choose the correct answer from the code given below:

Column I Water Quality	Column II pH Value
(A) Neutral	(i) 5
(B) Moderately acidic	(ii) 7
(C) Alkaline	(iii) 4
(D) Injurious	(iv) 8

Codes:	(A)	(B)	(C)	(D)
(a)	(ii)	(iii)	(i)	(iv)
(b)	(i)	(iii)	(ii)	(iv)
(c)	(ii)	(i)	(iv)	(iii)
(d)	(iv)	(ii)	(iii)	(i)

44. The maximum emission of pollutants from fuel sources in India is caused by:
(a) Coal
(b) Firewood
(c) Refuse burning
(d) Vegetable waste product

45. The urbanisation process accounts for the wind in the urban centres during nights to remain:
(a) faster than that in rural areas
(b) slower than that in rural areas
(c) the same as that in rural areas
(d) cooler than that in rural areas

46. The University Grants Commission was constituted on the recommendation of:
(a) Dr. Sarvapalli Radhakrishnan Commission
(b) Mudaliar Commission
(c) Sargent Commission
(d) Kothari Commission

47. Which one of the following Articles of the Constitution of India safeguards the rights of Minorities to establish and run educational institutions of their own liking?
(a) Article 19 (b) Article 29
(c) Article 30 (d) Article 31

48. Match List - I (Institutions) with List - II (Functions) and select the correct answer by using the code given below:

List-I (Institutions)
(A) Parliament
(B) C & A.G.
(C) Ministry of Finance
(D) Executing Departments

List-II (Functions)
(i) Formulation of Budget
(ii) Enactment of Budget
(iii) Implementation of Budget
(iv) Legality of expenditure
(v) Justification of Income

Codes:	(A)	(B)	(C)	(D)
(a)	(iii)	(iv)	(ii)	(i)
(b)	(ii)	(iv)	(i)	(iii)
(c)	(v)	(iii)	(iv)	(ii)
(d)	(iv)	(ii)	(iii)	(v)

49. Foundation training to the newly recruited IAS (Probationers) is imparted by:
(a) Indian Institute of Public Administration
(b) Administrative Staff College of India
(c) L.B.S. National Academy of Administration
(d) Centre for Advanced Studies

50. Electoral disputes arising out of Presidential and Vice-Presidential Elections are settled by:
(a) Election Commission of India
(b) Joint Committee of Parliament
(c) Supreme Court of India
(d) Central Election Tribunal

ANSWERS

1. (d)	2. (a)	3. (b)	4. (b)	5. (d)
6. (c)	7. (d)	8. (b)	9. (d)	10. (b)
11. (b)	12. (b)	13. (d)	14. (d)	15. (c)
16. (c)	17. (c)	18. (d)	19. (b)	20. (d)
21. (c)	22. (b)	23. (d)	24. (b)	25. (d)
26. (b)	27. (b)	28. (b)	29. (a)	30. (d)
31. (d)	32. (a)	33. (a)	34. (a)	35. (a)
36. (b)	37. (d)	38. (b)	39. (d)	40. (b)
41. (a)	42. (c)	43. (c)	44. (c)	45. (b)
46. (a)	47. (c)	48. (b)	49. (c)	50. (c)

PAPER–II

1. Who says that Harappa and Mohenjodaro were not the two capitals in the Indus Valley Civilisation?

(a) John Marshall
(b) R.D. Banerji
(c) F.R. Alchin
(d) Daya Ram Sahani

2. What was the evolutionary concept of the Vedic philosophy?
(a) Polytheism
(b) Henotheism
(c) Monotheism and Monism
(d) All the above

3. The founder of the Sankhya philosophy was:
(a) Patanjali (b) Nagarjuna
(c) Kapila (d) Kanada

4. The Nagarjuni Caves were erected by:
(a) Dasharatha (b) Kharavela
(c) Ashoka (d) Chandragupta II

5. The Hathigumpha inscription of Kharavela refers to the irrigational works of the:
(a) Mauryas (b) Nandas
(c) Sungas (d) Sakas

6. The river which formed the boundary between the Shakyas and the Koliyas is:
(a) Gandak (b) Saryu
(c) Achiravati (d) Rohini

7. The copper hoards are associated with the following wares:
(a) Painted Grey Ware
(b) Ochre Coloured Pottery
(c) Northern Black Polished Ware
(d) Black and Red Wares

8. Who spoke about the gold-drain of the Roman Empire?
(a) Herodotus (b) Strabo
(c) Pliny (d) Arrians

9. The Pallavas are stated to have the dockyard at:
(a) Nagapattinam (b) Tamaralipti
(c) Sopara (d) Kalyana

10. Match List I with List II and choose your answer from the code given below:

List I
(A) Rajaraja I
(B) Chandragupta Maurya
(C) Pushyagupta
(D) Rajendra Chola

List II
(i) Shravana Belagola
(ii) Brihdisvara Temple
(iii) Gangaikondacholapuram
(iv) Sudarshana Lake

Codes:	**A**	**B**	**C**	**D**
(a)	(i)	(iii)	(ii)	(iv)
(b)	(iv)	(iii)	(ii)	(i)
(c)	(i)	(ii)	(iv)	(iii)
(d)	(ii)	(i)	(iv)	(iii)

11. Match List I with List II and choose your answer from the codes given below:

List I
(A) Vasumitra (B) Patanjali
(C) Megasthenes (D) Harishena

List II
(i) Samudra Gupta
(ii) Chandragupta Maurya
(iii) Pushyamitra Shunga
(iv) Kanishka

Codes:	**A**	**B**	**C**	**D**
(a)	(i)	(iv)	(ii)	(iii)
(b)	(iv)	(iii)	(ii)	(i)
(c)	(iv)	(ii)	(iii)	(i)
(d)	(i)	(iii)	(iv)	(ii)

12. Given below are two statements, one labelled as Assertion (A), and the other labelled as Reason (R):
Assertion (A): The Pratitya-Samutapada is a concept of the Buddhist philosophy.
Reason (R): It believes in cause and effect.
In the context of the above two statements, which one of the following is correct?
(a) (A) is true, but (R) is false.
(b) (R) is true, but (A) is false.

(c) Both (A) and (R) are false.
(d) Both (A) and (R) are true.

13. Given below are two statements, one labelled as Assertion (A), and the other labelled as Reason (R):
Assertion (A): Heliodorus erected a garuda column at Vidisa.
Reason (R): He was an Indo-Greek ruler.
In the context of the above two statements, which one of the following is correct?
(a) (A) is true, but (R) is false.
(b) (A) is false, but (R) is true.
(c) Both (A) and (R) are true.
(d) Both (A) and (R) are false.

14. Arrange the correct genealogy of the following Later Gupta Kings as recorded in the Aphsad inscription.
(a) Krishna-gupta, Jivita-gupta I, Kumara-gupta, Harsha-gupta
(b) Harsha-gupta, Kumara-gupta, Jivita-gupta I, Krishna-gupta
(c) Krishna-gupta, Harsha-gupta, Jivita-gupta I, Kumara-gupta
(d) Kumara-gupta, Harsha-gupta, Krishna-gupta, Jivita-gupta I

15. How many Embassies were sent by the Chinese Emperor, Tai Tsung, to the court of Harshavardhana?
(a) One (b) Two
(c) Three (d) Four

16. Abu Raihan Biruni wrote his account of India in:
(a) Persian (b) Turki
(c) Arabic (d) Chaghtai

17. The first attempt to centralise administration during the Sultanate period was made by:
(a) Iltutmish
(b) Nasiruddin Mahmud
(c) Ghiyasuddin Balban
(d) Jalal-ud-Din Khalji

18. *Tabqat-i-Nasiri* throws light on the history of north India in the:
(a) 13th Century (b) 14th Century
(c) 15th Century (d) 16th Century

19. The following travellers visited India in medieval times. Point out the correct sequence:
(a) Marco Polo, Conti, Afanasi Nikitin, Varthema
(b) Conti, Varthema, Marco Polo, Nikitin
(c) Varthema, Marco Polo, Conti, Nikitin
(d) Nikitin, Varthema, Marco Polo, Conti

20. Which of the following is not a port?
(a) Cambay (b) Chaul
(c) Gulbarga (d) Masulipattam

21. Babur wrote autobiography in:
(a) Persian (b) Arabic
(c) Osmanli Turki (d) Chagtai Turki

22. Painting was patronized by:
(a) Humayun
(b) Humayun and Akbar
(c) Humayun, Akbar and Jahangir
(d) Humayun, Akbar, Jahangir and Aurangzeb

23. Indian traders in the 17th Century traded at:
(a) Mokha and Aden
(b) Mokha, Aden and Bander Abbas
(c) Mokha, Aden, Bander Abbas and Isfahan
(d) Mokha, Aden, Bander Abbas, Isfahan and Bukhara

24. In the XVII Century the English East India Company's main rival in India was the:
(a) Dutch East India Company
(b) French East India Company
(c) Danish East India Company
(d) Courteen Association

25. Whom Sri Jadunath Sarkar has called "the last constructive Hindu Genius"?

(a) Baji Rao I
(b) Shivaji
(c) Krishna Deva Raya
(d) Nana Phadnavis

26. The Khalsa Panth was established by:
(a) Guru Arjun
(b) Guru Tegh Bahadur
(c) Guru Gobind Singh
(d) Banda Bahadur

27. *Sadar-us-Sudur* under the Mughals was the Minister of:
(a) War
(b) Religious and Charitable Affairs
(c) Finance
(d) Trade

28. *Jains* were patronised by:
(a) Babur and Humayun
(b) Humayun and Akbar
(c) Akbar and Jahangir
(d) Jahangir and Aurangzeb

29. Given below are two statements, one labelled as Assertion (A), and the other labelled as Reason (R):
Assertion (A): Medieval Hindu Saints generally spoke against caste system.
Reason (R): They were influenced by Islamic idea of equality.
In the context of the above two statements, which one of the following is correct?
(a) Both (A) and (R) are true and (R) is the correct explanation of (A).
(b) Both (A) and (R) are true and (R) is not the correct explanation of (A).
(c) (A) is true, but (R) is false.
(d) (A) is false, but (R) is true.

30. After the arrival of the Portuguese, English, Dutch and French in India, the cultivation of:
(a) tobacco began
(b) tobacco and tomato began
(c) tobacco, tomato and red chillies began
(d) tobacco, tomato, red chillies and maize began

31. Which has been described as Dupleix's 'private' war?
(a) Second Carnatic War
(b) Second Sikh War
(c) Second Anglo-Maratha War
(d) First Carnatic War

32. Which Act abolished the monopoly of East India Company's trade in India?
(a) Regulating Act, 1773
(b) Charter Act, 1813
(c) Charter Act, 1833
(d) Government of India Act, 1858

33. Who introduced the Ryotwari Settlement in Madras?
(a) Sir Charles Grant
(b) Sir John Shore
(c) Sir Thomas Munro
(d) Lord Cornwallis

34. English was introduced as a medium of instruction by:
(a) Lord Macaulay, 1838
(b) Sir Charles Wood, 1854
(c) Lord Clive, 1857
(d) Lord Curzon, 1899

35. Revolutionary youth Madanlal Dhingra shot dead:
(a) Michael O' Dwyer
(b) Lord Curzon
(c) General Dyer
(d) Curzon Wylie

36. In 1917 Gandhi's intervention in the Ahmedabad Mill strike led to the enhancement of wages of the workers by:
(a) 25% (b) 30%
(c) 35% (d) 40%

37. The Indian National Congress had adopted the resolution on Fundamental Rights at its session held in:

(a) Gauhati (1926) (b) Madras (1927)
(c) Lahore (1929) (d) Karachi (1931)

38. Who argued that the Khilafat Movement was the result of the emergence of a "middle class" among Indian Muslims?
(a) Francis Robinson
(b) W.C. Smith
(c) Mushurul Hasan
(d) Moin Shakir

39. Who presided over the first session of the All India Trade Union Congress?
(a) M.N. Joshi (b) M.N. Roy
(c) Lala Lajpat Rai (d) SA. Dange

40. Which Commission recommended the adoption of a Famine Code for India?
(a) Campbell Commission, 1868
(b) Macdonnell Commission, 1898
(c) Strachey Commission, 1880
(d) Lyall Commission, 1901

41. Who prophesied that the railways would become the forerunner of modern industry?
(a) Karl Marx
(b) Dadabhoy Naoroji
(c) Lord Dalhousie
(d) Jamshedji Tata

42. Who was appointed in 1856 as the resident of Awadh by Dalhousie to give him reports about its administration?
(a) Henry Lawrence
(b) General Outram
(c) Colonel Sleeman
(d) General Havelock

43. Match List I with List II and select the correct answer:

List I
(A) Maulana Abul Kalam Azad
(B) Jawaharlal Nehru
(C) M.K. Gandhi
(D) Surendra Nath Banerjee

List II
(i) A Nation in the Making
(ii) Hind Swaraj
(iii) Al-Hilal
(iv) Glimpses of World History

Codes:	**A**	**B**	**C**	**D**
(a)	(iii)	(iv)	(i)	(ii)
(b)	(iv)	(iii)	(ii)	(i)
(c)	(iii)	(iv)	(ii)	(i)
(d)	(i)	(ii)	(iii)	(iv)

44. Given below are two statements, one labelled as Assertion (A), and the other labelled as Reason (R):
Assertion (A): Brahmo Samaj used the word 'Shuddhi Movement' for effecting socio-religious and political unity in India.
Reason (R): 'Shuddhi Movement' meant the reconversion of those Hindus who had once been willingly or forcibly converted into the other religions but were now willing to come back into the fold of Hinduism.
In the context of the above two statements, which one of the following is correct?
(a) Both (A) and (R) are true and (R) is the correct explanation of (A).
(b) Both (A) and (R) are true and (R) is not the correct explanation of (A).
(c) (A) is true, but (R) is false.
(d) (A) is false, but (R) is true.

45. The name of Col. Sleeman is associated with which event:
(a) The Sind Campaign
(b) The Suppression of Thugee
(c) Campaign against the Pindaris
(d) None of the above

46. The fee paid to the Lord for the use of the mill, brewery and bakery was known as:
(a) Banalite (b) Corvee
(c) Gabelle (d) Taille

47. The rise of bourgeosie to economic power, westernization of the world and revival of slavery were the consequences of:
   (a) Commercial Revolution
   (b) Feudalism
   (c) Industrial Revolution
   (d) Manorialism

48. Match the following:

Authors	Works
(A) Erasmus	(i) Divine Comedy
(B) Machiavelli	(ii) Utopia
(C) Thomas More	(iii) The Prince
(D) Dante	(iv) Praise of Folly

Codes:	A	B	C	D
(a)	(iii)	(ii)	(i)	(iv)
(b)	(ii)	(i)	(iii)	(iv)
(c)	(i)	(ii)	(iii)	(iv)
(d)	(iv)	(iii)	(ii)	(i)

49. Bullionism and the favourable balance of trade were the basic features of:
   (a) Colonialism
   (b) Commercialism
   (c) Free Trade
   (d) Mercantilism

50. Match List I with List II and select the correct answer:

List I
(A) Council of Trent
(B) Adolf Hitler
(C) Jean Jacques Rousseau
(D) Benito Mussolini

List II
(i) Social Contract
(ii) Duce
(iii) Counter-Reformation
(iv) Fuhrer

Codes:	A	B	C	D
(a)	(iv)	(i)	(ii)	(iii)
(b)	(ii)	(iv)	(i)	(iii)
(c)	(iii)	(iv)	(ii)	(i)
(d)	(iii)	(iv)	(i)	(ii)

ANSWERS

1. (c)	2. (c)	3. (c)	4. (a)	5. (b)
6. (d)	7. (d)	8. (c)	9. (d)	10. (d)
11. (b)	12. (d)	13. (c)	14. (c)	15. (b)
16. (c)	17. (c)	18. (a)	19. (a)	20. (c)
21. (d)	22. (c)	23. (d)	24. (b)	25. (d)
26. (c)	27. (b)	28. (c)	29. (a)	30. (d)
31. (a)	32. (b)	33. (c)	34. (a)	35. (d)
36. (c)	37. (d)	38. (c)	39. (c)	40. (c)
41. (a)	42. (c)	43. (c)	44. (d)	45. (b)
46. (b)	47. (c)	48. (d)	49. (b)	50. (d)

JUNE–2006

Note: This paper contains fifty (50) objective type questions, each question carrying two (2) marks. Attempt all the questions.

PAPER–I

1. Which of the following comprise teaching skill:
   (a) Black Board writing
   (b) Questioning
   (c) Explaining
   (d) All the above

2. Which of the following statements is most appropriate?
   (a) Teachers can teach.
   (b) Teachers help can create in a student a desire to learn.
   (c) Lecture Method can be used for developing thinking.
   (d) Teachers are born.

3. The first Indian chronicler of Indian history was :
   (a) Megasthanese (b) Fahiyan
   (c) Huan Tsang (d) Kalhan

4. Which of the following statements is correct?
   (a) Syllabus is a part of curriculum.
   (b) Syllabus is an annexure to curriculum.
   (c) Curriculum is the same in all educational institutions affiliated to a particular university.
   (d) Syllabus is not the same in all educational institutions affiliated to a particular university.

5. Which of the two given options is of the level of understanding?
   (I) Define noun.
   (II) Define noun in your own words.
   (a) Only I (b) Only II
   (c) Both I and II (d) Neither I nor II

6. Which of the following options are the main tasks of research in modern society?
   (I) to keep pace with the advancement in knowledge.
   (II) to discover new things.
   (III) to write a critique on the earlier writings.
   (IV) to systematically examine and critically analyse the investigations/ sources with objectivity.
   (a) IV, II and I (b) I, II and III
   (c) I and III (d) II, III and IV

7. Match List I (Interviews) with List II (Meaning) and select the correct answer from the code given below:

   List I (Interviews)
   (A) Structured interviews
   (B) Unstructured interviews
   (C) Focussed interviews
   (D) Clinical interviews

   List II (Meaning)
   (i) Greater flexibility approach
   (ii) Attention on the questions to be answered
   (iii) Individual life experience
   (iv) Pre determined question
   (v) Non-directive

Codes:	A	B	C	D
(a)	(iv)	(i)	(ii)	(iii)
(b)	(ii)	(iv)	(i)	(iii)
(c)	(v)	(ii)	(iv)	(i)
(d)	(i)	(iii)	(v)	(iv)

8. What do you consider as the main aim of inter disciplinary research?
   (a) To bring out holistic approach to research.
   (b) To reduce the emphasis of single subject in research domain.
   (c) To over simplify the problem of research.
   (d) To create a new trend in research methodology.
9. One of the aims of the scientific method in research is to:
   (a) improve data interpretation
   (b) eliminate spurious relations
   (c) confirm triangulation
   (d) introduce new variables
10. The depth of any research can be judged by:
   (a) title of the research.
   (b) objectives of the research.
   (c) total expenditure on the research.
   (d) duration of the research.

Read the following passage and answer the questions 11 to 15:

The superintendence, direction and control of preparation of electoral rolls for, and the conduct of, elections to Parliament and State Legislatures and elections to the offices of the President and the Vice-President of India are vested in the Election Commission of India. It is an independent constitutional authority.

Independence of the Election Commission and its insulation from executive interference is ensured by a specific provision under Article 324(5) of the constitution that the chief Election Commissioner shall not be removed from his office except in like manner and on like grounds as a Judge of the Supreme Court and conditions of his service shall not be varied to his disadvantage after his appointment.

In C.W.P. No. 4912 of 1998 (Kushra Bharat Vs. Union of India and others), the Delhi High Court directed that information relating to Government dues owed by the candidates to the departments dealing with Government accommodation, electricity, water, telephone and transport etc. and any other dues should be furnished by the candidates and this information should be published by the election authorities under the commission.

11. The text of the passage reflects or raises certain questions:
   (a) The authority of the commission can not be challenged.
   (b) This would help in stopping the criminalization of Indian politics.
   (c) This would reduce substantially the number of contesting candidates.
   (d) This would ensure fair and free elections.
12. According to the passage, the Election Commission is an independent constitutional authority. This is under Article No. :
   (a) 324 (b) 356
   (c) 246 (d) 161
13. Independence of the Commission means :
   (a) have a constitutional status.
   (b) have legislative powers.
   (c) have judicial powers.
   (d) have political powers.
14. Fair and free election means:
   (a) transparency
   (b) to maintain law and order
   (c) regional considerations
   (d) role for pressure groups
15. The Chief Election Commissioner can be removed from his office under Article:
   (a) 125 (b) 352
   (c) 226 (d) 324
16. The function of mass communication of supplying information regarding the processes, issues, events and societal developments is known as:

(a) content supply (b) surveillance
(c) gratification (d) correlation

17. The science of the study of feedback systems in humans, animals and machines is known as:
(a) cybernetics
(b) reverse communication
(c) selectivity study
(d) response analysis

18. Networked media exist in inter-connected:
(a) social environments
(b) economic environments
(c) political environments
(d) technological environments

19. The combination of computing, telecommunications and media in a digital atmosphere is referred to as:
(a) online communication
(b) integrated media
(c) digital combine
(d) convergence

20. A dialogue between a human-being and a computer programme that occurs simultaneously in various forms is described as:
(a) man-machine speak
(b) binary chat
(c) digital talk
(d) interactivity

21. Insert the missing number:

$\frac{16}{32}, \frac{15}{33}, \frac{17}{31}, \frac{14}{34}, ?$

(a) $\frac{19}{35}$ (b) $\frac{19}{30}$
(c) $\frac{18}{35}$ (d) $\frac{18}{30}$

22. Monday falls on 20th March 1995. What was the day on 3rd November 1994?
(a) Thursday (b) Sunday
(c) Tuesday (d) Saturday

23. The average of four consecutive even numbers is 27. The largest of these numbers is (a) 36 (b) 32 (c) 30 (d) 28

24. In a certain code, FHQK means GIRL. How will WOMEN be written in the same code?
(a) VNLDM (b) FHQKN
(c) XPNFO (d) VLNDM

25. At what time between 4 and 5 o'clock will the hands of a watch point in opposite directions?
(a) 45 min. past 4
(b) $40\frac{4}{11}$ min. past 4
(c) 50 min. past 4
(d) $54\frac{6}{11}$ min. past 4

26. Which of the following conclusions is logically valid based on statement given below?
Statement: Most teachers are hard working.
Conclusions: (I) Some teachers are hard working.
(II) Some teachers are not hard working.
(a) Only (I) is implied
(b) Only (II) is implied
(c) Both (I) and (II) are implied
(d) Neither (I) nor (II) is implied

27. Who among the following can be asked to make a statement in Indian Parliament?
(a) Any MLA
(b) Chief of Army Staff
(c) Solicitor General of India
(d) Mayor of Delhi

28. Which of the following conclusions is logically valid based on statement given below?
Statement: Most of the Indian states existed before independence.

Conclusions : (I) Some Indian States existed before independence.

(II) All Indian States did not exist before independence.

(a) Only (I) is implied
(b) Only (II) is implied
(c) Both (I) and (II) are implied
(d) Neither (I) nor (II) is implied

29. Water is always involved with landslides. This is because it:
(a) reduces the shear strength of rocks
(b) increases the weight of the overburden
(c) enhances chemical weathering
(d) is a universal solvent

30. Direction for this question:
Given below are two statements (a) and (b) followed by two conclusions (i) and (ii). Considering the statements to be true, indicate which of the following conclusions logically follow from the given statements by selecting one of the four response alternatives given below the conclusion:

Statements: (a) all businessmen are wealthy.

(b) all wealthy people are hard working.

Conclusions: (i) All businessmen are hard working.

(ii) All hardly working people are not wealthy

(a) Only (i) follows
(b) Only (ii) follows
(c) Only (i) and (ii) follows
(d) Neither (i) nor (ii) follows

31. Using websites to pour out one's grievances is called:
(a) cyberventing (b) cyber ranting
(c) web hate (d) web plea

32. In web search, finding a large number of documents with very little relevant information is termed:
(a) poor recall
(b) web crawl
(c) poor precision rate
(d) poor web response

33. The concept of connect intelligence is derived from:
(a) virtual reality
(b) fuzzy logic
(c) bluetooth technology
(d) value added networks

34. Use of an ordinary telephone as an Internet applicance is called :
(a) voicenet (b) voice telephone
(c) voice line (d) voice portal

35. Video transmission over the Internet that looks like delayed livecasting is called:
(a) virtual video
(b) direct broadcast
(c) video shift
(d) real-time video

36. Which is the smallest North-east State in India?
(a) Tripura (b) Meghalaya
(c) Mizoram (d) Manipur

37. Tamilnadu coastal belt has drinking water shortage due to:
(a) high evaporation
(b) sea water flooding due to tsunami
(c) over exploitation of ground water by tubewells
(d) seepage of sea water

38. While all rivers of Peninsular India flow into the Bay of Bengal, Narmada and Tapti flow into the Arabian Sea because these two rivers:
(a) Follow the slope of these rift valleys
(b) The general slope of the Indian peninsula is from east to west

(c) The Indian peninsula north of the Satpura ranges, is tilted towards the west
(d) The Indian peninsula south of the Satpura ranges is tilted towards east

39. Soils in the Mahanadi delta are less fertile than those in the Godavari delta because of:
(a) erosion of top soils by annual floods
(b) inundation of land by sea water
(c) traditional agriculture practices
(d) the derivation of alluvial soil from red-soil hinterland

40. Which of the following institutions in the field of education is set up by the MHRD Government of India?
(a) Indian council of world Affair, New Delhi
(b) Mythic Society, Bangalore
(c) National Bal Bhawn, New Delhi
(d) India International Centre, New Delhi

41. **Assertion (A):** Aerosols have potential for modifying climate
Reason (R): Aerosols interact with both short waves and radiation.
(a) Both (A) and (R) are true, and (R) is the correct explanation of (A)
(b) Both (A) and (R) are true, but (R) is not the correct explanation of (A)
(c) (A) is true, but (R) is false
(d) (A) is false, but (R) is true

42. 'SITE' stands for:
(a) System for International technology and Engineering
(b) Satellite Instructional Television Experiment
(c) South Indian Trade Estate
(d) State Institute of Technology and Engineering

43. What is the name of the Research station established by the Indian Government for 'Conducting Research at Antarctic?
(a) Dakshin Gangotri
(b) Yamunotri
(c) Uttari Gangotri
(d) None of the above

44. Ministry of Human Resource Development (HRD) includes:
(a) Department of Elementary Education and Literacy
(b) Department of Secondary Education and Higher Education
(c) Department of Women and Child Development
(d) All the above

45. Parliament can legislate on matters listed in the State list:
(a) With the prior permission of the President.
(b) Only after the constitution is amended suitably.
(c) In case of inconsistency among State legislatures.
(d) At the request of two or more States.

The following pie chart indicates the expenditure of a country on various sports during a particular year. Study the pie chart and answer Question Number 46 to 50.

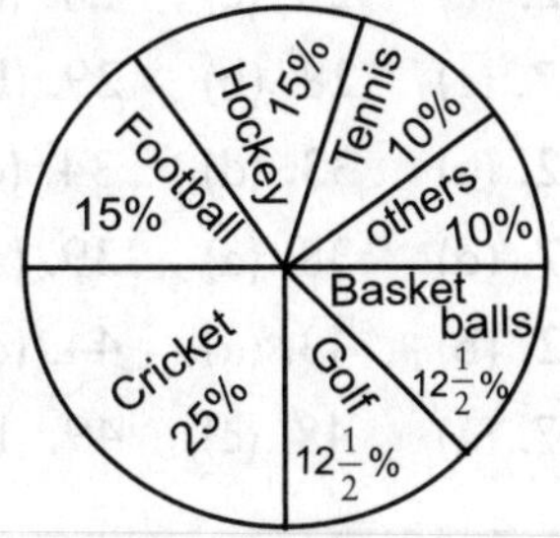

46. The ratio of the total expenditure on football to that of expenditure on hockey is:
(a) 1 : 15 (b) 1 : 1
(c) 15 : 1 (d) 3 : 20

47. If the total expenditure on sports during the year was Rs. 1,20,000,00 how much was spent on basket ball?

(a) Rs. 9,50,000 (b) Rs. 10,00,000
(c) Rs. 12,00,000 (d) Rs. 15,00,000

48. The chart shows that the most popular game of the country is:
(a) Hockey (b) Football
(c) Cricket (d) Tennis

49. Out of the following country's expenditure is the same on:
(a) Hockey and Tennis
(b) Golf and Basket ball
(c) Cricket and Football
(d) Hockey and Golf

50. If the total expenditure on sport during the year was Rs. 1,50,00,000 the expenditure on cricket and hockey together was:
(a) Rs. 60,00,000 (b) Rs. 50,00,000
(c) Rs. 37,50,000 (d) Rs. 25,00,000

ANSWERS

1. (d)	2. (b)	3. (d)	4. (a)	5. (b)
6. (a)	7. (a)	8. (a)	9. (b)	10. (b)
11. (d)	12. (a)	13. (a)	14. (b)	15. (d)
16. (a)	17. (a)	18. (d)	19. (d)	20. (d)
21. (d)	22. (a)	23. (c)	24. (c)	25. (d)
26. (c)	27. (c)	28. (b)	29. (b)	30. (a)
31. (a)	32. (a)	33. (d)	34. (c)	35. (d)
36. (c)	37. (d)	38. (a)	39. (a)	40. (c)
41. (a)	42. (b)	43. (a)	44. (d)	45. (d)
46. (b)	47. (a)	48. (c)	49. (b)	50. (a)

PAPER–II

Read the passage given below and answer the question that follow, based on the passage you understand:

Mahatma Gandhi was looked on by many, both Indian and European, as the epitome of Hindu tradition, but this is a false judgement for he was much influenced by western ideas. Gandhi believed in the fundamentals of his ancient culture, but his passionate love of the underdog and his antipathy to caste were unorthodox in extreme and owed more to European 19th Century liberalism than to anything Indian. His faith in non-violence was by no means typical of Hinduism. For Gandhi's pacifism we must look mainly to the 'Sermon on the Mount' and to Tolstoy. His championing of Women's rights is also the result of western influence. In his social context he was always rather an innovator than a conservative. Though some of his colleagues thought his programme of social reform too slow, he succeeded in shifting the whole emphasis of Hindu thought towards a popular and equalitarian social order in place of the hierarchy of class and caste. Gandhi and his followers gave a new orientation and new life to Hindu culture, after centuries of stagnation. Today politically and economically India faces many problems of great difficulty and no one can forecast her future with any certainty. However Indians of coming generations will not be unconvincing and self-conscious copies of Europeans but will be men rooted in their own traditions and aware of the continuity of their culture. Already the extremes of national self-denigration and fanatical cultural chauvinism are disappearing. In the past Hindu civilization has received, adapted and digested elements of many different cultures-Indo-European, Mesopotamian, Iranian, Greek, Roman, Scythian, Turkish, Persian and Arab. With each new influence it has somewhat changed. Now it is well on the way to assimilating the culture of the west. Hindu civilization will retain its continuity. The Bhagawat Gita will not cease to inspire men of action and the upanishads men of thought. The charm and the graciousness of the Indian way of life will continue, however much affected it may be by the labour saving devices of the west. People will still love the tales of the heroes of the Mahabharata and the Ramayana. The quite and gentle happiness which at all times pervaded Indian life where oppression, disease and poverty have not overclouded it will surely not vanish before the more hectic ways of the west. Much that was useless in ancient Indian Culture has already perished. Widows have long ceased to be burnt on their husbands pyres. Girls may not by law be married in childhood. In buses and trains all over India Brahmins rub shoulders with the lower castes without consciousness of grave pollution and the temples are open to all by law. Caste is vanishing, the process began long ago, but its pace is now so rapid that the more objectionable features of caste may have disappeared with a generation or so.

The old family system is adapting itself to present day conditions. In fact the whole face of India is altering, but the cultural tradition continues, and it will never be lost.

1. Which factor influenced Gandhi's ideas on Indian Culture most?
   (a) Believed in the fundamentals of ancient culture
   (b) Influenced by western ideas
   (c) 'Sermon on the Mount'
   (d) Tolstoy's ideas
2. Mention the most important social issue taken up by Gandhiji for reforms:
   (a) Religion
   (b) Caste
   (c) Women's status
   (d) Orthodoxy in Hinduism
3. Future of Indian Culture rests mostly on:
   (a) Relevance to the present society
   (b) Equalitariarism in society
   (c) Elimination of conservative trends in Indian Society
   (d) Eliminating European influences
4. Which ancient sacred text influenced the Indian mind most?
   (a) Bhagavat Gita (b) Puranas
   (c) Epics (d) Upanishads
5. Which factor influenced most to eliminate caste-system in India?
   (a) Rationalism
   (b) Job opportunities
   (c) Legislations
   (d) Liberal education
6. The southernmost site of the Harappan Culture is:
   (a) Lothal (b) Kot Diji
   (c) Daimabad (d) Rangapur
7. Which one of the following is a work on Tamil grammar?
   (a) Manimekhalai (b) Kural
   (c) Silappadigaram (d) Tolkappiyam
8. Which of the following relates to the Later Vedic period?
   (a) Dasarajna battle
   (b) Worship of Indra, Varuna and Surya
   (c) Crystallization of caste
   (d) Conflict with Dasyus and Panis
9. Which of the following Buddhist works mentions the Shodasa-mahajanapadas?
   (a) Anguttara Nikaya
   (b) Digha Nikaya
   (c) Dipavamsa
   (d) Mahavamsa
10. Which of the following edicts of Ashoka mentions his relations with the outside world?
    (a) Rock edict I
    (b) Rock edict XIII
    (c) Rummindei inscription
    (d) Sanchi inscription
11. "Milindapanha" contains the dialogue between Menander and:
    (a) Asvaghosha (b) Dingnaga
    (c) Nagasena (d) Nagarjuna

12. Which of the following texts mentions in detail the contract theory of the origin of the State?
(a) Digha Nikaya (b) Dipavamsa
(c) Kamandakiya (d) Mahavamsa

13. Match List I with List II and select the correct answer from the code given below:

List I
(A) Gunadhya (B) Vagbhatta
(C) Bhaskaracharya (D) Merutunga

List II
(i) Lilavati
(ii) Prabandha Chintamani
(iii) Brihatkatha
(iv) Ashtahgahridaya

Codes:	**A**	**B**	**C**	**D**
(a)	(i)	(ii)	(iii)	(iv)
(b)	(iv)	(i)	(ii)	(iii)
(c)	(ii)	(iii)	(i)	(iv)
(d)	(iii)	(iv)	(i)	(ii)

14. Which of the following educational institutions is arranged in a chronological order?
(a) Takshasila, Kanchipuram, Valabhi and Nalanda
(b) Kanchipuram, Takshasila, Nalanda and Valabhi
(c) Valabhi, Takshasila, Kanchipuram and Nalanda
(d) Takshasila, Valabhi, Kanchipuram and Nalanda

15. Match List I with List II and choose your answer from the code given below:

List I
(A) Dasavatara temple
(B) Gupta brick temple
(C) Meguti temple
(D) Parvati temple

List II
(i) Aihole (ii) Bhitargaon
(iii) Nachana Kuthar (iv) Deogarh

Codes:	**A**	**B**	**C**	**D**
(a)	(ii)	(i)	(iii)	(iv)
(b)	(i)	(ii)	(iii)	(iv)
(c)	(iv)	(ii)	(i)	(iii)
(d)	(iv)	(i)	(ii)	(iii)

16. The most famous stupa built by the Sailendras is located at:
(a) Anuradhapura
(b) Borobudur
(c) Angkor Vat
(d) Angkor Thorn

17. Which of the following dynasties patronised the famous Kailash temple at Ellora?
(a) Vakataka (b) Gupta
(c) Early Chalukya (d) Rashtrakuta

18. Given below are two statements, one labelled as Assertion (A), and the other labelled as Reason (R):

Assertion (A): Rajendra I undertook the Kadaram Campaign.

Reason (R): His desire was to spread Indian Culture in Southeast Asia.

In the context of the above two statements, which one of the following is correct?

Codes:
(a) (A) is correct, but (R) is wrong
(b) Both (A) and (R) are correct
(c) (A) is wrong, but (R) is correct
(d) Both (A) and (R) are wrong

19. Which of the following is chronologically correct?
(a) Gondophernes, Wima Kadphises and Kanishka
(b) Simuka, Satakarni and Krishna
(c) Mahendravarman, Dantivarman and Narasimhavarman
(d) Rajaraja, Parantaka and Aditya

20. Given below are two statements, one labelled as Assertion (A), and the other labelled as Reason (R):

Assertion (A): Buddha preached his sermons through the medium of Prakrit language.
Reason (R): He wanted to reach each and every section of the society.
In the context of the above two statements, which one of the following is correct?
Codes:
(a) (A) is correct, but (R) is wrong
(b) Both (A) and (R) are correct
(c) (A) is wrong, but (R) is correct
(d) Both (A) and (R) are wrong

21. Which of the following is not relevant for the Mamluk period?
(a) Khazian-u'l-Futuh
(b) Taj u'l Ma 'asir
(c) Tarikh-i-Feroz Shahi
(d) Tabaqat-i-Nasiri

22. Who among the following regarded Delhi as the largest city in the entire Islamic East?
(a) Alberuni (b) Amir Khusrau
(c) Ibn-Batuta (d) Shams Siraj Afif

23. Given below are two statements, one labelled as Assertion (A), and the other labelled as Reason (R):
Assertion (A): Balban sought to increase the prestige and power of the monarchy, and to centralize all authority in the hands of the sultan.
Reason (R): He followed the Islamic theory of sovereignty.
In the context of the above two statements, which one of the following is correct?
Codes:
(a) Both (A) and (R) are true and (R) is the correct explanation of (A)
(b) Both (A) and (R) are true, but (R) is not the correct explanation of (A)
(c) (A) is true, but (R) is false
(d) (A) is false, but (R) is true

24. Allauddin Khalji did not levy:
(a) Kharaj (b) Ghari
(c) Qismat-i-khoti (d) Charai

25. Match List I with List II and select the correct answer from the code given below:
List I
(A) Nizam u'd-Din Auliya
(B) Shaikh Nur u'd-Din
(C) Baha u'd-Din Ganjbakhsh
(D) Dadu
List II
(i) Naqashbandhiya (ii) Bhakti
(iii) Chishtiya (iv) Rishi

Codes:	A	B	C	D
(a)	(iii)	(ii)	(i)	(iv)
(b)	(iii)	(iv)	(i)	(ii)
(c)	(iii)	(i)	(ii)	(iv)
(d)	(i)	(iv)	(iii)	(ii)

26. Match List I with List II and select the correct answer from the code given below:
List I
(A) Wakil-i-dar
(B) Amir-i-hajib
(C) Mushrif-i-mumalik
(D) Barid-i-mumalik
List II
(i) Head of the state - news - agency
(ii) Officer incharge of royal household
(iii) Master of ceremonies at the court
(iv) The Accountant - General for the Sultanate

Codes:	A	B	C	D
(a)	(ii)	(iii)	(iv)	(i)
(b)	(i)	(ii)	(iii)	(iv)
(c)	(iii)	(ii)	(iv)	(i)
(d)	(iv)	(i)	(ii)	(iii)

27. Given below are two statements, one labelled as Assertion (A), and the other labelled as Reason (R):

Assertion (A): In the Adhi Granth the hymns of Kabir, Raidas, Namdev and Baba Farid are also included.

Reason (R): Sikhism was born in the milieu of strong bhakti tradition.

In the context of the above two statements, which one of the following is correct?

Codes:

(a) Both (A) and (R) are true and (R) is the correct explanation of (A)
(b) Both (A) and (R) are true, but (R) is not the correct explanation of (A)
(c) (A) is true, but (R) is false
(d) (R) is true, but (A) is false

28. Given below are two statements, one labelled as Assertion (A), and the other labelled as Reason (R):

Assertion (A): From the very beginning of the Bahmani Kingdom the foreigners wielded considerable influence in the politics of the kingdom.

Reason (R): Bahman Shaha never trusted the Deccani nobles.

In the context of the above two statements, which one of the following is correct?

Codes:

(a) Both (A) and (R) are true and (R) is the correct explanation of (A)
(b) Both (A) and (R) are true, but (R) is not the correct explanation of (A)
(c) (A) is true, but (R) is false
(d) (A) is false, but (R) is true

29. Who among the following gave the figure that there were some two hundred nayakas in Vijayanagara Kingdom?

(a) Domingo Paes
(b) Nicolo De Conti
(c) Varthema
(d) Fernao Nuniz

30. Match List I with List II and select the correct answer from the code given below:

List I

(A) Bhim Sen
(B) Amir Khusrau
(C) Al-Biruni
(D) Nizam u'd - Din Ahmad

List II

(i) Qiran us Sadain
(ii) Kitab Fi Tahqiq mā li 'l - Hind
(iii) Nuskha-i Dilkusha
(iv) Tabaqat-i Akbari

Codes:	**A**	**B**	**C**	**D**
(a)	(i)	(iii)	(iv)	(ii)
(b)	(iii)	(ii)	(iv)	(i)
(c)	(iv)	(i)	(ii)	(iii)
(d)	(iii)	(i)	(ii)	(iv)

31. Which of the following is not correctly matched?

(a) Chauth – One-fourth of the land revenue demanded by Shivaji as war expense
(b) Tanka – A copper coin
(c) Ijara – The system of farming-out revenue
(d) Hast-o-bud – A method of land revenue assessment

32. Sultan Muhammad Quli Qutub Shah was the contemporary of:

(a) Akbar
(b) Aurangzeb
(c) Shah Jahan
(d) Muhammad Shah

33. Which of the following statements is/are not correct?

(i) The mints in Mughal India worked on the basis of free coinage.
(ii) Each coin bore the name of the mint and the year of issue.

(iii) The number of rupee mints was fourteen under Akbar
(iv) The coins minted in the previous reign were called Khazana

Select the correct answer from the code given below.

Codes:

(a) (i), (ii) (b) (i), (iii), (iv)
(c) (ii), (iii) (d) (iv) only

34. Who among the following estimated the total population of India in 1600 at about 100 millions?
(a) Kingsley Davis (b) Moreland
(c) Irfan Habib (d) Ashok V. Desai

35. Who among the following does not subscribe to the "Mughal Centric" approach to the downfall of Mughal empire?
(a) Irfan Habib (b) Satish Chandra
(c) Muzaffar 'Alam (d) Athar Ali

36. Decline of the artisan communities in India was mainly due to:
(a) Industrial revolution
(b) Import of foreign goods
(c) Development of local and regional markets
(d) Monopoly of British trade

37. Under whose Chairmanship the Indian Education Commission of 1882 was appointed?
(a) Sir Charles Wood
(b) Lord Curzon
(c) W.W. Hunter
(d) Lord Lytton

38. Given below are two statements, one labelled as Assertion (A), and the other labelled as Reason (R):

Assertion (A): Introduction of modern communications affected the traditional self sufficient villages, local markets, caste and trade.

Reason (R): The modern communications were not introduced in India to demolish indigenous village life, including trade, caste and local markets.

In the context of the above two statements, which one of the following is correct?

Codes:

(a) Both (A) and (R) are true and (R) is the correct explanation of (A)
(b) Both (A) and (R) are true, but (R) is not the correct explanation of (A)
(c) (A) is true, but (R) is false
(d) (R) is true, but (A) is false

39. One of the following was not a nationalist Muslim but known for his communal views:
(a) Mirza Ismail
(b) Kasim Razvi
(c) Sir Ali Imam
(d) Badruddin Tayyabji

40. Match List I with List II and indicate the correct answer from the code given below:

List I

(A) Bhavani Mandir
(B) Anand Mutt
(C) Philosophy of Bomb
(D) Geetanjali

List II

(i) Rabindranath Tagore
(ii) Bhagavati Charan
(iii) Bankim Chandra Chatterjee
(iv) Birendra Kumar Ghosh

Codes:	**A**	**B**	**C**	**D**
(a)	(ii)	(i)	(iii)	(iv)
(b)	(iii)	(ii)	(iv)	(i)
(c)	(iv)	(iii)	(ii)	(i)
(d)	(i)	(iv)	(iii)	(ii)

41. Match List I with List II and choose your answer from the code given below:

List I

(A) Lord Ripon
(B) Lord Elphinston

(C) Lord Curzon
(D) Lord Dalhousie

List II
(i) Widow Remarriage Act
(ii) Educational Reforms
(iii) Local Self-Government
(iv) Governor

Codes:	**A**	**B**	**C**	**D**
(a)	(iii)	(iv)	(ii)	(i)
(b)	(iv)	(iii)	(i)	(ii)
(c)	(ii)	(iv)	(iii)	(i)
(d)	(i)	(ii)	(iv)	(iii)

42. Given below are two statements, one labelled as Assertion (A), and the other labelled as Reason (R):
Assertion (A): The main characteristic feature of Ramakrishna's religious precept was his belief in the truth of all religions.
Reason (R): Ramakrishna had no belief in any religion.
In the context of the above two statements, which one of the following is correct?
Codes:
(a) Both (A) and (R) are true and (R) is the correct explanation of (A)
(b) Both (A) and (R) are true, but (R) is not the correct explanation of (A)
(c) (A) is true, but (R) is false
(d) (A) is false, but (R) is true

43. Arrange the following in chronological order in the code given below:
(i) Individual Satyagraha
(ii) Salt Satyagraha
(iii) Swaraj Party
(iv) Constructive Programme
Codes:
(a) (iii), (iv), (ii), (i)
(b) (iv), (iii), (ii), (i)
(c) (i), (iii), (iv), (ii)
(d) (ii), (i), (iv), (iii)

44. One of the following leaders questioned Gandhi when he called off non-cooperation movement in 1922.
(a) C. Rajagopalachari
(b) Vallabhbhai Patel
(c) C.R. Das
(d) Maulana Azad

45. One of the following was not a member of Cabinet Mission:
(a) Sir Stafford Cripps
(b) Lord Wavell
(c) Sir Pethic Lawrence
(d) A.V. Alexander

46. Which of the following is not the salient feature of Annales school?
(a) Interdisciplinary approach
(b) Search for 'new sources'
(c) Long duree
(d) Region-Centric approach

47. Who among the following articulates that there can be no objectivity in history?
(a) Post-Modernists (b) Marxists
(c) Neo-Colonialists (d) Sub-alternists

48. Who among the following was not associated with the foundation of Non-Alignment Movement?
(a) Marshal Tito
(b) Jawaharlal Nehru
(c) Nelson Mandela
(d) President Sukarno

49. Protestantism was officially recognised in:
(a) Diet of Warms 1521
(b) Diet of Augnsburg 1555
(c) Diet of Spears 1526
(d) Diet of Augnsburg 1592

50. One of the following rulers was not associated with Enlightened Despotism
(a) Fredrick II of Prussia
(b) Peter the Great of Russia
(c) Louis XIV of France
(d) Joseph II of Austria

ANSWERS

1. (b)	2. (d)	3. (c)	4. (a)	5. (b)
6. (c)	7. (d)	8. (c)	9. (a)	10. (b)
11. (c)	12. (c)	13. (d)	14. (d)	15. (c)
16. (b)	17. (d)	18. (a)	19. (a)	20. (b)
21. (c)	22. (d)	23. (b)	24. (a)	25. (b)
26. (a)	27. (a)	28. (b)	29. (d)	30. (c)
31. (d)	32. (b)	33. (d)	34. (b)	35. (a)
36. (a)	37. (c)	38. (b)	39. (c)	40. (c)
41. (a)	42. (c)	43. (b)	44. (c)	45. (b)
46. (d)	47. (b)	48. (c)	49. (b)	50. (c)

DECEMBER–2005

Note: This paper contains fifty (50) objective type questions, each question carrying two (2) marks. Attempt all the questions.

PAPER–I

1. Team teaching has the potential to develop:
   (a) Competitive spirit
   (b) Cooperation
   (c) The habit of supplementing the teaching of each other
   (d) Highlighting the gaps in each other's teaching

2. Which of the following is the most important characteristic of Open Book Examination system?
   (a) Students become serious.
   (b) It improves attendance in the classroom.
   (c) It reduces examination anxiety amongst students.
   (d) It compels students to think.

3. Which of the following methods of teaching encourages the use of maximum senses?
   (a) Problem-solving method
   (b) Laboratory method
   (c) Self-study method
   (d) Team teaching method

4. Which of the following statement is correct?
   (a) Communicator should have fine senses
   (b) Communicator should have tolerance power
   (c) Communicator should be soft spoken
   (d) Communicator should have good personality

5. An effective teacher is one who can:
   (a) control the class
   (b) give more information in less time
   (c) motivate students to learn
   (d) correct the assignments carefully

6. One of the following is not a quality of researcher:
   (a) Unison with that of which he is in search
   (b) He must be of alert mind
   (c) Keenness in enquiry
   (d) His assertion to outstrip the evidence

7. A satisfactory statistical quantitative method should not possess one of the following qualities:
   (a) Appropriateness (b) Measurability
   (c) Comparability (d) Flexibility

8. Books and records are the primary sources of data in:
   (a) historical research
   (b) participatory research
   (c) clinical research
   (d) laboratory research

9. Which of the following statement is correct?
   (a) objectives should be pin-pointed
   (b) objectives can be written in statement or question form
   (c) another word for problem is variable
   (d) all the above

10. The important pre-requisites of a researcher in sciences, social sciences and humanities are:

(a) laboratory skills, records, supervisor, topic
(b) Supervisor, topic, critical analysis, patience
(c) archives, supervisor, topic, flexibility in thinking
(d) topic, supervisor, good temperament, pre-conceived notions

Read the following passage and answer the questions 11 to 15:

Knowledge creation in many cases requires creativity and idea generation. This is especially important in generating alternative decision support solutions. Some people believe that an individual's creative ability stems primarily from personality traits such as inventiveness, independence, individuality, enthusiasm, and flexibility. However, several studies have found that creativity is not so much a function of individual traits as was once believed, and that individual creativity can be learned and improved. This understanding has led innovative companies to recognise that the key to fostering creativity may be the development of an idea-nurturing work environment. Idea-generation methods and techniques, to be used by individuals or in groups, are consequently being developed. Manual methods for supporting idea generation, such as brainstorming in a group, can be very successful in certain situations. However, in other situations, such an approach is either not economically feasible or not possible. For example, manual methods in group creativity sessions will not work or will not be effective when : (1) there is no time to conduct a proper idea-generation session; (2) there is a poor facilitator (or no facilitator at all); (3) it is too expensive to conduct an idea-generation session; (4) the subject matter is too sensitive for a face-to-face session; or (5) there are not enough participants, the mix of participants is not optimal, or there is no climate for idea generation. In such cases, computerised idea-generation methods have been tried, with frequent success.

Idea-generation software is designed to help stimulate a single user or a group to produce new ideas, options and choices. The user does all the work, but the software encourages and pushes, something like a personal trainer. Although idea-generation software is still relatively new, there are several packages on the market. Various approaches are used by idea-generating software to increase the flow of ideas to the user. Idea Fisher, for example, has an associate lexicon of the English language that cross-references words and phrases. These associative links, based on analogies and metaphors, make it easy for the user to be fed words related to a given theme. Some software packages use questions to prompt the user towards new, unexplored patterns of thought. This helps users to break out of cyclical thinking patterns, conquer mental blocks, or deal with bouts of procrastination.

11. The author, in this passage has focussed on
    (a) knowledge creation
    (b) idea-generation
    (c) creativity
    (d) individual traits

12. Fostering creativity needs an environment of
    (a) decision support systems
    (b) idea-nurturing
    (c) decision support solutions
    (d) alternative individual factors

13. Manual methods for the support of idea-generation, in certain occasions,
    (a) are alternatively effective
    (b) can be less expensive
    (c) do not need a facilitator
    (d) require a mix of optimal participants

14. Idea-generation software works as if it is a:
    (a) stimulant
    (b) knowledge package
    (c) user-friendly trainer
    (d) climate creator
15. Mental blocks, bouts of procrastination and cyclical thinking patterns can be won when:
    (a) innovative companies employ electronic thinking methods
    (b) idea-generation software prompts questions
    (c) manual methods are removed
    (d) individuals acquire a neutral attitude towards the software
16. Level C of the effectiveness of communication is defined as:
    (a) channel noise
    (b) semantic noise
    (c) psychological noise
    (d) source noise
17. Recording a television programme on a VCR is an example of:
    (a) time-shifting
    (b) content reference
    (c) mechanical clarity
    (d) media synchronisation
18. A good communicator is the one who offers to his audience:
    (a) plentiful of information
    (b) a good amount of statistics
    (c) concise proof
    (d) repetition of facts
19. The largest number of newspapers in India is published from the state of:
    (a) Kerala (b) Maharashtra
    (c) West Bengal (d) Uttar Pradesh
20. Insert the missing number:
    8 24 12 ? 18 54
    (a) 26 (b) 24
    (c) 36 (d) 3 2
21. January 1, 1995 was Sunday. What day of the week lies on January 1, 1996?
    (a) Sunday (b) Monday
    (c) Saturday (d) None of these
22. The sum of a positive number and its reciprocal is twice the difference of the number and its reciprocal. The number is:
    (a) $\sqrt{2}$ (b) $\frac{1}{\sqrt{2}}$
    (c) $\sqrt{3}$ (d) $\frac{1}{\sqrt{3}}$
23. In a certain code, ROUNDS is written as RONUDS. How will PLEASE will be written in the same code:
    (a) LPAESE (b) PLAESE
    (c) LPAEES (d) PLASEE
24. At what time between 5.30 and 6.00 will the hands of an clock be at right angles?
    (a) $43\frac{5}{11}$ min. past 5
    (b) $43\frac{7}{11}$ min. past 5
    (c) 40 min. past 5
    (d) 45 min. past 5
25. **Statements:** I All students are ambitious
    II All ambitious persons are hard working
    Conclusions: (i) All students are hard-working
    (ii) All hardly working people are not ambitious
    Which of the following is correct?
    (a) Only (i) is correct
    (b) Only (ii) is correct
    (c) Both (i) and (ii) are correct
    (d) Neither (i) nor (ii) is correct
26. **Statement:** Most students are intelligent
    Conclusions: (i) Some students are intelligent
    (ii) All students are not intelligent

Which of the following is implied?
(a) Only (i) is implied
(b) Only (ii) is implied
(c) Both (i) and (ii) are implied
(d) Neither (i) nor (ii) is implied

27. **Statement:** Most labourers are poor
Conclusions: (i) Some labourers are poor
(ii) All labourers are not poor
Which of the following is implied?
(a) Only (i) is implied
(b) Only (ii) is implied
(c) Both (i) and (ii) are implied
(d) Neither (i) nor (ii) is implied

28. Line access and avoidance of collision are the main functions of:
(a) the CPU
(b) the monitor
(c) network protocols
(d) wide area networks

29. In the hypermedia database, information bits are stored in the form of:
(a) signals (b) cubes
(c) nodes (d) symbols

30. Communications bandwidth that has the highest capacity and is used by microwave, cable and fibre optics lines is known as:
(a) hyper-link
(b) broadband
(c) bus width
(d) carrier wave

31. An electronic bill board that has a short text or graphical advertising message is referred to as:
(a) bulletin (b) strap
(c) bridge line (d) banner

32. Which of the following is not the characteristic of a computer?
(a) computer is an electrical machine
(b) computer cannot think at its own
(c) computer processes information error free
(d) computer can hold data for any length of time

33. Bitumen is obtained from:
(a) Forests and Plants
(b) Kerosene oil
(c) Crude oil
(d) underground mines

34. Malaria is caused by:
(a) bacterial infection
(b) viral infection
(c) parasitic infection
(d) fungal infection

35. The cloudy nights are warmer compared to clear nights (without clouds) during winter days. This is because:
(a) clouds radiate heat towards the earth
(b) clouds prevent cold wave from the sky, descend on earth
(c) clouds prevent escaping of the heat radiation from the earth
(d) clouds being at great heights from earth absorb heat from the sun and send towards the earth

36. Largest soil group of India is:
(a) Red soil (b) Black soil
(c) Sandy soil (d) Mountain soil

37. Main pollutant of the Indian coastal water is:
(a) oil spill
(b) municipal sewage
(c) industrial effluents
(d) aerosols

38. Human ear is most sensitive to noise in the following frequency ranges:
(a) 1-2 KHz (b) 100-500 Hz
(c) 10-12 KHz (d) 13-16 KHz

39. Which species of chromium is toxic in water:
(a) Cr + 2 (b) Cr + 3
(c) Cr + 6 (d) Cr is non-toxic element

40. Match List I (Dams) with List II (River) in the following:

List-I (Dams)	List-II (River)
(A) Bhakra	(i) Krishna
(B) Nagarjunasagar	(ii) Damodar
(C) Panchet	(iii) Sutlej
(D) Hirakud	(iv) Bhagirathi
(E) Tehri	(v) Mahanadi

Codes:	A	B	C	D	E
(a)	v	iii	iv	ii	i
(b)	iii	i	ii	v	iv
(c)	i	ii	iv	iii	v
(d)	ii	iii	iv	i	v

41. A negative reaction to a mediated communication is described as:
(a) flak
(b) fragmented feedback
(c) passive response
(d) non-conformity

42. The launch of satellite channel by IGNOU on 26th January 2003 for technological education for the growth and development of distance education is:
(a) Eklavya channel
(b) Gyandarshan channel
(c) Rajrishi channel
(d) None of these

43. Match List-I with List-II and select the correct answer from the code given below:

List I (Institutions)	List II (Locations)
(A) The Indian Council of Historical Reasearch (ICHR)	(i) Shimla
(B) The Indian Institute of Advanced Studies (IIAS)	(ii) New Delhi
(C) The Indian Council of Philosophical Research (ICPR)	(iii) Bangalore
(D) The Central Institute of Coastal Engineering for fisheries	(iv) Lucknow

Codes:	A	B	C	D
(a)	ii	i	iv	iii
(b)	i	ii	iii	iv
(c)	ii	iv	i	iii
(d)	iv	iii	ii	i

44. Which of the following is not a Fundamental Right?
(A) Right to equality
(b) Right against exploitation
(c) Right to freedom of speech and expression
(d) Right of free compulsory education of all children upto the age of 14

45. The Lok Sabha can be dissolved before the expiry of its normal five year term by:
(a) The Prime Minister
(b) The Speaker of Lok Sabha
(c) The President on the recommendation of the Prime Minister
(d) None of the above

Study the following graph carefully and answer Q.No. 46 to 50 given below it:

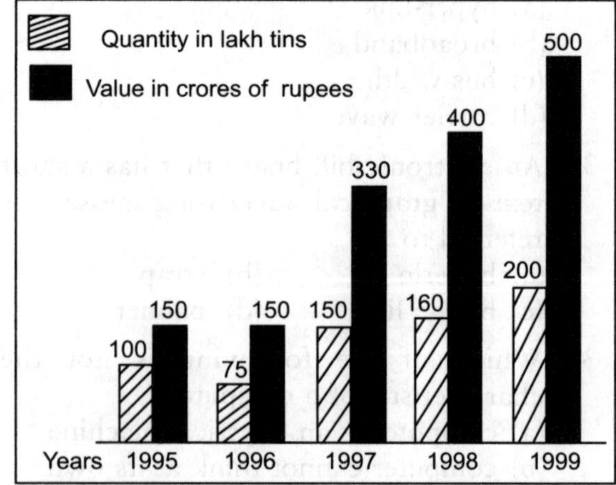

46. In which year the value per tin was minimum?
(a) 1995 (b) 1996
(c) 1998 (d) 1999

47. What was the difference between the tins exported in 1997 and 1998?
(a) 10 (b) 1000
(c) 100000 (d) 1000000

48. What was the approximate percentage increase in export value from 1995 to 1999?
(a) 350 (b) 330.3
(c) 433.3 (d) None of these

49. What was the percentage drop in export quantity from 1995 to 1996?
(a) 75 (b) 50
(c) 25 (d) None of these

50. If in 1998, the tins were exported at the same rate per tin as that in 1997, what would be the value (in crores of rupees) of export in 1998?
(a) 400 (b) 375
(c) 352 (d) 330

ANSWERS

1. (c)	2. (d)	3. (b)	4. (a)	5. (c)
6. (d)	7. (d)	8. (a)	9. (a)	10. (b)
11. (a)	12. (b)	13. (a)	14. (a)	15. (b)
16. (a)	17. (d)	18. (a)	19. (d)	20. (c)
21. (b)	22. (d)	23. (b)	24. (b)	25. (c)
26. (b)	27. (b)	28. (c)	29. (a)	30. (b)
31. (b)	32. (a)	33. (d)	34. (c)	35. (c)
36. (a)	37. (c)	38. (d)	39. (c)	40. (b)
41. (c)	42. (a)	43. (a)	44. (d)	45. (c)
46. (a)	47. (a)	48. (d)	49. (c)	50. (c)

PAPER–II

1. Where do we get the continuous sequence of the Harappan Ware and the Painted Grey Ware?
(a) Lothal (b) Kalibangan
(c) Alamgirpur (d) Bhagwanpura

2. Ashoka mentions some foreign rulers alongwith their states in his Rock Edict:
(a) 5th Rock Edict
(b) 13th Rock Edict
(c) 12th Rock Edict
(d) 10th Rock Edict

3. The *Rig-Veda* does not mention one of the following:
(a) Magadha (b) Sapt-Sindhu
(c) Dasyu (d) Varna

4. The site of Piparawah is identified with one of the following ancient towns:
(a) Kushinagara (b) Lumbini
(c) Kapilavastu (d) Sravasti

5. What is the language of Pliny's original work, the *Natural History*?
(a) Greek (b) Latin
(c) French (d) English

6. Which work refers to India's contacts with Baveru?
(a) Arthasastra (b) Dipavamsa
(c) Agamas (d) Jatakas

7. Match List I with List II and choose your answer from the code given below:

List I
(A) Bilhana (B) Someshvara
(C) Somadeva (D) Jayadeva

List II
(i) Manasollasa
(ii) Gita Govinda
(iii) Vikramankadevacharita
(iv) Kathasaritasagara

Codes:	**A**	**B**	**C**	**D**
(a)	(iii)	(i)	(iv)	(ii)
(b)	(i)	(iii)	(iv)	(ii)
(c)	(ii)	(iv)	(iii)	(i)
(d)	(iii)	(i)	(ii)	(iv)

8. Who converted Kumarapala, the Chalukyan King of Gujarat to Jainism?
(a) Hemachandra (b) Hemadri
(c) Vimal Suri (d) Jina Dutt Suri

9. The Pallavas used one of the following symbols:
(a) Trident and Lingam
(b) Fish and Ship
(c) Elephant and Lion
(d) Bull and Lingam

10. The earliest Vessara temple is carved at:
(a) Mahabalipuram
(b) Deogarh
(c) Aihole
(d) Nachna-Kuthara

11. Which of the following pairs is not matched correctly?
(a) Kalhana and Rajatarangini
(b) Dharamapala and Nalanda
(c) Ashoka and Buddhism
(d) Vakapatiraja and Harsha

12. Given below are two statements, one labelled as Assertion (A), and the other labelled as Reason (R):
Assertion (A): The concept of Syadavada in Jainism accommodates the views of others.
Reason (R): The Jainas are frightened by others views.
In the context of the above two statements, which one of the following is correct?
(a) (A) is true, but (R) is false
(b) (R) is true, but (A) is false
(c) Both (A) and (R) are true
(d) Both (A) and (R) are false

13. Given below are two statements, one labelled as Assertion (A), and the other labelled as Reason (R):
Assertion (A): Kharavela threatened Dimita, the King of Magadha, in his Hathigumpha inscription.
Reason (R): Dimita retreated to Mathura because he wanted to challenge him from there.
In the context of the above two statements, which one of the following is correct?
(a) Both (A) and (R) are true
(b) Both (A) and (R) are false
(c) (A) is true, and (R) is false
(d) (A) is false, and (R) is true

14. Match List I with List II and choose your answer from the codes given below:

List I	**List II**
(A) Diodorus	(i) Indica
(B) Arrian	(ii) Library of History
(C) Ptolemy	(iii) Geography
(D) Megasthenes	(iv) Indica

Codes:	**A**	**B**	**C**	**D**
(a)	(ii)	(i)	(iii)	(iv)
(b)	(i)	(iii)	(iv)	(ii)
(c)	(ii)	(iv)	(i)	(iii)
(d)	(iv)	(ii)	(iii)	(i)

15. Who was the founder of the Lingayat Sect?
(a) Appar (b) Sankara
(c) Ramanuja (d) Basavanna

16. Madhvacharya propagated Bhakti in:
(a) Karnataka (b) Andhra
(c) Orissa (d) Maharashtra

17. Gajpati rulers principally controlled:
(a) Bengal (b) Orissa
(c) Bihar (d) South Andhra

18. Amir Khusro was associated with:
(a) Slave rulers
(b) Slave and Khalji rulers

(c) Slave, Khalji and Tughluq rulers
(d) Tughluq and Sayyid rulers

19. Vijayanagar Empire was established in the:
(a) 13th Century (b) 14th Century
(c) 15th Century (d) 16th Century

20. The author of *Purush-Pariksha* was born in:
(a) Bengal (b) Orissa
(c) Bihar (d) Uttar Pradesh

21. Who among the Persian historians wrote mainly about Sher Shah?
(a) Abbas Khan Sherwani
(b) Nizamuddin Ahmed
(c) Abdul Qadir Badaoni
(d) Yahya Sirhindi

22. In the 17th Century major Portuguese settlements in India were at:
(a) Goa
(b) Goa and Daman
(c) Goa, Daman and Diu
(d) Goa, Daman and Cochin

23. Pondicherry was the main base on the Coromondel coast of the:
(a) Dutch East India Company
(b) French East India Company
(c) English East India Company
(d) Danish East India Company

24. The English East India Company exported from India to Europe in the XVII Century mainly:
(a) Cotton textiles
(b) Cotton textiles and indigo
(c) Cotton textiles, indigo and saltpetre
(d) Cotton textiles, indigo, saltpetre and spices

25. *Mansabdari* was instituted by:
(a) Babur (b) Humayun
(c) Akbar (d) Aurangzeb

26. *Adi-Granth* was given final form by:
(a) Guru Nanak
(b) Guru Angad
(c) Guru Arjun
(d) Guru Gobind Singh

27. Who among the following was not a peasant in medieval India?
(a) *Khudkashta* (b) *Muzarain*
(c) *Balahar* (d) *Pahikashta*

28. The Maratha Confederacy fell before the English because the Maratha Chiefs were:
(a) disunited
(b) disunited and militarily weak
(c) lacking in political foresight
(d) not able to correctly judge English intentions

29. Socio-religious movements in medieval India profoundly affected:
(a) Social life
(b) Economic life
(c) Cultural life
(d) Regional languages

30. Given two statements, one labelled as Assertion (A), and the other labelled as Reason (R):
Assertion (A): Under the Great Mughals architecture flourished.
Reason (R): Some of the Great Mughals were great patrons of architecture.
In the context of the above two statements, which one of the following is correct?
(a) Both (A) and (R) are true and (R) is the correct explanation of (A).
(b) Both (A) and (R) are true and (R) is not the correct explanation of (A).
(c) (A) is true but (R) is false.
(d) (A) is false but (R) is true.

31. After the Battle of Plassey the servants of East India Company carried on their private trade in Bengal through the:
(a) Authority of the Company
(b) Misuse of dastaks
(c) Nawab's of Bengal
(d) Servants of the Nawabs

32. Who introduced for the first time the Quaternary settlement in Bengal?
(a) Lord Clive
(b) Warren Hastings
(c) Lord Cornwallis
(d) Lord Wellesly

33. What is not correct about the Permanent Settlement?
(a) Proprietary Rights granted to the Zamindars
(b) Land Revenue fixed in perpetuity
(c) Proprietary Rights granted to the ryots
(d) Assessment of revenue at the double rates

34. Ishwar Chandra Vidyasagar founded the college in Calcutta called:
(a) Bethune College
(b) Hindu College
(c) Ripon College
(d) Presidency College

35. Which of the following measures was not taken up by Lord Curzon?
(a) The Partition of Bengal
(b) The Ancient Monuments Act
(c) Press Act
(d) The Indian Universities Act

36. Who amongst the following belonged to the Firangi Mahal School of Lucknow?
(a) Shibli Nomani
(b) Maulana Hasan Ahmed Madni
(c) Maulana Abdul Kalam Azad
(d) Maulana Abdul Bari

37. Who amongst the following was not associated with the Swarajist group in the Congress in 1922-23?
(a) Dr. Rajendra Prasad
(b) Motilal Nehru
(c) C.R. Das
(d) Hakim Ajmal Khan

38. Who presided over the first session of the All Indian Kisan Sabha?
(a) N.G. Ranga
(b) Raj Kumar Shukla
(c) Swami Sahjanand
(d) Baba Ramchandra Das

39. The symbol used in the Revolt of 1857 was:
(a) Rose and Bread
(b) Lotus and Cow
(c) Rose and Lamp
(d) Lotus and Bread

40. Who has argued that de-industrialization did not take place in India under the colonial rule?
(a) Anil Seal
(b) Dada Bhai Naoroji
(c) Morris D. Morris
(d) Amiya Bagchi

41. Match List I with List II and select the correct answer:

List I
(A) Vanchi Iyer
(B) T.K. Mahadevan
(C) Shrinivas Pillay
(D) E.V. Ramaswamy Naicker

List II
(i) Vaikom Satyagraha
(ii) Tinnevelli conspiracy case
(iii) The Hindu Progressive Improvement Society
(iv) Self Respect Movement

Codes:	A	B	C	D
(a)	(ii)	(iv)	(iii)	(i)
(b)	(iii)	(ii)	(iv)	(i)
(c)	(ii)	(i)	(iii)	(iv)
(d)	(i)	(ii)	(iv)	(iii)

42. Match List I with List II and select the correct answer:

List I
(A) Sir William Jones
(B) Hindu College
(C) Edward Thompson
(D) M.A.O. College

List II

(i) Rise and Fulfilment of the British Rule in India
(ii) Aligarh Muslim University
(iii) Bengal Asiatic Society and G.T. Garrett
(iv) Presidency College

Codes:	**A**	**B**	**C**	**D**
(a)	(i)	(iv)	(ii)	(iii)
(b)	(iii)	(iv)	(i)	(ii)
(c)	(iii)	(ii)	(i)	(iv)
(d)	(iv)	(iii)	(ii)	(i)

43. Who amongst the following was not included in the I.N.A. trial held in the Red Fort, Delhi?
(a) G.S. Dhillon
(b) Prem Sahgal
(c) Col Mohan Singh
(d) Shanawaz Khan

44. In 1946, the Interim Government was headed by:
(a) Liaqat Ali Khan
(b) Jawaharlal Nehru
(c) Maulana Abdul Kalam Azad
(d) Lord Mountbatten

45. Given below are two statements, one labelled as Assertion (A), and the other labelled as Reason (R):
Assertion (A): Woods' Despatch of 1854 is generally known as the Magna Carta of English Education in India.
Reason (R): It outlined a comprehensive plan for the future development of education system in India by the British Government.
In the context of the above two statements, which one of the following is correct?
(a) Both (A) and (R) are true and (R) is the correct explanation of (A).
(b) Both (A) and (R) are true and (R) is not the correct explanation of (A).
(c) (A) is true but (R) is false
(d) (A) is false but (R) is true

46. During Renaissance the interest in the study of Gracco-Roman classics came to be known as:
(a) Individualism (b) Hedonism
(c) Romanticism (d) Humanism

47. Who called commerce is 'a perpetual war of wit and energy among all nations'?
(a) Jean Bodin
(b) Jean Baptist Colbert
(c) Thomas Mun
(d) Thomas Hobbes

48. Who was universally acclaimed as the Prince of the Humanists?
(a) Erasmus
(b) John Colet
(c) Thomas More
(d) Francesco Petrarch

49. Calvinists in France were called:
(a) Puritans (b) Presbyterians
(c) Huguenots (d) Catholics

50. Who was the first Greek Historian?
(a) Thucydides (b) Herodotus
(c) Manetho (d) Homer

ANSWERS

1. (d)	2. (b)	3. (a)	4. (a)	5. (b)
6. (b)	7. (a)	8. (a)	9. (a)	10. (b)
11. (d)	12. (a)	13. (c)	14. (d)	15. (d)
16. (a)	17. (b)	18. (b)	19. (b)	20. (a)
21. (a)	22. (d)	23. (b)	24. (c)	25. (c)
26. (c)	27. (b)	28. (c)	29. (d)	30. (a)
31. (b)	32. (b)	33. (c)	34. (a)	35. (c)
36. (b)	37. (d)	38. (c)	39. (d)	40. (c)
41. (c)	42. (b)	43. (c)	44. (b)	45. (a)
46. (d)	47. (b)	48. (a)	49. (a)	50. (b)

JUNE–2005

Note: This paper contains fifty (50) objective type questions, each question carrying two (2) marks. Attempt all the questions.

PAPER–II

Read the passage given below and answer the questions that follow, based on your understanding of the passage:

The Guild (Srèni), a form of industrial and mercantile organisation which played as big a part in the economy of ancient India as it did in that of most other ancient or medieval civilisations. There are faint and uncertain references to some sort of guild organisations even in vedic literature, and by the time of composition of the Buddhist scriptures, guilds certainly existed in every important Indian town, and embraced almost all trades and industries, we even read of a guild of thieves.

The Guild united both the craftsmen's cooperatives and the individual workman of a given trade into a single corporate body. It fixed rules of work and wages, and standards and prices for the commodities in which its members dealt, and its regulations had the force of law and were upheld by the King and Government. Over its own members, the guild had judicial rights, which were recognized by the State. A guild court could, like a caste council, expel a refractory member, a penalty which would virtually preclude him from practising his ancestral trade and reduce him to beggary. We read in Buddhist literature of Guild Courts settling quarrels between members and their wives and the rules of the Buddhist Order lay down that a married woman may not be ordained a nun without a consent of her husband and his guild. Thus the guild had power not only over the economic, but also over the social life of its members. It acted as guardian of their widows and orphans, and as their insurance against sickness. Its powers and functions in this respect were very similar to those of caste councils in more recent times, and, though some authorities would disagree with us, we cannot but conclude that the guilds played an important part in the evolution of trade castes.

The Guild was headed by a chief usually called the "Elder" (jyeshthaka, in pali jetthaka), who was assisted by a small council of senior members. The office of elder was usually hereditary and held by one of the richest members of the guild. In the pali scriptures, the Elder is invariably described as a very wealthy man, often with much influence at the palace, and counselling the king himself. The Guilds had a corporate life, symbolized, as in medieval europe, by the possession of banners, and also of chauris, the ceremonial yak's tail fly-whisks which bear insignia of nobility. These and other emblems were sometimes granted by royal charter, and were carried in local religious processions by the guildsmen. Some guilds again like those of medieval Europe, had their own militias which served as auxiliaries of the kings' armies in time of need.

1. The author is mainly concerned with:
   (a) a discussion on the origin and development of the guild system
   (b) the Constitution and functions of the guilds
   (c) the judicial powers of the guilds over their members
   (d) the role of guilds in the socio-economic life in ancient India
2. According to the author, the principal role played by the guild was:
   (a) to act as guardian of the widows and orphans
   (b) to fix rules for work and wages
   (c) to make regulations for the members of the guild
   (d) to help the growth of trade and commerce
3. The term "Elder" (*jyeshthaka*) signifies:
   (a) a rich merchant
   (b) an elected merchant
   (c) a hereditary and wealthy merchant
   (d) a selected courtier
4. Which of the following was *not* used as a symbol of the guild?
   (a) chauris
   (b) militia
   (c) banners
   (d) insignia of nobility
5. The tone of the passage is:
   (a) laudatory (b) analytical
   (c) descriptive (d) critical
6. Which of the following Harappan sites has yielded evidence of furrow marks in cultivation?
   (a) Lothal (b) Banavali
   (c) Kalibangan (d) Dhaula Vira
7. Which of the following is *not* related to the vedic period?
   (a) Sabha (b) Samiti
   (c) Dharmasana (d) Vidatha
8. The theory of *syadvada* is associated with:
   (a) Buddhism
   (b) Jainism
   (c) Sankhya philosophy
   (d) Vedanta philosophy
9. Which of the following inscriptions refers to the erection of a Garuda Pillar by a Greek national?
   (a) Eran Inscription
   (b) Sanchi Inscription
   (c) Besnagar Inscription
   (d) Bharhut Inscription
10. The Gupta rulers had established matrimonial relations with a number of royal families. Give the answer as per the code.
    (a) Vakatakas (b) Lichchhavis
    (c) Nagas (d) Sakas
    Codes:
    (a) (a), (b) and (c)
    (b) (b) and (d)
    (c) (a) and (b)
    (d) (a), (b), (c) and (d)
11. Who among the following, granted for the first time, fiscal and administrative immunities, to the Buddhist monks?
    (a) Gautamiputra satakarni
    (b) Asoka
    (c) Hala
    (d) Yajna satakarni
12. Which of the following statements is true about the Kushana period?
    (a) Issue of silver coins on a large scale
    (b) flourishing of the Gandhara School of Art
    (c) patronage of Amarsimha
    (d) extension of the Kushana empire upto Bengal
13. Match List I with List II and select the correct answer from the code given below:

List I

(A) Harsha (B) Vijnanesvara
(C) Bhoja (D) Bana

List II

(i) *Harshacharita*
(ii) *Samarangan Sutradhara*
(iii) *Priyadarsika*
(iv) *Mitakshara*

Codes:	**A**	**B**	**C**	**D**
(a)	(i)	(ii)	(iv)	(iii)
(b)	(iii)	(ii)	(iv)	(i)
(c)	(iii)	(iv)	(ii)	(i)
(d)	(i)	(ii)	(iii)	(iv)

14. Match List I with List II and choose your answer from the code given below:

List I	**List II**
(A) Nivartana	(i) a tax
(B) Kara	(ii) a gold coin
(C) Sulka	(iii) a toll
(D) Gadyana	(iv) Land revenue

Codes:	**A**	**B**	**C**	**D**
(a)	(i)	(ii)	(iii)	(iv)
(b)	(iv)	(i)	(iii)	(ii)
(c)	(ii)	(i)	(iv)	(iii)
(d)	(iii)	(iv)	(i)	(ii)

15. Given below are two statements, one labelled as Assertion (A), and the other labelled as Reason (R):

Assertion (A): Indo-Roman trade activity declined in the 3rd-4th century A.D.

Reason (R): Brahmanical ascendancy in society led to the restrictions on sea-travel.

In the context of the above two statements, which one of the following is correct?

Codes:

(a) (A) is correct, but (R) is wrong
(b) Both (A) and (R) are correct
(c) (A) is wrong, but (R) is correct
(d) Both (A) and (R) are wrong

16. According to Ziauddin Barani the nobles of which of the following sultans were always heavily in debt to the great merchants and money lenders of Delhi?

(a) Balhan
(b) Jalaluddin Khalji
(c) Ghiyasuddin Tughlaq
(d) Muhammad Tughlaq

17. Match List I with List II and select the correct answer from the code given below:

List I

(A) Alaud-Din Khalji
(B) Ghiyas-ud-Din Tughlaq
(C) Muhammad Tughlaq
(D) Feroz Tughlaq

List II

(i) His policy of increasing agrarian taxation led to a peasant revolt
(ii) He introduced the system which later on came to be called as *kankut*
(iii) He abolished most of the agrarian cesses imposed by his predecessors
(iv) He gave concessions to *khuts* and *muqaddams*

Codes:	**A**	**B**	**C**	**D**
(a)	(i)	(iii)	(ii)	(iv)
(b)	(ii)	(i)	(iv)	(iii)
(c)	(i)	(iv)	(iii)	(ii)
(d)	(ii)	(iv)	(i)	(iii)

18. Given below are two statements, one labelled as Assertion (A), and the other labelled as Reason (R):

Assertion (A): Mohammad Tughlaq was the first sultan to visit the tomb of Muinuddin Chishti at Ajmer.

Reason (R): He was a strong believer in mysticism.

In the context of the above two statements, which one of the following is correct?

Codes:
(a) Both (A) and (R) are true and (R) is the correct explanation of (A)
(b) Both (A) and (R) are true, but (R) is not the correct explanation of (A)
(c) (A) is true, but (R) is false
(d) (A) is false, but (R) is true

19. Arrange the following in descending order to depict the hierarchical structure of the rural society. Select the answer from the code given below:
(i) khuts and mugaddams
(ii) reza riaya
(iii) rais and ranas
(iv) balhars
Codes:
(a) (i), (iii), (ii), (iv) (b) (iv), (ii), (iii), (i)
(c) (iii), (i), (ii), (iv) (d) (iv), (ii), (i), (iii)

20. The institution of slavery underwent a perceptible decline after the:
(a) 13th Century (b) 14th Century
(c) 15th Century (d) 16th Century

21. Match List I with List II and select the correct answer from the code given below:
List I (Vijayanagara ruler)
(A) Harihara II
(B) Devaraya I
(C) Virupaksha II
(D) Vira Narasimha

List II (Period)
(i) 1406–1422 (ii) 1377–1404
(iii) 1503–1509 (iv) 1465–1485

Codes:	**A**	**B**	**C**	**D**
(a)	(ii)	(i)	(iv)	(iii)
(b)	(i)	(iii)	(ii)	(iv)
(c)	(ii)	(iii)	(i)	(iv)
(d)	(iv)	(ii)	(iii)	(i)

22. Arrange the following in sequence in which they appeared, and select the answer from the code given below:
(i) Abdur Razzaq (ii) Bernier
(iii) Marco Polo (iv) Thomas Roe
Codes:
(a) (i), (iii), (iv), (ii) (b) (ii), (iv), (iii), (i)
(c) (iii), (i), (iv), (ii) (d) (iv), (ii), (i), (iii)

23. Who among the following Bahmani rulers shifted the Bahmani capital from Gulbarga to Bidar?
(a) Ahmad Shah
(b) Firuz Shah
(c) Muhammad Shah II
(d) Ghiyasuddin

24. Arrange the following in chronological order. Select the correct answer from the code given below:
(i) Lal Darwaza Masjid
(ii) Bara Sona Masjid
(iii) Tomb of Ghiyasuddin Tughlaq
(iv) Jami Masjid at Ahmedabad
Codes:
(a) (iv), (i), (iii), (ii) (b) (iii), (iv), (i), (ii)
(c) (ii), (iii), (i), (iv) (d) (i), (ii), (iv), (iii)

25. Given below are two statements, one labelled as Assertion (A), and the other labelled as Reason (R):
Assertion (A): The medieval Indian culture bears deep imprints of Persian and Central Asian traditions.
Reason (R): The ruling class patronized only the Persian and Central Asian culture.
In the context of the above statements, which one of the following is correct?
Codes:
(a) Both (A) and (R) are correct, and (R) is the correct explanation of (A)
(b) Both (A) and (R) are correct, but (R) is not the correct explanation of (A)
(c) (A) is true, but (R) is false
(d) (A) is false, but (R) is true

26. Which of the following is not correctly matched?
(a) Battle of Chausa – June, 1535
(b) Death of Sher Shah – May, 1545

(c) Bairam Khan's regency – 1556 to 1560
(d) Treaty of Purander – 1665

27. Which of the following was not a coin?
(a) muzaffari (b) muhar
(c) anna (d) do dami

28. Arrange the following in chronological order, and select the correct answer from the code given below:
(i) Introduction of the dagh system
(ii) Introduction of the dual rank (zat and sawar)
(iii) Creation of twelve subahs (provinces)
(iv) Introduction of the dahsala system
Codes:
(a) (i), (ii), (iv), (iii) (b) (ii), (i), (iv), (iii)
(c) (iii), (iv), (i), (ii) (d) (i), (iv), (iii), (ii)

29. The zabt system was established in the Deccan in the later years of Shahjahan's reign by:
(a) Murshid Quli Khan
(b) Shahji Bhosle
(c) Danishmand Khan
(d) Diler Khan

30. Given below are two statements, one labelled as Assertion (A), and the other labelled as Reason (R):
Assertion (A): During the first half of the Eighteenth century the Maratha confederacy achieved its zenith of power ruling over vast territory in western, central and northern India.
Reason (R): The Rajputs supported the Marathas against the Mughals.
In the context of the above two statements, which one of the following is correct?
Codes:
(a) Both (A) and (R) are true and (R) is the correct explanation of (A)
(b) Both (A) and (R) are true, but (R) is not the correct explanation of (A)
(c) (A) is true, but (R) is false
(d) (A) is false, but (R) is true

31. Given below are two statements, one labelled as Assertion (A), and the other labelled as Reason (R):
Assertion (A): The social, self respect ideological struggle of the Justice Party was to uphold their numerical majority in the society.
Reason (R): The leaders of the Justice Party tried to fight and lead the Non-Brahmin movement.
In the context of the above two statements, which one of the following is correct?
Codes:
(a) Both (A) and (R) are true and (R) is the correct explanation of (A)
(b) Both (A) and (R) are true, but (R) is not the correct explanation of (A)
(c) (A) is true, but (R) is false
(d) (A) is false, but (R) is true

32. Give the chronological sequence of the annexation of the following States by the British:
(a) Bengal, Marathas, Mysore, Sikhs
(b) Sikhs, Bengal, Marathas, Mysore
(c) Bengal, Mysore, Marathas, Sikhs
(d) Mysore, Bengal, Marathas, Sikhs

33. Which is the correct chronology of the following?
(i) Bombay Darpan of Balasastri Jambekar
(ii) Amrit Bazar Pataika of Sisir Kumar *et al.*
(iii) Marathi of Balagangadhar Tilak
(iv) Digdarshan of Balasastry
Codes:
(a) (iii), (iv), (ii), (i) (b) (iv), (iii), (ii), (i)
(c) (i), (iii), (iv), (ii) (d) (ii), (i), (iv), (iii)

34. Match the following Magazines/ Newspapers and their Editors:

(A) Dinabandhu (i) Dadabai Nouroji
(B) Voice of India (ii) Manmohan Ghosh
(C) The Statesman (iii) Jyotiba Phule
(D) Indian Mirror (iv) Robert Knight

Codes:	A	B	C	D
(a)	(ii)	(iv)	(iii)	(i)
(b)	(iii)	(i)	(iv)	(ii)
(c)	(iv)	(ii)	(iii)	(i)
(d)	(i)	(iii)	(ii)	(iv)

35. Match the movements/organisations in the princely states with the leaders/ princely states and select the correct answer from the code given below:

List I
(A) Nizams subjects League
(B) Sivapura Satyagraha
(C) Majlis-i-Ittehad ul Musalmeen party
(D) Punnapra Vaylar Satyagrara

List II
(i) Bahadur Yar Jung
(ii) Nizamat Jung Bahadur
(iii) Travancore State
(iv) Mysore State

Codes:	A	B	C	D
(a)	(ii)	(iv)	(i)	(iii)
(b)	(i)	(ii)	(iii)	(iv)
(c)	(iii)	(ii)	(i)	(iv)
(d)	(iv)	(iii)	(ii)	(i)

36. Match List I with List II and indicate the correct answer from the code given below:

List I
(A) Codification of Indian Laws
(B) First Governor General of India
(C) Second Round Table Conference
(D) The Last Governor General of British India

List II
(i) William Bentinck
(ii) Lord Irwin
(iii) Lord Canning
(iv) Lord Macaulay

Codes:	A	B	C	D
(a)	(i)	(iii)	(ii)	(iv)
(b)	(ii)	(iv)	(i)	(iii)
(c)	(iii)	(i)	(iv)	(ii)
(d)	(iv)	(i)	(ii)	(iii)

37. 'Paramountcy is Paramount' is the statement in the preamble of:
(a) Simon Commission (Indian Statutory Commission)
(b) Butler Commission (Indian States Commission)
(c) Hunter Commission (Indian Education Commission)
(d) Cabinet Mission

38. One of the following is not a colonial historiographer.
(a) Judith Brown (b) A.L. Basham
(c) Anil Seal (d) V.A. Smith

39. 'Ryothu Rakshana Yatra' from Ichapuram to Madras in the Madras presidency was organised in 1937-38 by:
(a) Indian National Congress
(b) Andhra Peasants Association
(c) Kisan Sabha
(d) Communist Party

40. Which of the following is not correctly matched?
(a) Surendranath Banerjee – India Today
(b) Jawaharlal Nehru – Discovery of India
(c) Subhash Chandra Bose – Fight for Freedom
(d) Pattabhi Seetharamaiah – History of Indian National Congress

41. Who among the following was not associated with Arya Samaj?
(a) Dayananda Saraswati
(b) Lala Hansraj
(c) Pandit Haradayal
(d) Lala Lajpat Rai

42. One of the following was not associated with social reform movement.
    (a) Behramji Malabari
    (b) Mohandas Karamchand Gandhi
    (c) Iswarchand Vidyasagar
    (d) R.C. Dutt
43. 'Hind Swaraj' was written by Gandhi while,
    (a) travelling from England to India by ship
    (b) in Sabarmati ashram
    (c) travelling from England to South Africa by ship
    (d) leading Champaran satyagraha
44. The British took over the following area for the Payment of arrears for Hyderabad contingency and retained it till 1947.
    (a) Berar
    (b) Raichur, Osmanabad and Berar
    (c) Ceded districts
    (d) Northern Circars
45. One of the following is not oral evidence:
    (a) Interviews
    (b) Tape Recording of events
    (c) Private papers of individuals
    (d) extracting oral evidence through coercive methods
46. Such judgements as:
    "Facts are sacred, opinion is free" allude to giving primacy to:
    (a) Facts over historian
    (b) Oral history over written history
    (c) Interpretation over facts
    (d) Fact over fiction
47. Which of the following is not the secondary source?
    (a) Ashoka and the Decline of Mauryan Empire
    (b) Peasant State and society in Medieval South India
    (c) Rulers, Townsmen and Bazars
    (d) Travels in the Mughal Empire
48. Humurabi's code belongs to:
    (a) Roman civilization
    (b) Greek civilization
    (c) Babylonian civilization
    (d) Chinese civilization
49. The Russian Social Democratic Party was founded by:
    (a) Karl Marx
    (b) Lenin
    (c) Melenkov
    (d) George Phekhanov
50. Mustafa Kamal Pasha terminated the concept of theocratic state in Turkey in the year:
    (a) 1927 (b) 1930
    (c) 1925 (d) 1937

ANSWERS

1. (d)	2. (d)	3. (c)	4. (b)	5. (b)
6. (c)	7. (c)	8. (b)	9. (c)	10. (a)
11. (a)	12. (b)	13. (c)	14. (b)	15. (a)
16. (d)	17. (d)	18. (d)	19. (c)	20. (a)
21. (a)	22. (c)	23. (a)	24. (b)	25. (b)
26. (a)	27. (d)	28. (d)	29. (a)	30. (d)
31. (d)	32. (c)	33. (c)	34. (b)	35. (a)
36. (d)	37. (d)	38. (a)	39. (c)	40. (a)
41. (c)	42. (d)	43. (b)	44. (d)	45. (c)
46. (c)	47. (c)	48. (c)	49. (b)	50. (b)

PRACTICE PAPERS

MOCK TEST–1
PAPER–I

1. A teacher is called the leader of the class because
   (a) he is autocratic emperor of his class
   (b) he masters the art of oratory like a political leader
   (c) he is a maker of the future of his students
   (d) he belongs to a recognised teachers' union
2. The aim of introducing career courses in schools and colleges is to
   (a) increase G.K. in students
   (b) develop the ability to make the intelligent choice of jobs
   (c) provide professional knowledge to students
   (d) All of the above
3. The most effective attribute for a teacher is
   (a) Teaching skills (b) Knowledge
   (c) Feedback (d) Management
4. Those teachers are preferred most by students who
   (a) are themselves disciplined
   (b) give important questions before examination
   (c) dictate notes in the class
   (d) can clear their difficulties regarding subject-matter
5. The qualities of a teacher is/are:
   (i) He must not give any false promise
   (ii) He must not have any bad habits
   (iii) He should be mentally and physically fit
   (iv) He must not be superstitious about his class and students
   (a) Only (iii), (iv) and (ii)
   (b) Only (iv), (i) and (ii)
   (c) Only (i), (iii) and (iv)
   (d) All of the above
6. A teacher is more effective who can
   (a) motivate students to learn
   (b) control the class
   (c) correct the assignments carefully
   (d) give more information in less time
7. A teacher ought to know the problems prevalent in the field of education because
   (a) he can tell the government about it
   (b) with this knowledge, he can have information about education
   (c) he can tell about the same to another teacher
   (d) only he can do something about solving them
8. We can judge the quality of a research by the
   (a) experience of researcher
   (b) relevance of research
   (c) depth of the research
   (d) methodology followed in conducting the research
9. The theory or model developed through the fundamental research to the actual solution of the problems is applied in
   (a) educational research
   (b) action research

(c) applied research
(d) basic research

10. A write-up based on studies of the census data of a given area is called
(a) Research paper (b) Article
(c) Research report (d) Thesis

Direction: (11-16) Study the following passage and give answer to the questions based on it.

Knowledge creation in many cases requires creativity and idea generation. This is especially important in generating alternative decision support solutions. Some people believe that an individual's creative ability stems primarily from personality traits such as inventiveness, independence, individuality, enthusiasm, and flexibility. However, several studies have found that creativity is not so much a function of individual traits as was once believed, and that individual creativity can be learned and improved. This understanding has led innovative companies to recognise that the key to fostering creativity may be the development of an idea-nurturing work environment. Idea-generation methods and techniques, to be used by individuals or in groups, are consequently being developed. Manual methods for supporting idea generation, such as brain-storming in a group, can be very successful in certain situations. However, in other situations, such an approach is either not economically feasible or not possible. For example, manual methods in group creativity sessions will not work or will not be effective when: (a) there is no time to conduct a proper idea-generation session; (b) there is a poor facilitator (or no facilitator at all); (c) it is too expensive to conduct an idea-generation session; (d) the subject matter is too sensitive for a face-to-face session; or (e) there are not enough participants, the mix of participants is not optimal, or there is no climate for idea generation. In such cases, computerised idea-generation methods have been tried, with frequent success. Idea-generation software is designed to help stimulate a single user or a group to produce new ideas, options and choices. The user does all the work, but the software encourages and pushes, something like a personal trainer. Although idea-generation software is still relatively new, there are several packages on the market. Various approaches are used by idea-generating software to increase the flow of ideas to the user. Idea Fisher, for example, has an associate lexicon of the English language that cross-references words and phrases. These associative links, based on analogies and metaphors, make it easy for the user to be fed words related to a given theme. Some software packages use questions to prompt the user towards new, unexplored patterns of thought. This helps users to break out of cyclical thinking patterns, conquer mental blocks, or deal with bouts of procrastination.

11. The author, in this passage has focused on
(a) individual traits
(b) knowledge creation
(c) creativity
(d) idea-generation

12. Idea-generation software works as if it is a
(a) user-friendly trainer
(b) stimulant
(c) climate creator
(d) knowledge package

13. Which among the following personality traits is not believed to be a factor contributing to an individual's creative ability?
(a) Flexibility (b) Individuality
(c) Sophistication (d) Enthusiasm

14. In certain occasions, manual methods for the support of idea-generation
(a) can be less expensive
(b) do not need a facilitator

(c) require a mix of optimal participants
(d) are alternatively effective

15. Mental blocks, bouts of procrastination and cyclical thinking patterns can be won when
(a) idea-generation software prompts questions
(b) individuals acquire a neutral attitude towards the software
(c) manual methods are removed
(d) innovative companies employ electronic thinking methods

16. Fostering creativity needs an environment of
(a) decision support systems
(b) alternative individual factors
(c) idea-nurturing
(d) decision support solutions

17. For controlling noise in a classroom, the best method of communication is
(a) remaining calm and just looking at student
(b) saying 'don't talk'
(c) continue teaching without caring for noise
(d) raising one's voice above students voice

18. In India, Education TV was first introduced in the year
(a) 1978 (b) 1959
(c) 1987 (d) 1998

19. The failure of the teacher to communicate his ideas well to students may result into:
I. Classroom indiscipline.
II. Decrease in attendance in class.
III. Loss of student's interest in class.
(a) Only II (b) Only III
(c) Only I (d) All of these

20. Visualisation in the instructional process cannot increase
(a) curiosity and concentration
(b) interest and motivation
(c) stress and boredom
(d) retention and adaptation

21. Communication helps in
(a) entertainment
(b) integration of country
(c) cultural promotion
(d) All of these

22. "Because you deserve to know" is the punchline used by
(a) *Hindustan Times*
(b) *The Telegraph*
(c) *The Times of India*
(d) *India Today*

23. Find the odd man out from the following groups of letters.
(a) UlmnE (b) AbcdE
(c) ApqrL (d) IfghO

24. The ambitious computerisation program of the Government of India aimed at connecting 60,000 government schools through internet is known as
(a) Vidya Vahini (b) Gyan Vahini
(c) Kalpana project (d) Vidya Vani

25. Find the wrong number in the following sequence.
225, 336, 447, 557, 669, 771
(a) 669 (b) 557
(c) 336 (d) 771

26. In this question two words are given which have certain relationship followed by four paired lettered words. Select the paired words, that has the same relation as original pair.
ROOF : FOUNDATION
(a) Plateau : Valley
(b) Peak : Valley
(c) Mountain : Grassland
(d) Hill : Mountain

27. "Communication is a verbal process by which we understand each other and reduce uncertainty through the use of

symbol." Who is the author of this statement?
(a) David K. Barlo
(b) Dance
(c) P.S.K. Serichavenko
(d) K.J. Newman

28. Find out the missing number:
8 24 12 ? 18 54
(a) 28 (b) 32
(c) 36 (d) 38

29. A D C F
C F E H
O R ? ?
(a) JK (b) RN
(c) SU (d) QT

30. 3, 12, 27, 48, 75, (?), 147.
(a) 111 (b) 108
(c) 117 (d) 122

31. In this question four words have been given, out of which three are alike in some manner and the fourth one is different. Choose the odd one out.
(a) Epigraphy (b) Ecology
(c) Archaeology (d) Palaeontology

32. Which of the following figures will represent the right relationship between, societies, societies who run schools, DPS society.

(a) 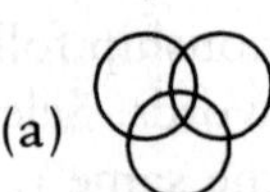 (b) 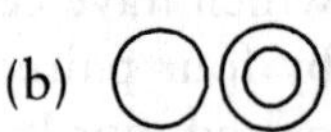

(c) 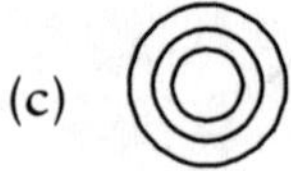 (d) 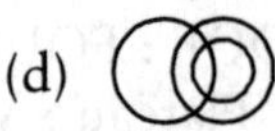

33. **Statements:**
I. All students are ambitious.
II. All ambitious persons are hard working.
Conclusions:
(i) All students are hard-working.
(ii) All hardly working people are not ambitious.
Which of the following is correct?
(a) Only (i) is correct
(b) Only (ii) is correct
(c) Both (i) and (ii) are correct
(d) Neither (i) nor (ii) is correct

34. In a certain code language:
'pit dit mit' means: 'Reena went to Delhi'.
'dit ket set' means: 'Delhi is closing'.
'mit set un' means: 'Reena' is educated.
Then what is the code for 'went'?
(a) dit (b) mit
(c) pit (d) None of these

35. EDITOR : MAGAZINE
Choose the pair from the answer choices that best expresses the relationship similar to that expressed by the question pair.
(a) Novel : Writer
(b) Director : Film
(c) Poem : Poet
(d) Chair : Carpenter

36. Should education in India be made free?
Arguments:
I. Yes, this is the only way to improve the level of literacy.
II. No, this would add already heavy burden on the exchequer.
(a) Only argument I is strong
(b) Only argument II is strong
(c) Both the arguments are strong
(d) None of these

Direction: (37-41) Study the table and answer the questions:

Export of Pulses and Import of Onion (in ₹ crores)

Year	Export of Pulses (in ₹ crores)	Import of Onion (in ₹ crores)
1998-99	44	58
1999-00	45	50

2000-01	60	54
2001-02	56	60
2002-03	92	68
2003-04	100	78
2004-05	68	60

37. During which year there was a maximum fall in export?
(a) 2004-05 (b) 2001-02
(c) 2003-04 (d) None of these

38. The percent of increase of imports in 2003-04 over 2002-03 is
(a) 14.9% (b) 14.7%
(c) 18.4% (d) 18.9%

39. In 1999-2000, the ratio of export to the import is
(a) 19:11 (b) 11:9
(c) 13:17 (d) 9:10

40. During which year there was maximum increase in import over its preceding year?
(a) 2003-04 (b) 2000-01
(c) 2001-02 (d) 2002-03

41. During which year there was minimum increase in import over its preceding year?
(a) 2003-04 (b) 2002-03
(c) 2001-02 (d) None of these

42. The sum of a positive number and its reciprocal is twice the difference of the number and its reciprocal. The number is:
(a) $\sqrt{3}$ (b) $\sqrt{2}$
(c) $\frac{1}{\sqrt{2}}$ (d) $\frac{1}{\sqrt{3}}$

43. Which one of the following states has the maximum number of Wildlife Sanctuaries (National Park and Sanctuaries)?
(a) Madhya Pradesh
(b) Rajasthan
(c) Uttar Pradesh
(d) West Bengal

Directions: (44-48) Answer the following questions based on the graph given below:

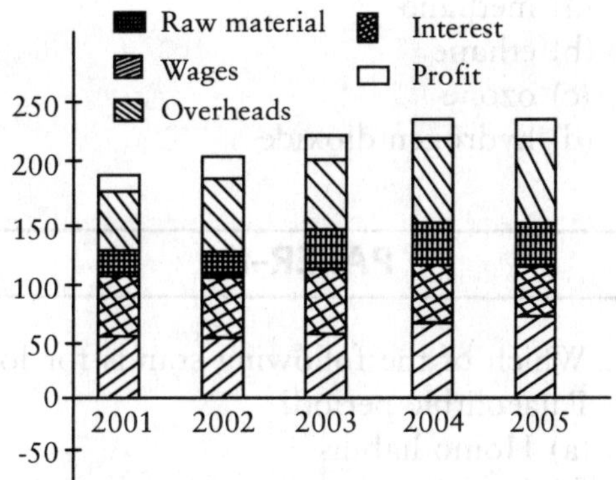

44. Which component of the cost of production has remained almost unchanged over the period 2001-2005?
(a) Wages (b) Interest
(c) Raw material (d) Overheads

45. In which year was the increase in raw material maximum?
(a) 2004 (b) 2002
(c) 2003 (d) 2001

46. What percent of costs did the profits form over the period?
(a) 7% (b) 5%
(c) 2% (d) 1%

47. In which period was the change in profit maximum?
(a) 2002-03 (b) 2001-02
(c) 2004-05 (d) 2003-04

48. If the interest component is not included in the total cost calculation, which year would show the maximum profit per unit cost?
(a) 2001 (b) 2002
(c) 2003 (d) 2005

49. How many types of emergencies have been envisaged by the Constitution?

(a) One (b) Two
(c) Three (d) Four

50. Photocopying and other electrical equipments produce
(a) methane
(b) ethane
(c) ozone
(d) hydrogen dioxide

PAPER–II

1. Which of the following stands for lower Palaeolithic period?
(a) Homo habilis
(b) Homo sapiens
(c) Homo sapiens sapiens
(d) Australoid

2. Which of the following is associated with Palaeolithic period?
(a) Crescent
(b) Triangle
(c) Polished Hand Axe
(d) Acheulian Hand Axe

3. Which of the following represents Mesolithic period?
(a) Ground tools (b) Olduwan
(c) Clactonian (d) Microliths

4. Which of the following stands for Neolithic?
(a) Scavenging
(b) Gathering – Hunting
(c) Food production
(d) Pastoralism

5. Which of the following is not associated with the first Urbanization?
(a) Town Planning
(b) Citadel
(c) Defence wall
(d) Coins

6. Match List I with List II and choose your answer from the codes given below

List I
(A) Harappa Civilization
(B) Aryans
(C) Gautami Putra
(D) Shravanabelgola

List II
(i) Spoked wheel
(ii) Copper technology
(iii) Jainism
(iv) Satavahana

Codes:	A	B	C	D
(a)	(ii)	(iv)	(iii)	(i)
(b)	(iii)	(ii)	(iv)	(i)
(c)	(ii)	(i)	(iv)	(iii)
(d)	(iv)	(iii)	(i)	(ii)

7. Match List I with List II and choose your answer from the codes given below

List I	List II
(A) Ayas	(i) Latin
(B) Aes	(ii) Sanskrit
(C) Ayari	(iii) English
(D) Iron	(iv) Avesta

Codes:	A	B	C	D
(a)	(ii)	(i)	(iv)	(iii)
(b)	(i)	(ii)	(iv)	(iii)
(c)	(ii)	(i)	(iii)	(iv)
(d)	(iii)	(ii)	(i)	(iv)

8. Match List I with List II and choose your answer from the codes given below

List I	List II
(A) Vajji	(i) Indraprastha
(B) Chedi	(ii) Kausambi
(C) Vats	(iii) Vaishali
(D) Kuru	(iv) Shaktimati

Codes:	A	B	C	D
(a)	(iv)	(i)	(iii)	(ii)
(b)	(iii)	(iv)	(ii)	(i)
(c)	(i)	(iii)	(ii)	(iv)
(d)	(ii)	(iv)	(i)	(iii)

9. Match List I with List II and choose your answer from the codes given below

List I
(A) Thirthankar
(B) Kathasaritasagar
(C) Bodhisatva
(D) Brihtakathamanjri

List II
(i) Buddhism (ii) Jainism
(iii) Somadeva (iv) Ksheminder

Codes:	**A**	**B**	**C**	**D**
(a)	(ii)	(iii)	(i)	(iv)
(b)	(i)	(iv)	(iii)	(ii)
(c)	(iii)	(ii)	(iv)	(i)
(d)	(iv)	(i)	(ii)	(iii)

10. Match List I with List II and choose your answer from the codes given below

List I
(A) Triratna
(B) Jataka
(C) Mudrarakshas
(D) Kathasaritasagar

List II
(i) Buddhism (ii) Jainism
(iii) Somadeva (iv) Vishakhadatt

Codes:	**A**	**B**	**C**	**D**
(a)	(ii)	(iii)	(iv)	(i)
(b)	(ii)	(i)	(iii)	(iv)
(c)	(iv)	(ii)	(i)	(iii)
(d)	(ii)	(i)	(iv)	(iii)

11. Given below are two statements, one labelled as Assertion (A) and the other labelled as Reason (R)

Assertion (A): The concept of 'Sarve Hitai and Sarve Sukhai' in Vedic Philosophy is for the upliftment of all the people.

Reason (R): It aims to work for the betterment of all human beings.

In the context of the above two statements, which of the following is correct?

(a) Both (A) and (R) are true.
(b) (A) is true but (R) is untrue.
(c) (A) is false but (R) is true.
(d) Both (A) and (R) are untrue.

12. Given below are two statements, one labelled as Assertion (A) and the other labelled as Reason (R)

Assertion (A): The concept of 'Bahujan Hitai and Bahujan Sukhai' in Buddhism is for the upliftment of the majority of the people.

Reason (R): It aims to relieve the majority of the population of its problems.

In the context of the above two statements, which of the following is correct?

(a) (A) is true but (R) is untrue.
(b) (R) is true but (A) is untrue.
(c) Both (A) and (R) are true.
(d) Both (R) and (A) are untrue.

13. Given below are two statements, one labelled as Assertion (A) and the other labelled as Reason (R)

Assertion (A): Kushana period was the golden age in ancient Indian history.

Reason (R): This period witnessed all round development.

In the context of the above two statements, which of the following is correct?

(a) (A) is true but (R) is false.
(b) (R) is true but (A) is false.
(c) Both (A) and (R) are false.
(d) Both (A) and (R) are true.

14. Given below are two statements, one labelled as Assertion (A) and the other labelled as Reason (R)

Assertion (A): Indian feudal system discouraged agriculture production.

Reason (R): It was enemical to agricultural growth.

In view of the above two statements, which of the following is correct?

(a) (A) is true but (R) is false.
(b) (R) is true but (A) is false.
(c) Both (A) and (R) are true.
(d) Both (A) and (R) are false.

15. Given below are two statements, one labelled as Assertion (A) and the other labelled as Reason (R)
Assertion (A): Pulkeshin-II defeated Harshvardhana.
Reason (R): He wanted to expand his empire in north India.
In the context of the above two statements, which of the following is correct?
(a) (A) is true but (R) is false.
(b) (R) is true but (A) is false.
(c) Both (A) and (R) are true.
(d) Both (A) and (R) are false.

16. Given below are two statements, one labelled as Assertion (A) and the other labelled as Reason (R)
Assertion (A): In spite of large and efficient army, Balban did not think of territorial expansion of his Sultanate.
Reason (R): Tughril's Revolt completely diverted his attention towards its suppression.
In the context of the above two statements, which one of the following is correct?
(a) Both (A) and (R) are true and (R) is the correct explanation of (A).
(b) Both (A) and (R) are true, but (R) is not the correct explanation of (A).
(c) (A) is true, but (R) is false.
(d) (R) is true, but (A) is false.

17. Which one of the following Sultans brought the Ashokan Pillar to Delhi?
(a) Giasuddin Tughlaq
(b) Muhammad-bin-Tughlaq
(c) Firoz Tughlaq
(d) Sikander Lodi

18. Who among the following in South India did not accept the sovereignty of Alauddin?
(a) Pandyas (b). Hoysalas
(c) Yadavas (d) Kakatiyas

19. 'Pushti Marg' was founded by:
(a) Chaitanya
(b) Vallabhacharya
(c) Ramanand
(d) Nimabark

20. In Bahamani Kingdom, 'Sadre-i-Jahan' was the chief of which department?
(a) Religious and judicial
(b) Military
(c) Foreign
(d) Revenue including land revenue

21. In 1595-96 the Mughal Mansabdars were classified into:
(a) 6 groups (b) 5 groups
(c) 4 groups (d) 3 groups

22. Vascodagama visited which one of the following ports?
(a) Goa (b) Madgoan
(c) Mangalore (d) Calicut

23. Given below are two statements, one labelled as Assertion (A) and the other labelled as Reason (R):
Assertion (A): The Chishti Silsila was the most prominent amongst the Sufi orders.
Reason (R): The Silsila had its sphere of influence in Rajasthan, Punjab, Bihar, Bengal, Orissa and the Deccan.
In the context of the above two statements, which one of the following is correct?
(a) Both (A) and (R) are true and (R) is the correct explanation of (A).
(b) Both (A) and (R) are true, but (R) is not the correct explanation of (A).
(c) (A) is true, but (R) is false.
(d) (R) is true, but (A) is false.

24. Struggle between Mughal forces with Maharana Pratap of Mewar which took place in June, 1576, has been described by Abul Fazal as the Battle of
(a) Haldighati (b) Gogunda
(c) Khamnor (d) Kumbhalgarh

25. Given below are two statements, one labelled as Assertion (A) and the other labelled as Reason (R):
Assertion (A): After five years of direct administration and experimentation, Akbar placed the lands of North India with the Mansabdars.
Reason (R): Akbar's treasuries obtained and augmented revenue from the new system.
In the context of the above two statements, which one of the following is correct?
(a) Both (A) and (R) are true and (R) is the correct explanation of (A).
(b) (A) is false but (R) is correct.
(c) (A) is correct but (R) is false.
(d) Both (A) and (R) are false.

26. Main export commodity of Vijayanagar Kingdom was....
(a) Black pepper (b) Textiles
(c) Salt (d) Silk

27. 'Pietra-dura' technique of surface ornamentation was first adopted in
(a) Itimad-ud-Daula's Tomb
(b) Taj Mahal
(c) Diwan-e-Am (Red Fort, Delhi)
(d) Moti Masjid (Agra Fort)

28. Who was the ruler of Mewar at the time of Akbar's attack on Chittor in 1567-1568 A.D.?
(a) Rana Sanga
(b) Rana Udai Singh
(c) Maharana Pratap
(d) Rana Amar Singh

29. Which was the most important commodity exported from India in the 17th Century?
(a) Spices (b) Cotton textile
(c) Indigo (d) Saltpetre

30. Given below are two statements, one labelled as Assertion (A) and the other labelled as Reason (R)
Assertion (A): By 1750 A.D., Peshwa became all powerful in Maratha Kingdom.
Reason (R): Peshwas shifted their head-quarter from Satara to Pune.
In the context of the above two statements, which one of the following is correct?
(a) (A) is correct, but (R) is wrong.
(b) Both (A) and (R) are correct, but (R) is not the correct explanation of (A).
(c) (A) is wrong, but (R) is correct.
(d) Both (A) and (R) are wrong.

31. The Permanent Settlement was made with the
(a) Zamindars
(b) Peasant Cultivators
(c) Village Communities
(d) Muqaddams

32. Parsi Social Reformer Behramji M. Malabari carried on his campaign against
(a) Infant and Child Marriage
(b) Polygamy
(c) Female Infanticide
(d) Widow remarriage

33. Which tribal leader was regarded as an incarnation of God and Father of the World (Dharti Aba)?
(a) Kanhu Santha (b) Rupa Naik
(c) Birsa Munda (d) Joria Bhagat

34. Who said "The British rule was a bleeding drain from India"?

(a) Dadabhai Naoroji
(b) M.G. Ranade
(c) R.C. Dutt
(d) Bal Gangadhar Tilak

35. In 1920 the All India Trade Union Congress was organized by:
(a) B.P. Wadia
(b) Mahatma Gandhi
(c) N.M. Joshi
(d) Jawaharlal Nehru

36. Which social reformer of Maharashtra became famous by the name of 'Lokhitwadi'?
(a) Atmaram Pandurang
(b) Bal Gangadhar Tilak
(c) Gopal Hari Deshmukh
(d) Gopal Krishna Gokhale

37. Raja Ram Mohan Roy raised his voice and agitated against which evil custom and practice?
(a) Caste Custom
(b) Kulinism
(c) Sati Pratha
(d) Widow remarriage

38. Who was not associated with the Aligarh Movement?
(a) Altaf Hussain Hali
(b) Nazir Ahmad
(c) Maulana Abul Kalam Azad
(d) Chiragh Ali

39. The Journal 'Bahishkrit Bharat' was started by
(a) Jyotiba Phule
(b) Dr. B.R. Ambedkar
(c) M.K. Gandhi
(d) Karsandas Mulji

40. Who took over the leadership of the Brahmo Samaj after the death of Raja Ram Mohan Roy?
(a) Dwarka Nath Tagore
(b) Keshav Chandra Sen
(c) Devendra Nath Tagore
(d) Ram Chandra Vidya Vagish

41. Who made the greatest contribution in organizing the Kisan Sabha Movement?
(a) N.G. Ranga
(b) Vallabh Bhai Patel
(c) Jawaharlal Nehru
(d) Swami Sahjanand Saraswati

42. The two greatest pioneers in the cause of widow's education were:
(a) D.K. Karve and Pandita Ramabai
(b) M.G. Ranade and R.G. Bhandarkar
(c) Ishwar Chandra Vidya Sagar and Keshav Chandrasen
(d) B.M. Malabari and K. Sridharlu Naidu

43. Under the 'Old Guarantee System' the British Companies investing in railways were assured a guarantee of
(a) 3% (b) 5%
(c) 8% (d) 10%

44. Who was the first President of the Harijan Sevak Sangha founded by Mahatma Gandhi?
(a) G.D. Birla
(b) Mahadev Desai
(c) Amritlal Thakkar
(d) Dr. B.R. Ambedkar

45. Adyar was the famous centre and headquarter of the:
(a) Aurobindo Ashram
(b) Madras Mahajan Sabha
(c) Theosophical Society
(d) Ramakrishna Mission

46. Whiteman's burden was theory of:
(a) Humanism (b) Imperialism
(c) Non-alignment (d) Socialism

47. During Renaissance the interest in the study of Graeco-Roman Classics came to be known as

(a) Individualism (b) Hedonism
(c) Romanticism (d) Humanism

48. Bandung Conference relates to
(a) Nazism (b) Non-alignment
(c) Apartheid (d) Imperialism

49. Calvinists in France were known as
(a) Puritans (b) Presbyterians
(c) Huguenots (d) Catholics

50. Who was the first Greek Historian?
(a) Thucydides (b) Herodotus
(c) Homer (d) Megasthenes

PAPER–III

1. What is history?
(a) Story of future events
(b) Story of the past events
(c) Story of present events
(d) All of the above

2. Who was the most prominent of the traditional Muslim scholars of the Deoband school who held the view that there was no conflict between Muslims and nationalism?
(a) Maulana Zafar Ali Khan
(b) Maulana Mohammad Ali
(c) Maulana Abul Kalam Azad
(d) Badruddin Tyabiji

3. *Varnasrama* refers to the Vedic social system, which organizes society into
(a) four occupational divisions
(b) four stages of life
(c) Both (a) and (b)
(d) None of the above

4. The Law of Karma is one of the fundamental doctrines in
(a) Hinduism (b) Buddhism
(c) Jainism (d) All of the above

5. **Assertion (A):** In South India agriculture was the principal occupation of the Megalithic people.
Reason (R): They introduced tank irrigation.
Codes:
(a) Both A and R are true and R is the correct explanation of A
(b) Both A and R are true but R is not the correct explanaton of A
(c) A is true but R is false
(d) A is false but R is true

6. Match Lists I and II and select the correct answer using the codes given below the lists:
List I (Edicts Sites)
(A) Sopara (B) Shahbazgarhi
(C) Manshera (D) Kalsi
List II (Region)
(i) Maharashtra (ii) Afghanistan
(iii) Pakistan (iv) Uttar Pradesh

Codes:	**A**	**B**	**C**	**D**
(a)	(i)	(ii)	(iii)	(iv)
(b)	(i)	(iii)	(ii)	(iv)
(c)	(ii)	(iii)	(iv)	(i)
(d)	(ii)	(iv)	(iii)	(i)

7. Which one of the following is not matched correctly?
(a) Ballalasena: Dayabhaga
(b) Lakshmidhara: Krityakalpataru
(c) Rajasekhara: Kavyamimamsa
(d) Uddyotana: Kuvalayamalakaha

8. In which of the following respects have the various Harappan sites marked uniformity?
(a) Town planning (b) Crafts
(c) Seals (d) Agricultural

9. Which were the earliest cereals grown by man?
(a) Millets
(b) Wheat and barley
(c) Maize
(d) Rice

10. When copper and stone implements were simultaneously used, the age is called

(a) Neolithic (b) Mesolithic
(c) Microlithic (d) Chaleolithic

11. The Indus Valley Civilization type was found in
(a) China (b) Egypt
(c) Sumer (d) All of the above

12. Consider the following statements
1. Evidence of double burial comes from Lothal.
2. The general burial practise was extended inhumation.
3. Traces of wooden coffin were found at Harappa by Mortimer Wheeler.
4. Fractional burial was not known to the people of Mohenjodaro.

Codes:
(a) 1 and 2 are true
(b) 2, 3 and 4 are true
(c) 1, 2 and 3 are true
(d) All are true

11. The religion of early Vedic-Aryans primarily depends on
(a) Knowledge
(b) Bhakti
(c) Image-worship
(d) Yajanas and Sacrifices

12. The river most mentioned in Early Vedic literature is
(a) Ganga (b) Sarasvati
(c) Sutudri (d) Sindhu

13. The Tantric cult was named after the scripture of
(a) *Bhagvad Gita* (b) *Ramayana*
(c) *Vedangas* (d) *Tantras*

14. When the Aryans first came into India, they were segregated primarily into three social classes. Identify the correct groupings
(a) warriors, aristocracy, priests
(b) warriors, priests, common people
(c) warriors, common, people, aborigines
(d) None of the above

15. In which Vedic text is the shudra first mentioned?
(a) *Atharaveda*
(b) *Sathapatha Brahmanas*
(c) *Purusasukta in the tenth mandala*
(d) *Vedangas*

16. Lord Buddha was born in
(a) 543 BC (b) 623 BC
(c) 507 BC (d) 563 BC

17. In Mahayana Buddhism, the Buddha is regarded not only as an enlightened being but also as the embodiment of truth and reality behind the universe and has various forms and attributes. These are the different Buddhas and Boddhisattvas, around each of whom there centres a popular cult. Match

List I
(A) The Buddha of Infinite light
(B) The Bodhisattva of wisdom
(C) The Bodhisattva of compassion
(D) The Bodhisattava of power

List II
(i) Manjushri Vajrapani
(ii) Vajrapani
(iii) Amitabh
(iv) Avalokitesvara

Codes:	**A**	**B**	**C**	**D**
(a)	(iii)	(ii)	(i)	(iv)
(b)	(ii)	(i)	(iii)	(iv)
(c)	(iv)	(iii)	(ii)	(i)
(d)	(ii)	(i)	(iv)	(iii)

18. **Assertion (A):** Lord Mahavira preached in the language of the masses that served as a powerful inspiration for his followers to adopt such languages for disseminating knowledge and producing works of literary significance.
Reason (R): On account of this fact different languages like Prakriti, Apabhramasa, Hindi, Rajasthani, Kannada, Tamil and Gujarati were enormously enriched.

Codes:
(a) Both A and R are true and R is the correct explanation for A.
(b) Both A and R are true but R is not the correct explanation for A.
(c) A is true but R is false.
(d) A is false but R is true.

19. Which of the following statements is true?
(a) Kashi lost its position to Kosala and Magadha
(b) Kosala lost its position to Kashi and Magadha
(c) Magadha lost its position to Kashi and Kosala
(d) None of the above

20. Mahaviracary's *Ganitasara Sangrahu* was an important book on mathematics. It found out
(a) the theory of zero
(b) a new rule to the use of logarithms
(c) the theory of relativity
(d) the decimal theory

21. Evidence of Roman trade with South India is available from the excavations at
(a) Kanyakumari and Kodungallur
(b) Arikamedu and Alagangulam
(c) Alagangulam, Arikamedu and Kodungallur
(d) Arikamedu and Kanyakumari

22. Animal remains found at the Belan valley in Mirzapur district of Uttar Pradesh reveal the fact that goats, sheep and cattle were domesticated around
(a) 200 B.C. (b) 500 B.C.
(c) 2,500 B.C. (d) 5,000 B.C.

23. Which of the following Buddhist priest was questioned by King Milinda in *Milind Panha*?
(a) Ananda
(b) Ashvaghosa
(c) Nagasena
(d) None of the above

24. The term 'Chaitya' describes
(a) a hall for assembly and religious purposes
(b) recreation of grounds for Buddhist monks
(c) sleeping quarters of the monks
(d) None of the above

25. A *Hundi* or 'Bill of Exchange' is a kind of legal negotiable instrument used to settle a payment
(a) At a future date
(b) On a previous date
(c) On the same day
(d) On any date

26. The formation of an Interim Government set up on September 2, 1946 was first envisaged by
(a) Cabinet Mission Plan
(b) Cripps Mission
(c) Wavell Plan
(d) None of the above

27. Who was made the Home Minister when Jawaharlal Nehru formed the interim Government in 1946?
(a) Liaqat Ali Khan
(b) Mohammad Ali Jinnah
(c) Sardar Patel
(d) Baldev Singh

28. Which one of the following archaeologists initially discovered the Mohenjodaro site of the Indus Valley Civilization?
(a) R.D. Bannerjee
(b) Sir John Marshal
(c) Sir Martimer Wheeler
(d) Daya Ram Sahni

29. Savalda culture, a local chalcolithic culture is located in
(a) Gujarat (b) West Bengal
(c) U.P. (d) Maharashtra

30. The mainstay of the economy of the chalcolithic culture was

(a) hunting and herding
(b) subsistence agriculture and stock-raising
(c) trade and commerce
(d) hunting

31. The period covered by the Ochre-coloured pottery culture may roughly be placed between
(a) 2000-1500 BC (b) 2000-1880 BC
(c) 2100-400 BC (d) 1400-700 BC

32. The philosophy of upanishads emphasises on
(a) Karma (b) Tapa
(c) Bhakti (d) Gyan

33. The basic unit of the Vedic nation was
(a) Kula (b) Grama
(c) Jana (d) Vish

34. King Ashvapati of the Upanishadic Age was the ruler of
(a) Sursena (b) Panchala
(c) Matsya (d) Kekaya

35. Which one of the following is the oldest smriti?
(a) *Manu smriti*
(b) *Yajnavalkya smriti*
(c) *Vishnu Dharmasastra*
(d) *Narada smriti*

36. The term 'Aryan' denotes
(a) A superior race
(b) A speech group
(c) A nomadic people
(d) An ethnic group

37. Which of the following statements regarding Vedic woman is not correct?
(a) The family was matriarchal
(b) Woman was allowed to have Vedic education
(c) Woman participated in sacrifices
(d) Woman attended assemblies

38. Who founded the Haryanka dynasty?
(a) Udayin (b) Ajatshatru
(c) Bimbisara (d) Bindusara

39. Which one of the following texts of ancient India allows divorce to a wife deserted by her husband?
(a) *Arthashastra*
(b) *Sukra Nitisara*
(c) *Manavadharmashastra*
(d) *Kamasutra*

40. During the rule of the Mauryans, normally the revenue was
(a) 1/8 of the produce
(b) 1/6 of the produce
(c) 1/4 of the produce
(d) 1/2 of the produce

41. There is similarity between the edicts of Ashoka and those of
(a) Darius
(b) Antiochus II
(c) Antigonus Gonatas
(d) Ptolemy II

42. The Greek sources call Amitrochates (Sanskrit, Amitraghata or killer of foes) to
(a) Ashoka (b) Bindusara
(c) Chanakya (d) Chandragupta

43. Mahavira emphasised the salvation through practice of three jewels. Strike out the one which is not included in the three
(a) Right conduct (b) Right faith
(c) Right knowledge (d) Right speech

44. The Bodhisatva Doctrine is associated with
(a) Hinayana Buddhism
(b) Mahayana Buddhism
(c) Theravada Buddhism
(d) Vajrayana Buddhism

45. The capital of the Haryanka King Bimbisara was
(a) Rajgir or Girivraya
(b) Champa
(c) Vaishali
(d) Ujjain

46. The 'dialectic of seven steps' (Saptabhanginaya) is a characteristic feature of
   (a) Jainism (b) Buddhism
   (c) Saivism (d) Vaisnavism
47. "Decay is inherent in all component beings. Work out your own salvation with diligence." These words are attributed to
   (a) Mahavira
   (b) Krishna
   (c) Sankaracharya
   (d) The Buddha
48. The veda which is partly a proved work is
   (a) Rigveda (b) Yajurveda
   (c) Samveda (d) Atharvaveda
49. The Jangama are
   (a) a Shaivite order of wandering religious mendicants
   (b) the priests or *gurus* of the Shaivite sect of Lingayats
   (c) Both (a) and (b)
   (d) None of the above
50. In the pre-Mauryan period, the history of Magadh is synonymous with the history of two dynasties. Which are they?
   (a) Gupta/Haryanka
   (b) Haryanka/Nandas
   (c) Nandas/Kushan
   (d) Kushan/Gupta

ANSWERS SHEET

PAPER—I

1. (c)	2. (c)	3. (a)	4. (d)	5. (d)
6. (a)	7. (d)	8. (b)	9. (c)	10. (b)
11. (d)	12. (a)	13. (c)	14. (c)	15. (a)
16. (c)	17. (a)	18. (b)	19. (a)	20. (c)
21. (d)	22. (a)	23. (c)	24. (a)	25. (b)
26. (b)	27. (b)	28. (c)	29. (d)	30. (b)
31. (b)	32. (c)	33. (a)	34. (c)	35. (b)
36. (b)	37. (a)	38. (b)	39. (d)	40. (a)
41. (d)	42. (c)	43. (a)	44. (b)	45. (c)
46. (b)	47. (d)	48. (b)	49. (c)	50. (c)

PAPER—II

1. (c)	2. (d)	3. (d)	4. (c)	5. (d)
6. (c)	7. (a)	8. (b)	9. (a)	10. (d)
11. (a)	12. (c)	13. (d)	14. (c)	15. (a)
16. (c)	17. (c)	18. (a)	19. (b)	20. (a)
21. (d)	22. (d)	23. (b)	24. (a)	25. (c)
26. (a)	27. (b)	28. (c)	29. (d)	30. (a)
31. (a)	32. (a)	33. (c)	34. (a)	35. (c)
36. (c)	37. (c)	38. (c)	39. (b)	40. (c)
41. (d)	42. (a)	43. (b)	44. (c)	45. (c)
46. (b)	47. (d)	48. (b)	49. (c)	50. (b)

PAPER—III

1. (b)	2. (c)	3. (c)	4. (d)	5. (a)
6. (a)	7. (a)	8. (a)	9. (b)	10. (c)
11. (c)	12. (c)	13. (c)	14. (b)	15. (c)
16. (d)	17. (d)	18. (a)	19. (a)	20. (b)
21. (b)	22. (d)	23. (c)	24. (a)	25. (a)
26. (a)	27. (c)	28. (a)	29. (d)	30. (b)
31. (a)	32. (d)	33. (a)	34. (d)	35. (a)
36. (b)	37. (a)	38. (a)	39. (a)	40. (a)
41. (b)	42. (b)	43. (b)	44. (a)	45. (a)
46. (a)	47. (d)	48. (b)	49. (c)	50. (b)

MOCK TEST–2
PAPER–I

1. Minimum program of guidance includes
   (a) occupational information service
   (b) data collector service
   (c) counselling service
   (d) All of these
2. If majority of students in a class is weak, a teacher should
   (a) not care about intelligent students
   (b) keep his speed of teaching fast so that students' comprehension level may increase
   (c) keep his teaching slow which can also be helpful-to bright students
   (d) keep his teaching slow along with some extra guidance to bright students
3. If the principal of your institution is not satisfied with your performance and charges you with the act of negligence of duties, how would you behave with him?
   (a) You would neglect him
   (b) You would take revenge by giving physical and mental agony to him
   (c) You would keep yourself alert and make his efforts unfruitful
   (d) You would take a tough stand against the charges
4. What makes people to undertake research?
   (a) Desire to get intellectual joy of doing some creative work
   (b) Desire to get a research degree along with its consequential benefits
   (c) Desire to face the challenge in solving the unsolved problems
   (d) All of these
5. Which of the following aims at probing into the phenomenon to formulate a more precise research problem or to develop a new hypothesis?
   (a) Descriptive research
   (b) Conclusive research
   (c) Diagnostic research
   (d) Exploratory research
6. Which of the following is not instructional material?
   (a) Transparency
   (b) Overhead projector
   (c) Printed material
   (d) Audio cassette
7. Of great importance in determining the amount of transference that occurs in the process of learning is the
   (a) knowledge of the teacher
   (b) IQ of the teacher
   (c) presence of identical elements
   (d) use of appropriate elements
8. The characteristic(s) of hypothesis is/are:
   I. It can be tested.
   II. It must consist of known facts.
   III. It must be objective and specific.
   (a) Only I and III (b) Only I and II
   (c) Only I (d) All of these
9. The guide for the research requires which of the following qualities?
   (a) Interdisciplinary expertise
   (b) Subject matter expertise
   (c) Methodological expertise
   (d) All of these
10. Which of the following indicates evaluation?
   (a) Seema got 195 marks out of 200
   (b) Sapna got 72 percent marks in English
   (c) Asha got First Division in final examination
   (d) All of the above

Direction: (11-16) Study the following passage and give answer to the questions based on it.

Much of the theoretical literature of archeology in the 1980s devotes considerable energy to bashing the 1970s, and the target often turns out to be the so-called New or Processual Archeology. While many of the attacks come from recent theorists who are attempting to replace it with post-processual archeology, some criticism comes from within what was New Archeology even from the hand of its original champion, Lewis Binford. If scholars from both outside and inside the theoretical developments of the 1970s are rejecting the New Archeology, why am I defending its importance to us today? The answer is very simple...for better or worse, it is us! As Alison Whylie has recently said the New Archeology of the 1960s quickly became everybody's archeology in the 1970s. Most of today's faculty members and senior archeologists were the people who, in one way or another, adopted the teachings of New Archeology. Although most archeologists did not claim to agree with all aspects of New Archeology nor could more than two or three people agree on what it was, virtually one rejected it outright. Typically, each one presented her or his version, often using a New Archeology text as a starting point for pedagogical purposes. Few wanted to be left out of the exciting new theoretical movement of those years, and New Archeology was passed on to the succeeding generation of students who reached maturity in the 1980s and are today's young professionals.

Criticisms now leveled against the New Archeology of the seventies do have merit, but by discounting that era as misguided, critics have overlooked its crucial importance. New Archeology has an important historical role in the developments of the field we have today and it has continuing importance because it is still guiding archeology's trajectory into the future. Equally troubling is that some critics ask us to reject the basic tenets of New Archeology and to replace them with a system often called post processualist archeology. I believe this is rhetoric that not only misrepresents the achievements of the New Archeology of the seventies, but also does not successfully articulate the potential contributions of its own position.

To put the New Archeology of the seventies into perspective, it is important to review the decades leading up to its development. In the first years following World War II, archeology was still a small field, but by the fifties and the sixties, it was expanding rapidly and taking itself quite seriously. Since the launching of Sputnik in 1957 there had emerged a frenzy in the United States to make all disciplines more scientific. Great strides were made in bringing science into archeology through new dating techniques a multidisciplinary approach, early experiments with the use of statistics, and devoting substantial attention to increasing the precision of artifact classification. The sixties provided the nation with both the optimistic Kennedy years, with an emphasis on science and the conviction that we were capable of accomplishing wondrous; things, and the cynical Vietnam era. Coming on the heels of a decade of civil rights unrest, the widespread dissatisfaction with the Vietnam conflict in the late sixties molded a generation of young Americans who were distrustful of established authority. In academic life, there was an increasing emphasis on environment, other cultures, and people oriented disciplines. Anthropology and archeology grew markedly because of these trends. Archeologists were urged to become concerned with sociological issues—the people behind the artifacts.

It was during these decades of rapid change that many of the core concepts of the New Archeology entered the literature. However, they were not, at first, assembled into a program for action that attracted a solid following. Water Taylor advocated the conjuctive approach with little effect, while Leslie White's evolutionism and Julian Styeward's cultural ecology attracted some attention, but largely among cultural anthropologists. Albert Spaulding led a one-man campaign to bring science and statistics into archeology. But the individual whose work catalyzed the New Archeology movement was Lewis Binford, who incorporated these earlier lines of thinking together with an explicit concern for scientific methods and field research designs. Much of Binford's thinking probably crystallised while he was at the University of Michigan, but was during his relatively few years at the University of Chicago that he changed the direction of modern archeology.

11. New Archeology refers to
    (a) newer techniques used in Archeology
    (b) newer inventions used in Archeology
    (c) newer theoretical foundations in Archeology
    (d) None of these

12. The author defends the Archeology of the 1970's because
    (a) he has a nostalgic feeling about it
    (b) it has research value
    (c) it paved way for newer traditions
    (d) it has historical value

13. The author suggests that
    (a) We should respect new Archeology as a movement in Archeology
    (b) We should go back to the tenets of processual Archeology
    (c) We should treat tenets of new Archeology with respect
    (d) All of the above

14. The importance of Archeology arose from
    (a) the end of World War II
    (b) an increasing scientific outlook
    (c) the launch of Sputnik in 1957
    (d) All of these

15. Which one of the following is not an area of focus for archeologist?
    (a) Study the interaction of people of small group
    (b) Studying cultures of other people
    (c) Study the social structure of the past societies
    (d) Study the man-environment relationship in the past

16. An archeologist is concerned with
    (a) classification of artefacts
    (b) maintenance of museums
    (c) digging of ancient cities
    (d) All of these

17. Rhetorics means
    (a) study of the technique and rules for using language effectively
    (b) using language effectively to please or persuade
    (c) excessive use of verbal ornamentation
    (d) All of the above

18. If a receiver replying on 'hmm-mm' or 'Isee'. This type of reply is known as
    (a) positive feedback
    (b) ambiguous feedback
    (c) negative feedback
    (d) None of these

19. Which of the following FM radio stations is owned by the Times of India group?
    (a) AIR
    (b) Radio Rainbow
    (c) Radio Mirchi
    (d) Red FM

20. Find the next number in the following sequence:
    9, 8, 25, 12, 49, 18, 121, 26, ?
    (a) 142, 36 (b) 169, 36
    (c) 225, 36 (d) 196, 36

21. **Statement:** Should there be complete ban on pouched tobacco products (like Gutka) in India?
    Arguments:
    (i) Yes, it is the most important cause of mouth cancer and mouth ulcer in our country.

(ii) No, there are many people employed in this industry right from manufacturing to retailing. This ban will hamper their livelihood.

(a) Only argument (i) is strong
(b) Only argument (ii) is strong
(c) Both the arguments (i) and (ii) are strong
(d) Neither (i) nor (ii) is strong

22. The relationship between Animal, Cows, Dogs can be shown by

(a) 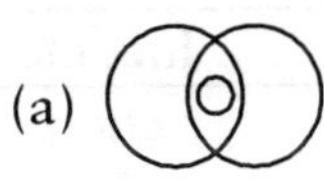 (b) 

(c) 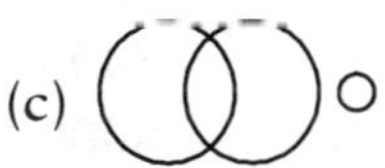 (d) 

23. If in a certain code:
'nso prt kli chn' means 'sharma gets marriage gift'.
'pit lnm wop chn' means 'wife gives marriage gift'. 'tti wop nhi' means 'he gives nothing'. What would mean gives:

(a) kli (b) tti
(c) wop (d) lnm

24. Characteristics of all informal and formal communications are

(a) Same (b) Structured
(c) Different (d) None of these

25. Three of the following four are alike in a certain way and so form a group. Find the one which doesn't belong to that group?

(a) Dog (b) Tiger
(c) Horse (d) Lion

26. What is research design?

(a) The methods used in analysis and finding the final conclusion is known as research design
(b) A researcher needs to prepare a plan of action for his study which is known as research design
(c) The presentation of final data is known as research design
(d) None of these

27. Recording a television program on a Set Top Box is an example of

(a) content reference
(b) time-shifting
(c) media synchronisation
(d) mechanical clarity

28. Which of the following statements say the same thing?

(i) "I am a teacher" (said by Arvind)
(ii) "I am a teacher" (said by Binod)
(iii) "My son is a teacher" (said by Binod's father)
(iv) "My brother is a teacher" (said by Binod's sister)
(v) "My brother is a teacher" (said by Binod's only sister)
(vi) "My sole enemy is a teacher" (said by Binod's only enemy)

Choose the correct answer from the codes given below:

Codes:

(a) (v) and (vi)
(b) (i) and (ii)
(c) (ii) and (vi)
(d) (ii), (iii), (iv) and (v)

29. In this question there are two statements followed by four conclusions numbered I, II, III and IV.

Statements:

A. All books are trees.
B. All trees are lions.

Conclusions:

I. All books are lions.
II. All lions are books.
III. All trees are books.
IV. Some lions are books.

Choose the correct answer.

(a) Only I and IV follow
(b) Only II and III follow

(c) None of conclusions follow
(d) All conclusion follows

Directions: (30-34) Answer the questions based on following table.

Machines X and Y can independently produce either product P or product Q. The time taken by machines X and Y (in minutes) to produce one unit of product P and Q are given in the table below. (Each machine works 8 hours per day.)

Product	X	Y
P	10	8
Q	6	6

30. If the number of units of P is to be three times that of Q, what is the maximum idle time to maximise total units manufactured?
(a) 8 minutes (b) 0 minute
(c) 12 minutes (d) None of these

31. If X works at half its normal efficiency, what is the maximum number of units produced, if at least one unit of each must be produced?
(a) 119 (b) 135
(c) 127 (d) 136

32. What is the maximum number of units that can be manufactured in one day?
(a) 250 (b) 160
(c) 270 (d) 195

33. If equal quantities of both are to be produced, then out of four choices given below the least efficient way would be
(a) 59 of each with 8 min. idle
(b) 71 of each with 9 min. idle
(c) 53 of each with 10 min. idle
(d) 48 of each with 4 min. idle

34. What is the least number of machine hours required to produce 30 pieces of P and 25 pieces of Q respectively?
(a) 6 hr 30 min. (b) 9 hr 30 min.
(c) 6 hr 40 min. (d) 8 hr 30 min.

35. Telematic is a combination of
(a) Telecommunication and computer
(b) Telecommunication and information
(c) Television and computer
(d) All of the above

36. Following is a part of balance sheet of Timas Pvt. Ltd. Study the table and give answer to the question given below:

(All values in ₹ crore)

Year	Expenditure	Income
1990	3400	4000
1995	3800	4500
2000	4500	5400
2005	6400	8000

Which of the following conclusions is not true?
(a) There has been a steady growth in % profit of the company
(b) There is around 90% increase in expenditure of the firm from 1990 to 2005
(c) Income of the company is doubled in 15 years
(d) Percentage profit in 2000 was 18%

37. If EFGHUK is coded as VUTSRQ then LIMIT can be coded as
(a) KNRNC (b) ORNRG
(c) JKOKG (d) RSTSG

38. The more is 'Resolution Power' of a printer better is its
(a) Speed (b) Colour
(c) Memory (d) Quality

39. Laterite soil develops due to
(a) deposits of alluvial
(b) deposition of loess
(c) leaching
(d) continued vegetation cover

40. Line access and avoidance of collision are the main functions of
(a) network protocols
(b) wide area networks
(c) the CPU
(d) the monitor

41. Communication satellites are placed in
(a) Geostationary Orbit
(b) Polar Orbit
(c) Both (a) and (b)
(d) None of these

42. DLL stands for
(a) Data Deriving Language
(b) Data Definition Language
(c) Data Design Language
(d) All of the above

43. Transistors were first used in
(a) 2nd generation computers
(b) 3rd generation computers
(c) 4th generation computers
(d) None of these

44. Which of the following is not provided in the constitution?
(a) Planning Commission
(b) Election Commission
(c) Finance Commission
(d) Public Service Commission

45. The 1st satellite launched in space was
(a) Early Bird (b) Sputnik-1
(c) Skylab (d) Aryabhatta-1

46. At what time between 5.30 and 6.00 will the hands of a clock be at right angles?
(a) 45 minutes past 5
(b) $43\frac{5}{11}$ minutes past 5
(c) $43\frac{7}{11}$ minutes past 5
(d) 40 minutes past 5

47. A person can be a member of Council of Ministers without being a member of Parliament for a maximum period of
(a) 45 days (b) 90 days
(c) 180 days (d) one year

48. Many engineers and architects use a different type of pen called a
(a) Pointer pen (b) Computer pen
(c) Light pen (d) Logical pen

49. Which of the following are wrongly matched?

Name of Volcano	**Country**
(a) Mt. Spur	USA
(b) Mt. Fuego	Guatemala
(c) Mt. Ag'ung	Indonesia
(d) Mt. Lascor	Equador

50. How many types of emergency can be declared by the President of India?
(a) 1 (b) 2
(c) 3 (d) 4

PAPER–II

1. Which of the following is not a Neolithic site?
(a) Taxila
(b) Kili Ghul muhammad
(c) Mundigak
(d) Mehrgarh

2. The veda which contains references to music is
(a) *Rigveda* (b) *Yajurveda*
(c) *Samaveda* (d) *Atharvaveda*

3. The first reaction against the vedic sacrifices is available in
(a) Buddhism (b) Jainism
(c) Ajivikas (d) Upanishads

4. How many kinds of slaves have been mentioned by Narada?
(a) 15 (b) 12
(c) 10 (d) 7

5. The script which has not been used in the Mauryan inscriptions is
   (a) Prakrit (b) Devanagari
   (c) Araimic (d) Greek

6. The first law-giver who supported the system of division of property was
   (a) Vishnu (b) Brihaspati
   (c) Manu (d) Yagnavalkya

7. Match List I with List II and choose your answer from the codes given below:

List I	**List II**
(A) Senani	(i) Maruts
(B) Purohit	(ii) Agni
(C) Gramani	(iii) Indra
(D) Yajamana	(iv) Brihaspati

Codes:	**A**	**B**	**C**	**D**
(a)	(ii)	(iv)	(i)	(iii)
(b)	(i)	(iii)	(iv)	(ii)
(c)	(iii)	(i)	(ii)	(iv)
(d)	(iv)	(ii)	(i)	(iii)

8. Match List I with List II and choose your answer from the codes given below:

List I
(A) Junagarh Inscription
(B) Iron pillar Inscription
(C) Banskhera Inscription
(D) Aihole Inscription

List II
(i) Harshavardhana
(ii) Pushyagupta
(iii) Chandergupta II
(iv) Pulkeshin II

Codes:	**A**	**B**	**C**	**D**
(a)	(ii)	(iii)	(i)	(iv)
(b)	(i)	(ii)	(iv)	(iii)
(c)	(iii)	(iv)	(ii)	(i)
(d)	(iv)	(i)	(ii)	(iii)

9. The later part of *kadambari* was written by:
   (a) Bana (b) Dandin
   (c) Mayura (d) Bhushan

10. The chola king who was devoted to shaivism but patronised Buddhism also was
    (a) Rajendra I (b) Rajendra II
    (c) Rajaraja (d) Rajadhiraja

11. Given below are two statements, one labelled as Assertion (A) and the other labelled as Reason (R):
    Assertion (A): Second urbanisation in India was caused by the use of iron technology.
    Reason (R): Iron technology was the moving force.
    In the context of the above two statements which of the following is correct?
    Codes:
    (a) (A) is true but (R) is untrue
    (b) (R) is true but (A) is untrue
    (c) Both (A) and (R) are true
    (d) Both (A) and (R) are untrue

12. Given below are two statements, one labelled as Assertion (A) and the other labelled as Reason (R):
    Assertion (A): The punch marked coins were inscribed in Brahami Script.
    Reason (R): It facilitated trade.
    In context of the above two statements which of the following is correct?
    Codes:
    (a) (A) is true but (R) is false
    (b) (R) is true but (A) is false
    (c) Both (A) and (R) are true
    (d) Both (A) and (R) are false

13. Given below are two statements, one labelled as Assertion (A) and the other labelled as Reason (R):
    Assertion (A): Sangam literature is a 'Sanskrit Kavya'.
    Reason (R): It offers information on the social conditions.
    In view of the above two statements which of the following is correct?

Codes:
(a) (A) is true but (R) is false
(b) (A) is false but (R) is true
(c) Both (A) and (R) are false
(d) Both (A) and (R) are true

14. Given below are the two statements, one labelled as Assertion (A), and the other labelled as Reason (R):
Assertion (A): The Aihole inscription of Pulakesin II mentions Harsha as a very popular ruler.
Reason (R): However, it happens to be an account of his defeat.
In the context of the above two statements, which one of the following is correct?
Codes:
(a) Both (A) and (R) are true and (R) is the correct explanation of (A)
(b) (A) is false, but (R) is correct
(c) (A) is correct, but (R) is false
(d) Both (A) and (R) are false

15. Match List I and List II and choose your answer from the codes given below:
List I
(A) Dandin (B) Vakapati
(C) Ashvaghosha (D) Rajashekhara
List II
(i) Gaudvaho
(ii) Buddhacharita
(iii) Karpura manjari
(iv) Dashakumaracharita

Codes:	**A**	**B**	**C**	**D**
(a)	(iv)	(i)	(ii)	(iii)
(b)	(ii)	(iii)	(iv)	(i)
(c)	(i)	(iii)	(iv)	(ii)
(d)	(iii)	(ii)	(iv)	(i)

16. Given below are two statements, one labelled as Assertion (A) and the other labelled as Reason (R):
Assertion (A): Iltutmish was not a usurper.
Reason (R): There was nothing to be usurped.
In the context of the above two statements, which of the following is correct?
Codes:
(a) Both (A) and (R) are true and (R) is the correct explanation of (A)
(b) Both (A) and (R) are true but (R) is not the correct explanation of (A)
(c) (A) is true, but (R) is false
(d) (A) is false, but (R) is true

17. Abdus Samad Khan was patronized by Akbar as:
(a) a Musician (b) an Author
(c) a Painter (d) an Architect

18. The office of Peshwa became independent during the rule of:
(a) Shivaji (b) Sambhaji
(c) RajaRam (d) Sahu

19. Which of the following is not associated with Mesolithic?
(a) Hunting-gathering
(b) Domestication of animals
(c) Domestication of plants
(d) Horticulture

20. The *Adi Granth* was compiled by:
(a) Guru Nanak
(b) Guru Angad
(c) Guru Amar Das
(d) Guru Arjun Dev

21. The post of Diwan-i-Mustkharaj was created by which of the following Sultans?
(a) Alauddin Khalji
(b) Ghiyasuddin Balban
(c) Razia
(d) Ibrahim Lodi

22. Match List I with List II and choose your answer from the codes given below:
List I (Battles)
(A) Battle of Rajmahal
(B) Second Battle of Panipat

(C) Battle of Khanwa
(D) Battle of Ghagara

List II (Year of the Battles)
(i) 1527 A.D.
(ii) 1529 A.D.
(iii) 1556 A.D.
(iv) 1576 A.D.

Codes:	A	B	C	D
(a)	(ii)	(iii)	(i)	(iv)
(b)	(iv)	(i)	(ii)	(iii)
(c)	(iii)	(iv)	(i)	(ii)
(d)	(iv)	(iii)	(i)	(ii)

23. Match List I with List II and choose your answer from the codes given below:

List I (Writter)
(A) Nizamuddin Ahmad
(B) Ali Muhammad Khan
(C) Gul Badan Begam
(D) Ibn Batuta

List II (Works)
(i) *Humayun Nama*
(ii) *Mirat - i -Ahmadi*
(iii) *Tabqat - i - Akbari*
(iv) *Rahela*

Codes:	A	B	C	D
(a)	(iii)	(ii)	(i)	(iv)
(b)	(iv)	(i)	(ii)	(iii)
(c)	(i)	(iv)	(iii)	(ii)
(d)	(iii)	(ii)	(iv)	(i)

24. Match List I with List II and select the correct answer from the codes given below:

List I
(A) R.P. Tripathi
(B) Ishwari Prasad
(C) K.S. Lal
(D) Agha Mehdi Husain

List II
(i) Tughlaq Dynasty
(ii) Twilight of the Delhi Sultanate
(iii) Some Aspects of Muslim Administration
(iv) History of Qarauna Turks

Codes:	A	B	C	D
(a)	(iii)	(iv)	(ii)	(i)
(b)	(ii)	(i)	(iii)	(iv)
(c)	(iv)	(ii)	(i)	(iii)
(d)	(i)	(iii)	(ii)	(iv)

25. What is the correct chronological sequence of the following Peshwas?
1. Bajirao I
2. Balaji Vishwanath
3. Balaji Bajirao
4. Madhavarao

Codes:

(a)	1	3	2	4
(b)	4	2	1	3
(c)	2	1	3	4
(d)	3	4	1	2

26. The Ryotwari settlement was made with the
(a) Zamindars
(b) Cultivators
(c) Village communities
(d) Muqaddams

27. Who remarked in 1834 that "The bones of the cotton weavers are bleaching the plains of India"?
(a) Lord Macaulay
(b) Lord William Bentinck
(c) Dadabhai Naoroji
(d) Raja Ram Mohan Ray

28. What is the correct sequence of the following?
1. Birth of Akbar
2. Arrival of Vasco-da-gama in India
3. Execution of Guru Teg Bahadur
4. Battle of Khanwa

Codes:
(a) 1, 2, 3, 4
(b) 4, 3, 2, 1
(c) 2, 4, 1, 3
(d) 3, 2, 4, 1

29. Match List I with List II and select correct answer from the codes given below the list

List I	List II
(A) Peshwa	(i) Indore
(B) Bhonsle	(ii) Baroda
(C) Holkar	(iii) Poona
(D) Gaekwar	(iv) Nagpur

Codes:	A	B	C	D
(a)	(i)	(ii)	(iii)	(iv)
(b)	(ii)	(iv)	(ii)	(iii)
(c)	(iii)	(iv)	(i)	(ii)
(d)	(iv)	(i)	(ii)	(iii)

30. Given below are two statements, one labelled as Assertion (A) and the other labelled as Reason (R)
    Assertion (A): The 'Zabti' system of land revenue was introduced by Akbar.
    Reason (R): Akbar wanted to collect the average of both the crops and the crops rates of last ten years.
    In the context of the above two statements, which one of the following is correct?
    Codes:
    (a) Both (A) and (R) are true and (R) is the correct explanation of (A)
    (b) Both (A) and (R) are true and but (R) is not the correct explanation of (A)
    (c) (A) is true, but (R) is false
    (d) (A) is false but (R) is true

31. Taluqdari settlement was made in:
    (a) Bihar (b) Orissa
    (c) Oudh (d) Madras

32. Who was not a founder member of Muslim League in 1906:
    (a) Agha Khan
    (b) Nawab Mohsin ul Mulk
    (c) M.A. Jinneh
    (d) Nawab Salimullah

33. Jacobin club at Sirangpattanam was established in 1797 by:
    (a) Napoleon (b) Hyder Ali
    (c) Col. Bussey (d) Tipu Sultan

34. Hind Mazdoor Sangh was founded by:
    (a) N.M. Joshi
    (b) V.B. Patel
    (c) G.L. Nanda
    (d) Dadabhai Naorozi

35. First textile mill in India was established in Ahmedabad in:
    (a) 1865 (b) 1870
    (c) 1859 (d) 1881

36. Who was the greatest Parsi Social Reformer of the 19th century?
    (a) Jamsetji Tata
    (b) Rustom Behramji
    (c) Behramji M. Malabari
    (d) Pheroz Shah Mehta

37. The credit of the victory of Port Novo goes to the British General:
    (a) Munro (b) Eyrecoot
    (c) Col. Fraser (d) Col. Bailey

38. Who gave the call—"One religion, one caste and one God for mankind"?
    (a) Jyotiba Phule
    (b) Swami Vivekanand
    (c) Shri Narayana Guru
    (d) Periyar Ramaswami Naikar

39. Servants of India Society was founded by:
    (a) G.K. Gokhale (b) M.G. Ranade
    (c) B.G. Tilak (d) V.D. Savarkar

40. He opposed the partition of Bengal but later on became a Sanyasi, who was he?
    (a) Barindra Ghosh
    (b) Bhupen Dutt
    (c) Aurobindo Ghosh
    (d) Vivekanand

41. Satya Shodhak Samaj was founded by:
    (a) Shahuji Maharaj
    (b) B.R. Ambedkar
    (c) Jyotiba Phule
    (d) Jagjivan Ram

42. Pakistan resolution was passed at:
(a) Lahore (b) Calcutta
(c) Lucknow (d) Karachi

43. Arrange the following events in chronological order
1. First Sikh war
2. First Afghan war
3. First Burmese war
4. Third maratha war

Codes:
(a) 4, 3, 2, 1 (b) 1, 2, 3, 4
(c) 4, 1, 2, 3 (d) 3, 1, 2, 4

44. Given below are two statements, one labelled as Assertion (A) and other labelled as Reason (R)
Assertion (A): Gandhiji supported the Khilafat movement.
Reason (R): He was against the British.
In the context of the above two statements, which one of the following is correct?
Codes:
(a) Both (A) and (R) are true, and (R) is the correct explanation of (A).
(b) Both (A) and (R) are true, but (R) is not the correct explanation of (A).
(c) (A) is true, but (R) is false.
(d) (A) is false, but (R) is true.

45. Match the following:
List I
(A) K.C. Sen (B) Lala Hansraj
(C) G.K. Gokhale (D) M.G. Ranade

List II
(i) Poona Sarvajanik sabha
(ii) Adi Brahma Samaj
(iii) Arya Samaj
(iv) Bharat Sevak Samaj

Codes:	A	B	C	D
(a)	(iii)	(iv)	(ii)	(i)
(b)	(i)	(ii)	(iii)	(iv)
(c)	(ii)	(iii)	(iv)	(i)
(d)	(iv)	(i)	(iii)	(ii)

46. Law code is related to:
(a) Hammurabi (b) Thucydides
(c) Strabo (d) Justin

47. Bandung Conference relates to:
(a) Nazism (b) Non-alignment
(c) Apartheid (d) Imperialism

48. Who amongst the following belongs to the sub-altern school of historiography?
(a) Bipan Chandra
(b) Romila Thapar
(c) Ranjit Guha
(d) Ramchandra Guha

49. Whitemen's burden was a theory of:
(a) Humanism (b) Imperialism
(c) Non-alignment (d) Socialism

50. Confucianism developed in:
(a) Korea (b) Malaysia
(c) China (d) Thailand

PAPER–III

1. Asvaghosh has composed by
(a) Budhacharita (b) Lalitawistara
(c) Mahavamsa (d) Mahavastu

2. Mahayana has one aspect that has adopted some features of tantrism like speech, charms, goddess worship. It is mentioned in
(a) Srava kayana (b) Tantrism
(c) Lotus Sutra (d) Mantrayana

3. The key note of Ashoka policy of dhamma was
(a) Kindness (b) Self-control
(c) Moderation (d) Charity

4. The Nagara, the Dravida the Vesara are:
(a) the three main linguistic divisions into which the languages of India can be classified
(b) the three main styles of Indian temple architecture

(c) the three main musical gharanas prevalent in India
(d) the three main racial groups of the Indian subcontinent

5. The Sunga rulers were followers of
(a) Buddhism (b) Jainism
(c) Bhagavatism (d) Shaivism

6. The founder of the Satavahana dynasty is
(a) Simuka
(b) Sri Satakarni
(c) Yajnasri Satakarni
(d) Pulamayi I

7. Which one of the following is not depicted on the abacus of the Sarnath Lion Capital of Ashoka?
(a) Elephant (b) Lion
(c) Deer (d) Horse

8. The fertile agrarian tract in the early 'Tamil' country is denoted by the term
(a) Marudam (b) Mullai
(c) Palai (d) Neydas

9. In the Mauryan administration the official designated as Rupadarsaka was
(a) examiner of silver and other metals
(b) examiner of coins
(c) manager of state
(d) superintendent of courtesans

10. The treatise written by Kautilya was called
(a) *Arthashastra*
(b) *Mudrarakshasa*
(c) *Indica*
(d) None of the above

11. Which one of the following assemblies protected the interests of traders under the Chola administration?
(a) Kuri (b) Nagaram
(c) Mahasabha (d) Perunguri

12. The Cholas, the Pandyas, the Keralaputras and the Satyaputras are mentioned as his neighbouring powers by Ashoka in
(a) Pillar Edict VII
(b) Minor Rock Edicts
(c) Rock Edict XI
(d) Rock Edict II

13. Kautilya mentions senior officials or superintendents as
(a) Nagarika (b) Sthanikas
(c) Gopa (d) Adhyakshas

14. Match List I with List II and select the correct answer by using the codes given below.

List I (Sources mentioned)
(A) Greek source
(B) Jain source
(C) Buddhist source
(D) Brahmanical source

List II (Information about Chandragupta Maurya)
(i) He was born in a humble family
(ii) He was the son of a Kshatriya
(iii) He was a Sudra
(iv) He was the son of a village headman's daughter
(v) He was a Jain

Codes:	**A**	**B**	**C**	**D**
(a)	(i)	(iii)	(iv)	(ii)
(b)	(iv)	(v)	(iii)	(i)
(c)	(iii)	(v)	(ii)	(iv)
(d)	(i)	(iv)	(ii)	(iii)

15. The Sangams were
(a) the Hindu religious texts written in Tamil
(b) the Buddhist religious texts
(c) societies of learned men
(d) titles of a south Indian dynasty

16. Small village assemblies during the Sangam Age were known as
(a) Podiyil (b) Avai
(c) Ambalan (d) Manaram

17. The Meenakhshi temple at Madurai is the monument of

(a) Cholas (b) Cheras
(c) Pallavas (d) Pandyas

18. Which among the following dynasties had the strongest navy
(a) Gupta (b) Pallava
(c) Chalukya (d) Chola

19. Which Satavahana ruler is credited with having increased the naval power of the empire which provided a fillip to trade with foreign countries?
(a) Vasishtiputra Sri Pulamayi
(b) Gautamiputra Satakarni
(c) Hala
(d) Apilaka

20. South of the Deccan plateau in the Sangam age, three kingdoms arose. Point the odd one out.
(a) Pandyas (b) Cheras
(c) Cholas (d) Pallavas

21. Coins with legends and portraits were first issued in India by the
(a) Indo-Greeks (b) Satavahanas
(c) Sungas (d) Sakas

22. Which of the following reasons is not correct about the attitude of the people in the Sangam Age towards war?
(a) The ideal of a conquering king was accepted and hailed
(b) They lusted for territorial expansion through conquests
(c) They did not provoke wars. They were never the aggressor but always the defender
(d) Their material spirits were eulogised by poets

23. Match List I with List II and select the correct answer by using the codes given below.

List I (Authors)
(A) Chekkilar
(B) Ottakutan
(C) Kulasekhara Alvar
(D) Cheraman Perumal Nayanar

List II (Their works)
(i) *Periya Puranam*
(ii) *Kalingattuparani*
(iii) *Perumal Tirumali*
(iv) *Adiyula*

Codes:	**A**	**B**	**C**	**D**
(a)	(iv)	(ii)	(iii)	(i)
(b)	(iv)	(iii)	(ii)	(i)
(c)	(i)	(iii)	(ii)	(iv)
(d)	(i)	(ii)	(iii)	(iv)

24. **Assertion (A):** Yajna Sri Satakarni was a lover of trade and navigation.
Reason (R): His love for navigation and overseas trade is shown by the representation of a ship on his coins.
(a) If both (A) and (R) are true and (R) is the correct explanation of (A).
(b) If both (A) and (R) are true but (R) is not the correct explanation of (A).
(c) If (A) is true but (R) is false.
(d) If (A) is false but (R) is true.

25. The Badami rock inscription of Pulakesin I is dated in the Saka year 465. If the same were to be dated in Vikrama Samvat, the year would be
(a) 407 (b) 330
(c) 300 (d) 601

26. Which of the following is not considered an Indo-Aryan language?
(a) Arabic (b) Persian
(c) Avesta (d) English

27. The term 'Mixed Economy' was coined by
(a) Anthony Crosland
(b) Pat Mullins
(c) Andrews Shonfield
(d) Harold Macmillan

28. In which Indian state is the Sun Temple of Konark located?

(a) West Bengal (b) Assam
(c) Tamil Nadu (d) Odisha

29. During the Swadeshi movement, of the several forms of struggle thrown up by the movement which one met with the greatest of success?
(a) Disobeying of unjust laws
(b) Boycott of foreign goods
(c) Boycott of the government educational institutions
(d) Development of Swadeshi industries

30. The first to establish trade contacts with the Roman empire were
(a) Vakatakas
(b) Western Sakas
(c) Tamil and Chera kingdom
(d) Kushanas

31. *Ugraditya* wrote a treatise in Sanskrit containing 8,000 shlokas known as *Kalyan Karak*. It deals with
(a) the principle of non-violence
(b) the philosophy of Jainism
(c) the way to Kaivalya
(d) the medicines to be taken by Jains

32. Who was writer of *Ramacharitamanas*?
(a) Surdas (b) Harsha
(c) Tulsidas (d) Kalidas

33. Which was not one of the pottery used by the neolithic people?
(a) Black and red ware
(b) Matt-impressed ware
(c) Black-burnished ware
(d) Grey ware

34. The term Dravidian refers to a stratum of Indian popultion who can be classified as
(a) Caucasoid
(b) Alpine
(c) Proto Australoid
(d) Palaeo-Mediterranean

35. Which of the following statements is/are true about the Iron age in South India?
(a) The earliest phase of Iron age in South India is recovered in the excavations at Piklihal, Hallur and the burial pits at Brahmagiri
(b) The use of iron in South India began sometime around 1100 B.C.
(c) The iron objects excavated from the grave goods shows uniformity in types
(d) All of the above

36. The exact number of stories of *Jatakas* tales is
(a) 260 (b) 500
(c) 750 (d) 820

37. Which of the following was not a centre of learning in ancient India
(a) Vikramshila (b) Nalanda
(c) Taxila (d) Koushambi

38. The *Rajatarangini* composed by Kalhana in the twelfth century is our main source on
(a) history of Assam
(b) history of Nepal
(c) history of medieval Kashmir
(d) post-Gupta economics

39. Which one of the following was a Sarva sect in ancient India?
(a) Isanasivagurudevapaddhati
(b) Mayamata
(c) Mattamayura
(d) Ajivika

40. The copper hoards are associated with the
(a) black and red ware
(b) lustrous red ware
(c) painted grey ware
(d) ochre-coloured ware

41. Bactria, which was a key region in the network of international trade in early times, was located in the area now known as
(a) Afghanistan (b) Iran
(c) Baluchistan (d) Punjab

42. Buddha allowed women to enter the Samgha to accommodate the wishes of
(a) Amrapali
(b) Gautami Prajapati
(c) Maya
(d) Yasodhara

43. Two versions known as the white and the black are available in
(a) *Samaveda* alone
(b) *Yajurveda* alone
(c) *Atharvaveda* alone
(d) *Rigveda* and *Yajurveda*

44. Jainism has derived its metaphysical thoughts from
(a) Samkhya philosophy
(b) Bhagavatas
(c) Ajivakas
(d) Buddhism

45. The Vajapeya and Rajasuya were
(a) the terms for treasurer and superintendent
(b) tribes in the later Vedic period
(c) sacrifices as a mark of paramountcy
(d) tribes of the early Vedic period

46. A scholar uses footnotes when
(a) a passing phrase is used
(b) all the strange, unknown assertions are used
(c) all the distinct elements of arguments are used
(d) All of the above

47. The Cold War means
(a) the war with sticks
(b) the war of words
(c) the war without arms
(d) the war in which the arms are not used but the whole atmosphere of war remains the same between the rival countries

48. Which of the following books was written by Julius Caesar?
(a) *The Commentaries on the Gallic war and the Civil war*
(b) *The Lives of the Caesar*
(c) *Second Punic War*
(d) *A National History of Rome*

49. In which of the following countries 'Renaissance' began first
(a) Italy (b) Germany
(c) Britain (d) France

50. The most famous bronze image of the Chola period belongs to
(a) Nataraja (b) Murugan
(c) Vishnu (d) Venkateshwar

ANSWERS SHEET

PAPER—I

1. (d)	2. (d)	3. (c)	4. (d)	5. (d)
6. (a)	7. (b)	8. (d)	9. (d)	10. (d)
11. (d)	12. (c)	13. (c)	14. (b)	15. (a)
16. (d)	17. (d)	18. (b)	19. (c)	20. (b)
21. (a)	22. (b)	23. (c)	24. (c)	25. (c)
26. (b)	27. (b)	28. (c)	29. (b)	30. (b)
31. (a)	32. (b)	33. (c)	34. (a)	35. (b)
36. (d)	37. (b)	38. (d)	39. (c)	40. (a)
41. (a)	42. (b)	43. (a)	44. (a)	45. (b)
46. (c)	47. (c)	48. (c)	49. (d)	50. (c)

PAPER—II

1. (d)	2. (c)	3. (d)	4. (a)	5. (b)
6. (c)	7. (d)	8. (a)	9. (d)	10. (c)
11. (c)	12. (c)	13. (d)	14. (d)	15. (a)
16. (c)	17. (c)	18. (b)	19. (d)	20. (d)
21. (a)	22. (d)	23. (a)	24. (a)	25. (c)
26. (b)	27. (c)	28. (c)	29. (c)	30. (c)
31. (c)	32. (c)	33. (d)	34. (a)	35. (c)

36. (c)	37. (b)	38. (b)	39. (a)	40. (c)
41. (c)	42. (a)	43. (a)	44. (c)	45. (c)
46. (a)	47. (b)	48. (c)	49. (b)	50. (c)

PAPER—III

1. (a)	2. (c)	3. (b)	4. (b)	5. (d)
6. (a)	7. (c)	8. (a)	9. (b)	10. (a)
11. (b)	12. (d)	13. (d)	14. (d)	15. (b)
16. (d)	17. (d)	18. (d)	19. (a)	20. (d)
21. (a)	22. (c)	23. (d)	24. (a)	25. (d)
26. (a)	27. (b)	28. (d)	29. (b)	30. (c)
31. (b)	32. (c)	33. (a)	34. (d)	35. (d)
36. (b)	37. (d)	38. (c)	39. (b)	40. (d)
41. (a)	42. (b)	43. (c)	44. (a)	45. (c)
46. (c)	47. (d)	48. (a)	49. (a)	50. (a)

MOCK TEST–3
PAPER–I

1. In the large group communications, effectively used media is
   (a) Radio
   (b) Television
   (c) Overhead Projector
   (d) Computer
2. A child may be suffering from hearing impairment if
   (a) he generally says 'please repeat' to the teacher
   (b) he speaks loudly unusually
   (c) he comes nearer to the speaker during conversation
   (d) All of the above
3. If a student is absent from the classes for a long time
   (a) Teacher should try to know the cause of his absence
   (b) Teacher should try to solve his problems or help him
   (c) Teacher should go to his home to meet him
   (d) Both (a) and (b)
4. The telecast materials are used to
   (a) increase retention power
   (b) enhances concentration and learning
   (c) reduces the burden of the teacher
   (d) All of the above
5. The main function of educational psychology is to provide prospective teacher with
   (a) how to deal with students and everyday class situation
   (b) research procedures for evaluating current teaching procedure
   (c) insight into the needs, problems and styles of behaviour of teacher
   (d) insight into various aspects of modern teaching education
6. Which of the following is not a method of research?
   (a) Historical (b) Observation
   (c) Philosophical (d) Survey
7. The communication which transpires inside a person is known as
   (a) group communication
   (b) intrapersonal communication
   (c) interpersonal communication
   (d) mass communication
8. The word research is derived from
   (a) Greek word (b) French word
   (c) Spanish word (d) Latin word
9. Educational quality is
   (a) Only a legal right
   (b) Fundamental right
   (c) Only a customary right
   (d) None of these
10. A good teacher is one who
   (a) has genuine interest in his student
   (b) is highly intelligent
   (c) lives simple life
   (d) has mastery over his teaching subject

11. Which of the following institutions is responsible for the implementation of reforms in teaching profession?
   (a) National Institute of Educational Planning and Administration
   (b) University Grants Commission
   (c) National Council for Teacher's Education
   (d) National Council for Educational Research and Training

12. The most important characteristic of Open Book Examination system is that
   (a) it compels students to think
   (b) students become serious
   (c) it improves attendance in the classroom
   (d) it reduces examination anxiety amongst students

13. Discussion in the class will be more effective if the topic of discussion is
   (a) informed to the student well in advance
   (b) not introduced
   (c) stated before the start of discussion
   (d) written on the board without introducing it

14. A person is not a successful communicator
   (a) who presents material in a precise and clear way
   (b) who sometimes becomes informal before the receiver and developes rapport
   (c) who knows a lot but is somewhat reserve in his attitude
   (d) who is able to adapt himself according to the language of communication

15. Which of the following provides more freedom for the learners to interact actively?
   (a) Small group discussions
   (b) Lecture by experts
   (c) Viewing of the TV
   (d) Use of film projector

16. In this question, four words are given, out of which three are alike in some manner and one is different. Choose the odd one out.
   (a) Diamond (b) Graphite
   (c) Coal (d) Pearl

17. Two objects or events are related in some way. Pick out that option which has the same type of relationship stated in the given two words:

   HANDS : FINGERS :: ?
   (a) Competition : Victory
   (b) Head : Hair
   (c) Skin : Colour
   (d) Machine : Tools

18. Human ear is most sensitive to noise in the range
   (a) 1-2 kHz (b) 100-500 Hz
   (c) 10-12 kHz (d) 13-16 kHz

Direction: (19-23) Study the following passage and give answer to the questions based on it.

A recent report in *News Week* says that in American colleges, students of Asian origin outperform not only the minority group students but the majority Whites as well. Many of these students might be of Indian origin, and their achievement is something that we can be really proud of. It is unlikely that these talented youngsters will come back to India, and that is the familiar brain drain problem. However, recent statements by the nation's policy makers indicate that the perception of this issue is changing. 'Brain Bank' and not the 'Brain Drain' is the more appropriate idea, they suggest that since the expertise of Indians abroad is only deposited in other places and not lost.

This may be so, but this brain bank, like most of other banks, is one that primarily serves customers in its neighbourhood. The skills of Asians now excelling in America's colleges will mainly help the USA. No matter how significant, what non-resident Indians do for India and what their counterparts do for other Asian lands is only a by-product.

But it is also necessary to ask, or be reminded why Indians study more fruitfully when abroad. The Asians whose accomplishments *News Week* records would have probably had a very different fate if they had studied in India. In America, they found an elbow room, books and facilities not available and not likely to be available here. The need to prove themselves in their new country and the competition of an international standard they faced there must have cured mental and physical laziness. But other things helping them in America can be obtained if we achieve a change in social attitudes, especially towards youth.

We need to learn to value individuals and their unique qualities more than conformity and respectability. We need to learn the language of encouragement to add to our skill in flattery. We might also learn to be less liberal with blame and less tight-fisted with appreciation, especially to those showing signs of independence.

19. It is a general belief that the talented young Indians studying in America
    (a) will not return to pursue their careers in India
    (b) have a reputation for being hard-working
    (c) have an opportunity to contribute in India's development
    (d) can solve the brain drain problem because of recent changes in policy
20. Among the many groups of students in American colleges, Asian students
    (a) have only a minority status like the blacks
    (b) are often written about in magazines like *News Week*
    (c) are the most successful academically
    (d) have proved that they are as goods as Whites
21. There is talk of the 'Brain Bank'. This idea
    (a) is based on plan to utilise foreign exchange remittances to stimulate research and development
    (b) is a solution to the brain drain problem
    (c) is a new problem caused partly by the brain drain
    (d) is a new way of looking at the role of qualified Indians living abroad
22. The students of Asian origin in America include
    (a) Indians who are the most hard-working of all
    (b) a fair number from India
    (c) a small group from India
    (d) persons from India who are very proud
23. Which of the following most appropriately sums up the intent of the author?
    (a) USA has excelled just because of the contributions from talented immigrants
    (b) We need to look at 'Brain Drain' in a positive way as 'Brain Bank'
    (c) Indians should take pride in the fact that fellow Indians have excelled in foreign lands against all odds
    (d) We need to think of the ways to help grow and retain the talent of our land
24. What should come in place of the question mark (?) in the following series?

    102, 99, 104, 97, 106 ?

    (a) 106 (b) 59
    (c) 95 (d) 64
25. **Statement:** Let us increase the taxes to cover the deficit.

Conclusions:

I. If the taxes are not increased, the deficit cannot be met.
II. The present taxes are very low.
III. Deficit in the budget are not desirable.

Choose the correct option.
(a) Only II and III are implicit
(b) Only I and III are implicit
(c) Only I and II are implicit
(d) All are implicit

26. **Statements:**

A. Some dogs are cats.
B. None of the cats is a cow.

Conclusins:

I. Some cats are not dogs.
II. Some cats are dogs.
III. Some cows are dogs.
IV. No dog is a cow.

Choose the correct option.
(a) Only II follows
(b) Only III follows
(c) Only I and III follows
(d) Only IV follows

Directions: (27-30) Using the following table answer the questions given below.

Yearly income (in ₹ '000)

Name/Year	2008	2009	2010	2011
Mahesh	1200	1600	2000	2400
Suresh	1000	1400	1600	2000
Ganesh	900	1200	1500	2000
Seema	2000	2500	3000	3700
Sapna	1200	1200	1500	1700

27. Whose average income for all the four years is ₹ 1400000?
(a) Mahesh alone
(b) Ganesh and Sapna both
(c) Mahesh and Suresh
(d) Sapna alone

28. How high is the total average income for four years of men as compared to that of women?
(a) 2133340 (b) 3500440
(c) 4320540 (d) 5440820

29. What is the round figure, the ratio between the total income of men and that of women for all years?
(a) 16:14 (b) 14:15
(c) 15:16 (d) 23:21

30. Can we say women earn more than men?
(a) No
(b) Yes
(c) Not sure
(d) Difference is not so significant

Directions: (31-35) Using the following graph answer the questions given below.

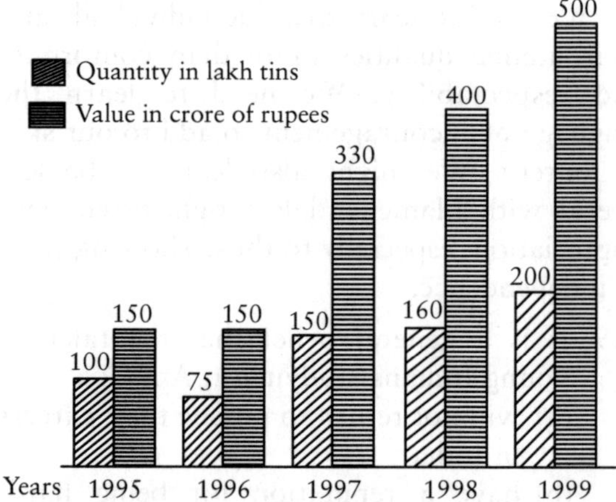

31. What was the approximate percentage increase in export value from 1995 to 1999?
(a) 435 (b) 395.5
(c) 422.8 (d) None of these

32. If in 1998, the tins were exported at the same rate per tin as that in 1997, what would be the value (in ₹ crores) of export in 1998?
(a) 375 (b) 352
(c) 395 (d) 392

33. In which year the value per tin was minimum?
(a) 1996 (b) 1998
(c) 1995 (d) 1999

34. What was the percentage drop in export quantity from 1995 to 1996?
(a) 25 (b) 46
(c) 52 (d) None of these

35. What was the difference between the tins exported in 1997 and 1998?
(a) 10 (b) 1000
(c) 100000 (d) 1000000

36. Which of the following statements is/are true about ozone layer?
(a) It is depleting due to human activities
(b) It is found in upper atmosphere, which absorbs UV rays
(c) It causes skin cancer and genetic disorder
(d) Both (a) and (b)

37. Study the figure and find the region which represents the students who study Physics and Chemistry but not Mathematics.

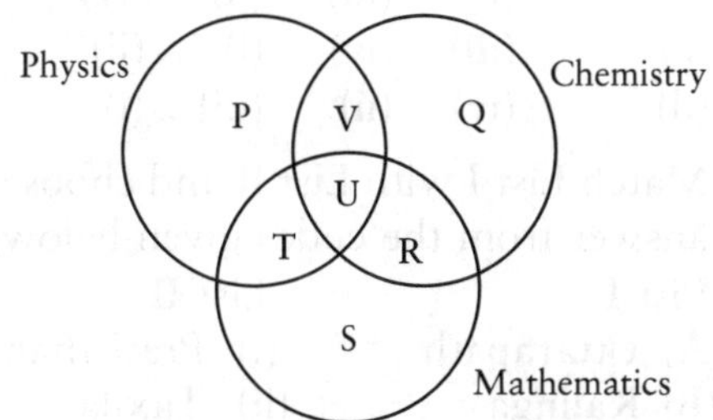

(a) P + T + S + R + U + V
(b) T
(c) P + T + S
(d) V

38. Which of the following is a non-point source of water pollution?
(a) Factories (b) Lawn
(c) Coal mines (d) None of these

39. The depletion of ozone layer causes
I. Skin cancer.
II. Damage to our immune system.
III. Damage to our eyes.
(a) Only III (b) Only I and II
(c) Only I and III (d) All of the above

40. **Statements:**
I. All the fruits are stones.
II. No tree is fruit.
III. All stones are rains.

Conclusion:
(a) Some rain is fruit
(b) No stone is a tree
(c) No rain is a tree
(d) None is true

41. Web designer is also known as
(a) Web maintainer (b) Web editor
(c) Web master (d) Web author

42. Which of the following schedule of our constitution is related to languages?
(a) Sixth (b) Eighth
(c) Seventh (d) Tenth

43. In the hypermedia database, information bits are stored in the form of
(a) Symbols (b) Signals
(c) Cubes (d) Nodes

44. Explosive volcanic eruption is caused by
(a) High water content in ground
(b) Low viscosity of magma
(c) High viscosity of magma
(d) None of these

45. The VIRUS is a
(a) Device
(b) Software program
(c) Hardware
(d) anti-piracy software

46. Appropriation Act of the General Budget is
(a) a Constitution Amendment Bill
(b) a Finance Bill
(c) a Money Bill
(d) an Ordinary Bill

47. If in a certain language, GERMANY is coded as HGUQFTF then how will you code NEOMAN?
(a) OFQQFT (b) OFQPES
(c) OGRQFT (d) None of these

48. Which of the following is biggest fresh-water lake in India?
(a) Loktak (b) Dal
(c) Sukhna (d) None of these

49. Different memories can be classified according to the concept of
(a) Transfer Rate
(b) Access mode/capacity
(c) Access Time
(d) All of the above

50. Which of the following diagrams represents the relation between red, clothes and roses most appropriately?

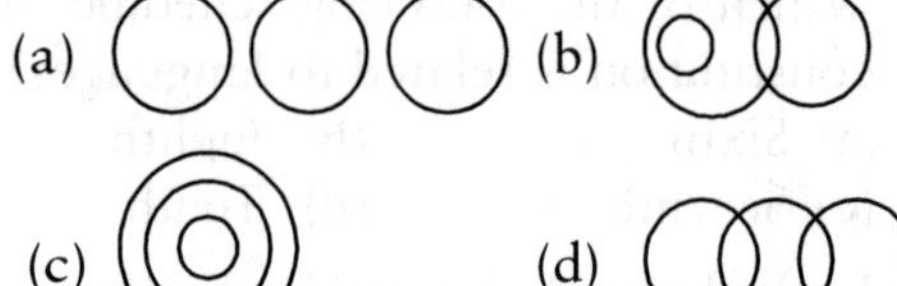

PAPER–II

1. The *Rigveda* does not mention one of the following:
(a) Magadha (b) Sapt-Sindhu
(c) Dasyu (d) Varna

2. What is the language of Pliny's original work, *The Natural History*?
(a) Greek (b) Latin
(c) French (d) English

3. Which work refers to India's contacts with Baveru(Babylon)?
(a) *Arthasastra* (b) *Dipavamsa*
(c) *Agamas* (d) *Jatakas*

4. Match List I with List II and choose your answer from the codes given below:

List I
(A) Bilhana (B) Someshvara
(C) Somadeva (D) Jayadeva

List II
(i) Manasollasa
(ii) Gita Govinda
(iii) Vikramankadevacharita
(iv) Kathasaritasagara

Codes:	A	B	C	D
(a)	(iii)	(i)	(iv)	(ii)
(b)	(i)	(iii)	(iv)	(ii)
(c)	(ii)	(iv)	(iii)	(i)
(d)	(iii)	(i)	(ii)	(iv)

5. Match List I with List II and choose your answer from the codes given below:

List I	List II
(A) Anga	(i) Giribraj
(B) Magadha	(iii) Champa
(C) Kosal	(iii) Vaishali
(D) Vajji	(iv) Shravasti

Codes:	A	B	C	D
(a)	(ii)	(i)	(iv)	(iii)
(b)	(i)	(iii)	(ii)	(iv)
(c)	(iii)	(iv)	(i)	(ii)
(d)	(iv)	(ii)	(iii)	(i)

6. Match List I with List II and choose your answer from the codes given below:

List I	List II
(A) Uttarapath	(i) Pratisthan
(B) Kalinga	(ii) Taxila
(C) Satavahana	(iii) Mahismati
(D) Avanti	(iv) Tosali

Codes:	A	B	C	D
(a)	(ii)	(iv)	(i)	(iii)
(b)	(iii)	(ii)	(iv)	(i)
(c)	(iv)	(iii)	(ii)	(i)
(d)	(i)	(iv)	(iii)	(ii)

7. Match List I with List II and choose your answer from the codes given below:

List I	List II
(A) Indika	(i) Banabhatta
(B) Harshacharita	(ii) Chandbardai
(C) Prithwiraj Raso	(iii) Megasthanese
(D) Rajatarangini	(iv) Kalhana

Codes:	A	B	C	D
(a)	(iv)	(iii)	(i)	(ii)
(b)	(iii)	(i)	(ii)	(iv)
(c)	(ii)	(iv)	(iii)	(i)
(d)	(i)	(ii)	(iv)	(iii)

8. Who converted Kumarapala, the Chalukyan King of Gujarat to Jainism?
(a) Hemachandra
(b) Hemadri
(c) Vimal Suri
(d) Jina Dutt Suri

9. The Pallavas used one of the following symbols:
(a) Trident and Lingam
(b) Fish and Ship
(c) Elephant and Lion
(d) Bull and Lingam

10. The earliest Vessara temple is carved at:
(a) Mahabalipuram
(b) Deogarh
(c) Aihole
(d) Nachna-Kuthara

11. Which of the following pairs is not matched correctly?
(a) Kalhana and Rajatarangini
(b) Dharamapala and Nalanda
(c) Ashoka and Buddhism
(d) Vakapatiraja and Harsha

12. Given below are two statements, one labelled as Assertion (A), and the other labelled as Reason (R):
Assertion (A): The concept of Syadavada in Jainism accommodates the views of others.
Reason (R): The Jainas are frightened by others views.
In the context of the above two statements, which one of the following is correct?
(a) (A) is true, but (R) is false
(b) (R) is true, but (A) is false
(c) Both (A) and (R) are true
(d) Both (A) and (R) are false

14. Match List I with List II and choose your answer from the codes given below:

List I	List II
(A) Diodorus	(i) Indica
(B) Arrian	(ii) Library of History
(C) Ptolemy	(iii) Geography
(D) Megasthenes	(iv) Indica

Codes:	A	B	C	D
(a)	(ii)	(i)	(iii)	(iv)
(b)	(i)	(iii)	(iv)	(ii)
(c)	(ii)	(iv)	(i)	(iii)
(d)	(iv)	(ii)	(iii)	(i)

15. Who was the founder of the Lingayat Sect?
(a) Appar (b) Sankara
(c) Ramanuja (d) Basavanna

16. Given below are two statements, one labelled as Assertion (A) and the other labelled as Reason (R):
Assertion (A): Tripartite struggle was the political struggle for the Supremacy of north India.
Reason (R): This was essential.
In the context of the above two statements which of the following is correct?
(a) (A) is true but (R) is false
(b) (A) is false but (R) is true
(c) Both (A) and (R) are false
(d) Both (A) and (R) are true

17. Gajpati rulers principally controlled:
(a) Bengal (b) Odisha
(c) Bihar (d) South Andhra

18. Amir Khusro was associated with:
(a) Slave rulers
(b) Slave and Khalji rulers

(c) Slave, Khalji and Tughluq rulers
(d) Tughluq and Sayyid rulers

19. Vijayanagar Empire was established in the:
(a) 13th Century (b) 14th Century
(c) 15th Century (d) 16th Century

20. The author of *Purush-Pariksha* was born in:
(a) Bengal (b) Odisha
(c) Bihar (d) Uttar Pradesh

21. Who among the Persian historians wrote mainly about Sher Shah?
(a) Abbas Khan Sherwani
(b) Nizamuddin Ahmed
(c) Abdul Qadir Badaoni
(d) Yahya Sirhindi

22. In the 17th Century major Portuguese settlements in India were at:
(a) Goa
(b) Goa and Daman
(c) Goa, Daman and Diu
(d) Goa, Daman and Cochin

23. Pondicherry was the main base on the Coromondel coast of the:
(a) Dutch East India Company
(b) French East India Company
(c) English East India Company
(d) Danish East India Company

24. The English East India Company exported from India to Europe in the XVII Century mainly:
(a) Cotton textiles
(b) Cotton textiles and indigo
(c) Cotton textiles, indigo and saltpetre
(d) Cotton textiles, indigo, saltpetre and spices

25. Mansabdari was instituted by:
(a) Babur (b) Humayun
(c) Akbar (d) Aurangzeb

26. Adi-Granth was given final form by:
(a) Guru Nanak
(b) Guru Angad
(c) Guru Arjun
(d) Guru Gobind Singh

27. Which of the following is not associated with New Stone age?
(a) Domestication of plants
(b) Iron
(c) Sedentary life
(d) Early village settlements

28. The Maratha Confederacy fell before the English because the Maratha Chiefs were:
(a) disunited
(b) disunited and militarily weak
(c) lacking in political foresight
(d) not able to correctly judge English intentions

29. Socio-religious movements in medieval India profoundly affected:
(a) Social life
(b) Economic life
(c) Cultural life
(d) Regional languages

30. Given two statements, one labelled as Assertion (A), and the other labelled as Reason (R):
Assertion (A): Under the Great Mughals architecture flourished.
Reason (R): Some of the Great Mughals were great patrons of architecture.
In the context of the above two statements, which one of the following is correct?
(a) Both (A) and (R) are true and (R) is the correct explanation of (A).
(b) Both (A) and (R) are true and (R) is not the correct explanation of (A).
(c) (A) is true but (R) is false.
(d) (A) is false but (R) is true.

31. After the Battle of Plassey the servants of East India Company carried on their private trade in Bengal through the:
(a) Authority of the Company
(b) Misuse of dastaks

(c) Nawab's of Bengal
(d) Servants of the Nawabs

32. The highest British Capital Investment in India was made in the:
(a) Tea, Coffee and the Indigo Plantation.
(b) Railways, Banking, Insurance and Shipping.
(c) Cotton Textile Industry.
(d) Jute Mills.

33. What is not correct about the Permanent Settlement?
(a) Proprietary Rights granted to the Zamindars
(b) Land Revenue fixed in perpetuity
(c) Proprietary Rights granted to the ryots
(d) Assessment of revenue at the double rates

34. Ishwar Chandra Vidyasagar founded the college in Calcutta called:
(a) Bethune College
(b) Hindu College
(c) Ripon College
(d) Presidency College

35. Which of the following measures was not taken up by Lord Curzon?
(a) The Partition of Bengal
(b) The Ancient Monuments Act
(c) Press Act
(d) The Indian Universities Act

36. Who amongst the following belonged to the Firangi Mahal School of Lucknow?
(a) Shibli Nomani
(b) Maulana Hasan Ahmed Madni
(c) Maulana Abdul Kalam Azad
(d) Maulana Abdul Bari

37. Who amongst the following was not associated with the Swarajist group in the Congress in 1922-23?
(a) Dr. Rajendra Prasad
(b) Motilal Nehru
(c) C.R. Das
(d) Hakim Ajmal Khan

38. Who presided over the first session of the All Indian Kisan Sabha?
(a) N.G. Ranga
(b) Raj Kumar Shukla
(c) Swami Sahjanand
(d) Baba Ramchandra Das

39. The symbol used in the Revolt of 1857 was:
(a) Rose and Bread
(b) Lotus and Cow
(c) Rose and Lamp
(d) Lotus and Bread

40. Who has argued that de-industrialization did not take place in India under the colonial rule?
(a) Anil Seal
(b) Dada Bhai Naoroji
(c) Morris D. Morris
(d) Amiya Bagchi

41. Match List I with List II and select the correct answer:

List I
(A) Vanchi Iyer
(B) T.K. Mahadevan
(C) Shrinivas Pillay
(D) E.V. Ramaswamy Naicker

List II
(i) Vaikom Satyagraha
(ii) Tinnevelli conspiracy case
(iii) The Hindu Progressive Improvement Society
(iv) Self Respect Movement

Codes:	**A**	**B**	**C**	**D**
(a)	(ii)	(iv)	(iii)	(i)
(b)	(iii)	(ii)	(iv)	(i)
(c)	(ii)	(i)	(iii)	(iv)
(d)	(i)	(ii)	(iv)	(iii)

42. Match List I with List II and select the correct answer:

List I
(A) Sir William Jones
(B) Hindu College

(C) Edward Thompson
(D) M.A.O. College

List II
(i) Rise and Fulfilment of the British Rule in India
(ii) Aligarh Muslim University
(iii) Bengal Asiatic Society and G.T. Garrett
(iv) Presidency College

Codes:	**A**	**B**	**C**	**D**
(a)	(i)	(iv)	(ii)	(iii)
(b)	(iii)	(iv)	(i)	(ii)
(c)	(iii)	(ii)	(i)	(iv)
(d)	(iv)	(iii)	(ii)	(i)

43. Who amongst the following was not included in the I.N.A. trial held in the Red Fort, Delhi?
(a) G.S. Dhillon
(b) Prem Sahgal
(c) Col Mohan Singh
(d) Shanawaz Khan

44. In 1946, the Interim Government was headed by:
(a) Liaqat Ali Khan
(b) Jawaharlal Nehru
(c) Maulana Abdul Kalam Azad
(d) Lord Mountbatten

45. Given below are two statements, one labelled as Assertion (A), and the other labelled as Reason (R):
Assertion (A): Woods' Despatch of 1854 is generally known as the Magna Carta of English Education in India.
Reason (R): It outlined a comprehensive plan for the future development of education system in India by the British Government. In the context of the above two statements, which one of the following is correct?
(a) Both (A) and (R) are true and (R) is the correct explanation of (A).
(b) Both (A) and (R) are true and (R) is not the correct explanation of (A).
(c) (A) is true but (R) is false.
(d) (A) is false but (R) is true.

46. During Renaissance the interest in the study of Gracco-Roman classics came to be known as:
(a) Individualism (b) Hedonism
(c) Romanticism (d) Humanism

47. Who called commerce is 'a perpetual war of wit and energy among all nations'?
(a) Jean Bodin
(b) Jean Baptist Colbert
(c) Thomas Mun
(d) Thomas Hobbes

48. Who was universally acclaimed as the Prince of the Humanists?
(a) Erasmus
(b) John Colet
(c) Thomas More
(d) Francesco Petrarch

49. Calvinists in France were called:
(a) Puritans (b) Presbyterians
(c) Huguenots (d) Catholics

50. Who was the first Greek Historian?
(a) Thucydides (b) Herodotus
(c) Manetho (d) Homer

PAPER–III

1. Match List I with List II and select the correct answer by using the codes given below:

List I (Major rock edicts)
(A) First (B) Third
(C) Fifth (D) Seventh

List II (Contents)
(i) Relationship between servants and masters and proper treatment of prisoners
(ii) Pleads for toleration amongst all sects
(iii) Prohibition of animal sacrifices and festivals gathering

(iv) Mention of the Yuktas, rajukas and the Pradesikas for the propagation of Dhamma

Codes:	**A**	**B**	**C**	**D**
(a)	(iv)	(iii)	(ii)	(i)
(b)	(iii)	(i)	(iv)	(ii)
(c)	(ii)	(iii)	(iv)	(i)
(d)	(iii)	(iv)	(i)	(ii)

2. Who was the first royal convert to Buddhism?
   (a) Akbar
   (b) Ajatashatru
   (c) Ashoka
   (d) Chandragupta Maurya
3. In which year of Ashoka coronation did the Kalinga war take place?
   (a) Third (b) Eighth
   (c) Fifteenth (d) Twentieth
4. The capital of the Sungas was
   (a) Agra (b) Sabala
   (c) Vidisa (d) Pataliputra
5. Many of Gandhiji's associates joined him in his political career during the course of various activities undertaken by him.

List I	**List II**
(A) Champaran indigo cultivators	(i) Anasuya Behn
(B) Ahmedabad textile workers	(ii) Vallabh Bhai Patel and Indulal Yagnik
(C) Kheda peasants	(iii) Rajendra Prasad, Braj Kishore Prasad, and JB Kriplani
(D) South Africa	(iv) Gokhale

Codes:	**A**	**B**	**C**	**D**
(a)	(i)	(iii)	(ii)	(iv)
(b)	(iv)	(i)	(ii)	(iii)
(c)	(iii)	(ii)	(i)	(iv)
(d)	(iii)	(i)	(ii)	(iv)

6. **Assertion (A):** The Himalayas is responsible for making the Indo-Gangetic plains a vast well-watered garden, swarming with population.
   Reason (R): This was the reason for Asian nomadism.
   (a) Both A and R are true and R is the correct explanation of A
   (b) Both A and R are true but R is not the correct explanaton of A
   (c) A is true but R is false
   (d) A is false but R is true
7. Who was the President of the Indian National Congress when India became free?
   (a) J.B. Kripalani
   (b) Sardar Patel
   (c) Mahatma Gandhi
   (d) Jawaharlal Nehru
8. The earliest painting of Ajanta caves belong to
   (a) 1st centruy AD (b) 2nd century AD
   (c) 3rd century AD (d) 4th century AD
9. Which of the following theories of education was very similar to the 20th century economic 'trickle-down' theory of development?
   (a) downward filtration
   (b) upward filtration
   (c) Western filtration
   (d) None of the above
10. The veda which is partly a proved work is
    (a) Rigveda (b) Yajurveda
    (c) Samveda (d) Atharvaveda
11. Who is remembered as the pioneer of economic nationalism?
    (a) G.K. Gokhale
    (b) Bipin Chandra Pal
    (c) Madan Mohan Malviya
    (d) R.C. Dutt

12. Charak-Samhita is a treatise on
    (a) Astronomy
    (b) Sanskrit grammar
    (c) Medicine
    (d) Astrology
13. Which one of the Harappan deities is not represented in Hindu religion?
    (a) Unicorn
    (b) Compound creatures
    (c) Pashupati Shiva
    (d) Seven mothers
14. The Chalukya King who had the title of Sri Prithvi-Vallabha and Parameswara was
    (a) Maharaja Kirthivarman
    (b) Pulakesin II
    (c) Mangalesa
    (d) Pulakesin I
15. Which of the following statements is the purpose of history?
    (a) To entertain the readers
    (b) To develop the basic I.Q.
    (c) To know the difference between past and future
    (d) To explain and understand the present
16. The IVC belonged to
    (a) Iron-age (b) Copper-age
    (c) Bronze-age (d) Stone-age
17. The history dealing with religion, morals, manners, food and dress culture, etc., is known as
    (a) Military History
    (b) Economic History
    (c) Social History
    (d) Diplomatic History
18. Where is Kalibangan, one of the sites of the Harappan civilization located?
    (a) Near Sind
    (b) Near Ropar on the Sutlej
    (c) Ganganagar district of Rajasthan
    (d) Near the Ghaggar valley
19. What are the basic considerations one should keep in mind for the selection of Project or Problem?
    (a) Language of the source material
    (b) To avoid the study of comparative history
    (c) Availability of source material
    (d) All of the above
20. In which region have traces of the Megalithic culture been located?
    (a) Northeast (b) South India
    (c) Northwest (d) North India
21. The black-and-red pottery is noteworthy of which phase
    (a) Bronze Age
    (b) Neolithic Age
    (c) Chalcolithic Period
    (d) Paleolithic Age
22. The word 'History' is derived from which of the following language?
    (a) Roman (b) Latin
    (c) Greek (d) French
23. Important crops like rice, wheat and barley, came to be cultivated in the sub-continent during the
    (a) Indus Valley around 2500 B.C.
    (b) Neolithic Age
    (c) Paleolithic Age
    (d) Seventh Millennium B.C.
24. *Tolkappiyam* is
    (a) A disciple of sage Agastya
    (b) A state in the Pandyan kingdom
    (c) A book on the Mauryan administration
    (d) An earliest standard treatise on grammar
25. In connection with the Indus Valley Civilization, we come across the name of
    (a) D.D. Kosambi
    (b) Sir Vincent Smith
    (c) Sir Mortimer Wheeler
    (d) Sir Alexander Cunningham
26. There was brisk commercial contact between Rome and Tamil Nadu during

the Sangam period. Many articles were exported from Tamil Nadu to Rome. Which one among the following items was not included in the export?

(a) Ivory (b) Wine
(c) Spices (d) Beryl

27. Identify the incorrect combination among the following
(a) Dholavira and single citadel
(b) Harappa and Granary
(c) Lothal and Dockyard
(d) Mohenjodaro and the great bath

28. Which Indian ruler conquered Java and Sumatra?
(a) Samudragupta
(b) Vikramaditya
(c) Rajaraja Chola I
(d) Rajendra Chola I

29. The largest concentration of Harappan sites has been found along the
(a) Ghaggar-Hakra (b) Sutlej
(c) Ravi (d) Indus

30. The first dynasty of the Vijayanagar Kingdom was
(a) Saluva (b) Tuluva
(c) Hoysala (d) Sangama

31. Which one of the following was not an Indus Valley Civilization site?
(a) Rangpur (b) Suktagendor
(c) Lothal (d) Patliputra

32. Which of the following historians was the author of *The Saxons in England*?
(a) Frederick York Powell
(b) John Richard Green
(c) John Mitchell Kemble
(d) Charles Harding Firth

33. Macth the following List I and II. Select the correct answers by using the codes given below the lists.

List I
(A) Mohenjodaro (B) Lothal
(C) Surkotda (D) Harappa

List II
(i) Pillared Hall (ii) Bones of Horse
(iii) Cemetery R-37 (iv) Double Burial

Codes:	A	B	C	D
(a)	(i)	(iv)	(ii)	(iii)
(b)	(iii)	(iv)	(i)	(ii)
(c)	(ii)	(i)	(iii)	(iv)
(d)	(iv)	(iii)	(ii)	(i)

34. Which one of the following assemblies protected the interests of traders under the Chola administration?
(a) Kuri (b) Nagaram
(c) Mahasabha (d) Perunguri

35. Discovery and exploration during 'Renaissance'
(a) gave new ideas about the world
(b) improved knowledge about sea, other countries and provided contact with out side the world
(c) opened up new trade routes
(d) All the above are correct

36. **Assertion (A):** At the intellectual level, the most serious challenge to Buddhism and Jainism was posed by Sankaracharya.
Reason (R): Sankaracharya's philosophy is called Advaitavada or the doctrine of non-dualism.
(a) If both (A) and (R) are true and R is the correct explanation of (A)
(b) If both (A) and (R) are true but (R) is not the correct explanaton of (A)
(c) If (A) is true but (R) is false
(d) If (A) is false but (R) is true

37. The Turks conquered the Constantipole in the year
(a) 1453 A.D. (b) 1454 A.D.
(c) 1455 A.D. (d) 1456 A.D.

38. Match the following List I and II. Select the correct answers by using the codes given below the lists.

List I

(A) Yadava kingdom
(B) Kakatiyas of Warangal
(C) Hoyasalas of Dvarsamudra
(D) Chalukyas of Vengi

List II

(i) Had matrimonial alliance with the Cholas
(ii) Polygonal or star-shaped temple architecture
(iii) Gave a great impetus to Telugu literature
(iv) Growth of a new religious sect the Mahanubhavas

Codes:	A	B	C	D
(a)	(iv)	(iii)	(ii)	(i)
(b)	(iii)	(ii)	(iv)	(i)
(c)	(iv)	(ii)	(iii)	(i)
(d)	(i)	(ii)	(iii)	(iv)

39. The Great Wall of China was built by a...who elected himself as emperor over all three States.
(a) Chi-ruler
(b) Chin-ruler
(c) Chu-ruler
(d) None is correct

40. The commercial importance of Korkai was that
(a) it was the place where pearls gathered from all places were sent
(b) it was an important administrative centre of the Pandyan kingdom
(c) it was the region where the pearl fisheries of the Pandyan kingdom were worked by condemned criminals
(d) None of the above

41. In which year did the French Revolution break out?
(a) 1789 A.D. (b) 1791 A.D.
(c) 1796 A.D. (d) None is correct

42. Which Hoysala ruler was first a Jain and then converted to Vaishnavism by Ramanuja?
(a) Vira Ballala
(b) Vishnuvardhana
(c) Both (a) and (b)
(d) None of the above

43. The people in the world are divided on the basis of
(a) Religion
(b) Cultural background
(c) Nationality
(d) All the above are correct

44. Which of the following is not one of the three-age system used in dividing up human pre-history?
(a) Stone Age (b) Bronze Age
(c) Copper Age (d) Iron Age

45. Name the writer who is generally regarded as "Father of History"
(a) Kalhana (b) Aristotle
(c) Herodotus (d) Thuchdides

46. Who was the first ruler of the Pala Dynasty of Bengal?
(a) Devapala (b) Gopala
(c) Dharmapala (d) Vigropala

47. Which Revolution fathered Russian Revolution?
(a) American Revolution
(b) Industrial Revolution
(c) French Revolution
(d) All of the above

48. In *Bhagvad Gita* there are three distinct paths or ways of salvation. Which of the paths given below was not one of its guide lines?
(a) Asceticism (b) Bhakti
(c) Jnana (d) Karma

49. Which one of the following is not related to Leonardo-da-Vinci
(a) Virginia Woolf
(b) The Virgin of the Rocks
(c) The Last Supper
(d) Monalisa

50. The two important centres of Gupta sculpture were
   (a) Gandhara and Ajanta
   (b) Mathura and Gandhara
   (c) Mathura and Sarnath
   (d) Pataliputra and Ujjain

ANSWERS SHEET

PAPER—I

1. (d)	2. (d)	3. (c)	4. (d)	5. (d)
6. (a)	7. (b)	8. (d)	9. (d)	10. (d)
11. (d)	12. (c)	13. (c)	14. (b)	15. (a)
16. (d)	17. (d)	18. (b)	19. (c)	20. (b)
21. (a)	22. (b)	23. (c)	24. (c)	25. (c)
26. (b)	27. (b)	28. (c)	29. (b)	30. (b)
31. (a)	32. (b)	33. (c)	34. (a)	35. (b)
36. (d)	37. (b)	38. (d)	39. (c)	40. (a)
41. (a)	42. (b)	43. (a)	44. (a)	45. (b)
46. (c)	47. (c)	48. (c)	49. (d)	50. (c)

PAPER—II

1. (a)	2. (b)	3. (d)	4. (a)	5. (a)
6. (a)	7. (b)	8. (a)	9. (d)	10. (c)
11. (b)	12. (a)	13. (d)	14. (a)	15. (d)
16. (a)	17. (b)	18. (c)	19. (b)	20. (c)
21. (a)	22. (c)	23. (b)	24. (d)	25. (c)
26. (c)	27. (b)	28. (b)	29. (b)	30. (a)
31. (a)	32. (d)	33. (c)	34. (a)	35. (c)
36. (d)	37. (a)	38. (c)	39. (d)	40. (c)
41. (c)	42. (b)	43. (c)	44. (b)	45. (a)
46. (d)	47. (a)	48. (a)	49. (c)	50. (b)

PAPER—III

1. (d)	2. (c)	3. (b)	4. (b)	5. (d)
6. (b)	7. (a)	8. (a)	9. (a)	10. (b)
11. (d)	12. (c)	13. (a)	14. (b)	15. (d)
16. (d)	17. (c)	18. (c)	19. (d)	20. (b)
21. (c)	22. (c)	23. (b)	24. (d)	25. (c)
26. (b)	27. (a)	28. (d)	29. (a)	30. (d)
31. (d)	32. (c)	33. (a)	34. (b)	35. (d)
36. (b)	37. (a)	38. (a)	39. (c)	40. (c)
41. (a)	42. (b)	43. (d)	44. (c)	45. (c)
46. (b)	47. (d)	48. (a)	49. (a)	50. (c)

MOCK TEST–4
PAPER–I

1. Dewry defines education as a
   (a) theoretical need
   (b) social need
   (c) personal need
   (d) psychological need

2. All of the following statements about a teacher are correct except the one.
   (a) A teacher changes his/her attitudes and behaviour according to the need of the society
   (b) A teacher is a friend, guide and philosopher
   (c) A teacher distinguishes between students
   (d) A teacher is the leader in the class

3. A person cannot be an effective teacher if he
   (a) teaches moral values
   (b) is a strict disciplinarian
   (c) knows his subject well
   (d) has no interest in teaching

4. The most important single factor in underlying the success of a teacher is
   (a) organisational ability
   (b) scholarship
   (c) communicative ability
   (d) personality and his ability to relate to the class and to the pupils
5. If you are irritated and show rashness because of the inadequate behaviour of another teachers, what do you think about your own behaviour?
   (a) Your behaviour is also a sign of maladjustment and so try to control yourself when you are maltreated
   (b) It is justified because behaviours are choice
   (c) Your behaviour is not good because elders have the right to behave you in this way
   (d) All of the above
6. The term 'SITE' stands for
   (a) Satellite Instructional Teachers Education
   (b) Satellite International Television Experiment
   (c) Satellite Instructional Television Experiment
   (d) Satellite Indian Television Experiment
7. Team teaching has the potential to develop
   (a) highlighting the gaps in each other's teaching
   (b) competitive spirit
   (c) cooperation
   (d) the habit of supplementing the teaching of each other
8. In any research one should
   (a) not try out anything blindly but wait until a sudden flash appears in his mind
   (b) know everything in the area without bothering to learn the details of any
   (c) know more and more about less and less in certain specific sub area
   (d) None of these
9. Determine the nature of the following definition:
   'Poor' means having an annual income of ₹ 10,000.
   (a) Lexical (b) Persuasive
   (c) Precising (d) Stipulative
10. Which of the following methods implies the collection of information by way of investigators own examination without interviewing the respondents?
    (a) Random probability sampling
    (b) Observation
    (c) Posting questionnaire
    (d) Schedule method
11. Why do teachers use teaching aid?
    (a) For students' attention
    (b) To make teaching fun-filled
    (c) To make students attentive
    (d) To teach within understanding level of students
12. On which of the following statements there is consensus among educators?
    (a) Disciplinary cases should be totally neglected in the class
    (b) Disciplinary cases should be sent to the principal only when other means have failed
    (c) Disciplinary cases should never be sent to principal's office
    (d) None of these
13. Good evaluation of written material should not be based on
    (a) Logical presentation
    (b) Comprehension of subject
    (c) Linguistic expression
    (d) Ability to reproduce whatever is read

14. A good researcher lays his hands on
    (a) any area as long as manpower and fundings are available in plenty
    (b) a specific area and tries to understand in minute details
    (c) several areas and tries to understand them at fundamental level
    (d) None of these
15. The basis on which assumptions are formulated
    (a) Universities
    (b) Cultural background of the country
    (c) Specific characteristics of the castes
    (d) All of these

Read the following passage and answer the questions 16 to 20:

India is dedicated to free institutions and principles of democracy. We are striving to give everyone an opportunity and raise the standard of living for all. A democracy is one where people have the right to live their own lives and develop themselves in their own way under the guidance of their chosen representatives. If our political democracy is to succeed, it is essential that it be buttressed by steps towards economic equality or what has been referred to as the 'socialistic pattern of society'. Poverty and unemployment hold the biggest threat to the successful working of our democratic system.

16. One may infer from the paragraph that in a socialistic pattern of society
    (a) to provide employment to all is the greatest problem
    (b) the socialist party dominates
    (c) all the inhabitants are treated equal
    (d) None of these
17. The successful working of Indian democratic system is under a threat of
    (a) economic inequality
    (b) poverty
    (c) unemployment
    (d) All the above
18. In a democratic system
    (a) commodities are freely bought and sold
    (b) government serves the people
    (c) the government is run by the people themselves
    (d) people do not have political freedom
19. The word buttressed in the paragraph means
    (a) Supported (b) Dictating
    (c) Declared (d) Guided
20. Democracy can fail if there is
    (a) opportunity for development
    (b) a weak government
    (c) economic inequality
    (d) unemployment
21. Aspect ratio of TV Screen is
    (a) 4:3 (b) 3:4
    (c) 2:3 (d) 2:4
22. Which of the following is not a product of learning?
    (a) Knowledge (b) Attitudes
    (c) Maturation (d) Concepts
23. The first paper for the human beings was developed by
    (a) The Aryans
    (b) The Babilonians
    (c) The Chinese
    (d) The Sumerians
24. Which sequence in turn will lead one to face the west direction from which one starts turning?
    (a) Right, right, left, right, left right
    (b) Left, right, left, left, right, right
    (c) Right, right left, left, right, right
    (d) Left, left, right, left, right, left
25. Fill in the blank with the most appropriate choice

_____ is the supreme medium to express yesterday, today and tomorrow with its own unique language.

(a) Television (b) Cinema
(c) Radio (d) Newspaper

26. In which language the newspapers have highest circulation?

(a) Tamil (b) English
(c) Bengali (d) Hindi

27. Amit is the son of Rahul. Sarika, Rahul's sister has a son Sonu and a daughter Rita. Raja is the maternal uncle of Sonu. How is Rita related to Raja.

(a) Aunt (b) Sister
(c) Daughter (d) Niece

28. **Statements:** A man must be wise to be a good wrangler. Good wrangler's are all talkative and boring.

Conclusions:

I. All the wise persons are boring.
II. All the wise persons are good wranglers.

Choose the correct option.

(a) Only conclusion I follows
(b) Only conclusion II follows
(c) Both I and II follow
(d) None of these

29. What is the number that comes next in the sequence?

2, 5, 9, 19, 37, ...

(a) 74 (b) 75
(c) 76 (d) 78

30. Match List I with List II and select the correct answer using the codes given below:

List I	List II
(A) Pandit Jasraj	(i) Hindustani vocalist
(B) Kishan Maharaj	(ii) Sitar
(C) Ravi Shankar	(iii) Tabla
(D) Udai Shankar	(iv) Dance

Codes:	A	B	C	D
(a)	(i)	(ii)	(iii)	(iv)
(b)	(i)	(iii)	(iv)	(ii)
(c)	(i)	(iii)	(ii)	(iv)
(d)	(iii)	(ii)	(i)	(iv)

31. Who developed the ability to speak?

(a) Aryans (b) Neanderthal
(c) Cro-Magnon (d) Dravidians

32. In what way does communication in small group differ from that in the large group?

(a) Large group communication provides better feedback
(b) Small group provides far more interaction among the participants
(c) Interaction in small group is more restrictive
(d) Small group takes less time to convey the message

33. What is the main aim and objective of provision for feedback in communication system?

(a) Understand more about the content
(b) To make communication better by adjusting at both ends of Encoder and Decoder
(c) Identify the defect of communication
(d) Make necessary modification in communication system

34. Communications bandwidth that has the highest capacity and is used by microwave, cable and fibre optics lines is known as

(a) Carrier wave (b) Hyper-link
(c) Broadband (d) Bus width

35. In a certain code, CLOCK is written as KCOLC. How would STEPS be written in that code?

(a) SPETS (b) SPEST
(c) SPSET (d) SEPTS

36. Which one of the following is not an argument?

(a) Ram is not at home, so he must have gone to town
(b) Ram insulted me so I punched him in the nose
(c) If today is Tuesday, tomorrow will be Wednesday
(d) Since today is Tuesday, tomorrow will be Wednesday.

Direction: (37-41) Study the following pie chart and answer the questions based on it. Following pie chart represents the investment done by Timas Finance Ltd. in the various sectors. (All investments are in ₹ crores)

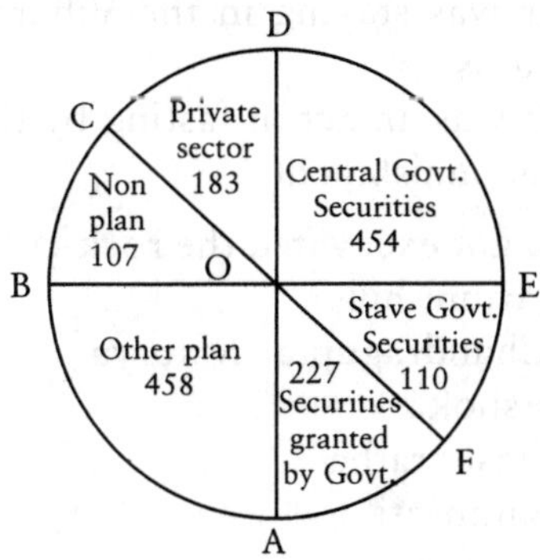

37. The percentage or gross investment in state government securities is nearly
(a) 7.1% (b) 9.2%
(c) 8.6% (d) 7.8%

38. The investment in plan and non-plan sector together is more or less than the investment in government securities (Central and State) by
(a) less, 106 crores (b) more, 4 crores
(c) more, 1 crores (d) more, 111 crores

39. The magnitude of ∠AOC is nearly
(a) 132° (b) 123°
(c) 126° (d) 115°

40. The ratio of area of the circle above ∠COF to the area of the circle below it is about
(a) 1 (b) 0.92
(c) 0.94 (d) 0.96

41. The investment in private sector is nearly what percent higher than the investment in State Government Security?
(a) 44% (b) 66%
(c) 54% (d) 46%

42. How many numbers between 100 and 300 begin or end with 2?
(a) 120 (b) 110
(c) 100 (d) 180

43. Which of the following operating system is used on mobile phones?
(a) Windows XP
(b) Windows Vista
(c) Android
(d) All of the above

44. Structure of logical argument is based on
(a) Linguistic expression
(b) Material truth
(c) Formal validity
(d) Aptness of examples

45. HTML is used to create
(a) machine language program
(b) high level program
(c) web page
(d) web server

46. Which of the following pollutants affects the respiratory tract in humans?
(a) Aerosols
(b) Sulphur dioxide
(c) Nitric oxide
(d) Carbon monoxide

47. Which of the following sources of energy has the maximum potential in India?
(a) Wind energy
(b) Solar energy
(c) Ocean thermal energy
(d) Tidal energy

48. In a deductive argument conclusion is
(a) Additional to the premises
(b) Entailed by the premises
(c) Summing up of the premises
(d) Not necessarily based on premises

49. What is the range of the numbers which can be stored in an eight bit register?
   (a) −127 to + 128 (b) −127 to + 127
   (c) −128 to + 128 (d) −128 to + 127

50. Universal Product Code (UPC), a pattern of bars printed on merchandise can be read by
   (a) Product Code Reader
   (b) Bar Code Reader
   (c) Code Reader
   (d) Card Reader

PAPER–II

1. What is the main achievement of the Neolithic revolution?
   (a) Animal husbandry
   (b) Agriculture
   (c) Nomadic life
   (d) Painting

2. Consider the following statements:
   (1) In Rig Vedic time the King was the absolute monarch.
   (2) Feudalism originated during the Rig Vedic period.
   (3) Purohita was the foremost among the functionaries of the King during the Rig Vedic time.

   Which of the statements given above is/are correct?
   (a) 1 and 2 (b) 2 and 3
   (c) 1, 2 and 3 (d) 3 only

3. Given below are two statements, one labelled as Assertion (A) and the other labelled as Reason (R):

   Assertion (A): The concept of middle path in Buddhism is to destroy all pains in human's life.

   Reason (R): It ends the extreme views.

   In the context of the above two statements which one of the following is correct?

   Codes:
   (a) (A) is true, but (R) is false
   (b) (R) is true, but (A) is false
   (c) Both (A) and (R) are true
   (d) Both (A) and (R) are false

4. What was Upavasatha (uposatha) in Buddhist order?
   (a) It was an act of general confession of Buddhist monks when they assembled every fortnight on the evenings of full and new moons
   (b) It was the vow taken by the newly admitted monks
   (c) It was staying in the Viharas during rains
   (d) It was an act of fasting by the monks as punishment

5. Who got excavated the rock-cut caves on Nagarjuni hills?
   (a) Chandragupta Maurya
   (b) Ashoka
   (c) Dasharatha
   (d) Samprati

6. Given below are two statements, one labelled as Assertion (A) and the other labelled as Reason (R):

   Assertion (A): Under Ashoka Mauryan monarchy had taken the shape of military despotism.

   Reason (R): Rock Edicts of Ashoka show him as remarking—"All men are my children".

   In the context of the above two statements which one of the following is correct?

   Codes:
   (a) (A) is correct, but (R) is wrong
   (b) Both (A) and (R) are correct
   (c) (A) is wrong, but (R) is correct
   (d) Both (A) and (R) are wrong

7. Hiuen Tsang visited Kanchi during the rule of which one of the following rulers of Pallava dynasty?

(a) Mahendra Varman–I
(b) Paramesvara Varman–I
(c) Narasimha Varman–I
(d) Narasimha Varman–II

8. Match List I with List II and choose your answer from the codes given below:

List I (Inscriptions)
(A) Bilahari Stone Inscription
(B) Mehrauli Pillar Inscription
(C) Hathigumpha Inscription
(D) Mandsaur Pillar Inscription

List II (Rulers)
(i) Yasodharman
(ii) Kharavela
(iii) Chandra
(iv) Yuvarajadeva

Codes:	A	B	C	D
(a)	(iv)	(ii)	(iii)	(i)
(b)	(ii)	(iii)	(i)	(iv)
(c)	(i)	(iv)	(iii)	(ii)
(d)	(iii)	(iv)	(i)	(ii)

9. Match List I with List II and select the correct answer from the codes given below:

List I (Authors)
(A) Buddha charita (B) Kiratarjuniyam
(C) Brihatsamhita (D) Rajatarangini

List II (Works)
(i) *Bharavi* (ii) *Ashvaghosha*
(iii) *Varahamihira* (iv) *Kalhana*

Codes:	A	B	C	D
(a)	(i)	(ii)	(iv)	(iii)
(b)	(ii)	(i)	(iv)	(iii)
(c)	(iii)	(iv)	(ii)	(i)
(d)	(iv)	(iii)	(i)	(ii)

10. Dhoyi was the court poet of which one of the following rulers of the Sena dynasty of Bengal?
(a) Hemantasena
(b) Vijayasena
(c) Vallalasena
(d) Lakshmanasena

11. Who among the following described Delhi as the largest city in the entire 'Islamic East'?
(a) Alberuni (b) Amir Khusrav
(c) Ibn Battuta (d) Shms Siraj Afif

12. The Portuguese captured Goa from the Sultan of Bijapur in:
(a) 1496 (b) 1510
(c) 1524 (d) 1558

13. Which of the following works deal with music?
(1) Man-kutuhal
(2) Tuhfat-ul Hind
(3) Madhavanala-Kamkandala
(4) Kitab-i-Nauras

Codes:
(a) 1, 2, 3 (b) 1, 3, 4
(c) 2, 3, 4 (d) 1, 2, 4

14. Which of the following represents Palaeolithic?
(a) Microliths
(b) Madras industry
(c) Neoliths
(d) Megaliths

15. Which among the following is associated with Mesolithic?
(a) Sohan (b) Burzahom
(c) Bhimbitaka (d) Shortughai

16. Which of the following stands for New Stone age?
(a) Hunting
(b) Pastoralism
(c) Scavenging
(d) Food production

17. Which among the following denotes Harappa Civilization?
(a) Malwa Culture
(b) Gandhar Grave Culture

(c) Megalithic Culture
(d) Sothi Culture

18. Given below are two statements, one labelled Assertion (A) and the other labelled Reason (R):
Assertion (A): Kushan period in ancient Indian history is the most prosperous period.
Reason (R): We witness all round development during this period.
Read the above statements and select the correct answer from the codes given below:
Codes:
(a) (A) is correct, but (R) false
(b) (A) is false, but (R) true
(c) Both (A) and (R) are incorrect
(d) Both (A) and (R) are correct

19. Given below are two statements, one labelled Assertion (A) and the other labelled Reason (R):
Assertion (A): Beginning of land grants in Gupta period is associated with the inception of feudalism.
Reason (R): This was imperative for economic development.
Read the above statements and select the correct answer from the codes given below:
Codes:
(a) (A) is correct, but (R) is incorrect
(b) (A) is false, but (R) true
(c) Both (A) and (R) are incorrect
(d) Both (A) and (R) are true

20. Given below are two statements, one labelled Assertion (A) and the other labelled Reason (R):
Assertion (A): Arabs invaded India in the first half of the 8th century A.D.
Reason (R): They were inspired by the imperialistic considerations.
Read the above statements and select the correct answer from the codes given below:
Codes:
(a) Both (A) and (R) are true
(b) Both (A) and (R) are incorrect
(c) (A) is true, but (R) is false
(d) (A) is untrue, but (R) is true

21. Arrange the following into sequential order and select the correct answer from the codes given below:
1. Chalcolithic age 2. Iron age
3. Bronze age 4. Stone age
Codes:
(a) 3, 2, 1, 4 (b) 2, 1, 4, 3
(c) 4, 3, 1, 2 (d) 1, 4, 2, 3

22. Arrange the following into sequential order and select the correct answer from the codes given below:
1. *Rajatarangini*
2. *Harsh Charit*
3. *Prithvi Raj Raso*
4. *Sangam literature*
Codes:
(a) 4, 3, 2, 1 (b) 3, 4, 1, 2
(c) 1, 3, 2, 4 (d) 4, 2, 1, 3

23. Arrange the following in chronological sequence and select the correct answer from the codes given below:
1. Chakravartin 2. Maharaja
3. Maharajadhiraj 4. Rajan
Codes:
(a) 3, 2, 1, 4 (b) 4, 3, 2, 1
(c) 2, 1, 3, 4 (d) 4, 2, 3, 1

24. Which of the order below is correct? Select the correct answer from the codes given below:
1. Ganga kingdom
2. Arab invasion
3. Mahender Pallava
4. Rise of Hoysala power

Codes:
(a) 3, 2, 1, 4 (b) 4, 3, 2, 1
(c) 2, 1, 4, 3 (d) 1, 2, 3, 4

25. Match List I with List II and select the correct answer from the codes given below:

List I
(A) Sabha and Samiti
(B) Northern Black Polished Ware
(C) Girnar inscription
(D) Devanam Piyon

List II
(i) Rudradaman
(ii) Gangetic plain
(iii) Ashoka
(iv) Vedic period

Codes:	A	B	C	D
(a)	(ii)	(iv)	(iii)	(i)
(b)	(ii)	(iv)	(i)	(iii)
(c)	(iv)	(ii)	(i)	(iii)
(d)	(ii)	(i)	(iv)	(iii)

26. Match List I with List II and select the correct answer from the codes given below:

List I
(A) Bodhisattva
(B) Dravid Style of architecture
(C) Mihirkula
(D) Chandella

List II
(i) Jejakbhukti (ii) Huna
(iii) South India (iv) Buddhism

Codes:	A	B	C	D
(a)	(iv)	(iii)	(i)	(ii)
(b)	(i)	(iii)	(ii)	(iv)
(c)	(iv)	(iii)	(ii)	(i)
(d)	(i)	(iv)	(ii)	(iii)

27. Match List I with List II and select the correct answer from the codes given below:

List I
(A) Etched Carnelian bead
(B) Copper
(C) Bary gaza
(D) Tamralipti

List II
(i) Bengal (ii) Port
(iii) Harappa (iv) Rajasthan

Codes:	A	B	C	D
(a)	(iv)	(ii)	(iii)	(i)
(b)	(iv)	(i)	(ii)	(iii)
(c)	(iv)	(iii)	(ii)	(i)
(d)	(iii)	(iv)	(ii)	(i)

28. When did Sher Shah Suri annex Malwa?
(a) 1540 (b) 1541
(c) 1542 (d) 1543

29. Who was awarded the title of Mirza Raja?
(a) Bhar Mal (b) Jai Singh
(c) Jaswant Singh (d) Raj Singh

30. In Maratha administration, *Majumdar* was?
(a) Accountant
(b) Secretary
(c) Government Official
(d) Cashier

31. Battle of Haldighati was fought between:
(a) Mughals and Amber
(b) Mughals and Kota
(c) Mughals and Mewar
(d) Mughals and Marwar

32. Arrange the following in correct sequence:
(a) Alauddin Masud Shah, Razia Sultan, Moizuddin Bahramshah, Ruknuddin Firuzshah
(b) Ruknuddin Firuzshah, Razia Sultan, Moizuddin Bahramshah, Alauddin Masud Shah
(c) Razia Sutlan, Alauddin Masud Shah, Ruknuddin Firuzshah, Moizuddin Bahramshah
(d) Moizuddin Bahramshah, Alauddin Masud Shah, Ruknuddin Firuzshah, Razia Sultan

33. The Act of 1919 provided for:
    (a) a separate and simultaneous ICS examination to be held in India.
    (b) a separate, but not simultaneous, ICS examination to be held in India.
    (c) reservation for Indians in the ICS examination.
    (d) holding of the ICS examination in Bombay, Calcutta and Madras.

34. Which of the following concepts is not associated with the non-cooperation movement?
    (a) Atmasakti (b) Non-violence
    (c) Boycott (d) Charka

35. The filature is a system related to:
    (a) cotton weaving (b) iron-smelting
    (c) silk-reeling (d) copper working

36. Who had evolved the concept of the drain of wealth?
    (a) Bankim Chandra Chatterjee
    (b) Romesh Dutt
    (c) Dadabhai Naoroji
    (d) Bipin Chandra

37. Given below are two statements, one labelled Assertion (A) and the other labelled Reason (R):
    Assertion (A): The Revolt of 1857 marked an important watershed in the evolution of British policies towards the Indian states.
    Reason (R): The Revolt of 1857 ended the rule of the East India Company.
    In the context of the above two statements, which one of the following is correct?
    Codes:
    (a) Both (A) and (R) are true and (R) is the correct explanation of (A).
    (b) Both (A) and (R) are true but (R) does not explain (A).
    (c) (A) is true and (R) is false.
    (d) (A) is false and (R) is true.

38. Given below are two statements, one labelled Assertion (A) and the other labelled Reason (R).
    Assertion (A): Gandhi for the first time had made untouchability an issue of public concern.
    Reason (R): He wanted to broaden the social base of the Congress.
    In the context of the above two statements, which one of the following is correct?
    Codes:
    (a) Both the statements are false.
    (b) (A) is true and (R) is false.
    (c) Both (A) and (R) are true but (R) does not explain (A).
    (d) Both (A) and (R) are true and (R) explains (A).

39. The Nazi Soviet Pact was signed in:
    (a) 1937 (b) 1938
    (c) 1939 (d) 1940

40. Which country disagreed with England and France over colonial issues in 1940s?
    (a) America (b) Russia
    (c) Germany (d) Italy

41. Identify the non-commonwealth country from the following:
    (a) Pakistan (b) Nepal
    (c) Sri Lanka (d) Myanmar

42. Research is a studious search for :
    (a) Identification (b) Facts
    (c) Hunt for material (d) Hypothesis

43. Match List I with List II and select the correct answer form the codes given below:
    List I
    (A) Ali Muhammad Khan
    (B) Zia-ud-din Barani
    (C) Bhim Sen
    (D) Inayat Khan
    List II
    (i) Nuskha-i-Dilkusha
    (ii) Mirat-i-Ahmadi

(iii) Shahjahan Nama
(iv) Fatawa-i-Jahandari

Codes:	**A**	**B**	**C**	**D**
(a)	(ii)	(iv)	(i)	(iii)
(b)	(i)	(iii)	(iv)	(ii)
(c)	(iv)	(ii)	(i)	(iii)
(d)	(iii)	(iv)	(ii)	(i)

44. Match List I with List II and select the correct answer form the codes given below:

List I	**List II**
(A) Shah Mir	(i) Jajnagar
(B) Zafar Khan	(ii) Khandesh
(C) Malik Raja	(iii) Kashmir
(D) Jauna Khan	(iv) Gujarat

Codes:	**A**	**B**	**C**	**D**
(a)	(i)	(iv)	(ii)	(iii)
(b)	(ii)	(i)	(iii)	(iv)
(c)	(iii)	(iv)	(ii)	(i)
(d)	(iv)	(ii)	(iii)	(i)

45. Given below are two statements, one labelled as Assertion (A), and the other labelled as Reason (R):
Assertion (A): During the seventeenth century India, the economic growth stimulated by the growing importance of a new external connection : the link between Mughal India and early modern Europe.
Reason (R): Each trading concern in Mughal India operated under a Royal Charter which granted it exclusive national rights to carry out the India trade.
In the context of the above two statements, which one of the following is correct?
Codes:
(a) (A) is correct, but (R) is wrong
(b) Both (A) and (R) are correct
(c) (A) is wrong, but (R) is correct
(d) Both (A) and (R) are wrong

46. Given below are two statements, one labelled Assertion (A) and the other labelled Reason (R):
Assertion (A): What occured in India under British rule was at the most aborted modernization, typical of modern colonial economic structure.
Reason (R): British persistently followed the policy of turning India into an agriculture country.
In the context of the above two statements, which one of the following is correct?
Codes:
(a) Both (A) and (R) are true and (R) is only the partial explanation of (A).
(b) Both (A) and (R) are true and (R) fully explains (A).
(c) (A) is true and (R) is false.
(d) Both (A) and (R) are false.

47. Arrange the following in chronological order:
1. Age of Consent Act
2. Deccan Agricultural Relief Act
3. Police Act
4. Universities Act

Codes:
(a) 1, 3, 2, 4 (b) 3, 2, 1, 4
(c) 3, 1, 2, 4 (d) 3, 2, 4, 1

48. Match the List I with List II using the code:
List I
(A) Prosperous British India
(B) The History of British India
(C) The Economic History of India
(D) Origins of Nationality in South Asia

List II
(i) C.A. Bayly (ii) R.C. Dutt
(iii) William Digley (iv) James Mill

Codes:	**A**	**B**	**C**	**D**
(a)	(ii)	(iii)	(i)	(iv)
(b)	(iii)	(iv)	(ii)	(i)
(c)	(iii)	(i)	(ii)	(iv)
(d)	(iv)	(iii)	(ii)	(i)

49. Match the List I with List II using the code:

List I
(A) Permanent Settlement
(B) Ryotwari Settlement
(C) Mahalwari Settlement
(D) Bombay Survey System

List II
(i) Alexander Reed
(ii) Thomas Law
(iii) Holt Mackenzie
(iv) G. Wingate

Codes:	A	B	C	D
(a)	(ii)	(i)	(iv)	(iii)
(b)	(ii)	(i)	(iii)	(iv)
(c)	(iii)	(iv)	(ii)	(i)
(d)	(iv)	(iii)	(ii)	(i)

50. Match the List I with List II using the code:

List I
(A) William Jones
(B) Charles Grant
(C) Thomas Macaulay
(D) Thomas Munro

List II
(i) Evangelicalism (ii) Utilitarianism
(iii) Orientalism (iv) Liberalism

Codes:	A	B	C	D
(a)	(iv)	(ii)	(iii)	(i)
(b)	(iii)	(i)	(iv)	(ii)
(c)	(iii)	(ii)	(i)	(iv)
(d)	(iii)	(iv)	(ii)	(i)

PAPER–III

1. **Assertion (A):** The megaliths emerged around the end of the second and beginning of the first millennium B.C.
Reason (R): They were known not from their actual settlements but from their graves, which are called megaliths as the graves were encircled by big pieces of stone.
(a) Both (A) and (R) are true and (R) is the correct explanation of (A)
(b) Both (A) and (R) are true but (R) is not the correct explanation of (A)
(c) (A) is true but (R) is false
(d) (A) is false but (R) is true

2. One consistent feature found in the history of southern India was the growth of small regional kingdoms rather than large empires because of
(a) the scarcity of manpower
(b) the absence of vast areas of fertile land
(c) too many divisions in the social structure
(d) the absence of minerals like iron

3. The *Chronographis* is written by
(a) Erich Brandenburg
(b) Sigebert of Gemblous
(c) Freytag
(d) Richer

4. The Indus Valley Civilization people built up their homes of
(a) Baked-bricks (b) Unbaked-bricks
(c) Mud (d) Stones

5. Who has associated history with political science?
(a) James Mill
(b) Renier
(c) Prof. Seeley
(d) None of the above

6. Match the following List I and II. Select the correct answers by using the codes given below the lists.

List I
(A) Kalibangan (B) Lothal
(C) Mohenjodaro (D) Harappa

List II
(i) This place seems to have been an outpost for sea trade with contemporary West Asian societies.

(ii) In terms of its size and variety of objects discovered, it ranks as the premier city of the Harappan civilization.
(iii) This settlement was located along the dried-up-bed of the river Ghaggar and has yielded evidence for the existence of Pre-Harappan and Harappan habitation.
(iv) Excavations begun at this site in 1912 show that people lived here for a very long time and went on building and rebuilding houses at the same location so that the height of the remains of the building and the debris is above 20 metres.

Codes:	A	B	C	D
(a)	(ii)	(iii)	(iv)	(i)
(b)	(iii)	(iv)	(i)	(ii)
(c)	(iii)	(i)	(iv)	(ii)
(d)	(iv)	(ii)	(iii)	(i)

7. Which one of the following poets of the Sangam Age has referred to a Mauryan expedition against a Tamil chieftain?
(a) Paranar (b) Avvaiyar
(c) Ilango Adigal (d) Mamulanar

8. At Lothal, which was an important industry that was adopted?
(a) Terracota toys (b) Ship-building
(c) Bead making (d) Pottery

9. Voltaire wrote which of the following books?
(a) *History of Charles XII, King of Sweden*
(b) *The Age of Louis XIV*
(c) Both (a) and (b)
(d) None of the above

10. The first metal to be used was
(a) Bronze (b) Copper
(c) Iron (d) Silver

11. Which of the following is/are the constituent/s of historical research?
(a) Sub-ordination of the data to a principle.
(b) Addition of New area.
(c) New interpretation of known data.
(d) All of the above.

12. Technological developments during the Neolithic Age led to a gradual production of surplus foodstuffs which supported what has been called
(a) Green revolution
(b) Industrial revolution
(c) Agricultural revolution
(d) Urban revolution

13. Tondaiman Ilandiraiyan, a contemporary of Karikala, himself a poet ruled the territory known as
(a) Kaveri (b) Nangur
(c) Kanchipuram (d) Auvaiyar

14. Agriculture was practised in Rajasthan and Kashmir as far back as
(a) 3000 B.C. (b) 5000 B.C.
(c) 6000 B.C. (d) 8000 B.C.

15. *Parallel Lives* is written by which author?
(a) Diodorus Siculus (b) Strabo
(c) Dio Cassius (d) Plutarch

16. 'Numismatics' is the branch of science dealing with
(a) Study of Rocks
(b) Study of Coins
(c) Study of Plants
(d) Study of Fossils

17. Important crops like rice, wheat and barley, came to be cultivated in the sub-continent during the
(a) Indus Valley around 2500 B.C.
(b) Neolithic Age
(c) Paleolithic Age
(d) Seventh Millennium B.C.

18. Which of the following historical books was not written by L.B. Namier?
(a) *The Structure of Policies at the Accession of George III*

(b) *The Rise of the Century*
(c) *1848: The Revolution of the Intellectuals*
(d) *England in the Age of the American Revolution*

19. Which among the following excavated sites is related to Malwa culture?
(a) Eran (b) Azadnagar
(c) Navadatoli (d) Nagda

20. South of the Deccan plateau in the Sangam age, three kingdoms arose. Point the odd one out.
(a) Pandyas (b) Cheras
(c) Cholas (d) Pallavas

21. No trace of ______ has been found in the Indus Valley civilisation
(a) barley (b) sesamum
(c) mustard (d) sugarcane

22. The story of Kannagi and Kovalan that refer to the Pattini cult, i.e. worshipping the Kannagi as an ideal wife is found in
(a) Viyalur
(b) Kodukar
(c) Silappadikaram
(d) Senguttuvan

23. Which of the given below features is not applicable to the Indus sites?
(a) Artifacts of royal trappings were identified
(b) The roads were straight and intersected each other at right angles thus dividing the cities into large rectangular blocks
(c) The commodious houses of the citizenry being double-storied were made of burnt bricks and stone
(d) Its separation of the city into two parts, a citadel consisting of monumental buildings and a lower town where the citizens lived

24. **Assertion (A):** The Bhakti movement in the South was led by a series of popular saints called Nayanars and Alvars.
Reason (R): There were 63 Nayanars (Shaiva saints) the most important being Appar, Nanasambandhar and Sundaramurti.
Codes:
(a) If both (A) and (R) are true and (R) is the correct explanation of (A)
(b) If both (A) and (R) are true but (R) is not the correct explanaton of (A)
(c) If (A) is true but (R) is false
(d) If (A) is false but (R) is true

25. Which of the statements regarding Samudragupta's conquests is incorrect?
(a) The king of Ceylon paid tribute
(b) The tribal chief of Central India and the Deccan were defeated and accepted suzerainty
(c) The Malavas and Yaudheyas (republics) were compelled to accept the Gupta supremacy
(d) He conquered four Northern kingdoms around Delhi

26. Which of the following was the most commonly seen form during the Black Death?
(a) Bubonic plague
(b) Pneumonic plague
(c) Septicemic plague
(d) Freckle-like spots and rashes

27. Who built the famous Kailashanath Temple of Kanchipuram?
(a) Nandivarman II
(b) Rajasimha
(c) Narsimhavarman I
(d) Aparajita

28. The objectives of the Commonwealth first outlined in the 1971 Singapore Declaration are a commitment to

1. world peace and free trade
2. promotion of representative democracy and individual liberty
3. the pursuit of equality and opposition to racism
4. the fight against poverty, ignorance, and disease

Codes:

(a) 1, 2 and 3 (b) 1, 3 and 4
(c) 2, 3 and 4 (d) 1, 2, 3 and 4

29. Which new route was added for foreign trade during Gupta period?
(a) Overseas route to Alexandria
(b) Overseas route to South Africa
(c) Overland route to North Russia
(d) Overland route to China

30. **Assertion (A):** The Himalayas is responsible for making the Indo-Gangetic plains a vast well-watered garden, swarming with population.
Reason (R): This was the reason for Asian nomadism.
Codes:
(a) If both (A) and (R) are true and (R) is the correct explanation of (A)
(b) If both (A) and (R) are true but (R) is not the correct explanaton of (A)
(c) If (A) is true but (R) is false
(d) If (A) is false but (R) is true

31. Match List I with List II and select the correct answer from the codes given below the lists

List I

(A) Napoleon
(B) Jean Jacques
(C) Croce
(D) Madame Roland

List II

(i) 'A history is Bonaparte contemporary history'
(ii) 'Liberty what Rousseau crimes are committed in thy name'
(iii) 'Man is born free but everywhere he is in chains'
(iv) 'I am the Child of Revolution'

Codes:	**A**	**B**	**C**	**D**
(a)	(iv)	(iii)	(i)	(ii)
(b)	(i)	(ii)	(iii)	(iv)
(c)	(ii)	(iii)	(iv)	(i)
(d)	(iii)	(iv)	(ii)	(i)

32. In the regions ruled by which one of the following dynasties, the state formation had been described as Secondary State?
(a) Chalukyas (b) Satavahanas
(c) Rashtrakutas (d) Gangas

33. "Return home with your shield or on it". The meaning of the saying of Romans was
(a) return home safely.
(b) run away from the battle field with your/Shield if enemy is stronger than you.
(c) return home from the battle with your arms.
(d) either return with victory or die in battle field.

34. In Sanskrit plays written during the Gupta period women and sudras speak
(a) Sauraseni (b) Pali
(c) Prakrit (d) Sanskrit

35. The large residential university established in ancient time was at
(a) Nalanda (b) Harappa
(c) Cochin (d) Vaishali

36. The Rishi *Silsilah* refers to an order of sufi saints in:
(a) Kashmir (b) Ajmer
(c) Hyderabad (d) Agra

37. Which of the features listed below were inapplicable to Bhagavata religious sect?
(a) The Bhagavata religion centred round idea of a supreme God
(b) It was related to the worship of Vasudeva Krishna

(c) The Bhagvatas also had a pantheon of lesser gods
(d) This religion accepted the view that salvation was possible by His grace alone

38. Which Gupta emperor has been called 'Lichchhavi-dauhitra'?
(a) Chandragupta I
(b) Shrigupta
(c) Samudragupta
(d) Chandragupta II

39. Samudragupta's achievements are mentioned in the
(a) *Indica*
(b) *Allahabad Prasasti*
(c) *Kaling edict*
(d) *Hathigumpha edict*

40. Who spoke the following words:
"Long years ago we made a tryst with destiny"?
(a) Jawaharlal Nehru
(b) Gopal Krishna Gokhale
(c) Gandhiji
(d) Raja Rammohan Roy

41. In which year was India's capital shifted from Calcutta to Delhi?
(a) 1911 (b) 1929
(c) 1935 (d) 1900

42. The Central Establishment Board was set up in
(a) 1977 (b) 1970
(c) 1958 (d) 1957

43. Government share in public sector should be more than
(a) 80% (b) 75%
(c) 51% (d) 26%

44. Which of the following peasant movements is not properly matched with the state in which it was launched?
(a) Moplah rebellion — Kerala
(b) Pabna Agrarian League — Maharashtra
(c) Kisan Sabha and Ekta (unity) movements — Uttar Pradesh
(d) Bardoli Satyagraha — Gujarat

45. During the pre-reforms period, Industrial license was issued by
(a) Finance Ministry
(b) Industry Ministry
(c) Planning Commission
(d) Director General of Technical Development

46. Which of the following statements about Harappan civilization are true?
1. The Harappans seem to have used both the foot and the cubit systems of measurement simultaneously
2. The Harappan bricks were mainly made in an open mould
3. Their foot system of measurement ranged from 16 to 32 cm and cubit from 48 to 64 cm.
4. At Harappa, a fragmentary bronze rod, broken at both ends seems to have been based on the standard cubit

Codes:
(a) 1, 2 and 4 (b) 2, 3 and 4
(c) 1, 2 and 3 (d) All of the above

47. Jawaharlal Nehru was influenced by
(a) Leninist socialism
(b) Maoist socialism
(c) Fabian socialism
(d) Marxist socialism

48. When did majority of countries adopt the Panch Shila?
(a) 1960 (b) 1975
(c) 1956 (d) 1955

49. What is the full form of AITUC?
(a) All India Trade Union Conglomerate
(b) All India Trade Union Congregation
(c) All India Trade Union Corporation
(d) All India Trade Union Congress

50. In South India the main theatre of tribal upsurge was

(a) Palkonda
(b) Gumsur
(c) Visakhapatnam (agency)
(d) Madras Presidency

ANSWERS SHEET

PAPER—I

1. (b)	2. (c)	3. (d)	4. (d)	5. (a)
6. (c)	7. (d)	8. (c)	9. (c)	10. (b)
11. (b)	12. (b)	13. (a)	14. (b)	15. (b)
16. (c)	17. (d)	18. (b)	19. (a)	20. (c)
21. (a)	22. (c)	23. (c)	24. (b)	25. (b)
26. (b)	27. (d)	28. (d)	29. (b)	30. (c)
31. (c)	32. (b)	33. (b)	34. (c)	35. (a)
36. (b)	37. (a)	38. (c)	39. (a)	40. (c)
41. (b)	42. (b)	43. (c)	44. (b)	45. (c)
46. (c)	47. (b)	48. (b)	49. (d)	50. (b)

PAPER—II

1. (b)	2. (d)	3. (b)	4. (a)	5. (b)
6. (c)	7. (c)	8. (d)	9. (b)	10. (d)
11. (c)	12. (b)	13. (d)	14. (a)	15. (c)
16. (d)	17. (d)	18. (d)	19. (a)	20. (c)
21. (c)	22. (d)	23. (d)	24. (a)	25. (a)
26. (c)	27. (d)	28. (c)	29. (b)	30. (a)
31. (c)	32. (b)	33. (a)	34. (d)	35. (c)
36. (c)	37. (a)	38. (d)	39. (c)	40. (a)
41. (b)	42. (b)	43. (a)	44. (c)	45. (b)
46. (a)	47. (b)	48. (b)	49. (a)	50. (d)

PAPER—III

1. (a)	2. (b)	3. (b)	4. (a)	5. (c)
6. (c)	7. (d)	8. (b)	9. (c)	10. (b)
11. (d)	12. (d)	13. (c)	14. (c)	15. (d)
16. (b)	17. (b)	18. (b)	19. (c)	20. (d)
21. (d)	22. (c)	23. (a)	24. (b)	25. (b)
26. (a)	27. (b)	28. (d)	29. (b)	30. (b)
31. (a)	32. (c)	33. (d)	34. (c)	35. (a)
36. (a)	37. (c)	38. (a)	39. (b)	40. (a)
41. (a)	42. (d)	43. (c)	44. (b)	45. (d)
46. (a)	47. (c)	48. (d)	49. (d)	50. (c)

MOCK TEST–5
PAPER–I

1. Which among the following gives more freedom to the learner to interact?
   (a) Small group discussion
   (b) Lectures by experts
   (c) Use of film
   (d) Viewing country-wide classroom program on TV
2. While designing communication strategy feed-forward studies are conducted by
   (a) Media (b) Audience
   (c) Communicator (d) Satellite
3. A theory is correct because
   (a) its derivations match with most observations
   (b) its advocate has written a big volume to establish it
   (c) it is supported by a large number of scholars
   (d) it has a large number of followers
4. Which of the following are true about the concepts?
   I. Concepts have different meanings in different contents.
   II. Concepts are the blocks from which theories are built.
   III. Concepts are ideas, abstractions, that do not have meaning in themselves.
   (a) Only II (b) I and III
   (c) I and II (d) All of these

5. The most sensible idea about teaching and research is that
   (a) they interfere with each other
   (b) they are two entirely different kinds of activities
   (c) they cannot go together
   (d) they are two sides of the same coin
6. Which of the following is quality of a teacher?
   (a) He should know the child psychology
   (b) He should evoke curiosity of the pupils by presenting the subject matter in an effective manner with clear explaining leading to better understanding of the matter
   (c) He should be trained in various teaching methodologies
   (d) All of these
7. Which of the following is/are true about research?
   (i) Gives emphasis to the development of theories, principles and generalisation, which are very helpful in accurate prediction regarding the variable understudy.
   (ii) It is always directed towards the solution of a problem.
   (iii) It is always based upon empirical or observable evidences.
   (a) Both (i) and (ii)
   (b) Both (i) and (iii)
   (c) Both (ii) and (iii)
   (d) All of the above
8. Which of the following methods of teaching encourages the use of maximum senses?
   (a) Team teaching method
   (b) Problem-solving method
   (c) Laboratory method
   (d) Self-study method
9. A non-fictional literary composition that forms an independent part of a publication, as a newspaper or magazine is known as
   (a) Symposium (b) Paper
   (c) Article (d) None of these
10. Photo bleeding means
    (a) Photo placement
    (b) Photo cropping
    (c) Photo colour adjustment
    (d) Photo cutting
11. Attitudes, concepts, skills and knowledge are products of
    (a) Explanation (b) Learning
    (c) Research (d) Heredity
12. To study the relationship of family size with income a researcher classifies his population into different income slabs and then takes a random sample from each slab. Which technique of sampling does he adopt?
    (a) Systematic Sampling
    (b) Random Sampling
    (c) Stratified Random Sampling
    (d) Cluster Sampling
13. In business communication, the major obstacles arise because of the
    (a) psychological barriers
    (b) physical barriers
    (c) organisational barriers
    (d) mechanical barriers
14. The most important question that a researcher is interested to use statistical techniques in his problem then he has to see
    (a) whether worthwhile inferences could be drawn
    (b) whether the data could be quantified
    (c) whether appropriate statistical techniques are available
    (d) whether analysis of data would be possible
15. How can the objectivity of the research be enhanced?
    (a) Through its validity
    (b) Through its impartiality

(c) Through its reliability
(d) All of these

16. Which one of the following is not correct? A belief becomes a scientific truth when it
(a) can be replicated
(b) is established experimentally
(c) is arrived by logically
(d) is accepted by many people

17. **Statements:** All cars are ducks. All ducks are birds.

Conclusions:
(i) All birds are cars.
(ii) All cars are birds.
Choose the correct one.
(a) Only conclusion (i) follows
(b) Only conclusion (ii) follows
(c) Both (i) and (ii) follow
(d) Neither (i) nor (ii) follows

18. Research can be conducted by a person who
(a) is a hard worker
(b) has studied research methodology
(c) holds a postgraduate degree
(d) possesses thinking and reasoning ability

19. Action-research is
(a) A longitudinal research
(b) An applied research
(c) A research carried out to solve immediate problems
(d) All of the above

Read the following passage and answer the questions 20 to 24:

The genesis of service tax emanates from the ongoing structural transformation of the Indian economy, whereby presently more than one-half of GDP originates from the services sector. Despite the growing presence of the services sector in the Indian economy it remained out of the tax net prior to 1994-95, leading to a steady deterioration in tax-GDP ratio. The service tax was introduced in 1994-95 on a select category of services at a low rate of five percent. While the service tax rate and the coverage of services being taxed have increased ever since, the combined tax-GDP ratio of the Centre and States, nevertheless, deteriorated from 16.4 percent in 1985-86 to 14.1 percent in 1999-2000. It may be noted that between 1990-91 and 1998-99, the share of industrial sector in GDP dropped by 6.4 percentage points whereas almost 64 percent of the tax revenue was generated by indirect taxes for which industrial sector continues to be the principal tax base. On the other hand, during the same period, the share of services sector in GDP has increased by 10 percentage points and this sector has still remained poorly taxed.

The rationale for service tax, therefore, lies not only in arresting the falling tax-GDP ratio but also in *ipso facto* improving allocative efficiency in the economy as well as promoting equity. Against this backdrop, the service tax needs to be designed taking into account the fact that (i) the share of services in GDP is expanding; (ii) failure to tax services distorts consumer choices and encourages spending on services at the expense of goods; (iii) untaxed service traders are unable to claim Value Added Tax (VAT) on service inputs, which encourages businesses to develop in-house services, creating further distortions; and (iv) most services that are likely to become taxable are positively correlated with expenditure of high-income households and, therefore, service tax improves equity.

In the Indian context, taxation of services assumes importance in the wake of the need for improving the revenue system, ensuring a measure of neutrality in taxation between goods and services and eventually helping to evolve an efficient system of domestic trade taxes, both at the Central and the State levels.

20. What, according to the passage, was the impact of exclusion of service tax till the first half of the last decade of the past century?
    (a) Service sector used to flourish exorbitantly
    (b) There was no impact as there was no service tax
    (c) There was a steady deterioration in the GDP
    (d) Tax-GDP ratio had steadily and gradually aggravated

21. Levying service tax is most likely to achieve which of the following?
    (i) Promoting equity.
    (ii) Check on reducing tax-GDP ratio.
    (iii) Enhancement in allocative efficiency.
    (a) Both (ii) and (iii)
    (b) Both (i) and (iii)
    (c) Both (i) and (ii)
    (d) All the three

22. The origin of service tax is attributed to
    (a) metamorphosis of our country's economy
    (b) increase in Gross Domestic Product (GDP)
    (c) existence of service sector
    (d) tax of the future

23. Which of the following factors helps service tax to improve fairness across different economic strata of society?
    (a) It improves revenue system
    (b) Taxable services are mostly those that are utilised by the rich
    (c) Untaxed service traders are prevented from claiming value added tax
    (d) Encouragement to in-house services is effected

24. Which of the following is most likely to provide neutrality to various economic activities?
    (a) Consistency in tax structure and revenue buoyancy
    (b) Increase in revenue buoyancy
    (c) Fairness in tax administration
    (d) Equity and efficiency in various activities

25. Which of the following is classified in the category of the developmental research?
    (a) Descriptive research
    (b) Philosophical research
    (c) Action research
    (d) All the above

26. The education aims at the fullest realisation of all the potentialities of children. It implies that
    I. it is necessary that their attitudes are helpful, encouraging and sympathetic.
    II. teacher and parents must know what children are capable of and what potentialities they possess.
    III. they should provide suitable opportunities and favourable environmental facilities which are conducive to the maximum growth of children.

    Choose the correct one.
    (a) II and III (b) I and III
    (c) I and II (d) All of them

27. How many times has the preamble of Indian constitution been amended so far?
    (a) Once (b) Twice
    (c) Thrice (d) Never

28. The relationship between earth, mountains and forests can be represented as

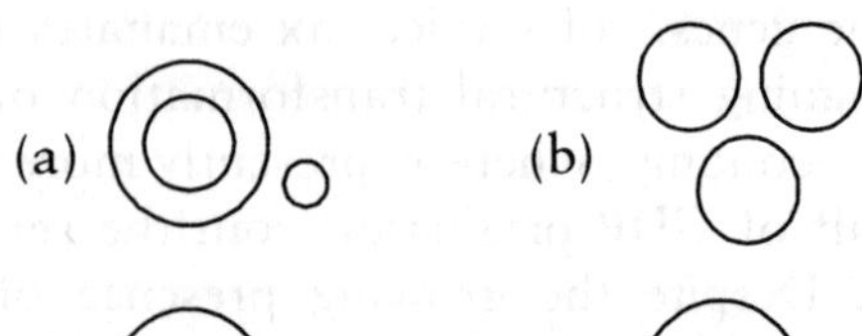

29. Central Fuel Research Institute is situated in
(a) Pune (b) Jadugoda
(c) Lucknow (d) Kolkata

30. The letters in the first set have certain relationship. On the basis of this relationship what is the right choice for the second set?

AST : BRU :: NQV : ?
(a) OPW (b) ORW
(c) MPU (d) MRW

31. The number of students in four classes A, B, C, D and their respective mean marks obtained by each of the class are given below:

	Class A	Class B	Class C	Class D
Number of students	10	40	30	20
Arithmetic mean	20	30	50	15

The combined mean of the marks of four classes together will be
(a) 15 (b) 32
(c) 50 (d) 20

32. Communication with oneself is known as
(a) Organisational communication
(b) Interpersonal communication
(c) Intrapersonal communication
(d) Grapevine communication

33. The number system which is not a positional notation system is
(a) Binary (b) Octal
(c) Roman (d) Decimal

34. Which of the following options will complete the series?
AZ, GT, MN, ?, YB.
(a) TS (b) KF
(c) RX (d) SH

35. If '367' means 'I am happy'; '748' means 'You are sad' and '469' means 'Happy and sad' in a given code, then which of the following represents 'and' in that code?
(a) 4 (b) 6
(c) 3 (d) 9

36. What is the excess 3 code?
(a) self-algebraic code
(b) cyclic complimenting code
(c) cyclic algebraic code
(d) self-complimenting code

37. Which of the following is not created by the Act of Parliament?
(a) Railway Board
(b) Atomic Energy Commission
(c) Backward Class Commission
(d) University Grants Commission

38. Which of the following is radioactive pollutant?
(a) Nickel (b) Iron
(c) Chlorine (d) Thorium

39. The first Indian experimental geostationary communication satellite was
(a) Skylab (b) Apple
(c) INSAT-1A (d) INSAT-1B

40. Which one of the following is a research tool?
(a) Diagram (b) Questionnaire
(c) Graph (d) Illustration

41. Which article of the constitution provides safeguards to Naga Customary and their social practices against any act of Parliament?
(a) Article 371 B (b) Article 371 A
(c) Article 263 (d) Article 371 C

42. **Statement:** Although the city was under kneedeep water for a week in this monsoon, there is no outbreak of any water borne disease.
Assumptions:
(i) Waterborne disease usually spreads in monsoon.
(ii) Water concentration at a place leads to waterborne disease.

Choose the correct option.
(a) Only assumption (i) is implicit
(b) Only assumption (ii) is implicit
(c) Both (i) and (ii) are implicit
(d) Neither (i) nor (ii) is implicit

43. Books and records are the primary sources of data in
(a) laboratory research
(b) historical research
(c) participatory research
(d) clinical research

44. The Kothari Commission's report was entitled on
(a) Learning to be adventure
(b) Education and National Development
(c) Education and socialisation in democracy
(d) Diversification of Education

45. What is the term used for a half byte?
(a) word (b) bit
(c) nibble (d) bug

46. C-band transponder in satellites uses the frequency range
(a) 12 GHz to 14 GHz
(b) 4 GHz to 6 GHz
(c) 2 GHz to 4 GHz
(d) None of these.

47. Which of the following water pollutants is the cause of sterility in human beings?
(a) Manganese (b) Mercury
(c) Arsenic (d) None of these

48. Controlled group condition is applied in
(a) Descriptive Research
(b) Survey Research
(c) Experimental Research
(d) Historical Research

49. Match List I with List II and select the correct answer using the codes given below.
List I (Institutes)
(A) Central Arid Zone Institute
(B) Space Application Centre
(C) Indian Institute of Public Administration
(D) Headquarters of Indian Science Congress

List II (Cities)
(1) Kolkata (2) New Delhi
(3) Ahmedabad (4) Jodhpur

Codes:	**A**	**B**	**C**	**D**
(a)	4	3	2	1
(b)	4	2	1	3
(c)	3	1	2	4
(d)	1	2	4	3

The total CO_2 emissions from various sectors are 5 mmt. In the Pie Chart given below, the percentage contribution to CO_2 emissions from various sectors is indicated.

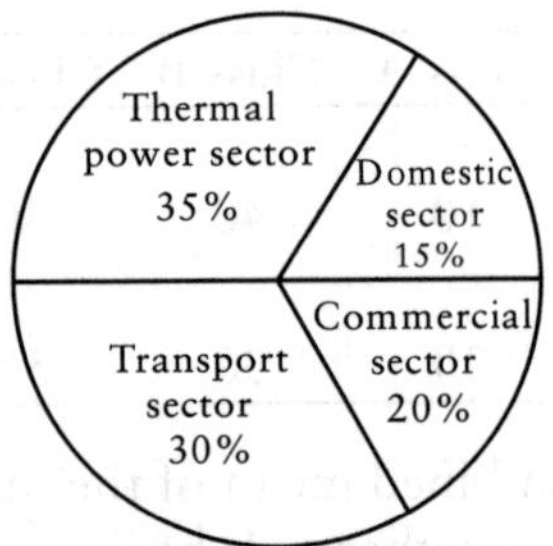

50. What is the absolute CO_2 emission from domestic sector?
(a) 1.75 mmt (b) 0.75 mmt
(c) 1.5 mmt (d) 2.5 mmt

PAPER–II

1. Which of the following is associated with the lower Palaeolithic period?
(a) Homo erectus
(b) Neanderthal
(c) Homo sapiens
(d) Homo sapiens sapiens

2. Which among the following represents the Mesolithic period?
(a) Olduwan tools (b) Hand axe
(c) Triangle tools (d) Polished tools

3. Which among the following denotes the Neolithic period?
(a) Kunal (b) Lothal
(c) Daimabad (d) Chirand

4. Given below are two statements, one is labelled as Assertion (A) and the other is labelled as Reason (R):
Assertion (A): Harappa civilization was developed with the application of copper tools.
Reason (R): This enabled people to make better use of the available natural resources.
Read the above statements and select the correct answer from the codes below:
Codes:
(a) (A) is incorrect, but (R) is true.
(b) Both (A) and (R) are incorrect.
(c) Both (A) and (R) are true.
(d) (A) is correct, but (R) is false.

5. Given below are two statements, one is labelled as Assertion (A) and the other is labelled as Reason (R):
Assertion (A): During the Rig Vedic period the society was pastoral.
Reason (R): The mode of subsistence was primarily based on pastoralism.
Read the above statements and select the correct answer from the codes below:
Codes:
(a) (A) is correct, but (R) is false.
(b) (A) is untrue, but (R) is true.
(c) Both (A) and (R) are false.
(d) Both (A) and (R) are correct.

6. Given below are two statements, one is labelled as Assertion (A) and the other is labelled as Reason (R):
Assertion (A): The rise of religious movements in the 6th century BC was an outcome of prevalent social and economic unrest.
Reason (R): The improved economic condition of the deprived sections of the society embolden them to seek their rightful place.
Read the above statements and select the correct answer from the codes given below:
Codes:
(a) (A) is correct, but (R) is false.
(b) (A) is incorrect, but (R) is true.
(c) Both (A) and (R) are correct.
(d) Both (A) and (R) are incorrect.

7. Given below are two statements, one is labelled as Assertion (A) and the other is labelled as Reason (R):
Assertion (A): Kushana period witnessed large scale cultural integration.
Reason (R): Kushana Kings advocated themselves it by example.
Read the above statements and select the correct answer from the codes given below:
Codes:
(a) (A) is correct, but (R) is incorrect.
(b) (A) is false, but (R) is true.
(c) Both (A) and (R) are false.
(d) Both (A) and (R) are true.

8. Arrange the following into sequential order and select the correct answer from the codes given below:
1. Janapada 2. Mahajanapada
3. Empire 4. Jana
Codes:
(a) 2, 3, 1, 4 (b) 3, 4, 2, 1
(c) 4, 1, 2, 3 (d) 4, 2, 1, 3

9. Arrange the following into sequential order and select the correct answer from the codes given below:
1. Malvikagnimitra 2. Harshacharita
3. Ashtadhyayi 4. Rajatarangini

Codes:
(a) 2, 3, 4, 1 (b) 3, 2, 1, 4
(c) 4, 2, 1, 3 (d) 3, 1, 2, 4

10. Arrange the following into sequential order and select the correct answer from the codes given below:
    1. Pulkeshin–II
    2. Pushyamitra Shunga
    3. Shankaracharya
    4. Chandabaradai

    Codes:
    (a) 2, 1, 3, 4 (b) 1, 3, 2, 4
    (c) 3, 4, 2, 1 (d) 4, 1, 3, 2

11. Match List I with List II and select the correct answer from the codes given below:

    List I
    (A) Levirate
    (B) Punch-marked coins
    (C) Varmanas
    (D) Nalanda

    List II
    (i) Kamrup
    (ii) Rig Veda
    (iii) Bihar
    (iv) Early Historical Period

Codes:	A	B	C	D
(a)	(ii)	(iii)	(i)	(iv)
(b)	(ii)	(iv)	(i)	(iii)
(c)	(iii)	(ii)	(iv)	(i)
(d)	(iv)	(iii)	(ii)	(i)

12. Match List I with List II and select the correct answer from the codes given below:

    List I
    (A) Second (B) Kharavela
    (C) Gautamiputra (D) Vikramadeva

    List II
    (i) Satavahana Urbanization Dynasty
    (ii) Bilhana
    (iii) Orissa
    (iv) Iron Charita

Codes:	A	B	C	D
(a)	(iv)	(i)	(ii)	(iii)
(b)	(iii)	(ii)	(iv)	(i)
(c)	(ii)	(iv)	(iii)	(i)
(d)	(iv)	(iii)	(i)	(ii)

13. Match List I with List II and select the correct answer from the codes given below:

    List I
    (A) Nagar style of
    (B) Shravanabelagola
    (C) Tantrayan
    (D) Mahenderavarman

    List II
    (i) Buddhism architecture
    (ii) Pallava dynasty
    (iii) North India
    (iv) Karnataka Shailey

Codes:	A	B	C	D
(a)	(iii)	(iv)	(i)	(ii)
(b)	(iv)	(i)	(ii)	(iii)
(c)	(ii)	(iv)	(iii)	(i)
(d)	(iv)	(iii)	(i)	(ii)

14. Who among the following Delhi Sultans enlarged the Quwwat-ul-Islam mosque?
    (a) Iltutmish
    (b) Balban
    (c) Alaud-Din Khalji
    (d) Firozshah Tughlaq

15. Who among the following Sultans of Delhi advocated the policy that "follow the middle course in realizing the Kharaj"?
    (a) Balban
    (b) Jalalud-Din Khalji
    (c) Ghyasuddin Tughlaq
    (d) Firoj Tughlaq

16. Which of the following statements are not true about Sultan Ghyasud-Din Tughlaq?
    1. He befriended Shaikh Nizamuddin Aulia.
    2. He gave certain concessions to Khots and Muqaddams.

3. He sent his son Ulugh Khan to recover arrears of tribute from Pratapa Rudra.
4. He levied a tax termed haqq-i-shurb.
Select the correct answer from the codes given below:

Codes:
(a) 1, 2 and 3 (b) 1 and 3
(c) 2 and 3 (d) 2 and 4

17. Match List I with List II and select the correct answer from the codes given below:

List I (Event)
(A) The Mughal conquest of Malwa
(B) Introduction of the Ilahi Era
(C) Annexation of Kashmir in Mughal empire
(D) Conquest of Orissa

List II (Year)
(i) 1584 (ii) 1592
(iii) 1585 (iv) 1561

Codes:	A	B	C	D
(a)	(iii)	(ii)	(i)	(iv)
(b)	(iv)	(i)	(iii)	(ii)
(c)	(i)	(iii)	(iv)	(ii)
(d)	(iii)	(i)	(ii)	(iv)

18. Shahu was set free from the Mughal captivity by:
(a) Aurangzeb
(b) Prince Azam
(c) Prince Kam Bakhsh
(d) Jahandar Shah

19. By which act the British Parliament had abolished the monopoly of East India Company's trade in India?
(a) Regulating Act, 1773
(b) Charter Act, 1813
(c) Charter Act, 1833
(d) Government of India Act, 1858

20. Arrange the following British Legislations concerning women in chronological order:
1. Hindu Widow Remarriage Act
2. The Native Marriage Act (Civil Marriage Act)
3. Abolition of Sati in Bengal Province
4. The Age of Consent Act

Codes:
(a) 3, 1, 2, 4 (b) 1, 2, 3, 4
(c) 4, 2, 1, 3 (d) 2, 3, 4, 1

21. Maulana Shibli Nomani belonged to the
(a) Aligarh School
(b) Deoband Madarsa
(c) Firangi Mahal
(d) Nadwat-ul-ulema

22. Gandhiji's intervention in the Ahmedabad Mill Strike of 1917 led to the enhancement of wages of the workers by
(a) 25% (b) 30%
(c) 35% (d) 40%

23. The chief grievance of the peasants in Champaran Satyagraha (1917) was against the
(a) awabs or illegal cesses
(b) oppression of the landlords
(c) land revenue demand
(d) tinkathia system

24. Who argued that de-industrialization did not take place in India under the colonial rule?
(a) Amiyo Baghchi
(b) Bipan Chandra
(c) Morris D Morris
(d) Toru Matsui

25. Who founded the Hindu College of Calcutta in 1817?
(a) David Hare
(b) William Jones
(c) H.T. Princep
(d) Henry Vivian Derozio

26. Match List I with List II and select the correct answer.

List I
(A) Maulana Abul Kalam Azad
(B) Dadabhai Naoroji
(C) Sir Syed Ahmad Khan
(D) Subhash Chandra Bose

List II
(i) The Indian Struggle
(ii) Asbab-i-Baghawat-i-Hind
(iii) Poverty and Un-British Rule in India
(iv) India Wins Freedom

Codes:	A	B	C	D
(a)	(iv)	(iii)	(ii)	(i)
(b)	(iii)	(ii)	(i)	(iv)
(c)	(ii)	(iv)	(iii)	(i)
(d)	(i)	(ii)	(iii)	(iv)

27. Paramountcy is the position of permanent power enjoyed by the British Government in relation to the
(a) Zamindars
(b) Princely states
(c) Peasants
(d) Christian Missionaries

28. The Congress Ministry in Madras during 1937-39 was headed by
(a) T. Prakasham
(b) Subramanium Bharti
(c) C. Rajgopalachari
(d) K. Kamraj

29. Who was the Chairman of the Drafting Committee of the Indian Constitution?
(a) Dr. Rajendra Prasad
(b) Dr. B.R. Ambedkar
(c) B.N. Rau
(d) Jawaharlal Nehru

30. Arrange the following events in their chronological order:
1. Cripps Mission
2. Quit India Movement
3. Individual Satyagraha
4. August Offer

Codes:
(a) 1, 2, 3, 4 (b) 4, 3, 1, 2
(c) 3, 4, 2, 1 (d) 2, 1, 4, 3

31. Who was known as the father of 'Humanism'?
(a) Dante (b) Erasmus
(c) Machiavelli (d) Petrarch

32. Bullionism and the favourable balance of trade were the basic features of
(a) Colonialism
(b) Commercialism
(c) Free Trade
(d) Mercantilism

33. Match List I with List II and select the correct answer from the codes given below the lists:

List I	List II
(A) Erasmus	(i) Divine Comedy
(B) Machiavelli	(ii) Utopia
(C) Thomas More	(iii) The Prince
(D) Dante	(iv) Praise of Folly

Codes:	A	B	C	D
(a)	(iii)	(ii)	(i)	(iv)
(b)	(ii)	(i)	(iii)	(iv)
(c)	(i)	(ii)	(iii)	(iv)
(d)	(iv)	(iii)	(ii)	(i)

34. Which of the following Harappan sites has yielded evidence of furrow marks in cultivation?
(a) Lothal (b) Banavali
(c) Kalibangan (d) Dhaula Vira

35. Which of the following is not related to the vedic period?
(a) Sabha (b) Samiti
(c) Dharmasana (d) Vidatha

36. The theory of syadvada is associated with:
(a) Buddhism
(b) Jainism
(c) Sankhya philosophy
(d) Vedanta philosophy

37. The Gupta rulers had established matrimonial relations with a number of royal families. Give the answer as per the code.
    1. Vakatakas 2. Lichchhavis
    3. Nagas 4. Sakas

    Codes:
    (a) 1, 2 and 3 (b) 2 and 4
    (c) 1 and 2 (d) 1, 2, 3 and 4

38. Which of the following statements is true about the Kushana period?
    (a) issue of silver coins on a large scale
    (b) flourishing of the Gandhara School of Art
    (c) patronage of Amarsimha
    (d) extension of the Kushana empire upto Bengal

39. Arrange the following in sequence in which they appeared, and select the answer from the code given below:
    1. Abdur Razzaq 2. Bernier
    3. Marco Polo 4. Thomas Roe

    Codes:
    (a) 1, 3, 4, 2 (b) 2, 4, 3, 1
    (c) 3, 1, 4, 2 (d) 4, 2, 1, 3

40. Who among the following Bahmani rulers shifted the Bahmani capital from Gulbarga to Bidar?
    (a) Ahmad Shah
    (b) Firuz Shah
    (c) Muhammad Shah II
    (d) Ghiyasuddin

41. Arrange the following in chronological order. Select the correct answer from the code given below:
    1. Lal Darwaza Masjid
    2. Bara Sona Masjid
    3. Tomb of Ghiyasuddin Tughlaq
    4. Jami Masjid at Ahmedabad

    Codes:
    (a) 4, 1, 3, 2 (b) 3, 4, 1, 2
    (c) 2, 3, 1, 4 (d) 1, 2, 4, 3

42. Given below are two statements, one labelled as Assertion (A), and the other labelled as Reason (R):
    Assertion (A): The medieval Indian culture bears deep imprints of Persian and Central Asian traditions.
    Reason (R): The ruling class patronized only the Persian and Central Asian culture.
    In the context of the above statements, which one of the following is correct?

    Codes:
    (a) Both (A) and (R) are correct, and (R) is the correct explanation of (A)
    (b) Both (A) and (R) are correct, but (R) is not the correct explanation of (A)
    (c) (A) is true, but (R) is false
    (d) (A) is false, but (R) is true

43. Which of the following is not correctly matched?
    (a) Battle of Chausa - June, 1535
    (b) Death of Sher Shah - May, 1545
    (c) Bairam Khan's regency - 1556 to 1560
    (d) Treaty of Purander - 1665

44. Which of the following was not a coin?
    (a) Muzaffari (b) Muhar
    (c) Anna (d) Do dami

45. Given below are two statements, one labelled as Assertion (A), and the other labelled as Reason (R):
    Assertion (A): During the first half of the Eighteenth century the Maratha confederacy achieved its zenith of power ruling over vast territory in western, central and northern India.
    Reason (R): The Rajputs supported the Marathas against the Mughals.
    In the context of the above two statements, which one of the following is correct?

    Codes:
    (a) Both (A) and (R) are true and (R) is the correct explanation of (A)
    (b) Both (A) and (R) are true, but (R) is not the correct explanation of (A)

(c) (A) is true, but (R) is false
(d) (A) is false, but (R) is true

46. Give the chronological sequence of the annexation of the following States by the British:
(a) Bengal, Marathas, Mysore, Sikhs
(b) Sikhs, Bengal, Marathas, Mysore
(c) Bengal, Mysore, Marathas, Sikhs
(d) Mysore, Bengal, Marathas, Sikhs

47. Given below are two statements, one labelled as Assertion (A), and the other labelled as Reason (R):
Assertion (A): Indo-Roman trade activity declined in the 3rd-4th century A.D.
Reason (R): Brahmanical ascendancy in society led to the restrictions on sea-travel.
In the context of the above two statements, which one of the following is correct?
Codes:
(a) (A) is correct, but (R) is wrong
(b) Both (A) and (R) are correct
(c) (A) is wrong, but (R) is correct
(d) Both (A) and (R) are wrong

48. According to Ziauddin Barani the nobles of which of the following sultans were always heavily in debt to the great merchants and money lenders of Delhi?
(a) Balhan
(b) Jalaluddin Khalji
(c) Ghiyasuddin Tughlaq
(d) Muhammad Tughlaq

49. Who among the following was not associated with Arya Samaj?
(a) Dayananda Saraswati
(b) Lala Hansraj
(c) Pandit Haradayal
(d) Lala Lajpat Rai

50. One of the following was not associated with social reform movement.
(a) Behramji Malabari
(b) Mohandas Karamchand Gandhi
(c) Iswarchand Vidyasagar
(d) R.C. Dutt

PAPER–III

1. **Assertion (A):** A major factor in the growth of communalism was the existence of several religions in India.
Reason (R): Communalism was not inspired by religion, nor was religion the object of communal politics—it was only its vehicle.
Codes:
(a) (A) and (R) is both true and (R) is the correct explanation for (A).
(b) (A) and (R) is both true but R is not the correct explanation for (A).
(c) (A) is true, (R) is false.
(d) (A) is false, (R) is true.

2. What was the extremely novel and original method initiated by Mahatma Gandhi to solve the peasants' problems during the Champaran Satyagraha of 1917-18?
(a) He started a Civil Disobedience Movement including non-payment of taxes
(b) He conducted a systematic and authoritative enquiry into the sufferings of the peasants
(c) He induced the peasants to court arrest for refusal to obey the directives of the indigo planters
(d) He undertook a fast unto death

3. Match List I with List II and select the correct answer from the codes given below the lists

List I

(A) Meerut conspiracy case

(B) The enunciation of the new British policy of 'discriminating protection' by the fiscal commission

(C) The laying down of discriminatory policy against the sons of soil in their employment in high position in the government.

(D) The reorganisation of Communist part of India under the leadership of P.C. Joshi after the meeting of Seventh Communist International

List II

(i) 1935 (ii) 1793

(iii) 1921 (iv) 1929

Codes:	A	B	C	D
(a)	(i)	(ii)	(iii)	(iv)
(b)	(ii)	(iv)	(i)	(iii)
(c)	(iv)	(iii)	(ii)	(i)
(d)	(iii)	(i)	(iv)	(ii)

4. In which plan was the lowest growth rate achieved?
   (a) First (b) Second
   (c) Third (d) Fourth

5. As early as 1908 the Indian National Congress had demanded a 'Dominion Status' for India. After how long was it accepted again?
   (a) 21 years (b) 22 years
   (c) 23 years (d) 29 years

6. Bijauliya Movement was related to
   (a) Assam (b) Orissa
   (c) Kerala (d) Rajasthan

7. Who was the person to be arrested in the Kanpur conspiracy case?
   (a) Bhagat Singh
   (b) S.A. Dange
   (c) M.N. Roy
   (d) Ram Prasad Bismil

8. NAM stands for
   (a) National Aid Mission
   (b) Non-Aligned Movement
   (c) National Aeronautical Mission
   (d) Non-Availability Margin

9. When was the first Kisan Sabha formed?
   (a) April 11, 1936 (b) April 19, 1936
   (c) April 22, 1936 (d) None of the above

10. Who is incharge of administrative and executive functions of the Planning Commission?
    (a) Deputy Chairman
    (b) Finance Minister
    (c) Prime Minister
    (d) President of India

11. Which of the following peasant struggles gained prominence in the pre-independence period?
    (a) Wahabi movement
    (b) Bakasht movement
    (c) Telengana movement
    (d) Gadar movement

12. Where was the Asian Relations Conference held?
    (a) Bangkok (b) New Delhi
    (c) Jakarta (d) Peking

13. What were not some of the problems faced in the teething period by the trade union leaders?
    (a) The proprietors of factories etc. used to sue the trade union on criminal charges of instigating the workers
    (b) The British government used to use repressive measures to break the union meetings
    (c) Lack of financial resources
    (d) The lack of willingness on the part of members to enroll as members

14. Which of these is not a source for irrigation?

(a) Water pump (b) Canals
(c) Tanks (d) Wells

15. While the determination of the Indian nationalists leaders grew, they were helped by revolutionaries from abroad. Which party was formed in the United States in 1913?
(a) Indian National Army
(b) Indian Home Rule Society
(c) Ghadar Party
(d) Independence movement in West Asia

16. India is a guiding star for the world in achieving objectives
(a) without tolerating foreign interference
(b) without violence
(c) through democratic means
(d) All the above are correct

17. Where was the decision to boycott the Simon Commission taken?
(a) At the Madras session of the Congress
(b) At the Lucknow session of the National Congress
(c) At the Nagpur session of the Congress
(d) At the Ahmedabad session of the Congress

18. When Gandhiji called off the Satyagraha movement which turned violent in Chauri Chaura in Gorakhpur district without consulting others, some of them protested and called it a national calamity. Who among these is not included?
(a) Abul Kalam Azad
(b) Bal Gangadhar Tilak
(c) Subhas Chandra Bose
(d) Motilal Nehru

19. What was the name of the movement started by Khan Abdul Gaffar Khan against the British?
(a) Red Shirt movement
(b) Khilafat movement
(c) Muslim League
(d) None of the above

20. Self reliance refers to
1. Dependence on foreign aid
2. Ownership in the hands of government
3. Reduction in imports
4. Increase in domestic production

Codes:
(a) 1 and 2 (b) 3 and 4
(c) 1, 2 and 3 (d) 2, 3 and 4

21. Which of the following was not one of the founder office-bearers of the Hindu Mazdoor Sevak Sangh formed in 1938?
(a) Gulzarilal Nanda
(b) N.M. Joshi
(c) Sardar Vallabhbhai Patel
(d) None of the above

22. Match List I with List II and select the correct answer from the codes given below the lists

List I
(A) Social Justice
(B) Freedom of religion
(C) Right to equality
(D) Welfare State

List II
(i) Secularism
(ii) Fundamental rights
(iii) Directive Principles
(iv) Removal of economic inequalities

Codes:	**A**	**B**	**C**	**D**
(a)	(iv)	(i)	(ii)	(iii)
(b)	(i)	(ii)	(iii)	(iv)
(c)	(iii)	(i)	(ii)	(iv)
(d)	(ii)	(iv)	(iii)	(i)

23. **Assertion (A):** Irrigation is an important technological advance in the agricultural sector.
Reason (R): No five year plan outlaid any strategy for increasing irrigation facilities.

Codes:

(a) Both (A) and (R) are true and (R) is the correct explanation for (A)
(b) Both (A) and (R) are true but (R) is not the correct explanation for (A)
(c) (A) is true but (R) is false
(d) (A) is false but (R) is true

24. The first modern trade union founded in India was
(a) Madras Labour Union
(b) Clerks' Union, Bombay
(c) Indian Seamen's Union, Calcutta
(d) M.S.M. Railway Union, Madras

25. Which of the following statements are true with respect to Revivalism in India?
1. Revivalism as an influential tendency emerged only during the second half of the nineteenth century.
2. Bankim Chandra Chatterji, Dayananda Saraswathi and Swami Vivekananda are generally considered the early protagonists of Revivalism.
3. Antagonism against other religions and communities was not a part of the Revivalist perspective.
4. Revivalist perspective was communitarian rather than communal.

Codes:

(a) 1 and 2 only (b) 2 and 4 only
(c) 1, 3 and 4 (d) 1, 2, 3 and 4

26. The word 'bhudan' meant
(a) problems of old age
(b) gift of land
(c) intellectual
(d) old people

27. The historical site wherein an early inscription referring to the five heroes of the Vrishnis is found in
(a) Ghoshandi (b) Mathura
(c) Dwaraka (d) Besnagar

28. The Greek accounts which throw light on ancient Indian history do not include
(a) Megasthenes' *Indica*
(b) Ptolemy's *Geography*
(c) Periplus of the Erythrean Sea
(d) Pliny's *Naturalis Historia*

29. What made possible the transition from the Paleolithic to the Neolithic age?
(a) Making wheels
(b) Learning a script
(c) Making a fire
(d) Growing grain

30. Technological developments during the Neolithic Age led to a gradual production of surplus foodstuffs which supported what has been called
(a) Green revolution
(b) Industrial revolution
(c) Agricultural revolution
(d) Urban revolution

31. **Assertion (A):** The Indo-Aryans came to India from somewhere in central Asia, possibly from the region south of the Urals and east of the Caspian sea.
Reason (R): They had been defeated by the Indo-European neighbours.
(a) Both (A) and (R) are true and (R) is the correct explanation for (A).
(b) Both (A) and (R) are true but (R) is not the correct explanation for (A).
(c) (A) is true but (R) is false.
(d) (A) is false but (R) is true.

32. Many early linguistic expressions were as sociated with cattle as
(a) Cattle raids and lost cattle frequently led to tribal fights
(b) Vedic Aryans were pastoral people
(c) Cow was the measure of value
(d) All the above

33. Alexander remained in India for _____ months

(a) 19 (b) 28
(c) 24 (d) 32

34. Which one of the following was initially the most powerful city state of India in the 6th century B.C.?
(a) Kamboj (b) Gandhar
(c) Magadh (d) Kashi

35. The Jaina text which contains the history of the Tirthankaras is known as
(a) Adi Purana (b) Kalpasutra
(c) Uvasagadasao (d) Bhagavati sutra

36. The name by which Ashoka is generally referred to his inscriptions is
(a) Priyadarsi (b) Chakravarti
(c) Dharmakirti (d) Dharmadeva

37. The Hinayana and Mahayana Schools differed on the issue of fundamental doctrines. But they agreed upon which of the following feature?
(a) Hinayanism accepted the fundamental doctrines of the old school. The Mahayanists introduced the concept of image worship as also the deification of Buddha
(b) Hinayanists regarded salvation of individuals as the goal; whereas the other emphasised on the salvation of all beings
(c) High and lower castes were allowed as devotees
(d) The school of Hinayanism stated that the path to salvation was through observance of the prescribed moral precepts. The Mahayanism school differed and laid stress on worship of Buddha and Boddhisattvas

38. Which one of the following statements regarding Ashokan stone pillars is incorrect?
(a) These are parts of architectural structures
(b) The shaft of pillars is tapering in shape
(c) These are monolithic
(d) These are highly polished

39. The Kushans issued coins of
(a) Gold and Silver
(b) Gold only
(c) Gold, Silver and Copper
(d) Gold and Copper

40. The commercial superintendent in the Mauryan period was known as
(a) Sitadhyaksha
(b) Panyadhyaksha
(c) Shulkadhyaksha
(d) Pautavadhyaksha

41. Nicbur and Ranke were associated with which period?
(a) Pre-Renaissance period
(b) Post-Renaissance period
(c) Renaissance period
(d) None of the above

42. The term 'dharmasthiya' used by Kautilya denoted
(a) judicial court
(b) department of revenue
(c) religious institution
(d) educational institution

43. Which of the following historical books was not written by L.B. Namier?
(a) *The Structure of Policies at the Accession of George III*
(b) *The Rise of the Century*
(c) *1848: The Revolution of the Intellectuals*
(d) *England in the Age of the American Revolution*

44. Who among the following joined Mir Qasim and Shuja-ud-Daula in declaring war upon the English East India Company and was later defeated by the British at the Battle of Buxar?
(a) Farrukhsiyar
(b) Jahandar Shah

(c) Shah Alam II
(d) Muhammad Shah

45. Who united all the Sikhs and founded a kingdom in the Punjab?
(a) Guru Teg Bahadur
(b) Guru Nanak
(c) Guru Gobind Singh
(d) Maharaja Ranjit Singh

46. In July 1763, the English declared war against Mir Qasim for he had
(a) objected to the duty-free trade by the Company's servants
(b) exempted all merchants from the payment of duties
(c) objected to the collection of revenue at a higher rate than ordered by the Company
(d) objected to the harsh methods of the collection of revenue by Company servants

47. With it, Jawaharlal Nehru began his 'wanderings among the Kisans', which has been described vividly in his autobiography. The reference here is to the
(a) Indigo cultivators agitation in Bihar
(b) Eka Movement in Awadh
(c) Kisan Sabha agitation in Awadh
(d) None of the above

48. Which of the following journals was not started by Sadharana Brahmo Samaj?
(a) *Indian Messenger*
(b) *Modern Review*
(c) *Sabad Kaumudi*
(d) *Tattva Kaumudi*

49. The book *India Ravaged* has been written by
(a) George Bernard Shaw
(b) Reginald Coupland
(c) Henry Brailsford
(d) Annie Besant

50. Prince Dara Shikoh was one of the greatest scholars that Mughal India produced. Which of the following was not one of the Sanskrit works to be translated into Persian under the patronage of Dara Shikoh?
(a) *Bhagavad Gita*
(b) *Bhagavata Purana*
(c) *Upanishads*
(d) *Yoga Vashist*

ANSWERS SHEET

PAPER—I

1. (a)	2. (c)	3. (a)	4. (d)	5. (d)
6. (d)	7. (d)	8. (c)	9. (b)	10. (c)
11. (b)	12. (c)	13. (c)	14. (b)	15. (d)
16. (b)	17. (a)	18. (d)	19. (c)	20. (d)
21. (d)	22. (a)	23. (b)	24. (a)	25. (d)
26. (d)	27. (a)	28. (d)	29. (b)	30. (a)
31. (b)	32. (c)	33. (c)	34. (d)	35. (d)
36. (d)	37. (a)	38. (d)	39. (b)	40. (b)
41. (b)	42. (c)	43. (b)	44. (b)	45. (c)
46. (b)	47. (a)	48. (c)	49. (a)	50. (b)

PAPER—II

1. (a)	2. (b)	3. (d)	4. (a)	5. (a)
6. (a)	7. (b)	8. (a)	9. (d)	10. (c)
11. (b)	12. (a)	13. (d)	14. (a)	15. (d)
16. (a)	17. (b)	18. (c)	19. (b)	20. (c)
21. (a)	22. (c)	23. (b)	24. (d)	25. (c)

26. (c)	27. (b)	28. (b)	29. (b)	30. (a)
31. (a)	32. (d)	33. (c)	34. (a)	35. (c)
36. (d)	37. (a)	38. (c)	39. (d)	40. (c)
41. (c)	42. (b)	43. (c)	44. (b)	45. (a)
46. (d)	47. (a)	48. (a)	49. (c)	50. (b)

PAPER—III

1. (d)	2. (b)	3. (c)	4. (b)	5. (a)
6. (d)	7. (b)	8. (b)	9. (a)	10. (a)
11. (c)	12. (b)	13. (a)	14. (a)	15. (c)
16. (d)	17. (a)	18. (b)	19. (a)	20. (b)
21. (b)	22. (a)	23. (c)	24. (a)	25. (d)
26. (b)	27. (b)	28. (d)	29. (d)	30. (d)
31. (c)	32. (d)	33. (a)	34. (c)	35. (b)
36. (a)	37. (c)	38. (a)	39. (c)	40. (b)
41. (c)	42. (a)	43. (b)	44. (c)	45. (d)
46. (b)	47. (c)	48. (c)	49. (a)	50. (b)